# HOLDING THEIR BREATH

# HOLDING THEIR BREATH

## HOW THE ALLIES CONFRONTED THE THREAT OF CHEMICAL WARFARE IN WORLD WAR II

## M. GIRARD DORSEY

CORNELL UNIVERSITY PRESS

*Ithaca and London*

First published 2023 by Cornell University Press

Library of Congress Cataloging-in-Publication Data

Names: Dorsey, M. Girard, 1971– author.
Title: Holding their breath : how the Allies confronted the
   threat of chemical warfare in World War II / M. Girard
   Dorsey.
Description: Ithaca, NY : Cornell University Press, 2023. |
   Series: Battlegrounds: Cornell studies in military history |
   Includes bibliographical references and index.
Identifiers: LCCN 2022023433 (print) | LCCN 2022023434
   (ebook) | ISBN 9781501768361 (hardcover) |
   ISBN 9781501768378 (epub) | ISBN 9781501768385 (pdf)
Subjects: LCSH: World War, 1939–1945—Chemical
   warfare. | Chemical warfare—Great Britain—
   History—20th century. | Chemical warfare—
   UnitedStates—History—20thcentury. | Chemicalwarfare—
   Canada—History—20th century.
Classification: LCC D810.C38 D67 2023 (print) | LCC
   D810.C38 (ebook) | DDC 940.54/85—dc23/eng/20220601
LC record available at https://lccn.loc.gov/2022023433
LC ebook record available at https://lccn.loc.gov/2022023434

*For my family,*
*the most important people in my life*

# Contents

*Acknowledgments*   ix

Introduction: Where the Story of
Chemical Warfare and World War II
Began                                                      1

1. Chain, Tool, Shield: The Role of an
   International Treaty in Chemical
   Weapons Arms Control before
   World War II                                            17

2. Is There Any Hope? Defensive
   Preparations against the Dreaded and
   Expected Gas War                                        41

3. The Sole Exception to the Rule:
   There Will Be No Chemical Conflicts,
   but Just in Case . . .                                  76

4. The Limits of Friendship: The Influence
   of Chemical Weapons on Alliances as
   World War II Expanded                                   110

5. Rolling the Dice: Risking Gas Warfare
   in Europe                                               133

6. Critical Timing: The Increasing
   Likelihood of Chemical Warfare in the
   Pacific                                                 166

Epilogue: "I Am Fear": Legacies of
Silent Chemical Warfare                                    203

*Notes*   211

*Bibliography*   269

*Index*   279

# ACKNOWLEDGMENTS

Although my name is listed as the author, this book is the result of material and intangible support from a variety of institutions and individuals. I have done my best to name them all, but I know I owe so many more than I have included here. Thank you.

First, thank you to the libraries and archives, as well as the experts who worked there, at The National Archives in Kew; the Imperial War Museum (especially Dave McCall); the Liddell Hart Centre for Military Archives at King's College, London; the Mass Observation Archive, University of Sussex; the National Archives and Records Administration in College Park, Maryland; the Air Force Historical Research Agency at Maxwell Air Force Base in Alabama; the Institute of World War II and the Human Experience at Florida State University; the Auckland War Memorial Museum; the Library and Archives Canada in Ottawa; and the University of New Hampshire Library. In particular, Kathrine Aydelott found books upon books for me, and Linda Johnson provided not only assistance but also asked her colleagues at other institutions for help for me. I am grateful to Paul Domenet whose artwork inspired the opening to the epilogue and who permitted me to include his poster in this book.

My colleagues—faculty and staff—at the University of Hampshire (UNH), especially in the history department and the Justice Studies Program, provided encouragement and intellectual support, whether conversing informally in the hallway, attending on-campus talks, or organizing lunches where several of us could share our progress. I appreciate the support the University of New Hampshire has provided, including a Faculty Scholars leave. My deep thanks to the dean of the College of Liberal Arts at the University of New Hampshire, Michele Dillon, and her predecessors and staff, for providing summer funding, approving sabbaticals, and naming me the Lamberton Professor of Justice Studies with the material support that position provided. The Center for the Humanities offered not only fellowships but also an opportunity to present some of my work on campus. The Hamel Center for Undergraduate Research put me in contact with a talented student who helped me find material one summer.

I have also been fortunate to receive funding—and the validation as well as the concrete support funding provides for student assistance, travel, and more—from UNH, including the College of Liberal Arts Summer Funding, the Michael Carney Gift Fund, the Alumni Gift Fund, an International Development Grant, the History Department Gift Fund, the Wheeler Fund, a Graduate School Summer Faculty Fellowship, and the Dunfey Fund. Thank you to the Institute on World War II and the Human Experience Cundy Grant, which allowed me to visit an incredible archive and gather material for two projects.

Students, from John Green, Anna Brown, Elisabeth Iaccono, Paul Goodman, Melanie Johnson, and Aaron Kronstadt, to those who listened to me talk about chemical warfare in class, have all alerted me to important information and helped me sort through it.

Outside of UNH, I appreciate colleagues, friends, and editors, in particular Kathy Barbier for introducing me to opportunities and being a wonderful friend, and Kurt Piehler, for chance to gather material, meet other scholars, and share ideas. Thank you to David Silbey, Bethany Wasik, Emily Andrew, Susan L. Smith, Walter Grunden, Asher Orkaby, Mike Rollin, Thomas Faith, Robin Clewley, Roy MacLeod, Brian Cuddy, and many people who have sat on panels, asked wonderful questions, and reviewed my writing, often multiple times. Thank you, too, to organizers of panels and conferences including the Society for Military History; the Transatlantic Studies Association; Weapons, Wounds, and Warfare Seminar at the University of Auckland; the World War I Centennial Symposium at Hawaii Pacific University; War, Peace, and International Order?: The Legacies of 1899 and 1907 organized by the Faculty of Arts at the University of Auckland and the New Zealand Centre for Human Rights Law, Policy and Practice; the History of Science Society; the Legacies of World War I Conference of Chestnut Hill College; the Southern Conference on British Studies; and the North American Conference on British Studies. I appreciate, too, the anonymous reviewers and everyone else who helped transform my manuscript into a book, improving it at every phase, especially those at Cornell University Press and Westchester Publishing Services.

Most of all, thank you to my family—from my dad who has always let me know that he appreciates my love of scholarship to my mom who kept an external hard drive safe when my family spent a semester abroad, protecting hundreds of photographs of primary sources. They provided so much motivation and practical support. My sons, Luke and Nick, tolerated a mom who talked about poison gas in the car and dragged them to meetings with other academics during vacations. I cannot ignore the dogs who spent countless hours in the office while I, rudely, typed rather than walked them. Most of all, thank you to my husband, Kurk, who not only made sure the family ate when I faced a deadline, provided moral support, talked about the concepts in the book with me, sent me interesting sources (including a tweet just today), read the manuscript (more than once!)—and, best of all, not only brought me perspective when I needed it (and, writing about poison gas, I needed it!) but made me laugh. Thank you.

# HOLDING THEIR BREATH

# Introduction
## Where the Story of Chemical Warfare and World War II Began

Gas! GAS! Quick, boys!—An ecstasy of fumbling
Fitting the clumsy helmets just in time,
But someone still was yelling out and stumbling
And flound'ring like a man in fire or lime.—
Dim through the misty panes and thick green light,
As under a green sea, I saw him drowning.

In all my dreams before my helpless sight,
He plunges at me, guttering, choking, drowning.
. . . . . . . . . . . . . . . . . . . . . . . . . . . . . . . . . . . . .
And watch the white eyes writhing in his face,
His hanging face, like a devil's sick of sin;
If you could hear, at every jolt, the blood
Come gargling from the froth-corrupted lungs,
Obscene as cancer, bitter as the cud . . .

—Wilfred Owen, "Dulce et Decorum Est"

Wilfred Owen's poem describes the ravages of a World War I gas attack on soldiers, conveying not only the physical trauma of the victim but also the emotional impact on his watching comrade. The unwilling observer is helpless to assist the dying man and franticly attempts to protect himself by donning a respirator.[1] It is hard even more than one hundred years later not to recoil at Owen's account. The excerpt effectively represents the human suffering that underlies popular associations with poison gas and helps illustrate its nature as an intangible as well as physical weapon. After World War I, gas engendered so much fear about its potential future use that societies agonized about it during the peacetime of the interwar period as well as during the fighting in World War II. How they interacted with gas and how the idea, potential, and reality of gas influenced them during that period is the focus of this book: chemical warfare can cause mental, emotional, and physical damage whether it is deployed or threatened. Its very presence in the global arsenal means that its role in World War II must be examined to understand both the conflict and the actions of those who strove to prevent its release or manage the suffering it could deliver. Gas can cause individual pain, but societies, militaries, diplomats, politicians, and others decide whether and when it can be deployed.

This book examines the experiences of the World War II Western Allies—Britain, the United States, and Canada—with gas. The Western Allies may not have released gas physically as a weapon, but the perception that chemical weapons (hereafter abbreviated as CW) threatened them and their cobelligerents, and the debates about joint retaliation protocols as well as when to release gas, all proved costly in terms of fear, cost, supplies, time, and expertise.[2] Gas was not used in the traditional or expected way, but it was a powerful weapon that influenced behavior in World War II. Britain, the United States, and Canada's experiences with CW offer new insights into one of the potentially devastating aspects of World War II, as well as lessons about the power of and restraints possible for a rogue weapon that is on the rise in the contemporary world. This book also ties together the legal, social, political, and military factors that shaped decisions to keep a weapon that is one of the symbols of World War I from becoming a leading tool of the deadliest war in modern history.

On May 29, 1945, the acting secretary of state, Joseph Grew, met with the secretary of war, Henry Stimson, about ending the war with Japan. General George Marshall was in attendance, as was the assistant secretary of war, John J. McCloy. McCloy recorded Marshall's assertion that his goal "to avoid the attrition we were suffering from such fanatical but hopeless defense methods [by the Japanese] . . . requires new tactics." Marshall, according to McCloy, "also spoke of gas and the possibility of using it in a limited degree, say on the outlying islands where operations were now going on or were about to take place. He spoke of the type of gas that might be employed. It did not need to be our newest and most potent—just drench them and sicken them so that the fight would be taken out of them."[3] Recommendations would follow. Of course, what really followed—just ten weeks later—was the atomic bomb, making the consideration of gas use in Japan moot.

In fact, those who lived during the interwar period—from politicians to soldiers, from laymen to disarmament supporters—expected future wars to be filled with gas attacks, ones that targeted civilians as well as military men. Logic based on gas use in past wars supported this conviction. World War I, well within the memory of those in power in the 1920s and 1930s, had hosted the advent and escalation of gas warfare. Colonial conflicts in Ethiopia and Morocco in the decades that followed the Great War illustrated that gas, although disliked by many, remained in the arsenal. Of course, any major war that followed would involve gas; that was simple logic.

The opposite emotion—in particular, fear—also supported assumptions about future gas use. World War I had been brutal. The introduction of modern technologies, such as airplanes, and the erosion of limitations, such as the general sanctity of civilians, led to deeper and wider destructiveness that continued even after the war ended.[4] While Britain witnessed zeppelins bombing London in World War I, the world beheld planes bombarding Guernica in the Spanish Civil War. The pattern seemed clear. These were horrifying developments, and it made sense that they inspired actions, including efforts to ban gas through the Geneva Gas Protocol, and words, such as Lord Halsbury's apocalyptic novel featuring a gas war, *1944*.[5] With these examples as guides, there was a conviction that the next war would use gas.[6]

But it did not. World War II contained almost unimaginable horrors, and air power certainly became a prominent part of it, but the conflict did not include regular poison gas attacks on the battlefield or an enemy's home front. There were experiments and periodic uses by the Japanese in China between 1937 and 1941, before the Western Allies—the United States, Canada, and Britain—recognized China as an ally, but these weapons were neither openly used nor part of a standard policy of deployment.[7] The most well-known use of toxic gas during World War II was in the Holocaust, when the Nazis used Zyklon B in some of the concentration camps. Yet, as deplorable as this was, this use was not against international enemies on a battlefield (and even the enemy's home front could be a battlefield); this was gas used on an imprisoned population. Neither scholars nor the public has chosen to classify that as chemical warfare as it is commonly understood. Thus, despite the common usage of poison gas on the Western Front in World War I, despite the common conviction by multiple nations that it would be used in World War II, it was not.

Why not? Even as chemical, military, and historical experts have raised doubts about the effectiveness of gas as a weapon in World War I, it is still widely known as one of the horrors of that conflict.[8] The common perception of its inhumanity was reinforced by the living reminders of disabled veterans and exacerbated by the expectation that gas would be released from the air and on the home front in future wars. The result would affect numerous civilians as well as military victims. Whether or not gas was more, or even as, effective physically as artillery or guns in World War I is less relevant than the belief that it might cause more suffering and death in the next wars. So, the leaders and laymen of great powers prepared for it, offensively and defensively. They worried about it. They discussed it. For over twenty-five years, from the end of World War I until the end of World War II, they spent enormous time and resources on a threat that never materialized physically.

Historians intrigued by this mystery have offered assorted explanations. During World War I, armies deployed gas from stationary weapons against entrenched or slowly moving targets. It is possible, but unlikely, that the fact that World War II was a war of movement, unlike the static Western Front of World War I, explains why gas was not used in the former. Perhaps the personal and publicly proclaimed abhorrence of gas by President Franklin Delano Roosevelt and Führer Adolf Hitler made a difference.[9] Or, some suggest, deterrence, unpreparedness, or a combination of factors inhibited gas use in World War II.[10] Limited inventory meant there were periods when responses would have been slow, localized, and short rather than the preferred strategy of rapid and sustainable attacks; although bomb and plane shortages existed, especially early in the war, they did not prevent retaliation everywhere.[11] While these and other reasons have merit, a wider and deeper examination of World War II reveals that the issue is more complicated.

The first step is to realize that the most useful question is not "Why didn't the Allies use gas?" This suggests that it was a one-time decision and that all the Western Allies used the same rationale. In fact, the Allies repeatedly made the decision to refrain from gas, sometimes from different motivations. So, "Why did the Allies, despite temptation and crises, refrain repeatedly from deploying gas?" is more accurate.

Even that is not the right question. Gas did not have to be deployed physically to be a weapon. Yes, gas was not released on the battlefield or on the enemy's home front via a deliberate policy, but in some ways, it *was* used. If one looks back at World War I, armies released gas on the battlefield, but the weapon's nature made it valuable not only because of the casualties it caused but also because of the fear it engendered in soldiers who dreaded it. It was a weapon of terror simply because it existed, and it forced militaries and others to change their behavior in anticipation of its use. Soldiers participated in anti-gas drills and learned how to put on respirators in seconds. Men carried gas masks, burdening themselves and bearing a constant reminder of the gas threat. Physicians struggled to determine how to treat gas cases, sometimes uselessly.[12] It did not have to be used physically to cause damage. It did not have to cause bodily harm to soldiers or civilians to influence the belligerents' wartime policies and actions, or even to cause anxiety.

Gas generated physical and intangible threats in World War II as well. The energy put toward preparing for a gas war—offensively and defensively on the home front (more of a fear for the British Empire than for Canada and the United States) and the battlefront—was inspired by both logic and fear. As a psychological and physical weapon, gas certainly shaped the war effort of the major belligerents. Gas, or at least the anticipation of it, consumed limited material, strained available human resources, and influenced nations' plans.

Thus, while one goal of this book is to comprehend why the Western Allies made the decision, repeatedly and despite great temptation, not to deploy gas on the battlefields, another purpose is to answer the question, "How did the existence of CW influence the course of their war?" Gas was an active weapon, even if not deployed in the traditional sense. Both the presence of a gas threat and weapons, and perceptions about it, affected British, US, and Canadian actions at home, with each other, and toward the enemy. These attitudes changed over time, impacting behaviors and policies regarding gas, including limits on restraints against using gas.

As the war continued, events illuminated boundaries that, if crossed, meant that the Western Allies almost certainly would decide to deploy gas. Those in power during World War II never considered absolute the taboo or norm against gas use that we speak of today. If national survival or national identity was at stake, for instance, Britain would have chosen to become a global pariah if that meant that it had to use gas to survive a German invasion. Canada possessed less motivation to start an offensive gas war deliberately, but not only was it allied with both Britain and the United States, who might, but also it engaged in offensive and defensive actions that had the potential to trigger Germany to start a gas war. For example, in the morass of calculations and bluffs in World War II, Canada's desire to inoculate its soldiers against botulism—considered a chemical weapon then—generated resistance from its Allies who thought that Germany might see a vaccination program as a hint that Canada was about to use botulism itself or as a justification for a Nazi preemptive chemical strike.

However, the boundaries shifted. One of the key factors that eroded gas restraints was the growing brutality of the war—and the concomitant desensitization of leaders and the public. Demonstrated by actions by both sides, from Germany's Vengeance rockets (more frequently known as the V-1 and V-2 rockets) lobbed at Britain to the UK and US carpet bombing of Germany and the US firebombing of Tokyo, this escalation combined with the conflict's length lessened the Western Allies' restraint. By the end of the war, it was not desperation but exhaustion and animosity that nearly provided the critical push for the Allies, particularly the United States, to start a gas war. As threats to national survival itself decreased after Victory in Europe (V-E) Day because belligerents were less likely to face enemy retaliation in kind, the Allies had the luxury of viewing what were less urgent challenges as their current greatest ones. They did not cross the chemical warfare line, likely because the war ended abruptly with the atomic bomb and the Russian declaration of war on Japan. These obviated US plans that probably would have led to an Allied gas attack on Japanese forces. By mid-1945, in other words, for at least some influential figures in the United States and Britain who had the power to propose or formulate chemical warfare policy, concerns about national survival had given way to surviving the war with energy to finish the job and without sacrificing more Allied lives than need be, however that had to be done. There was nothing inevitable about their decisions not to use gas in World War II.

This book focuses on Britain, Canada, and the United States—the Western Allies. Unlike the other two major Allies, the Soviet Union and China, these three were the nations who had the ability to produce and use gas, and who also possessed democratic systems in which governmental policies responded to public opinion and actions as well as military judgments and political assessments; there were many opportunities to make choices about gas or for policies to be influenced by a range of individuals. These nations cooperated, piecemeal, by sharing gas research, equipment, and scientific experts. More important, they were distinct from the USSR and China because they created a joint chemical warfare policy. In contrast, as future chapters will show, Britain and the United States distrusted the Soviet Union and China to tell the truth about Axis gas use against their populations. Britain, the United States, and Canada form a cohort in the gas story of World War II.

For myriad reasons, each Western Ally's leadership (re)considered gas at different times and in different ways. More specifically, Britain was one of the first nations involved in World War II that potentially faced an immediate threat by a chemical attack. It continued to be active in the war, and its former colony, Canada, was the most involved of the Commonwealth countries in cooperating not only with Britain but also with its neighbor, the United States. It was the only dominion who negotiated ably, and whose perspectives were considered seriously by Britain and the United States, during the establishment of the joint chemical warfare policy. Canada's role differed substantially from that of other members of the Commonwealth and Empire, although it did remain a junior partner of Britain and the United States.

The latter soon became the most powerful member of this coalition. After Pearl Harbor, understanding gas policy for all three also meant comprehending both the US position and that the other two nations had a wary eye on the United States. The fact that the United States—unlike the other two—was not bound by the Geneva Gas Protocol, the dominant prewar treaty banning gas, made the alliance relationship rocky at times.[13] This means that an analysis of chemical warfare restraint by the Western Allies is as much a story of alliance politics, international law, and diplomacy as it is an account of military machinations. The three nations struggled to balance the threats to their individual nations, manage their relationships with one another, build a unified gas policy, and calibrate their interest in winning World War II; gas was just an element of that complexity.

To study these issues among and within the Western Allies requires a transnational approach, going beyond traditional international diplomatic history. Transnational elements, as historian Jay Winter defines them, add complexity and nuance to the analysis. A transnational analysis includes factors that span national borders such as scientific debates, moral considerations, limits to national sovereignty, and considerations of lay people.[14] These approaches also offer multiple angles through which to study the perspectives and relationships of the three major Allies.

Studying the actions and considerations of three Allies over the course of a six-year war does not lead to simple conclusions. Although the three Allies in question certainly shared a chemical warfare policy, and many other interests, they also differed in a variety of ways, from vulnerabilities and geography to resources and leaders. For example, the British fought the war much longer than the United States and faced damage to their homeland more regularly than did the North American Allies. Winston Churchill, Britain's prime minister for most of the conflict, was much more open-minded about utilizing CW than was Franklin Roosevelt, the United States president. Canada, unlike the United States and Britain, was a relatively small power seeking the opportunity to gain great influence and respect as it worked with the other Allies on a chemical warfare policy.

Despite the differences, one of the similarities at the root of why the Western Allies developed a no-first-use gas policy arose before World War II began: the fundamental barrier to choosing to deploy gas arose out of interwar decisions to ban gas use via international law. In particular, the Geneva Gas Protocol of 1925 (in force in 1928) provided the foundation for decision-making and an ideological framework that led the Western Allies as a whole to decide repeatedly to avoid a gas war.

This restraint existed despite the fact that, even at inception, signatories recognized that the agreement was a flawed, and even weak, treaty. While the Geneva Gas Protocol seemed broad and inclusive on the surface with language that prohibited using "bacteriological" weapons and CW, there were no enforcement mechanisms in the treaty itself. Some signatories added reservations that permitted retaliation in kind as a deterrent and sanction, but such clauses weakened the protocol because they permitted gas use in certain circumstances rather than banning it entirely. Perhaps more important, the great powers and future World War II belligerents the United States and Japan never ratified it until well after World War II, thus limiting the number of countries constrained by it.[15] Just as relevant was the memory of Germany's violation of the 1899 Hague Convention that banned gas; popular and political opinions feared it would break the newer treaty in the next conflict. The protocol was not a solid shield against the potential catastrophe of a gas attack. However, its existence was sufficient, in the end, to serve as a basis to resist gas use. Among other reasons discussed more deeply in later chapters, those who signed did not want to break the treaty and thus did not prepare fully, in material or in mind, for a gas war.

Concern about the protocol influenced reluctance to open World War II with CW, but it did not determine that position for the course of the conflict. Because several crises emerged as the war continued—real emergencies, such as chemical warfare leaks in Bari, Italy, in 1943, and those based solely on perceptions of Axis intentions, such as the conviction that Germany would invade Britain during the war—the Allies had to enhance their abilities to wage gas warfare and to reassess repeatedly their choices not to do so. Independent national interests influenced them, but so did the relationships between the Allies. The result was a balancing act of military, political, legal, psychological, social, and diplomatic factors. Sometimes a country selected the alliance or a gas ban as a way to save national identity and security, but sometimes it prioritized gas warfare as the way to do the same, ready to use CW if the right triggering event occurred. The repeated national and alliance decisions to refrain from gas use depended on each country determining whether gas use would weaken or save its national identity as a respecter of international law and humane behavior and even its survival as an independent, sovereign nation, although the cost of the decisions might be its adherence to international law, the nation's ethical reputation, and even its citizens' lives. Each nation's perspective on gas included not only international considerations but also internal ones that depended on negotiations about power at the lay and expert level.

The definitions of national survival and identity may have varied a bit over time and in each nation, as did the assessment of whether a country believed it was under threat enough to use gas, and these evaluations did not necessarily occur in sync with those of the other Western Allies. The war ended before chemical warfare reappeared as a major physical weapon, and that left the gas taboo in place. As the war continued, the temptation to use gas increased, and it is likely that it would have been used by the United States as part of Operation Downfall, the planned invasion of Japan.

Thus, I argue that because the possible use of gas armaments provoked responses among experts and laymen in the Western Allies, they were active weapons that shaped belligerents' policies and actions. Unlike in World War I or even Syria today, they were not used physically, openly, and systematically in

World War II. Furthermore, while the Western Allies honored barriers against physical use, they did not perceive these prohibitions as absolute or immutable. Maintaining an allied gas policy was trumped only by the need for surviving the war intact. Changing threat levels and national priorities demanded flexibility, even if more positive attitudes toward CW would conflict with values such as protecting individual lives in one's own nation, long-supported backing of international legal bans, or anti-gas public opinion. World War II might well have ended with a physical gas war—and it could have been started by some of its original strongest opponents, the Western Allies.

## What Is Gas?

It is easy enough to bandy the terms "poison gas" or "chemical weapon" around, but what is gas, and why does it have such an unusual position among armaments?

The answers can be confusing. The name gas is often used interchangeably and colloquially with CW, but it is a slight misnomer. Gas is any substance that uses chemicals to harm people. It does not, contrary to its name, need to be in a gas form. In addition, the consensus is that the targets are human, and thus chemical substances like Agent Orange, defoliants used in Vietnam, are not classic CW.[16] However, as will be discussed in chapter 5, some weapons may not seem like CW at first glance, but they are. In World War II, a key example was botulism, which can be categorized as a biological weapon, or, in the parlance of the interwar era, a bacteriological weapon, because the illness is caused by bacteria. Since the organism harms humans by creating a toxin, however, it injures through chemical means according to the reasoning at the time, and thus it was managed by chemical warfare committees.

Also, weapons are not CW just because the military units that deploy them are CW specialists. CW services deployed what has traditionally been called poison gas, but they may have used other nontraditional weapons such as incendiaries as well. Still, their core weapons—and the focus of this book—are poison gases.

Scientists formulated and weaponized a variety of gases during World War I. Chlorine, phosgene, and especially mustard remain the classic CW today, with variations of mustard being the key weapon considered by the Allies in World War II. These are usually classified by their effects, such as harassing, incapacitating, or persistent.[17] The first include tear gases, chemicals not intended to produce lasting harm.[18] The last include mustard gas, a toxin that can linger for days, burning through clothing and other materials, causing blisters, blindness, lung ailments, and even death. Some of these gases are still core CW used today. For instance, police around the world deploy tear gas against crowds, and Saddam Hussein used mustard gas against the Kurds in 1988. The Organisation for the Prohibition of CW confirmed the use of a kind of mustard gas in Syria, and other gases are alleged to have been used.[19]

New generations of gases emerged into the public realm after World War II. During most of the interwar period, the Allies remained convinced that there were no new classes of gas to create. There could, however, be developments in protective gear and aerial deployment. During World War II, however, the Germans developed a new class, nerve gases, such as sarin and tabun, although they did not use them.[20] Gases in this organophosphate category of CW are often fast-acting, can alter blood pressure and heart rate, and might cause "loss of consciousness . . . convulsions . . . paralysis" and even death.[21] The Germans believed that the Allies had nerve gases and dared not give them an excuse to retaliate in kind with them. In fact, their existence "came as a terrible shock" to Britain and the United States at the end of the European war.[22] These nerve gases were notorious when deployed in the postwar years, such as when the terrorist group Aum Shinrikyo deployed sarin in the Tokyo subway; the UN confirmed its release in Khan Shaykhun in Syria in 2017; and the Russians poisoned a pardoned defector, Sergei Skirpal, in Salisbury, England, with a Novichok nerve agent in 2018.[23]

Even the classical categories of gas—the pre-nerve gases—are considered weapons of mass destruction (WMDs); they are potentially lethal, but they are also different in kind from other weapons. Gas can indeed kill masses if it spreads over enough targets in a thick concentration or is a sufficiently lethal compound, but so can a high explosive bomb. It is the intangible qualities of gas that make it different in kind, not just degree, than most weapons. It is poisonous, and poison has always been a weapon of ill repute. The original gases killed by suffocating the victim, a method of killing that instinctively seems ghastly. It was not really a problem that it was a weapon that could kill masses because cannons and machine guns could too. For other reasons, though, many saw it as barbaric and inhumane—and that was before it had ever been used.

Both gas and bombs were feared and anticipated before World War II. Aerial bombs were a dominant weapon of World War II, their use escalating in numbers and strength over the course of the war to create the terror of the long-lasting Blitz, the inferno of firebombed Dresden, and the shock of radiation-filled Hiroshima. Gas, although not released and not the product of escalation in World War II, had some parallels to conventional aerial bombs. In addition, many experts expected gas as well as conventional bombs to be dropped from planes; gas would have been a product of air power that seemed more horrible than regular bombs.

Unlike planes, though, gas had always had a negative association, rational or not, seen in efforts to outlaw it in the international 1899 Hague Conventions years before it existed as a working modern weapon. It certainly did not have the counterbalancing positive associations that flight did, such as the Wright brothers' miracle of aviation in 1903 and Charles Lindbergh's stunning solo journey across the Atlantic in 1927. Gas was its own weapon, feared for its own reasons, even if experts and laymen thought it might be released with the assistance of air power efforts; gas was a separate weapon and deserves to be seen as one.[24]

Gas can be a devastating weapon, but not all chemicals are or can be weapons. Even if a chemical compound is deadly, it may not be a suitable weapon. To be effective, gases must be able to be manufactured (reasonably) safely and inserted into a delivery mechanism (such as a shell) in such a concentration or quantity that it will create damage. At the same time, the gas and the weapon container must be stable enough to travel and be stored safely in a variety of temperatures and climates from the jungles of the Pacific Rim to the snowy winters of northern Europe. The gases cannot react with the containers in which they are stored; they cannot change the compound nor degrade the vessel. Then there must be a way to deploy the weapon effectively. If it is dropped from a plane, for instance, will the bomb explode at the right time? If it is released from a canister, as done in World War I, and carried by the wind, will the breeze maintain a steady direction—or will it blow the toxins back on the army that just released it?[25] If all of this works, will the weapon do the job it was meant to do—whether scare, annoy, or hurt the enemy? Will their gas masks be impermeable and thus neutralize the attack? Or will the gas masks exhaust the neutralizing agents in the respirators, the components that clean the foul air before the wearer inhales, if it lingers?

If scientists manage to produce a marriage of deployment mechanism and CW, gas can be delivered through a variety of means, from canisters to artillery shells to aerial bombs. It is a versatile weapon, sometimes brutality effective, especially against unprotected victims. Some gases can attack men who think they are safe, hidden deep in caves or bunkers, but are vulnerable to toxic mists creeping through holes. Others can float on the air, sometimes in a colorful cloud, a visible and inexorable threat to soldiers in their path. Mustard gas, a particularly persistent substance can linger close to the ground for days, poisoning anyone who comes into contact with it in the air or on an object coated or permeated by it, such as equipment or food. In World War I, some casualties were poisoned when they drank tea made from shell-hole water tainted by gas.[26] Furthermore, gas keeps injuring victims as long as it is in in contact with them. Patients who were covered in mustard gas had to remove saturated clothing to stop the substance from continuing to burn them.[27] In other cases, gas can kill rapidly, such as the World War I soldiers who, unknowingly gassed with phosgene, died of overexertion hours later. It can also lead to lingering deaths; some men who were doused with mustard gas survived their initial encounter but with lungs so weakened that they labored for years just to breathe and survive colds. From longitudinal observation, it is clear that some gases are connected to emphysema, cancers, and other diseases.[28]

Yet gases—at least the ones developed before the age of nerve gases—are one of the simplest weapons against which to defend. Security can be collective or individual. Groups can retreat to gas-proof shelters, whether tent-like structures in some cases or bunkers or buildings in others. As long as there is clear air to breathe and barriers to prevent skin-gas contact (especially against mustard), people can survive. On an individual level, gas masks are the core defense. These allow people to breathe safely—although not comfortably—for a few hours. Some models even allow wearers to exert themselves strenuously while protected. In World War I, for example, soldiers drilled with masks while engaged in activities, and in World War II human subjects of gas testing might be asked to cross testing fields during a trial.[29] There were even masks tailored to animals and to babies as well as to various facial configurations. Masks can accommodate the beards of Sikhs (a British concern in World War I) and the smaller faces of children.[30]

Since mustard gas, unlike other gases that primarily target pulmonary function, also wreaks dermatological havoc in the form of blisters, scientists also experimented with protective clothing, such as capes for World War II. Unfortunately, as unpleasant as masks were to wear—some felt they were suffocating—the other defensive gear was unpopular too. It was one more piece of equipment, and in a humid, hot climate like the tropics it was miserable to wear and made it challenging to move.[31] Still, the fact that Allied scientists continued to work on offensive and defensive aspects of gas warfare showed a commitment to it and a recognition that it could evolve—even if they, unlike the Germans, did not realize that it could be revolutionized by developing a new class of CW.

## World War I: Modern Battlefield Gas Use Begins

Modern poison gas has been despised and feared since it was conceived. By the end of the nineteenth century, the era of modern chemistry was well established. One could envision deliberately making chemical armaments. Some compounds used for peacetime uses were hazardous anyway, such as chlorine or arsenic. If these could be weaponized, then there would be a new category of arms. So, in 1899 when delegates of many of the great powers met in The Hague to discuss ways to put legal limits on wars, one proposed was a ban on gas, along with rules about treatment of the wounded and outlawing dum dum bullets.[32] However, since there were no gas weapons yet, the delegates to the conference had to predict what poison gas would be like in order to describe what they were prohibiting. In an era of rapid developments in artillery, it made sense to characterize imagined gas weapons as "projectiles the object of which" was asphyxiation.[33]

Not every delegate to the convention embraced the proposed ban. Admiral Alfred Mahan, the US naval expert, for example, dismissed it. Why should gas be prohibited if it was acceptable to drown sailors by sinking ships?[34] Was asphyxiation on land less humane than drowning at sea? Still, most nations' representatives signed, whether because they believed the law would work, they figured it was better than nothing, they did not think too deeply about its flaws, or simply to show that they too wanted to be members of the club of self-perceived civilized nations.

As most people who have studied World War I know, however, the ban failed nine months into the conflict. There is some suggestion that the French tried a version of chemical warfare by releasing police gases—tear gases—as some point. The Germans also reportedly released some gas on the Eastern Front. However, in the former case, there was no real damage, and, in the latter, it was an abysmal failure—the Russians did not even notice the gas.[35]

The real advent of modern chemical warfare began on April 22, 1915, at Ypres when the Germans released chlorine gas stored in cylinders through pipes that targeted the Canadian and French Algerian lines. This was part of a desperate effort to break the stalemate on the Western Front. In other words, the German army released poison gas much as one would release oxygen or helium from a series of tanks linked together by pipes. Turn a knob and let it hiss out, carried by the wind. As even the British prime minister, Herbert Asquith, acknowledged in his private correspondence to King George V, Germany's actions did not violate the letter of the law.[36] In public, though, the British reaction matched the general international reaction, which was less nuanced. As the secretary of state for war, Lord Horatio Kitchener, announced in the House of Lords, using gas was a "pernicious practice," while in the House of Commons Lord Robert Cecil called it "barbarous."[37]

The physical damage and the mental terror that ensued among the Allied troops nearly allowed the Germans to break the enemy lines at Ypres, each side's main goal on the Western Front.[38] This was prevented only because the Germans did not have enough confidence in the gas and did not have reinforcements ready to exploit the weakened Allied positions. This combined with bravery on the part of the Canadians, many of whom did not abandon their posts even as they suffocated, saved the day.[39]

After that, gas never had the benefit of total surprise. Soldiers dreaded facing gas at any moment, let alone actually confronting it if the enemy did use it. CW changed the way the war was fought, as the military added it to the preliminary stages of attacks, as industry turned to supplying defensive masks and offensive weapons, as scientists explored more and more lethal toxins, and as nations came to terms with new horrors of war. Once the Allied governments made the decision to retaliate with gas, chemical warfare escalated in frequency.

Germany paid in suffering since its opponents began retaliating within months. As Lord Kitchener stated in the House of Lords on May 18, 1915, a month after the Germans used gas, British soldiers could not be denied any weapon available (as gas now was). It would be detrimental—presumably to their safety as well as their morale.[40] The rest of the belligerents on the Western Front followed suit.

Still, there were limits. The British explicitly established a policy through which they would prepare to meet any German escalations, but they would not instigate them. One of the consequences of this policy, and of the fact that chemical warriors often deployed gas through static weapons such as cylinders or mortars, meant that chemical warfare remained limited to the Western Front. It never became a standard weapon in every theater. In addition, while civilians feared gas attacks, there were no concerted efforts to harm them with CW either.

The United States was another nation that prepared for enhanced chemical warfare. Although it entered the conflict in 1917, two years after the advent of chemical warfare, scientists from the Bureau of Mines had begun work in CW defense before that.[41] The United States added to the offensive arsenal, but not efficiently; they invented lewisite weapons, more closely related to mustard gas than to the earlier compounds used in the war, but the United States had to depend on European armaments. Although the United States began producing CW, the American Expeditionary Force did not have any ready to use in Europe before the end of the war.[42]

Still, belligerents used gas with increasing frequency, and they developed more casualty-producing weapons over time. For example, the British war production plans for 1919 included consideration about making more gas than even in the previous year.[43]

# Efforts to Ban Gas Use after World War I

The continued use of CW meant that laymen and experts alike developed an understanding of gas warfare and its potential, whether they based that knowledge on practical experience, scientific knowledge, or rumor. One did not need to know the exact chemical composition of a weapon or the precise schematics of the next delivery system to see that toxins and the armaments that housed them became more sophisticated over time. One result was an interwar debate about the future of gas in national arsenals. This coincided with the horror that World War I had been so destructive and a consequent rise in interest in arms control by grassroots groups internationally. To achieve these goals, politicians immersed themselves in an effort to embrace collective security as a way to prevent, or at least limit, warfare. The result included attempts to restrict CW in the Versailles Treaty and the Washington Naval Conference agreements. The most important result was the Geneva Gas Protocol of 1925, a ban on the use of CW and, for the first time, biological weapons. (The latter had been envisioned but not used on the battlefield.)[44] This treaty served as the governing document in international law regarding gas use and restraint until the Chemical Weapons Convention of 1993 (which entered into force in 1997).

Thus, the story of gas restraint in World War II really begins in 1925 and continues throughout World War II. Decisions made about the Geneva Gas Protocol—whether to sign it and how to respond to its limits in terms of offensive and defensive preparations—set the Western Allies on the courses they followed for the next twenty-five years. Britain felt compelled to sign the treaty or risk international condemnation. It also felt obliged to refrain from gas use for a long time, even relatively benign use of tear gas in the colonies, out of respect for the law.[45] Simultaneously, it acknowledged the flaws in the law—there was not a way to enforce compliance by other signatories or by nonsignatories—and thus prepared to defend against gas in the future. Canada, another signatory who wanted to refrain from a gas attack, differed from Britain in key ways. Across the Atlantic, it felt less vulnerability about world events. It sought to make its own sovereign decisions about gas needs.[46] The United States refused to sign until the 1970s, and, despite police forces that embraced gas for riot control and an active chemical lobby that championed CW, remained anti-gas at the executive level. President Franklin Roosevelt, in particular, abhorred gas. These restraints helped lead the three countries to abstain from strong offensive preparations for gas warfare. It also made the United States a weak link on the anti-gas front, since it was personal preference more than legal international commitments that determined US policy.

Yet all three Allies meshed their chemical warfare policies, sometimes painfully and slowly. The process by which this occurred, and examples of situations in which it was debated, illuminate the pitfalls of alliance politics and additional challenges to the weak protocol. The restraint wobbled at times. Episodes where this occurred include the anticipated invasion of Britain by Germany, the planning for the amphibious landing at Normandy, Britain's vulnerability to the V-1/V-2 rockets, and the proposed invasion of the home islands of Japan.

All the events mentioned occurred during World War II, but the story about the influence of gas on the Western Allies during that war requires opening the tale in the interwar period since the preparations for World War II gas use and defense are based on the fears held and actions taken before the conflict began. Whether during the prewar era or during the global hostilities, there were times when different Allies took the lead in the gas war and its key turning points. Britain has a prominent role in the first three chapters, as the nation most vulnerable to Germany and its strongest opponent in the first years of the war. It was particularly active in the interwar negotiations about gas bans and in efforts to establish domestic defenses again CW. It also faced the initial threat of German gas use during the conflict in 1940–1941 when a Hitlerian invasion of Britain, Operation Sea Lion, seemed most likely, and thus British leadership confronted the temptation to change its gas policy from no-first-use to offensive deployment first. Canada illustrated alliance tensions, and its actions are most apparent in the middle of the war when the countries developed their joint gas policy. The US's later entry into the war gave it a smaller part to play in the early chapters; its dominant role in the Pacific means that it is the focus of the last chapter about plans to use gas on Japan. This book illustrates the above-mentioned circumstances and includes the important episodes when the three cooperated and challenged one another at the policy level, even as they faced domestic trials and the Axis threat.

The story of World War II includes repeated decisions by key Western nations, alone and in concert, not to deploy gas, but it also includes gas as an active weapon, shaping perceptions and behaviors, even when it was not released. But as 1945 opened, increased ability to use CW, war-weariness, desensitization to destruction, and reduced fear of retaliation brought gas warfare closer to reality. Ironically, the atom bomb removed the need for the Western Allies to face a monumental decision about CW.

# CHAPTER 1

# Chain, Tool, Shield

## The Role of an International Treaty in Chemical Weapons Arms Control before World War II

> One lesson from the experience of the [First World] war is that we should not bind ourselves to observe any rules of war unless those who sign them with us undertake to uphold them by force, if need be, against an enemy who breaks them. We kept the rule against the use of poison gas [established in the Hague Conventions] till the Germans broke it, and when they did break it we had neither gas nor protection against gas ready. The rule was nothing but a disadvantage to us, for its violations by the Germans brought no help to us. To bind ourselves by rules which we intend to keep and others intend to break is unreasonable, so long as those who break them do it with impunity.
>
> —Lord Grey in *Twenty-Five Years*, quoted in the Committee of Imperial Defence, 1926

Before World War I, the great powers twice had prohibited chemical warfare: first in the 1899 Hague Conventions by banning asphyxiating projectiles, and then in the 1907 Hague Conventions by restricting poisonous and cruel weapons. Not every power had signed or ratified these treaties; the United Kingdom, France, Germany, Japan, and Russia did, but the United States did not join the 1899 Declaration against gas, although it did become a party to the 1907 Convention. As a result, Germany surprised the Allies when it released chlorine gas in 1915, but they, especially the British, prepared, retaliated, and learned to wage chemical warfare offensively and defensively throughout the rest of the conflict.

Lord Grey (formerly Sir Edward Grey) recounts this in the quotation at the beginning of this chapter, and his frustration and disillusionment with the treaties that were supposed to have protected Britain resonated in a Committee of Imperial Defence meeting over a decade later.[1] So, why did Britain, Canada, and the United States keep supporting interwar attempts to create treaties prohibiting chemical weapons (CW) including, eventually, the one that governed World War II gas use? Depending on the national perspective, the treaties were tools, shields, or chains—tools to gain political power at home or abroad, shields against gas attacks by enemies, but also chains to limit the flexibility of a country's gas policy.

While the Geneva Gas Protocol of 1925 governed international law regarding chemical warfare during World War II, there were multiple efforts to restrict and even prohibit wartime use of gas after World War I. The 1919 Treaty of Versailles, the 1922 Treaty Regarding the Use of Submarines and Noxious Gases in Warfare negotiated at the Washington Naval Conference hereinafter the Noxious Gases Treaty, and the failed 1930s World Disarmament Conference (WDC) all wrestled with ways to ban chemical warfare. For example, the Treaty of Versailles ostensibly banned only Germany from using gas, while the 1921–1922 Washington Naval Conference gas treaty was not ratified by enough signatories, and key powers refused to remain at the negotiating table during the World Disarmament Conference of the 1930s. The Geneva Gas Protocol of 1925 came into force, but even it had numerous flaws.

The British government participated in the negotiations for each one and accepted the first three, despite explicitly recognizing their frailties in private and public discussions. On the other side of the Atlantic, US diplomats negotiated and signed all the completed interwar treaties banning gas, even when the US Senate did not consent to any of them. In fact, United States delegations proposed the anti-gas clauses in the 1922 Noxious Gases Treaty and the 1925 Geneva Gas Protocol.[2] Presidents Herbert Hoover and Franklin Roosevelt spoke in favor of a CW ban, as part of a larger disarmament effort, at the WDC in 1932 and 1933, including *"all* chemical warfare [emphasis added]" by the former and offensive weaponry by the latter.[3] The Canadians, transitioning to an independent foreign policy in the interwar period, played a minor role in the negotiations and wielded little influence in creating and empowering the documents. They did participate and demonstrate recognition of the importance of the topic and complexity of the issues in both their Senate and House. Although each treaty played a role in increasing commitments—moral and legal—to anti-gas policy among the Western Allies during the interwar period, the Geneva Gas Protocol was the most important and powerful document—the one that dictated World War II chemical warfare law, despite being recognized as weak—and thus the one that will be emphasized in this chapter along with the perspective of Britain, the most vocal and active of the Western Allies regarding this treaty.

The underlying motivations for these gas bans, particularly the Geneva Gas Protocol, rose from multiple sources in each nation, including sentiment from on high in government as well as public opinion. A variety of factors shaped each country's views and political decisions, including national values, first-hand military experiences, respect for international law, and differing geographical vulnerabilities. Yet, rationales behind anti-gas policies in Britain, the United States, and Canada meant that although these countries all contained constituencies and politicians who wrestled with the question of whether gas was a humane weapon—or at least whether it was more inhumane than others available during the interwar period—they developed different attitudes toward gas. These were not radically different—it was not that the United States was wholeheartedly pro-gas and the British Empire emphatically against it, for example. It was more that the lay and public political attitude against gas in the latter was more dominant than it was in the United States. There were enough similarities, namely rejection of gas by enough leaders to make a no-first-use combined gas policy among the Western Allies possible, but there were enough differences to generate tension and doubts about the robustness of the policy. Overall, Britain was more vulnerable to gas and more legally restrained from using it, Canada felt less vulnerable but was just as legally inhibited, and the anti-gas attitudes in the United States dominated enough to produce an anti-gas policy championed by the executive branch, but no firm legal bindings. Since a gas war when a nation or population was particularly vulnerable, whether because of a lack of defensive equipment, the inability to retaliate locally, or the risk of a gas war spreading to global possessions, could realistically prove to be "catastrophic," as the British Joint Planning Staff stated bluntly, the stakes were high to fight a gas-free war.[4]

For Britain, although the treaties were nominally a shield, in reality they were a tool and a chain. Public opinion and political pressure encouraged the government to sign treaties banning gas so that they could serve as shields for the country against the anxiety and destruction of future chemical warfare. While the British government did not believe that the treaties could guarantee the country's safety, and in fact they might hamper it if weak ones constricted its behavior and choices but not an adversary's, the country did continue to participate in negotiations and sign the interwar treaties as they developed. The result was that the British poison gas policy developed during the interwar period was a simple one on its face: it would not start a gas exchange, but it reserved the right of retaliation in kind. This policy may not seem surprising today, in an era in which gas is a taboo and illegal weapon for great powers, but during World War I and in its immediate aftermath, neither stricture was inevitable. The British, and most of the other major belligerents, had used gas extensively, and increasingly, during the Great War—and they expected to continue to do so if the war had continued.

Britain followed this course of action while protecting its national security. From the government discussions behind closed doors, it is clear that politicians made decisions about gas laws based on realistic assessments of the treaties and of the international situation; practicalities, not philosophical interpretations about the humane or barbaric nature of gas, guided the conclusions. Yet while the law might have been only a weak shield, the government also believed it could be useful as a tool to discourage the onset of gas warfare or to put an employer of gas at a moral disadvantage in the court of global public opinion. In addition, the government ensured that the chain remained loose enough to allow the military to engage in research and other efforts to protect the nation legally; Britain resisted efforts to tighten it too much. The result was a series of interwar gas laws—including the Geneva Gas Protocol—that were weak on their face and, as scholars have noted, failed to achieve chemical disarmament.[5] Britain recognized these flaws even as they were signed, but in the end the treaties protected British national security interests regarding chemical warfare as it prepared for the next war. While imperfect, they enabled Britain to maintain an adequate gas policy: the treaties could not guarantee protection against gas, but they did not leave Britain completely vulnerable to it either. This situation shaped Britain's gas policy and actions toward CW in the interwar and World War II.

Canada had a minimal role in the interwar gas discussions, and it viewed the treaty as more than just a document about gas. As a dominion, it had little say in the Treaty of Versailles or the Noxious Gases treaty. By 1925, it had gained independent authority to approve the Geneva Gas Protocol, and most of the parliamentary debate about it demonstrated that approval was not just about gas.[6] Approval meant following Britain's lead, and its own inclinations, but did it want to do that blindly, or did it want to make it clear that it was making its own decision? Did it feel closer to the United States, its strong neighbor to the south, or to the mother country across the Atlantic? These tensions were not unique to debates about gas, but they do illustrate that CW policy was wrapped up in discussions about Canadian sovereignty during the interwar years, not just in World War II. The fact that Canada, like the United States, was less at risk for a future gas attack on the home front is likely to have made it more feasible for Canada to argue about gas from a political perspective with an eye to increasing its power and enhancing its specific identity in the international community rather than that of a potential victim. Gas treaties could be possible shields against a foe's temptation to start a gas war as well as tools for helping Canada establish its place among nations. Thus, while the Geneva Gas Protocol influenced Canada's gas policy, and limited its sovereignty, Canada's geographical position and level of diplomatic power meant that chemical warfare was less of a threat early in the war just as the gas threat was less of a factor in Canada's thinking and behavior during that period than it was for Britain and the United States, who faced German and Japanese attacks more directly.

The United States struggled with chemical warfare, too, but the national debates contained less angst than in Britain; the treaty was a weak shield and a tool, but not a chain. Some powerful people, such as General John Pershing, the commander of the American Expeditionary Force during World War I and thus familiar with CW targeting soldiers, argued vociferously against gas because of its potential to harm civilians. By 1926 he feared that future gas use of any kind could lead to "the possible poisoning of whole populations of non-combatant men, women, and children."[7] President Hoover decried gas as inhumane and argued that it should be prohibited.[8] A range of other factors entered the debate. For example, although it is worth noting that the US Chemical Warfare Service (CWS) was not the only one targeted for contraction in the early 1920s, the postwar trend of cutting the military budget meant that some anti-gas factions focused less on the nature of gas than on its cost.[9] Grassroots movements, such as the Women's International League for Peace and Freedom (WILPF), had broad disarmament goals, but sometimes they focused on gas explicitly.[10]

On the other hand, some were true believers, such as Major General Amos Fries, the Army's lead chemical warfare officer in Europe during World War I, who wanted to expand the chemical branch in the military as well as enhance its reputation.[11] In 1919 he celebrated the "'humanness' [sic] of chemical weapons," but he declared that gases, presumably nonlethal ones, would be "'exceedingly inviting' for police work."[12] In 1923 he went further, touting gas to cleanse cotton of the boll weevil, docks of teredo, and ships of barnacles.[13] Others favored gas for more commercial reasons as well; two of the most active organizations throughout the early interwar period were the American Chemical Society and the industry-sponsored National Association for Chemical Defense, formed to respond to the Geneva Gas Protocol.[14] The American Legion, as part of its general support for the military, was another proponent. While some of the debate, therefore, was about questions of humanity and peace, other elements focused on commercial and military power struggles.[15] These latter were strong not only because their supporters were more organized than the anti-gas lobby but also because they could draw on traditional US values such as business enterprise (chemistry was a key part of business success) and patriotism (veterans wanted powerful tools for soldiers).

The anti-gas lobby could marshal some compelling appeals, especially emotional ones. Will Irwin, a famous journalist who published *The Next War* in 1921, four years later decried visions of gas attacks on civilians in *The New York Times* in response to Secretary of the Navy Curtis Wilbur's dismissal of

**FIGURE 1.**    Amos Fries, chief of the US Chemical Warfare Service, championed the use of gas in war and peace. (Imago History Collection/Alamy Stock Photo)

those horrified by visions of future warfare. Irwin responded with a graphic image, "[a] flood of this killer [Lewisite gas] rolling over a city: that fatal dew everywhere; men, women and children burning in a dozen places."[16] While he was one of many speakers, he had a loud voice and large platform. Still, these appeals were not enough to overcome concerns that treaties would obligate permanent entanglements in world affairs or the need to maintain business health. Factors unrelated to gas meant that the United States did not ratify the Treaty of Versailles and that the Washington Naval Conference's Noxious Gas agreement did not come into force, so the US stance is most apparent in its actions regarding the Geneva Gas Protocol. In the end, the United States felt less threatened by gas, refusing to ratify the Geneva Gas Protocol.

In fact, the United States opened the door for some gas use by incorporating tear gas into domestic control, both by the military when it responded to riots and in the police arsenal. Its insistence that this be permitted meant that the United States interpreted international arms control prohibitions to allow some gas, regardless of whether other parties wanted complete bans.[17] It also compelled Britain to consider opening the door to nonlethal gas use in the colonies.

The result was more of a stalemate than the situation that emerged in Britain: there was no clear position for or against gas in the United States, and both sides debated whether gas, and treaties prohibiting it, could be a tool for the future, if not always a successful one for either side.[18] This meant that the president could shape the US gas policy; as long as he was firm, the CW stance remained stable. Yet, that meant that the US policy could change more quickly than that of any other nation. In the eyes of its Allies, this meant that the United States had the weakest restraints of all. And, by failing to add its own support to the legal bans, it removed a potentially powerful prop from them. Thus, some of the weaknesses in the legal gas bans are the United States' responsibility.

In sum, the United States was not a leader in the pro-gas or anti-gas movements, even though it was the nation that proposed some of the international gas bans and was the most powerful one to reject any of the bans. The United States helped muddy the waters, although it did not bear full onus for the prohibitions' weaknesses. All countries who permitted vague treaties have to answer for that—it is merely why and how much they bear responsibility that varies. It is ironic that the United States was one of the most powerful countries in World War II but had failed to take a leadership role with gas in the run up to it.

In the meantime, the Western Allies shared some anti-gas values about first strikes, and even general dislike of gas use, despite differing about the extent of that rejection, the roots of the anti-CW attitudes, and the fact the United States had not ratified the Geneva Gas Protocol. While all three countries entered World War II with a superficially similar no-first-use attitude toward chemical warfare, the three governments' divergent attitudes to the Geneva Gas Protocol show the underlying tensions that would plague their attempt at a common policy in World War II. At the same time, the British commitment to that policy was much stronger, grounded as it was in legal principles, and not simply personal anti-gas preferences and political machinations of its people and leaders. Thus, while all three countries had military rationales to maintain their anti-gas policies during World War II, Britain's reasons were wider and deeper, rooted not simply in the battlefield but in real dangers to its civilians at home and in the Empire. The reasons to choose, repeatedly, to avoid using gas involved more complexities, as subsequent chapters will show. However, over the course of the war, the tensions between these perspectives led to challenges that almost destroyed the agreement not to engage in to offensive gas warfare—something that would have shocked millions of people who were convinced that gas warfare might destroy civilization as they knew it.

## Interwar Public Opinion

The uneven diplomatic efforts to ban gas reflected the public ambivalence about CW.[19] After the Armistice, in Britain and globally, there were public efforts to debate the nature of gas and to outlaw it again. The discussions about gas revolved around several issues, but the central one was the nature of CW: were they inhumane? In Britain, for example, private individuals, such as H. G. Wells, and former servicemen, such as Lord Halsbury, provided loud and influential voices in public debate and continued to speak out into the 1930s.[20] H. G. Wells was a well-known novelist, and his words about destructive gases in books like *The Shape of Things to Come* would be read widely, even if they were fictional. Lord Halsbury wrote both fiction and nonfiction. His 1932 apocalyptic article in the *British Legion Journal* about gas use in the next war was profiled in *The New York Times*, quoting his argument that "people would be driven mad by the pain and misery [of future CW] and would lose all mental control," and if that were not dire enough, "London cannot be defended."[21] The Union for Democratic Control (UDC), a political organization founded in 1914 whose members crossed party lines, was among the influential citizen groups that opposed gas.[22] It certainly caught attention; one letter to the editor of the London *Times* described its gas pamphlet as "calculated to make the flesh of a rhinoceros creep."[23]

Some opinions were logical, based on known scientific information, and others emotional, inspired by fears of suffering and destruction. These beliefs challenged the gas-tolerant supporters, often scientists and soldiers who had worked with gas during the war, such as J. B. S. Haldane and Charles Foulkes, respectively.[24] While not all of those who tolerated gas enthusiastically embraced it, some did. Winston Churchill, a former minister of munitions, was one of its strongest, and bluntest, advocates, as befit his practical, dramatic, and adventurous nature. In 1919 he opened a memo by declaring "[t]he objections of the India Office to the use of gas against natives are unreasonable. Gas is a more merciful weapon than high explosive shell . . . There can be no conceivable reason why it should not be resorted to." Lest it seems like Churchill only supported internal or colonial use of, perhaps, nonlethal gases, he continued: "We have definitely taken the position of maintaining gas as a weapon in future wars."[25]

Others simply thought that chemical warfare could be managed, as did Henry Thuillier, a former head of the gas service and an interwar organizer of air raid precautions. He thought that proper training and distribution of gas masks would prevent a future gas war from becoming catastrophic.[26] After all, gas drills and defensive equipment had offered effective protection to many soldiers during the previous conflict. In the end, the more emotional and focused anti-gas side prevailed; British and global public opinion coalesced against chemical warfare, providing a force that was difficult for governments to challenge outright.

As important, both gas groups shared certain assumptions, especially that there would be a future war in which gas would be used widely and that it would be dropped from planes on civilians as well as soldiers.[27] Ironically, most of these predictions were incorrect. There was another war, of course, and civilians did suffer from aerial bombing, but gas was not a key component. Understanding that these beliefs were deeply and widely held, though, helps explain, when added to the loud anti-gas voices, the repeated attempts during the interwar period by governments and multinational organizations (such as the League of Nations) to prevent a gas war through international negotiations and treaties. This was the case even when realists, including some politicians and international groups who acquiesced to the treaties, doubted that the law could guarantee a ban on gas warfare.

In Britain, these voices arose originally not because of Nazi Germany's threat or dire events of the 1930s, but early in the post–World War I period. In Britain, as early as 1922, the London *Times* stated authoritatively: "It is obvious to every layman that civilization itself may be overthrown if chemical warfare develops, as was foreshadowed during the later stages of the Great War. It is obvious, too, that the progress of aviation exposes all to perils hitherto undreamed of, and what with explosive bombs, poisonous gases, and the like enormous damage may be done with little profit to anyone."[28] At about the same time, one can see that the experts also thought gas and planes would be linked. General staff officer J. F. C. Fuller gave a lecture to British physicians. His words and the implications of his talk were heard even across the Atlantic. *Time* magazine reported in its June 25, 1923, issue that, "[t]he purpose of the lecture was to prepare medical men for coping with thousands of gas cases, and to popularize methods of self-protection among the civilian population. Five hundred planes could capture London by anaesthetizing the entire population—if the attacking fleet were humane enough to avoid poison gas. When the matter-of-fact British seriously consider such possibilities, there is little doubt that the next phase of aerial warfare might spell the destruction of civilization."[29]

Within five years of the Armistice, therefore, the assumption was that a major European or world war would come again, and planes would have a powerful role.[30] To make matters more dreadful, planes would target civilians. This would be the next step in breaking the rules of war that the self-perceived civilized nations liked to pretend they held at the turn of the twentieth century. Civilians were supposed to be beyond the lines of fire, despite the fact that many were involved in World War I, arguably the first modern total war. Furthermore, while one of the supporters, Fuller, did allude to the possibility that CW could make war humane—if belligerents used relatively harmless sleeping gas—the article also made it clear that such restraint was unlikely. Considering that the trajectory of gas weaponry in World War I was one in which increasingly powerful and damaging mixtures appeared and were deployed in greater numbers over time, the pessimistic assumption about lethal gases being used was reasonable.

The British were far from alone in proclaiming that this combination of gas weapons, airplane delivery systems, and civilian targets was the future of war. These ideas, and the discussion about them, were international in scope, although, unsurprisingly, the Canadians more rarely addressed the issue of future gas use. When the national press did include stories, they tended to surface around the time of international negotiations. The Toronto *Globe and Mail*, for example, contained only a half dozen or so relevant stories in the decade after World War I, including a rare letter to the editor that queried "Has it occurred to you that . . . [gas] . . . will be the means of preventing wars in the future[?] Will any sensible nation declare war in the modern era with the certain conviction that if the enemy planes reach their territory, not only will their troops be wiped out, but also entire cities?"[31] While acknowledging the potential danger of future gas use, the author was not worried about Canada as much as about the civilians of the world. Other stories were generally in favor of bans but were reporting actions in Europe or the United States, rather than emphasizing Canadian views or actions.[32] The parliamentary debates were similar in scope and frequency.

On the other hand, the US section of the WILPF argued against weapons and war in general, but it also focused directly on gas at times.[33] It engaged in lobbying to get scientists and Congress on its side. For example, in an effort to generate political support for the Geneva Gas Protocol, in 1927 it circulated a pamphlet titled, "Can We Outlaw Poison Gas?"[34] In the document, the group listed a range of dire consequences if the United States failed to ratify the protocol, including hypocrisy, dashing people's hope of peace, and wasting resources (making gas and defenses rather than something more beneficial); it offered, therefore, moral and practical rationales to broaden the appeal of its argument. By 1931, *Time* magazine proclaimed this bluntly and openly; the call for arms limitation stretched beyond activists to mainstream journalism. It opened an article in the medicine section by stating: "The next war, militarists agree, will be a war of gas. It will be waged on civilians as well as soldiers."[35] There was open pressure against gas.

# Opening Rounds of Negotiation

The interwar efforts to ban gas had started modestly in the Treaty of Versailles of 1919. Article 171 prohibited Germany from "use. . [,] manufacture and importation" of gas.[36] The core text of 171 mirrored the essence of Article 23 of Section II of the Hague Convention of 1907 that stated it was "especially forbidden . . . to employ poison or poisoned weapons," but more relevantly, Britain believed that 171 directly referred to the existence of the earlier treaty, thus indicating that gas was still outlawed for all the Hague signatories, including itself.[37] The peace treaty, therefore, did not restrict Germany uniquely with regard to gas use (although it did with regard to gas manufacturing).

There was some ambiguity in this interpretation, though, which was important because official British chemical warfare policy had not been set firmly yet. During World War I, British policy permitted offensive use of any gas already deployed by the Germans.

This was different than the eventual international interwar efforts banning offensive gas use by all parties. In the immediate postwar years, the British government's attitude toward gas—both lethal compounds such as mustard as well as irritants like tear gas—was still being debated behind closed doors. Unlike the general public's debate about the humane nature of gas, one of the immediate issues for the British government was the practical question of whether gas was a useful weapon—a beneficial tool—and, in particular, whether it would be advantageous in the Empire. Mustard gas (the toxin most commonly mentioned by name) might solve some problems by taming rebellions at a low human and material cost for Britain.[38] As Winston Churchill, then secretary of state for the colonies, stated in a 1919 memo advocating gas in Afghanistan, "Gas . . . compels an enemy to accept a decision with less loss of [British] life than any other agency of war."[39] Some of his colleagues clearly agreed with him because the British considered using gas, especially tear gas, in Iraq, another trouble spot, in 1920 to put down a rebellion.[40]

Across the Atlantic, the United States government had already begun to embrace the anti-gas attitude, even as the CWS and some other groups continued to champion the weapon. The United States included the language from Article 171 in its own later peace settlement with Germany.[41] Soon afterward, the United States led the efforts to draft a new treaty that explicitly prohibited all signatories from using gas by proposing to include it in the arms control treaties negotiated in 1921 and 1922 at the Washington Naval Conference in the District of Columbia and later.[42] All of the future Western Allies ratified or otherwise approved of the extension of the ban; it was not one of them, but rather France, that nullified the limitations on gas when it rejected the restrictions on submarines in the same agreement.

## The League Takes the Biggest Step

The most important interwar developments occurred in 1924 when the League of Nations' Temporary Mixed Commission on Armaments finally produced a report, based on the opinions of international scientific experts and its own members, in an attempt to create a ban on gas that restrained more nations than the few at the Washington Naval Conference.[43] The report confirmed a widespread rejection of gas because its use, especially against civilians, "would be too horrible . . . the conscience of mankind would revolt at it."[44] It also admitted that, because of the nature of gas weapons and the chemical industry, the conversion of peacetime procedures and products to military ones was inevitable. No complete safeguards were possible: "Noting . . . the vital danger to which a nation would expose itself if it were lulled into security by over confidence in international treaties and conventions[,]" the nations needed to gain a full awareness of the danger of chemical warfare.[45] This seemed to be a warning to the lay population as well as to governments not to be soothed by treaties; while they appeared to be the only path toward protection on the international front at this point, perhaps there were national steps that could be taken to shield countries as well.

In Britain, the result was a renewed determination not to get caught by surprise as it had been in World War I when Germany violated the Hague Conventions. Internal proposals suggested augmenting Britain's current research and defensive work because it was clear that no law would ever completely protect the country. Even if it did not want to use gas offensively, Britain must take steps to retaliate if someone else did. Basically, therefore, the report did not change Britain's gas policy; it confirmed the fears that underlay it.

In the United States during this same period, the CWS struggled. After the war, it wanted, if possible, to enhance its status, but at the very least, it wanted to minimize any of the budget and personnel cuts that were rife in the interwar period.[46] The General Staff restrained the CWS from working on anything but defensive activities, with that restriction largely in place until the middle of the next decade.[47] As part of its efforts to gain authority and prestige during this time, the CWS lobbied to promote its usefulness outside of war too. One of key areas was its work in pesticides for rodents and insects.[48]

The efforts to draft an effective anti-gas treaty heated up again in the mid-1920s. In 1925, during the Arms Traffic Conference in May and June, the League of Nations tried to enhance international bans when a new anti-gas proposal arose. The result, the Geneva Gas Protocol, was the most rigorous and successful of the interwar CW treaties, and, in fact, it lasted until the Chemical Weapons Convention came into force in 1997.[49] The Geneva Gas Protocol contained the same core prohibitions as the earlier agreements.[50] Gas, defined as it was in the Treaty of Versailles and Article V of the Noxious Gases treaty, would not be used, although the clauses against the manufacture and importation of gas, present in the World War I treaty, were absent. Perhaps this was because gas was seen as uncivilized, "justly condemned by the . . . civilized world" according to the preamble, and, in fact, already banned in some eyes by customary international law.[51] This last statement articulated the position that, strictly speaking, countries were bound by it regardless of signing it; it was customary law for nations, although signing an agreement and thus showing conscious acceptance often seemed to add more force to a legal standard.

The new elements included a ban on biological weapons, armaments that had been discussed but not used in World War I; experts predicted that they could well be developed and employed in the future.[52] As with the original bans on gas in the Hague Conventions, the goal here was to prevent the use of a weapon before it had been introduced.

The other noteworthy component was that many more countries had the opportunity to sign this treaty from the beginning; it was not restricted to the few leading naval powers that had been invited to the Washington Conference. Essentially, the Geneva Gas Protocol tried to open the 1922 treaty, not in force because of France's refusal to approve it, to other nations.[53]

As with the earlier treaties, the British government wrestled with its position on this agreement. The British officials did not challenge the inclusion of new elements, namely the prohibition of bacteriological weapons or additional signatories, but rather the debate centered on the traditional concerns. Would this new agreement bind Britain in a way that would be detrimental to its national security? Should it sign the new treaty?[54] Would Britain still be able to conduct effective research and training regarding gas?[55]

The treaty did not restrict gas use against those who did not ratify, and those included some of the great powers such as the United States and Japan, countries that had signed the Noxious Gases treaty.[56] Although those holdouts could have ratified the treaties at any time, after a few years it was unlikely that they would do so. It was also unlikely that those who refused to ratify would agree with the idea that there was a customary ban on gas that restricted them from using CW, whether or not they signed a treaty. In some ways the protocol was an improvement over the Noxious Gases treaty. The larger pool of signatories was a benefit because more countries could bind themselves explicitly and reject gas, at least officially. However, did the agreement really protect ratifiers from some of the nations, such as Japan, that were most likely to be able to have the supplies and skills to wage a chemical war?

Perhaps the key issue was that yet again there was no real enforcement mechanism even listed or suggested in the body of the protocol; this was not unique to interwar agreements, but it was significant because many signatories carefully reserved the right of retaliation when they ratified the protocol, something that the drafters had not intended.[57] As one scholar mentioned, this meant that the treaty was simply an agreement to avoid first use of gas.[58] In the end, it did not advance gas prohibitions very far. It certainly did not mean that Britain or other nations could abandon their defensive or retaliation preparations with confidence because "[i]t is . . . hard to believe" that a country "less scrupulous than Great Britain . . . would not avail himself of such a powerful weapon of surprise."[59] If that happened, how would a country effectively punish a nation with which it was already at war other than by responding in kind? Would neutrals agree to enter war on behalf of a country that had been gassed? Would a nation trust an ally who claimed that a common enemy started a gas war and that all the allies should retaliate in kind?

Yet, inertia in the form of past condemnation of gas warfare, from the Hague Conventions to the Versailles Treaty and Noxious Gases treaty, made it hard to change directions. In other words, was Britain already "under the moral, though not legal obligation" to avoid gas use?[60] Added to this was public pressure, including from the International Committee of the Red Cross (ICRC). It not only pressed to have the Geneva Gas Protocol ratified but also wanted nations to share defensive information to allow the ICRC to assist victims if chemical warfare ever came to pass.[61] The latter, one might imagine, would not be popular with militaries or manufacturers, but it might make laymen everywhere feel better.

Regardless, it was not an easy decision for signatories to ratify the protocol. For reasons of politics and precedence, it was almost impossible to protest or reject the new treaty in a nation where those factors provided strong pressure to act. Even so, the protocol was not much more of a shield or chain than earlier bans except for the possibility that violating it would be even more offensive in global eyes since so many nations had adhered to the agreement.

Still, Britain did start to enhance its plans for future warfare with an eye to its own safety and that of its worldwide empire, which also demonstrates its use of the law as a tool that could be used to reinforce the abandonment of offensive gas use and bolster the right of retaliation. Even before ratifying, on February 18, 1925, the government decided to follow France's proposal: at the beginning of future conflicts it planned to contact belligerents, if they had also signed the

Geneva Gas Protocol, and ask if they planned to adhere to the protocol during the forthcoming war.[62] The query would contain a clear deterrent: "If this engagement [to avoid offensive gas use] is not obtained [from the recipient of the message], the French government will reserve its liberty to act according to circumstances."[63] By following the French lead, the British clearly retained the right to retaliation, a power they were careful not to lose in the rest of the interwar period.

A bit closer to home, London wanted the Empire to present a common front regarding gas and to hold a unified policy, especially regarding the ratification.[64] This was the first postwar gas focused treaty that most of the dominions were eligible to sign—and thus the first time London lobbied them. The Empire and Commonwealth provided resources, soldiers, and bases, but it also created vulnerabilities. The latter included potential loci of disturbances in the Middle East, Africa, India, and beyond. Unity is about harnessing strength and coordinating defenses, but as important is avoiding the appearance and actuality of weaknesses. Considering Britain's sensitivity to standing afoul of public opinion if it were to be the only country seemingly to embrace the now vilified weapon if it protested the ban strongly or even failed to sign it, it is not surprising that it looked to the Empire for allies. In addition, Britain would expect to fight alongside the colonies and the dominions in a future conflict as demonstrated by the existence of the Committee of Imperial Defence. This group, composed of civilian and military representatives, offered advice to the cabinet for the Empire, and had been established to consider crisis and security issues. A compatible philosophy regarding gas was all the more necessary.

Once Britain and the dominions formulated a general common policy, and Britain did not feel so alone, the next step was to determine when or how to ratify the Geneva Gas Protocol officially. Britain did not want to hamstring itself by restricting its own actions legally if others were not bound in the same way. Once signed, the law had to be honored. The cabinet settled on a wait-and-see plan in which the nation would not ratify the protocol until other nations did.[65] Perhaps the stakes seemed higher with each new agreement, whether because the dangers of war grew closer or because each one provided additional pressure to abstain from gas.

Still, although it seemed like the repeated conversations about the timing of ratification and the efforts to achieve it meant that the gas policy was more or less established, the issue was not as settled as it might have seemed. As late as November 1927, a cabinet meeting included a discussion about whether Britain should radically change its policy regarding gas. Should it begin to argue that it was a humane and thus legitimate weapon, giving warning that it intended to use it and, presumably, refuse to ratify the treaties in the end? After all, at this point, Britain was not firmly legally committed to Geneva (or even the Noxious Gases agreement), although politically and perhaps morally it was. As the cabinet meeting summary noted: "The main point submitted for the decision of the Cabinet was the general policy to be adopted in regard to Chemical Warfare; that is to say, should we change the policy we have hitherto adopted of denouncing Gas as a method of warfare, or should we in future advocate the international recognition of this weapon as legitimate and not necessarily inhuman?"[66]

Some of the military experts had pressed that view all along, marshalling statistics and charts to prove their point, or at least to promote the idea that gas was no more inhumane than the other major weapons of modern war.[67] Yet part of what caused the issue to arise seriously again was probably the awareness that the Soviet Union was examining gas intently. In other words, it seemed that chemical warfare might be an even more real and immediate threat than previously considered, and thus self-restrictions invoked by signing the treaties were more dangerous.[68]

In the end, Britain decided to maintain its rejection of gas use—at least first use—partially, it appears, because of the effort of trying to change generally negative public and legal attitudes about gas and partly because of the risks civilians might face in a gas war regardless of what any treaty promised in terms of protection. In addition, Britain certainly was unwilling to suffer condemnation for violating norms and legal bans against gas.[69] Besides, its current policy of promising not to initiate a gas war but preparing to defend against one could continue. This policy did not provide it as much security as a policy that allowed it to use freely a potentially valuable weapon on its own terms, but it was a compromise that garnered it the rights to prepare defensively, limit its armament spending (especially during economic hard times), reserve retaliatory prerogatives, keep legal respect, maintain the support of public opinion, and perhaps constrain some of its enemies.

Despite these reasons, it was not until 1929 that the British ratified the Geneva Gas Protocol, and this was only after yet more debate.[70] While the cabinet and Committee on Imperial Defence did not specify in their conclusions why they decided the time was right, the votes occurred soon after circulation of a note by Hugh Trenchard, the chief of the air staff, on March 25, 1929. He distilled the situation into five reasons: (1) almost everyone else (i.e., the great powers) had ratified while reserving the right to be bound only with regard to other signatories and holding the right to retaliate; (2) signing would not change Britain's ability to continue to engage in defensive measures; (3) not ratifying might give an enemy "some excuse" for using gas; (4) Britain was unlikely to start a gas war, so the implication was that it was not giving up anything; and (5) a widely ratified protocol might discourage a gas war. Interestingly, there was no reference to the biological warfare components in the protocol.[71] It was clear from the preliminary meetings in Geneva that the forthcoming World Disarmament Conference, in which gas, yet again, was on the agenda, was also a factor. According to Lord Cushendun, the British consul in Geneva, Britain would have more credibility and status in the negotiations if it spoke from a position of full legal bona fides.[72]

Still, mimicking France, Britain adhered with two key reservations. Britain stated that the protocol only "bound [it with regard to] those other States which have signed and ratified the Protocol or adhered thereto . . . [and it] ceases to be bound . . . [with regard to] any enemy State whose armed forces or whose allies do not respect the Protocol."[73] This drastically limited the original reach of the agreement that planned to ban all gas use. It also meant that Britain did not really change its policy on gas: it could maintain defensive research and some offensive preparations.

While the British government carried on debates about the protocol, considering Britain's position as well as that of the Empire and dominions, Canada turned its attention to the treaty too. Canada had signed the Geneva document on its own, but, as a dominion, still felt tied to Britain. It could make its own decision about ratification, yet when the issue arose in Parliament in Ottawa, Prime Minister Mackenzie King presented the motion as one in which the goal was for the "Dominion government to ask the approval of parliament" so Canada could ratify the treaty "as the same time . . . as it is ratified . . . in Great Britain."[74] Raoul Dandurand in the Senate noted that Canada planned to follow Britain's lead and ratify, too, with the standard reservations that made the treaty a "no first use" treaty applicable only to those who also ratified.[75] In some ways, it was an easy decision for Canada. Both houses approved the protocol, and each did so within one day of debate. Even the opposition, in the person of the conservative leader Richard Bennett, later prime minister himself, had quickly made it known "that this is a purely formal matter." He added to the interpretation that the goal was worthy because "[w]e are endeavouring to prevent a form of warfare . . . that has met with the universal reprobation of mankind."[76] Edward Garland pointed out something that was hard to dispute: Canada has "the least to fear of any nation" from warfare, partly because of its geographical distance from most major threats.[77] Furthermore, as James Ralston, the minister of national defense, stated bluntly: the core of the treaty would not change Canada's policy; it had, after all, ratified the Noxious Gases treaty, and thus its principles had been set.[78] The loyalty to Britain, the belief in the value of eradicating gas, the geographical insulation, and Britain's reservations likely all made it easier to trust in the Geneva Gas Protocol and not worry as much as the other countries if it was a naïve trust.

Yet, some politicians, including veterans who had faced gas threats personally in World War I, were not blind to potential flaws in the treaty or to the implications that merely following Britain's foreign policy could have. Robert Manion, a Conservative politician from Ontario who was a veteran of World War I and a winner of the Military Cross—someone who thought about gas treaties from a political perspective but knew about gas from a soldier's experience—voiced the same doubt that was felt in Britain and the United States: could the treaty be trusted?[79] He feared that there was a potential parallel between the Hague Conventions that had been violated in World War I and the potential for the Geneva Gas Protocol to be broken in a future war.[80] In the Senate, the issue arose again, as William Griesbach, a veteran of the Battle of Vimy Ridge, expressed what he thought was the view of the "[t]he average person" who also doubted that the treaty would hold if it were a question of national survival, as well as offering a reason for someone to vote for a flawed treaty. He noted that "human nature" would not permit a country to follow the rules in that case. Against gas himself, he said he would "vote for the resolution [to ratify the protocol] as it can do no harm, but it would be the height of folly for any person to be misled into thinking that our approval . . . settles the question of gases in warfare." He "gravely doubt[s] the value of treaties . . . of this kind."[81]

There was also some resistance because of Canada's relationship with Britain and the United States, not just because of the protocol itself. James Woodsworth, a member of the Independent Labour Party, did not think that his country should follow Britain's lead blindly as far as incorporating the two reservations. This debate was an opportunity to "gradually enter upon a better understanding in our foreign relationships."[82] Griesbach wondered what to do if the United States had not ratified Geneva yet and was told it had not.[83] Canada was in an awkward position politically, geographically, militarily, and culturally. Britain traditionally had managed Canada's foreign policy, and, of course, Canada still had firm cultural and political ties to the Empire. On the other hand, Canada's neighbor was the United States, a rising power and one that proposed gas bans. The protocol could be a vehicle for testing where Canada's loyalty lay and how much independence it felt it could exert in making diplomatic and military decisions. In the end, there was enough support for the ban that these questions of sovereignty did not play a large role in the parliamentary debates, but they are worth noting because the tensions influenced Canada's actions and the World War II gas alliance between the three countries.

Canada then, in discussions that proved to be much shorter and filled with less conflict than those in Britain and the United States, agreed to ratify the Geneva Gas Protocol the same year the British did. While it is perhaps true that Canada had the luxury of being more idealistic because it was less physically vulnerable than Britain or other nations, it did not have to be visionary. It ratified with some hope, but also with open eyes and an awareness that the original goal, according to Mackenzie King, was to "help establish international law."[84] It was also done with the realistic view that, as Raoul Dandurand noted: "[i]t is true that some nation may violate" it, but its real impact may be "to have a powerful moral effect," thus "planning for the future of humanity."[85] More relevant to the three Allies' future relationship, Canada was more optimistic than the United States in thinking that there was no harm, and possibly some good, in approving a treaty that was likely to be broken. In addition, while Canadian politicians used the ban to explore gently its sovereignty and allegiances in foreign policy, the US counterparts found it to be a vehicle for domestic political wrangling.

In fact, the United States failed to ratify the protocol more because of internal political conflict than because of a change of heart about the nature or practicality of gas. Although the terms of the protocol were in the public eye, courtesy of detailed newspaper articles as well as peace and disarmament activists, that was not enough to provide sufficient pressure for ratification.[86] Furthermore, those in the community who favored the treaty did not exert themselves much to support it, while the chemical industry and the military organized to present arguments against the protocol. Perhaps the proponents thought that they did not need to do so. Regardless, the fact that the Senate did not approve the protocol (until 1975) reveals that public and political fear of gas was not overwhelming. The protocol generated debate over serious issues, however. As *The New York Times* opined, "The debate on poison gas promises to be a spectacular one, for the subject lends itself to oratorical contention. There is much dispute about the facts past, present and potential: but whatever the truth may be an immense leeway for opinion and emotion exists."[87] Senator James W. Wadsworth, Jr., chair of the Senate Committee for Military Affairs, argued that gas was as humane as other weapons, while Senator William E. Borah, chair of the Senate Foreign Relations Committee, favored restraint on CW.[88] Borah had powerful allies, too, such as General John Pershing, whose letter of support he entered into the Congressional Record.[89]

The debate about the protocol brought the public into the political fray. The secretary of the American Chemical Society (ACS), Charles Parsons, exchanged letters with the secretary of state, Frank Kellogg; *The New York Times* coverage of the missives ensured public distribution of key sections. While their discussion focused on the accuracy of facts surrounding past negotiations, Kellogg argued that the United States had agreed to some previous anti-gas treaties, although not the 1899 Hague Declaration II against gases. Parsons's letter to the ACS members spoke out in vehement terms: ratification would be "a national calamity," and he urged them to write to their senators to lobby them.[90] Each man made logical points, but some of Parson's language revealed emotional undertones while Kellogg presented the face of an impassive diplomat. From World War I through World War II, usually anti-gas advocates were the ones who expressed emotional condemnations about CW policy; here it is clear that gas supporters felt deeply invested and motivated to act too.

The American Legion, another well-organized group, joined in the public debate, most noticeably by producing for distribution twenty-five thousand copies of its argument that gas was not inhumane. In fact, the chair of the American Legion's Legislative Committee, John Thomas Taylor, dismissed the anti-gas contingent as "pacifists . . . not . . . practical soldiers." He thought that the facts, including data amassed by the American Legion, showed that gas "makes for shorter wars, with less loss of life and subsequent misery" because it often just caused temporary incapacitation. The Legion also feared that the treaty would become a chain, "being honest-minded [the United States] would have no gas-service, nor any means to meet a gas attack by a pledge-breaking enemy."[91] In case a detailed article in *The New York Times* was not enough to spread their views, the Legion also convinced a senator to incorporate their pamphlet into the *Congressional Record* along with several other telegrams by local chapters and by other veterans' groups supporting the Legion's stance. Later, reading the transcripts of the 1929 debate about the protocol, one can hear the language and arguments of the Legion's pamphlet opposing a ban on gas.[92]

Thus, there were powerful words and voices on both sides of the deliberations, sometimes buffeting the protocol from different sides simultaneously. For example, in December 1926, the time that the Senate heard about Pershing's support for the protocol was the same time that the Senate considered returning the protocol to the Foreign Relations Committee for reconsideration (which it did, essentially burying it there) and that, outside of the Capitol, the ACS's president, Professor Norris, spoke to a professional body against the protocol.

While the general public may not have heard all of these arguments directly, they could read all about them in papers, including the well known *New York Times*.[93] Each individual senator may have had his own private reasons for his vote on ratification, but the context in which the politicians debated was a public one. Vocal lobbyists against the treaty spoke up at presentations, in letters to the

Senate, and through articles in newspapers in ways that made the debate a truly national one, not just one focused in Washington. Perhaps it is not surprising that the United States failed to ratify the protocol then, despite its strong support in Geneva when it was drafted: the lay voices speaking out were all against the treaty, and they had the commercial power of the chemical industry as well as the expertise of some of the military behind them. They did not necessarily stress these special qualifications, instead confronting the fears of the anti-gas groups on the latter's terms. They spoke of the humanity of gas compared to other weapons, even though neither side could really provide what a future gas war would be like. They also stressed the weakness of diplomacy, arguing that the protocol would only be a chain that would limit the US ability to fight back against anyone who did use gas. As Senator Lawrence Tyson noted, it would inhibit readiness because "even if we did go ahead and conduct the manufacture of chemicals for warfare, ultimately we would greatly decrease the preparation for this service and sooner or later it would come almost into disuse." In contrast, other countries might be ready, and, because of dual-use chemicals—ones that can be used for peaceful or military purposes—"no one will know it."[94]

This does not mean that the pro-gas lobby convinced the entire Senate, or even one party (note that Wadsworth was a Republican while Tyson was a Democrat), or even the US public. It did mean that the chief anti-gas advocate in the Senate, Senator Borah, did not think that two-thirds of his colleagues would vote not just *against* gas but *for* a treaty that could bind the United States' military might, especially when both sides considered the treaty unlikely to stop any nation from using gas. This distrust appeared repeatedly in debates about the Geneva Gas Protocol. Senator Wadsworth, the leader of the anti-Geneva group, believed that it would never be possible "to control the weapons used if they are militarily effective. When a nation is fighting for its life, like an individual, it will seize any weapon which will save its life."[95] Days later, Senator Joseph Ransdell echoed him, and the protocol's strongest supporter, Senator Borah, agreed.[96] Even in 1929, the last time the Geneva Protocol was discussed in detail before World War II, Congressman Roy Fitzgerald expressed the same sentiment more dramatically. He requested that those in favor of the protocol "give us security that any such agreement . . . will be observed by foreign nations, give us the assurance that the American people will not court punishment for the folly of putting naïve faith in what experience should teach us that others, under stress, may regard but as a 'scrap of paper.'"[97] No one was able to offer proof that the treaty would be viewed by enemies any more seriously than Germany had viewed Britain's guarantee of Belgian neutrality (anecdotally dismissed as just a "scrap of paper" by the Germans) before World War I; no one even tried to do so.

Although there were a few attempts to revive debate about the protocol between 1926 and 1929, such as when appropriations bills arose or when gas disasters occurred—even if these were not because of war gases—interest in the protocol rose in Congress only temporarily.[98] After 1929, consideration of the protocol went into hiatus for decades in the United States, and national opinion of gas remained unsettled. At least this way, though, the senators did not have to risk political opprobrium by voting against what they believed was the popular opinion; they could just let the treaty languish quietly out of sight.

The Geneva Gas Protocol, therefore, never became a chain for the United States in the way that it did for Britain or Canada, nor was it an effective tool to prod the United States into codifying a general ban on gas. As a result, though, it was the cause of the greatest tensions between the Western Allies on the chemical warfare front during World War II; even if the Western Allies recognized that the Geneva Gas Protocol could and might well be a weak shield that could be broken by a belligerent, Britain and Canada would not violate it lightly. Binding themselves to the powerful United States, a country that was not as vulnerable to gas as Britain for geographical reasons nor as hamstrung legally, made the unified chemical warfare policy between these three countries fragile.

The Geneva Gas Protocol is the key agreement from the interwar years and the last one ratified, but it was not because the signatories stopped trying to improve gas treaties and make them stricter and more effective. The WDC, also known as the Conference for the Reduction and Limitation of Armaments, was another attempt by the League to draft a treaty reducing weapons of all sorts. The real problem was not keeping CBW on the conference agenda, but rather keeping the conference alive. Germany's withdrawal from the League in October 1933 severely limited its accomplishments and, thus, the conference. Japan had withdrawn a few months earlier. There was no point in continuing trying to revise the gas, and even arms, agreements without the participation of some of the most potentially dangerous nations like Germany and Japan; thus the Geneva Protocol was left as the guiding document for gas use during World War II.

Nothing new had been settled, and Britain avoided having to commit again to a potentially flawed treaty or to cause an uproar by rejecting it.[99] Canada was in the same position. Britain's legal position and general wartime lethal gas policy remained unchanged, even as its conviction that a gas war was coming closer grew. In the Empire, air raid precautions stepped up, including ones to handle gas attacks on civilians.[100] The one real change to Britain's policy was that its plan to send telegrams to enemy belligerents at the start of a conflict, asking if each would obey the Geneva Gas Protocol, broadened to include any foe, even signatories to that agreement who should, theoretically, be legally constrained and trustworthy. Foreign Secretary Lord Halifax said that this was inspired by Germany and the idea that "since 1935 . . . conditions had changed. Gas had come more into the picture, and there was increasing evidence that enemy Governments seem less likely to honour their word."[101] Still the law could be a useful tool, even in this sort of situation. Rejections of queries about adherence to the protocol could be publicized, and, in an era in which public opinion was valuable and powerful, rejection or later violation of the protocol could "be of considerable propaganda value."[102]

The United States was not a member of the League, of course, but it had expressed support for the conference through ambassadorial and presidential communications. Politically, though, the United States maintained a national policy, based on presidential rejection of gas, throughout the interwar period.

At first glance, it seems that international attempts to formulate an international gas law that inspired trust in the interwar period was a failure or, at best, an uphill battle in which treaty signatories were forced to accept chains that severely limited their freedom of behavior and failed to form an effective shield. Doubts about legitimate shields, as well as doubts that gas was an inhumane weapon or even a real threat to North America, meant that the United States took a different path than Britain and Canada. The US Senate rejected the major interwar gas treaty, the Geneva Gas Protocol, although the United States government was split on its attitude toward gas, with a divide between the legislative and executive branches as well as within the legislative branch itself. Although the United States had been a leader in proposing anti-gas treaties, it failed to create an effective tool that would lend itself to a firm anti-gas stance, even one that would deter through an ability to retaliate with gas. There were repeated indications that both the anti-gas and pro-gas factions had power; this is part of what enabled the United States to be in the position to develop a chemical warfare policy with Britain and Canada during World War II that honored the gas prohibitions the latter two wanted to respect. It also meant that Canada and Britain could not trust completely an US anti-gas policy that was rooted in the chief executive's will, and thus something that could change when a new president came into office or if he changed his mind.

Canada did not seem to feel the angst that Britain did about the sturdiness of the anti-gas bans, perhaps because of its geographical safety net setting it apart from the threats London faced on continental Europe. The protocol, however, did provide a restraint that removed an incentive for Canada to change its policy and begin to prepare intensively for a gas war. Thus, while supporting gas bans, and seeing them as a possible shield and political tool,

Canada did not wrestle with all the nuances and implications of the protocol before ratifying it and did not find that it demanded much action even if the protocol itself did not guarantee protection.

However, the protocol served Britain—not perfectly, but adequately. The United Kingdom never gained an impeccable shield, but then it did not expect that one could be developed. Instead, by signing the protocol it placated the anti-gas public opinion and maintained its credibility as one of the great power nations perceived to be civilized. It restricted its expenditures on gas production and offensive training; while there are no hints that these limits were major goals, it is clear that Britain was cutting defense costs as part of its budget-tightening. The United Kingdom gained a tool; it believed it could pressure opponents to adhere to the treaty or shame them in the world's eyes if they did not. At the same time, and most importantly, Britain maintained enough leeway that it could continue its offensive research and defensive preparations, the very steps that would protect it the most and would give it the information needed to begin offensive production for retaliatory gas warfare quickly, even if it did not have a stockpile ready to use the day a war began. Whether or not gas was a humane weapon, Britain very practically provided itself with sufficient freedom to decide whether to use gas in the future. Trying to determine whether that critical point had arrived, and trying to prepare to defend its own people if it did, was a challenge it confronted repeatedly during World War II.

# Chapter 2

# Is There Any Hope?

## Defensive Preparations against the Dreaded and Expected Gas War

> The mass of British public opinion sees that the attempt at collective security and the attempt to translate that into collective action at Geneva [with the League of Nations] has failed.
>
> —Robert Boothby (later Baron Boothby), House of Commons, April 9, 1936

> If . . . gas has been used [by Italy], then I suggest that that is an issue of the very first importance and an issue which affects not merely Abyssinia but indeed the whole future of civilisation . . . What, after all, would be the use of any treaties, of any protocols, of any international documents of any kind, if they could be violated entirely with impunity at the convenience of any nation.
>
> —Viscount Cranborne, House of Commons, April 9, 1936

In the interwar period, Britons confronted their fears of future gas wars. After the Italian aerial gas attacks on the Ethiopians in 1935 and 1936, the realization that gas bombs could, indeed, be dropped from the air on civilians and soldiers shaped how the British prepared for a gas war in the years immediately before World War II.[1] Because of its proximity to Nazi Germany and Fascist Italy, Britain, much more than Canada or the United States, prepared for gas attacks on the domestic front as well as the international one, although none of them ignored the possibility. In Britain, domestic efforts were multifaceted, involving pressure by the press and public as well as planning and persuasion at the government level: readying for a total war meant that individuals throughout society had a role to play in defense against gas. For these reasons, Britain will be the focus of this chapter.

Instead of coalescing into a monolithic reaction that either gas could be managed or all would be lost, the British government both faced pressure from civilians to provide gas defenses and found itself in the position of pushing civilians to take the gas threat (and thus defensive preparations against it) seriously. While domestic and international efforts overlapped chronologically, Britain began to ramp up official anti-gas efforts at home with the failure of the World Disarmament Conference (WDC) in 1933, the increasing intransigence of countries like Hitlerian Germany, and the Italo-Abyssinian War in the mid-1930s. There were multiple assessments about the severity of the gas threat, and perceptions about this looming danger continued to vary once World War II arrived. The government wanted to protect laypeople from a rain of chemical weapons (CW), and by doing so it promoted the message that Britons would not be victims, if they so chose. Furthermore, a show of civilian anti-gas preparedness might deter the future Axis countries' gas attacks just as much as military, offensive CW-preparedness.

There was some lay cooperation. A few months into the war some British civilians feared and anticipated gas attacks, but a large number seemed to relax their common prewar view that a gas attack might occur. This trend intensified as the war continued and, despite bombardments of conventional explosives during the Blitz, no gas appeared. The government could not afford to be lackadaisical, though; if Germany ever used gas—and the government considered the threat viable even after Operation Barbarossa began in mid-1941—the greatest devastation would come if civilians panicked and did not follow rudimentary gas precautions.[2] No one had proof that masks, gas-proof rooms, and decontamination centers would work adequately in a city, but, if properly used, they provided the only means of defense in a gas attack. Thus, the government wrestled with the way to balance wariness of gas and maintain lay preparedness without panicking the population. That was never fully successful, but Britain fortunately never had to pay a price for failing to achieve that balance. Britain's need to confront a domestic gas threat in ways that Canada and the United States did not makes it all the more noteworthy that the three Western Allies developed a joint gas policy later in the war; they had to meld different perspectives about the dangers of gas to create protocols that would dictate their behavior about offensive and defensive CW use.

## Attacks on Ethiopia as Harbingers of Future War

In December of 1935, and then repeatedly in 1936, the Italians released 350 tons of gases, most notably mustard, in Ethiopia, wounding and killing soldiers and civilians in their efforts to conquer the country.[3] *The Times* of London carried a report from the executive secretary of the Ethiopian Red Cross, T. A. Lambie, about "the permanent blinding and maiming of hundreds of helpless women and children . . . with the most dreadful of all dreadful agencies . . . mustard gas . . . this monstrous weapon, which surpasses in fearfulness the wildest dread of a disordered imagination."[4] Newspapers in other countries reported the human and military tragedy too. In May of 1936, the *Los Angeles Times* printed a story that linked "the use of outlawed poison gas and the indiscriminate slaughter of civilians, including women, children[,] and Red Cross workers" as reasons for Italy's victory.[5] Likewise, the *Toronto Star Weekly* wrote about the "dew of death" that tormented civilians so that "their skins would be burning with ferocious heat that water wouldn't cool, and they would be going blind and screaming to God."[6]

It was not just the gas itself, as bad as that was, that evoked a reaction. It was also that the Ethiopian soldiers were not equipped to face the gas. The Ethiopian army was not like the militaries that met on the Western Front in late World War I who had been equipped with the latest gas masks. Also, because mustard burned the skin as well as the lungs, and because it lingered on the ground long after being deployed, the Ethiopians were particularly vulnerable; they often fought barefoot or in sandals.[7] While the Italian and Ethiopian armies were not evenly matched, the major belligerents' militaries in a future great power war were likely to be more closely balanced in terms of equipment. However, their civilian populations at this point were not well prepared to face a gas war. Thus, the events in Ethiopia were more than horror for those suffering. They also concerned the great powers, especially Britain, because they seemed like a harbinger of the devastation of future warfare that even they might face on the battle and home fronts.

The events in Ethiopia provided something that the interwar disarmament promoters, pacifists, and even anti-gas fiction writers could not: proof that mustard gas could be deployed from the air and confirmation that it could agonize civilian targets.[8] Perhaps Britain's physical location closer to the perpetrators, and thus more vulnerable to future gas attacks by European rogues, explains why there were more intense analyses of the Ethiopian attacks in Britain than in Canada and the United States. The fact that Britain took the Geneva Gas Protocol more seriously than the United States may have made its violation more wrenching to the former as well. The Italians' action did not endanger the Western Allies' immediate physical safety, but those who were savvy about the broader legal implications of the gas use recognized that Italy's actions—violating the Geneva Gas Protocol and thus breaking international law to deploy gas—threatened their own nations' future physical safety because gas laws would not protect them from rogues.[9]

Within Britain, one of the most vociferous condemnations occurred on March 30, 1936, when Viscount Cecil of Chelwood said in the House of Lords: "I want to point out that this is perfectly clearly a breach—if it has been committed—of [the Geneva Gas Protocol,] a very definite undertaking into which the Italian Government have entered."[10] Lord Cecil's concern was fair. At first, Italy denied it had used gas, then it claimed it had used nonlethal gases, and it justified its actions as a kind of retaliation in kind, in this case, response to alleged Ethiopian atrocities.[11] In reality, it seems that the Ethiopians had proven to be more challenging opponents than Mussolini had expected, and the first gas attacks occurred soon after an Ethiopian advance.[12] Thus, since the protocol had been ratified by both the Ethiopians and the Italians, the treaty governed conflict between the two nations, and Italy did break it. This legal equality may have trumped what one scholar has argued was a willingness by Britain, if not other white great powers, to allow weapons deemed inappropriate for "civilized" or Western peoples, such as dum dum bullets, against nonwhites.[13]

In addition to expressing horror at the description of civilian suffering and condemning Italian treaty violations, Lord Cecil was disturbed that the law the Italians violated was one that Britain had also signed.[14] While Ethiopia was the obvious target of Italy's actions, Cecil argued that Italy had treated Britain contemptuously by this dismissal of a shared treaty and that it threatened its well-being as well. As a result, he argued, Britain must compel the League of Nations to end the war, "for . . . unless [Italy's use of gas] . . . is repudiated and penalized, it will be evidently a precedent for any war in which this country is engaged, with the consequences which have been described in this House." Added to the potential danger for Britain and its civilians was the fear for civilization as a whole. Lord Cecil demonstrated the depth of his concern when he said that the combination of the violation of the law and the gassing of civilians meant that Italy's behavior was "perhaps as horrible and shameless a thing as has ever been done, even in the bloody annals of warfare."[15] This was an astonishingly strong condemnation considering all of the tribulations of the recent Great War.

The archbishop of Canterbury, Cosmo Gordon Lang, dwelt on the legal implications too. In his speech in the House of Lords, this was less because of sanctity for the law itself and more because of concern about the law's strength as a shield for civilization. He lamented, "Things are worse if, in order to prevent the use in future of these appalling methods of human destruction, conventions are carefully arranged and solemn signature are appended and then, whenever it appears to be convenient, they are torn aside by the very nations that entered into these solemn obligations." He concluded that Britain must respond.[16] As much as the archbishop decried the suffering of the Ethiopians, in Parliament he was at least as concerned with the implications for the safety of the British.

THE DAWN OF PROGRESS.

"BUT HOW AM I TO SEE IT? THEY'VE BLINDED ME."

FIGURE 2.    Bernard Partridge's cartoon in the April 8, 1936, issue of *Punch*, "The Dawn of Progress," illustrated the British condemnation of the Italian mustard gas attack on unprepared Abyssinians (Ethiopians) in 1935–1936 in an era in which many countries had sought to exclude inhumane and terrifying weapons, including chemical ones, through treaties. (*Punch* Cartoon Library/TopFoto)

Robert Gascoyne-Cecil, Viscount Cranborne (and later 5th Marquess of Salisbury), put it more bluntly in the same debate, as noted in the quotation at the start of the chapter: "What, after all, would be the use of any treaties, of any protocols, of any international documents of any kind, if they could be violated entirely with impunity at the convenience of any nation?"[17] It was not the current situation that was the problem, as disturbing as that was, as much as the implications: "if we cannot abolish the use of gas in warfare, it seems to me that we are very nearly at the end of our civilisation. . . . After all, where are you going to stop?"[18]

Collective security, one of the tools that, along with treaties, was expected to protect Britain and civilization, was at risk too. As can be seen in the quotation that opened the chapter, Boothby proclaimed that the majority of British opinion held that the League's inability to stop Italy's attacks on Ethiopia signaled the failure of the League in particular, and collective security in general. The hints had already been there when economic sanctions, imposed months before the gas attacks, did not deter Italy from escalating the war.

Italy's action was confirmation of the predictions discussed in the last chapter that countries would, as Germany had in 1915, violate the law and use gas. This made fears of gas particularly urgent because it brought the threat of gas close to home and close in time. Gas actually had been used, and as the world seemed to march closer to another large European war in the 1930s, the prospect of facing gas at home became imminent. Steps had to be taken to face it.

## Fighting Gas at Home

Engaged in diplomacy since 1918 to prevent a gas war, Britain was one of many nations that simultaneously turned to domestic efforts to prepare to face that war. During the interwar period, governmental bodies and civilians both discussed future gas threats. Some participants were not convinced that anything could stop gas. Others, in an era when air power theorists projected that unstoppable bombers would smash the resistance of a city, and when Stanley Baldwin, a former prime minister, told Britons that those planes would carry gas, put their faith in disarmament and their hope that the international community could create effective treaties banning CW. Another set may not have had a solution, but they found a role publicizing the extreme destruction possible in a gas war through speeches, letters to the editor, and fiction, whether as a cry for someone to create a solution, simply as a warning, or out of despair. Some of the novels written during this period helped create a dramatic and emotional image of gas warfare and provided a public venue for laymen to share their anxieties.[19]

Not all governmental bodies and civilians embraced the direst view, though. While no one who spoke up thought CW were innocuous, some experts did believe that it was a manageable threat for the home front. With proper precautions—ones that protected the body from toxins and the mind from panic—civilians could survive gas with their health and will intact. Enough laymen embraced this hope that domestic individual and group shields against gas were possible, even if international legal ones and collective security were not inviolable, that it led to popular pressure for government preparations for domestic CW defense measures in the interwar period. These measures were met at times with popular critiques about their effectiveness as well as the burdens that anti-gas preparations entailed. There were even commercial efforts to join the gas defense effort, suggesting that enough people worried about gas threats—and felt that the government could not provide enough protection—that there was a market.

In the interwar period, then, the threat of gas led to domestic conversation and actions, not just international ones. Gas was a global threat and one that targeted laymen as well as soldiers; it was an issue that led to democratic discussion. If everyone was a target, civilians felt that they should have a say about the extent of the threat and how to handle it. Even during peacetime, gas influenced public policy, and civilian attitudes, without being deployed.

## Imagining Future Disasters

While diplomats and activists worked through rational, measured, and legal discussions and frameworks and studied the physical events in Ethiopia, fiction authors offered graphic stories of potential gas wars to come, even if the latter did not propose specific solutions or prepare physical defenses. Gas, therefore, was not solely the concern of the diplomats and grassroots activists. Regardless of the authors' personal stances on government policies regarding gas, these accounts took advantage of the liberties possible in fiction and made their works quite dramatic. These writers may have incorporated CW simply because it was a trendy weapon to use in a popular contemporary genre, but it is clear that some authors had more serious goals in mind.[20] The ones that included CW showed the tragedies that could arise if gas were utilized, emphasizing the fears of gas that were present in societies and perhaps enhancing them. At the very least, these stories simply helped to keep CW concerns in the public view.

A vivid example is *Theodore Savage*, written by Cicely Hamilton and published in 1922. Hamilton, a journalist, playwright, feminist, and suffragette, later received a Civil List pension for her services from her writing. Despite, or perhaps because of, her work with an ambulance unit and hospital during World War I, some of Hamilton's works, such as *William: An Englishman*, written in 1919, critiqued the brutality of war.[21] *Theodore Savage* condemned war's potential destructiveness even further. It was, according to one reviewer, a "story . . . to make one's flesh creep, especially at this time," a period so soon after World War I when chemical warfare would have been in everyone's memories.[22] Hamilton's work focused on the title character, Theodore Savage, who lived in a time when the League of Nations fails, war erupts, and gas helps destroy civilization. Savage himself becomes brutal to survive in the post-apocalyptic society but retains memories of the civilized period, which he shares with fascinated youth. Perhaps this ability to know how low he had fallen makes him particularly tragic. This interwar apocalyptic tale was not the only one in which civilization was destroyed with the help of gas. In this case, the reviewer judged that "Miss Hamilton would seem to be the very queen of pessimists. But perhaps she is only telling a tale, with some deficiency of imaginative power."[23] She was not overly impressed by the author as a novelist, despite Hamilton's honors and awards, but Hamilton's book played on common fears that since World War I had escalated in destructiveness over time, the next war would be worse; one way for that to happen would be to expand the use of gas.[24]

Soon after the release of Hamilton's book, Lord Halsbury published a work that incorporated just as much destruction, if not more horror, and was clearly inspired by his beliefs about gas, not a publishing career. His novel, 1944, features a Russian gas attack on Britain as part of a war that destroys civilization (so much so that cannibalism even appears in the tale), leaving just a few people alive to restart it, thanks to the foresight of a handful of prepared individuals.[25] Since Halsbury had also written a nonfiction article about the dangers of gas in 1933, in which he declared that "One single bomb filled with modern asphyxiant gas would kill everybody in an area from Regent's Park to the Thames," it is clear that his earlier foray into fiction was for the purposes of calling attention to the dangers of gas.[26]

Whether for political or defensive reasons or for other motivations, artists continued to keep the gas threat in the public eye. The prolific and famous H. G. Wells wrote *The Shape of Things to Come* in 1933, adding a new twist to the catastrophic gas war story. In his novel, gas not only kills, but it influences daily life as people worry about gas attacks, ones that kill painfully in the many imagined wars that would take place over the course of the next two centuries.[27] Perhaps most creatively, in one of the novel's conflicts China deploys "Sterilizing Inhalation" gas, a compound that prevents human and animal reproduction; in the pronatalist interwar era, this would be particularly horrifying.[28]

Yet, by 1937, with the war seeming more likely, novelist Mary Rose Coulton, under the pseudonym Sarah Campion, published *Thirty Million Gas Masks*.[29] She did this the year after the *News Chronicle*, a newspaper that later became part of the *Daily Mail*, published an article with the subheading "30 Million Masks to be Made," about the government's plan to manufacture and store that number of respirators for free use by adults.[30] Coulton chose as the book's epigraph a couplet from the article by Hubert Phillips of the *News Chronicle*:

"Thirty million gas masks in the making; Thirty million wearers wondering why."[31] To answer that question, she told a grim tale, bringing the tale closer to home by situating the plot in real locations in Britain, particularly Cambridge. With a title that left no doubt as to one of the core subjects of the book, Campion's main character, Judith, a committed pacifist and a woman who lost a brother in World War I, soon finds herself caught up in a new war in 1939. In this conflict, gas kills many, despite the fact that the government opened shelters and distributed masks. Not wanting to engage in this war, Judith rejects the protection of a mask, allowing herself to be gassed.

The novel continues after her death, allowing us to see Judith's imagining of the world to come, if she had lived. In that future gas not only kills widely but also contaminates, providing lingering effects. On one hand, after the war, tourists in the abandoned city of Cambridge have to wear gas masks; gas is there, but it is almost as if people have allowed it to become a travel destination for those who are horrified at the past war and preparing for future threats. On the other hand, in this story, by 1944 Judith has become a leader in Cambridge, one that is so ruthlessly pacifist that she participates in the killing of those who are not, in an effort to set up her utopian society and save everyone from further war. Champion, in her plot and the section titles in the book, likens Judith to the Biblical Judith who killed her people to save them. Yet, in the end, she recognizes the perversion of her actions and that her fellow leaders are not true pacifists. Her colleagues see nothing wrong in fighting to defend their way of life, in this case a hopeless and ghostly fight against the living soldiers of Free Britain that is coming to cleanse Cambridge of gas in preparation of resettlement. She resigns from her post as the others march off to war.

As some authors imagined, gas indelibly changed British society, and not for the better: even the pacifists became murderers. Campion ends the novel with a despairing conclusion: "Is there no other way out but this, that we must kill or be killed? As we now are, none."[32] Preparedness, education, pacifism, and other options could not protect modern society from gas. The novel was a cry for pacifism—despite its flaws—but it was also a desperate warning about the dangers of gas.

These stories were not simply for a British audience or by British authors. Soon afterward, in 1938, Robert Sherwood from the United States wrote *Idiot's Delight*, a work that not only won a Pulitzer for drama but became a movie with Clark Gable in 1939; it was well known on both sides of the Atlantic. Typically for Sherwood, *Idiot's Delight* "denounce[s] war in general terms," but in this case it does so partly through the actions of a German character who "on the eve of discovering a cure for cancer" returns home to make gas at the advent of the war, the ultimate contrast. In fact, everyone in the play either returns to work for this national war effort or perishes in the conflict.[33] Although the play is antiwar, it is telling that when the play was written in 1938, the enemy was not only a German but also a chemist, one who moved from the height of humanitarian work to the depths of barbaric work. Perhaps it was simply a condemnation of Germans at a time when Hitler's nation had become increasingly aggressive, but there was a question of whether any chemist, or even any humanitarian, had the potential to turn to destructive goals.

Fiction could draw attention, reflect or influence moods, or simply be enjoyed, but it would not produce solutions to the gas threat by itself. Authors were often aware of events and political attitudes in the societies in which they wrote; Halsbury and Campion are two strong examples of that. Still, what they wrote was fiction. Gas posed a physical threat exceeded only by its psychological threat; it had to be tackled with both dangers in mind, yet interwar events on the international stage and in domestic conversations often reinforced the fear of gas during this period, thus threatening readiness on both the physical and mental fronts. To survive a gas attack required physical and mental defenses. Both were needed—sufficient tools, such as gas masks, and plans, such as how to seek shelter, could protect one's body, but if an individual did not believe that these preparations could work, he or she might not remain calm enough and become too depressed or fatalistic to act effectively. Furthermore, one had to remain firm in the belief that gas might come; denial or dismissal of the danger would leave one unprepared. The British government recognized that it needed to create physical defense strategies and equipment while simultaneously maintaining mental readiness, yet it struggled before and during the war with both.

## How to Manage It All

It was not only the artists who drew attention to the gas threat on the home front during the interwar period. The press, particularly popular magazines on both sides of the Atlantic, such as the *Illustrated London News (ILN)*, *Time*, and *Maclean's*, used both words and images to address the gas issue. While some of the articles addressed disarmament options, the ones analyzed in this chapter kept gas in the public's view and offered recommendations about how the government should prepare their populations for gas threats. These articles were more than merely informative; some of the defensive and protective measures they described would be quite similar to the ones Britain finally began to implement late in the interwar period. The United States may not have felt the same national danger, but many of its citizens still had a visceral concern about gas; it is not surprising that well-known periodicals published updates about the issue. For both the United States and Britain, though, their very contents showed how seriously other nations took the potential gas threat and how one could combat it if laws were not viable shields.

For example, in 1927, the *ILN* included a two-page article, "Town-Planning against Air Attack," depicting urban public works in the Soviet Union that were designed to be "defended against poison gas and from those heavy shells which might penetrate the earth and reach them."[34] The caption was by Lord Halsbury, the same man who wrote the novel, *1944*, demonstrating both his widespread involvement in the gas awareness campaign and the breadth of the connections in the lay conversation about gas. The type of observation of and admiration of foreign efforts appeared repeatedly in articles.[35]

The *ILN* also reproduced fearsome sketches originally published in the *Berliner Illustrirte Zeitung* predicting the impact of gas warfare on civilian populations in the future. In the two illustrations, Berlin (or at least an urban area) is covered with swirling, writhing gas. The city is a ghost town. There are cars, abandoned, with doors thrown open, in the middle of streets. In the foreground of one image there is a family, probably middle-class based on the clothing, collapsed in the street, dead—all unprepared for gas. Father, mother, and young child are faceless because of the position of the gas and the bodies; the implication is that gas will spare no one. The caption drove home the point that many people doubted the effectiveness of anti-gas laws.[36] This image was so powerful that the *ILN* used it again to illustrate a 1936 article on "The Menace of Gas Warfare."[37]

The Canadian magazine *Maclean's* published a similar story in 1937, but, unlike the British articles, it merely reported what others were doing without including the suggestion that Canada was behind in its preparations. Furthermore, in "Poison Gas Protection," it used a secondhand account, one from *Scientific American*, to talk about Parisian drills filled with sirens and gas shelters. It stressed the government's efforts, too: "the French Municipal Council recently passed a law making it obligatory for every new building to be equipped with gas-proof shelters which meet with the approval of army engineers." While it applauded the ten million masks the government had produced for civilians, it did not note that these would protect only a quarter of the population.[38] The author did, however, emphasize the fear that abounded in Paris: in special police, in the construction industry, in the Parisian government, and in medical care. As the article ended: "[y]ou have a picture of what happens when the entire population of a country is imbued with the idea of impended war," and it was clear that that war would involve gas attacks on the home front.[39]

Perhaps individual protection in the form of gas masks was the answer, or at least a key part of the solution. Making and distributing gas masks was a tangible step that the government and people could take to protect individuals, from World War I onward. The mask, therefore, became not just a tool but also a symbol of gas protection and government action by multiple nations contemplating gas.[40] For example, in a caption to a photographic essay in the *ILN*, the text ritually noted that while it was hoped that the gas treaties, specifically the Geneva Gas Protocol of 1925, would make anti-gas equipment moot, gas masks might provide the true protection. One image titled "Civilians Gas-Masked: Precautions Geneva May Render Superfluous" showed seven scenes of Russian civilians and domesticated animals wearing masks, including Russian seamstresses, "an eerie figure" disarming a gas bomb, and typists with helmets, among others. The press confirmed that provision of masks and the drills associated with them were widespread. There were references to French drills and German ones (the latter at a race track in Bremen) too.[41] This led to questions about British efforts, especially in the face of potential enemy Germany's mask manufacturing, as another photo essay made clear.[42] Again and again, in fact, the *ILN*, a widely read magazine, informed the British people about Germany's anti-gas efforts, showing a Germany that was prepared to protect its population with masks and with good training. Photographs of elaborate anti-gas drills teaching people how to handle the fallout from a gas attack appeared under headlines such as "Everyone's Doing it but Us!"[43] Nor was this periodical the only source promulgating such a message.

There were some experts in different countries who believed that CW attacks could be survived. For example, in a 1937 article, one major magazine stated that "the prospect of aero-gas-attack on cities has become a horrid spectre held up to palpitating civilians by excited publicists. Military experts in chemical warfare cry out to a man that this spectre has been grossly exaggerated."[44] Consider US Lt. Col. Augustin M. Prentiss, author of *Chemicals in War*, which is still a classic in the field of poison gas. He believed that gases had not developed much since their World War I days.[45] Gas proved manageable then, for the most part; it was not a superweapon, and well-trained and carefully equipped troops suffered relatively few injuries from it. Although he was a chemist, he thought incendiary bombs and high explosives would be more destructive.[46]

Some magazines also took it upon themselves to educate the public with the message that gas did not necessarily mean catastrophe. In 1938, *Life* magazine, well known for its imagery, included a double-page spread of fifteen pairs of pictures from the Austrian Ministry of Defense about the correct and incorrect ways to act in an air attack; four images focused on gas. Men as well as women are featured in the instructional images. In the first, the male character is surrounded by clouds, swatting away at them. In the second image, portraying the "right" way to act, a gentleman in a well-tailored suit strides purposefully (but not blindly) to a safe haven with a cloth over his nose, his hat still centered and his head upright. The caption reads: "'If gas bombs are dropping, don't stand still waving gas clouds away with your hands . . . Put your handkerchief over your mouth and nose, run into wind away from gas." What was unsaid was that people did not need to panic. In another image, a fashionable woman, absorbed by her outfit, is told, "If a chemical spatters on your clothes, don't try to brush it off with your hand . . . Wipe it off with [a] handkerchief but be careful to keep [the] chemical way from your skin."[47] Women might be stereotyped, as in this ad, as focused on clothes, but they were still considered to be educable and level-headed enough in a crisis to avoid harm from gas. In turn, the threat of gas could be defeated, even by civilians. At this point, though, there was also the underlying message that Germany and its allies were in the lead in terms of preparations; it was their plans that the future Allies publicized.

As important as the lessons themselves was the tone. As the author in *Life* noted, "The drawings are almost casual in tone. This nonchalance is purposeful. . . . What defending countries fear most is not that a few hundred defenseless civilians will be killed, but that whole cities will be shocked into mad panic."[48] Many believed that laws would fail and gas war would come, but they were not abandoning hope. Managing gas warfare was possible—or at least that was the official message seen from abroad, and it was a message that the British government would broadcast as well.

The conversations about gas among those who believed it was a threat included public participants from laymen and artists to journalists, not just discussants behind closed doors in the military and government or around tables at diplomatic conferences; the talks took place at multiple levels and in various genres. Domestically, the conversation about gas and fears about the extent of its destructive potential was kept alive throughout the interwar period in fiction and in the mainstream press; just as civilians were potential targets, they were also participants in the discussion. Emotional language and dramatic stories focused the reader on the idea that gas could be devastating. In contrast, governments and some laymen tried to manage the emotional fears and the rational threats. If gas threatened the home front, then some of the defensive actions had to take place at home, and the people at risk would have to take part; they could not wait for the results of some distant conference with other nations to protect them.[49]

## Domestic Preparations in Various Homelands

Preparing citizens and soldiers for gas attacks on the home front was a monumental task for Britain. The government, for example, developed masks,

**FIGURE 3.**  The key piece of defensive equipment for soldiers and civilians was a gas mask, but some nations also provided soldiers with capes, eye shields, ointments, and other protective clothing or tools. As with masks, these may have provided safety, but because they were both uncomfortable, especially in warm and humid climates, and took up valuable space, servicemen did not always carry this gear. (Imperial War Museum, CH 448)

anti-gas ointment, anti-gas eye shields, gas detectors, and curtains for shelters for auxiliary services at home, and all of that plus anti-gas capes, uniforms impregnated with anti-gas chemicals, and animal respirators for the armed services. The country produced them, for the military alone, in quantities ranging from nearly sixty thousand equine face masks to 262 million anti-gas clear or tinted eye shields to twenty-five million capes and seventy-five million jars of just one kind of anti-gas ointment. Accounting for military and civilian inventory from 1939 to 1945, there were more than 125 million respirators and the attendant bags for carrying them.[50] This did not include materials made in dominions like Canada.[51]

These defensive preparations took place earlier and more thoroughly in Europe than in North America, probably because the nations near Germany and Italy felt more threatened by gas than did those across the Atlantic. *Time* magazine praised Polish, German, Russian, and Italian efforts to implement anti-gas efforts among their populations, nearly eight years before World War II began. At the same time, the French Congress of Hygiene began pressing its government to take action by providing masks, providing training to civilians about how to use respirators, offering gas shelters, and constructing "outside of each community . . . gas safety zones."[52] Whether because of that, or for other reasons, by early 1936 a *Boston Globe* story reported that in France twenty-five thousand gas shelters had been built already, and that did not count the training and organization setup to prepare civilians for gas attacks from the air.[53] Across Europe, nations recognized the immediacy of a gas war threat.

In contrast, Canada did not engage in extensive defensive research until 1937 or so; as one scholar noted, until then, "The accepted wisdom was that Canada could rely on British technology in the event of another war."[54] Canadian development was partly because of necessity. Some Canadian officers, such as Major G. P. Morrison, had begun exploring domestic mask substitutes as early as 1932 when he conversed with mining companies about respirators. The limited cooperation, and even resistance, from Britain combined with the lack of necessary rubber and manufacturing techniques severely inhibited Canada's public-private attempts to develop its own gas mask industry. During the interwar period the country made slow progress, but it was not until 1939, just months before the war, that Canada managed to produce all the required parts in sufficient quantities to be useful.[55]

Gas masks were only one part of the defensive preparations, but Canada was slower than Britain in other areas too. The Toronto *Globe and Mail*, for example, reported on an optional training exercise in Winnipeg in 1937. Not only was that one of the only civilian defense opportunities reported, but it was all the way in another province, suggesting that there were not any options closer at that time. The article did suggest that others would be offered in each province under the auspices of the St. John Ambulance Brigade, not the government. Few other specifics were offered, though.[56]

Even more than Canada, the United States' behavior was minimal when compared to Britain's actions. In the United States, the Chemical Warfare Service (CWS) leadership, including Amos Fries, advocated future offensive use and defensive roles for that organization.[57] However, it found itself preoccupied during the 1920s with, as scholar Thomas Faith says, a struggle for survival. As he noted, in 1919 the US Army chief of staff Peyton C. Marsh told Congress that "the War Department believes that the CWS ought to be abolished." It does not get much more brutal than to have a parent organization try to eliminate a unit, and the diplomatic efforts to draft the international treaties discussed in chapter 1 would have gutted the CWS, if not led to its eradication, if Congress and the army absolutely believed the treaties were trustworthy shields negating the need for the CWS.[58] In a period in which popular opinion, some personal politically influential opinions, and economics argued against spending money on gas, legislators held hearings to consider reorganizing the army. One of the major issues was whether to disband the CWS: it was unpopular, expensive, and potentially unnecessary in the face of anti-gas treaties. The CWS lobbied astutely and maintained its separate organization and identity, but it was the disfavored stepchild of the army during this period.[59] One of the consequences was that it did not receive adequate funding to develop widespread anti-gas training programs or acquire stockpiles of supplies for gas defense. In contrast, during the war, the United States certainly took the mission of equipping the military seriously, acquiring the standard protections of masks, anti-gas ointments, and eye shields, in addition to unusual items such as aprons for medical use. Key items, like masks, were constantly evolving.[60] US soldiers would have the best equipment available.

The interwar CWS may not have enjoyed all of the support and status its leaders wanted, but it did ensure a role for itself between the wars. For example, although there was a struggle within the General Staff, by 1936 the body had been convinced to allow the CWS to "manufacture and supply toxic chemicals," partly because the secretary of war agreed with 1934 Joint Board advice for the United States to be prepared to release gas in any war. It had taken two years, but at least the CWS would be ready to wield gas, if needed.[61]

In terms of protecting the home front from gas, there was not a lot of discussion about threats to civilians at home, at least in public, unlike in Britain. Throughout the 1930s, the War Department General Staff did consider civilian protection, partly inspired by preparations and events in Europe.[62] There was a tension between those who did not want laymen to panic at the thought of gas attacks on them, and those who thought that preparatory plans had to be made. It was not until 1937 that the CWS settled on a pattern for a civilian gas mask, but these were not manufactured *en masse* until after Pearl Harbor.[63] In 1939 the CWS recognized that it had to make plans for distributing information to laymen, manufacture of civilian masks, and the institution of anti-gas training. Yet that year defensive training had been limited to the creation of two hundred copies of a secret pamphlet distributed to the appropriate commanders at home and abroad.[64] There were other efforts to protect the public, the most successful of these being short courses set up around the country that trained civilians in defensive measures; these educational efforts expanded during the first years of the war, but the steps the United States took to protect United States civilians against gas paled in comparison to what the British did.[65] Overall, the United States came late to the game, really beginning to pay attention to CW and defensive explanation during the "emergency period," the period after World War II began in Europe and before Pearl Harbor.[66]

This means that the story of anti-gas defense for civilians during the interwar, and even wartime, period was largely a British one. The British showed a sincere belief in the vulnerability of the nation to a real threat of gas even before World War II began that was unmatched by the attitudes in Canada and the United States.

## Preparing for Gas at Home in Britain

So, what did the British government do in the years before the war? A 1929 newspaper article noted that, "After the air exercises last summer there was criticism, in certain quarters, of the apparent apathy of the authorities in regard to providing London with some form of defence against poison gas attacks. Without going into detail, it can be said that the authorities are alive to the necessity of an effective form of defence, and are searching for an antidote for civilian use."[67] The article also noted public criticism of previously considered civilian defenses such as underground bunkers; while they might be good for high explosives, they would not protect against gas, which can winnow through cracks.[68] This story emphasizes two of the main themes of this time. The first was that the public questioned how and how well the government was protecting, or even could protect, people. The second was that there was a conflict between the requirements of providing anti-gas protection and those of providing high-explosive havens, yet both would be necessary in a future conflict.

Because of the complexities that would be involved in developing anti-gas measures, the British leadership was unable to make plans and equip the public quickly. Some laymen pushed London to work faster, and they questioned what it did. Yet while journalists could publicize other nations' efforts to develop anti-gas equipment and defenses for civilians, setting up a physical gas defense system was not easy—it was expensive, complicated, and time-consuming. Some efforts took place behind closed doors, of course, as officials assessed how to produce, fund, and distribute equipment, and then train lay people about how to use it on individuals from babies to adults; some took place in public venues to reassure the laymen that action could and would be taken. The defensive plans also had a mental and emotional element; anti-gas measures had to protect bodies, but they also needed to avert panic. Individuals were more likely to use anti-gas equipment and follow the chemical warfare defense protocols properly if they could think clearly.

Even if training equipment led one to think that a gas war was manageable, a nation would only survive if soldiers and civilians had sufficient defensive equipment and training. While Britain did maintain some anti-gas training and research for its armed services during the interwar years, until World War II became imminent, these were minimal. One reason was simply budgetary.

Britain instituted its famous Ten-Year Rule in 1919, formalizing it in 1928, and ending it in the early 1930s. This policy enshrined the view that Britain would not face a major war for at least ten years from the current date, and thus military spending could be reduced to reflect the lesser military needs of the immediate future.

In addition, as illustrated in the previous chapter, the British government had considered carefully how much gas preparation it could do legally, even in the early 1920s, as it sought League of Nations interpretations of the new treaties. While Britain consistently approved a small amount of defensive planning, effective anti-gas arrangements depended somewhat on offensive research so that respirators and other defensive equipment could match attacking capabilities. Thus, anti-gas work continued, but not as intensively as it might have.

Behind the scenes, as well as in front, the British government ministries such as the Home Office strove to prepare British civilians for the forthcoming war. The Air Raid Precautions (A.R.P.) Committee, with regular members from all the military services, the Home Office, the Ministry of Health, the police, and other civilian agencies, began to meet in 1924, and in various forms and differing regularity, continued until 1935, essentially charged with "examin[ing] all means by which the civil authorities could co-operate to make the policy of the Fighting Services effective."[69] The committee evolved into a Home Office department in 1935 that began to involve local government until, after the Munich Pact, preparations transformed civil defense into a ministerial-level organization, the Ministry of Home Security, once the war began.[70] Critically, no matter the administrative situation, the whole time A.R.P.'s brief included thinking about gas, although the extent of the threat and attention grew over time, "notwithstanding the prohibition of the use of poison gas in war contained in the Gas Protocol of 1925."[71]

The government may not have moved quickly in terms of developing gear, plans, and training, all of which were complex, but it continued to believe that the danger was real. Anti-gas plans kept evolving well into World War II. This maintenance demanded intellectual as well as physical energy and resources. Of course, defense meant more than approving effective gas mask designs; it also entailed ensuring their provision—a political and economic issue—for everyone. It included thinking about other ways to protect civilians and their possessions from gas. It meant that plans had to be made to handle decontamination and casualties, two problems that required specialized treatment. It involved the organization of national and local plans and infrastructure prepared to respond to a gas emergency. Finally, it demanded educational campaigns, not only to train civilians about how to defend themselves but also to ensure that laypeople believed in the anti-gas measures.[72] One of the lessons from World War I was that panic negated defense; anti-gas measures could be unpleasant since breathing through respirators, as one soldier described it, still felt like suffocating.[73]

Even after intelligence reports in 1937 showed that Germany "had made remarkable progress in its preparations for gas warfare, which are considerably ahead of this country," developments were slow.[74] A soldier, for instance, needed a heavy-duty mask so that he could continue his work in a gas-filled environment. A civilian's mask needed only to get him to a safe spot where he could wait out the attack; it could have a more limited lifespan. Thus, while the approaches to gas defense were similar for both groups of people, the particular issues considered when making design and production decisions differed. Different groups, such as the military services and the Home Office, submitted reports at different times, making it difficult to create an accurate, up-to-date picture of preparedness as late as June 13, 1939.[75] Even worse, the Home Office summary said "completion of delivery" of the children's and babies' respirators (for those from birth to age four) would not occur until "August and September 1939, respectively," potentially after the date when the war began.[76] Trials of masks for individuals who could not use standard designs because of asthma, tracheotomies, and other reasons continued into late 1939 and beyond.[77]

## Commercial Efforts: What the Government Cannot Do

While it is clear that some laymen and elements of the government supported action, protection was not left in the hands of the government alone. Businesses, too, participated in commercial efforts to develop and provide anti-gas measures. One of the most active companies was Carrier Engineering Co. which, in 1936, showed off "London's First Gasproof Office: Shelter for Ten" in a photo in which businessmen are seated, comfortably reading on a bench in a long rectangular room. The temporary quarters were rather utilitarian, but the men look comfortable and busy. What more could any industrialist want? The caption accompanying this photo detailed the filtration used to make not only this chamber but the office building habitable during a gas attack (although there was no mention of the damage that high explosives could do).[78] It does make one wonder what sort of business would be conducted during a gas attack, and how many people believed that the protective gear would work well enough that an attack could be ignored enough to concentrate on something else. But more important, the image proved that some people believed that gas could be managed.

In 1938 the A.G.P. Co., Ltd. hawked the A.G.P. Anti Gas Protection Outfit, which was "A complete supply of gas-proof materials for protecting homes

and offices. . . . Always ready, does no damage and can be used repeatedly."
Available for the small price of 40/- (British shillings, or two pounds in 1938),
this somewhat mysterious panacea seems like quack medicine for the desperate.[79] People with more cash to spare might be attracted to British Indestructo
Glass, Ltd.'s offering of glass that "will keep the room entirely gas-proof" by
preventing windows from shattering and allowing in gas.[80] These protections,
generally appearing to be equipment to save groups rather than individuals,
appeared in a major magazine and were marketed to the business and individual consumer.

It was not all about business, though. *The Star*, in 1932, advertised gas masks
and kennels for dogs. Military masks for dogs, horses, and pigeons had been issued during World War I, so masks for animals were not new, but proposing
them for pets rather than working animals was. *The Star*'s ad encouraged readers: "Many dog owners will welcome the fact that a gas mask for dogs can now
be bought. With it is supplied a training hood—a kind of mock-mask, by which
the animal is trained, with a minimum of inconvenience, to wear the real thing.
There are eight sizes, from quite tiny ones to 'giants.'" As the article noted later,
"gasproof kennels are now on the market also." Not only can they save a dog
but also "an owner's anxiety is considerably lessened."[81] No matter how much

FIGURE 4. Nations developed a variety of gas masks to protect their civilian and military
populations, but some people wanted to save their pets too. (Imperial War Museum, D 447)

one cares for one's pet, this was essentially a luxury item. At least for some optimistic companies and customers, gas masks were more than simple necessities.

These items were not always just for the wealthy, though. In 1938, *The Times* announced that the People's Dispensary for Sick Animals of the Poor, a charitable organization established in 1917, had "perfected a gas-proof kennel for dogs and cats . . . [that] contains filters identical with those in the standard gas masks. The movement of the animal either walking round or breathing actuates suction valves ensuring an ample supply of filtered air."[82] Your pet could be safe from gas, and it could also enjoy freedom of movement, presumably enhancing its comfort if it were to be restricted to the kennel for some time. At least some people believed that cherished pets, not just people, could survive gas attacks.

## Group Protection: Shelters Are the Key

Shelters are examples of group protection, just as masks were the quintessential individual defense; specific dilemmas arose when planning for each. Gas masks might not be enough. Standing on a street corner with a mask might suffice during a phosgene or chlorine attack, since the mask would protect the lungs, but it was not enough during a mustard attack because that chemical burned through clothing to blister the skin. This meant, to anyone who considered gas a threat, that civilians had to have gasproof havens. And if pilots mixed high explosive bombs with gas bombs, the combination would be particularly deadly, as some chemists predicted. The only way to defend against high explosives would be to take shelter, which was more reason for safe rooms. The problem, as the government began to realize, was that it was tricky to construct a room that could do both. For that matter, it was challenging to build a gasproof room at all. Any place meant to harbor people for a substantial time had to have ventilation. Gasproofing required eliminating all cracks, crevices, and other openings. A truly gasproof room, therefore, required elaborate air filtration systems to permit clean air in and remove contaminated air.[83] Although the Carrier Engineering Company advertised this in the interwar period, its version was neither available nor affordable to the average citizen.[84]

Furthermore, not everyone in a city had access to an underground shelter, one deep enough to withstand a hit from high explosives, and there were debates about the types of public shelters, especially underground stations, that should be available.[85] A room that might be gasproof at the start of an attack might be open to the elements if the bombs damaged it. Even if bombing did not break a window, simply opening the door to allow victims to enter could contaminate a room and require occupants to keep their masks on—at least as long as they would work.[86] Since throwing up one's arms in defeat was not an option for the British, the government worked to encourage the public to gasproof rooms in their dwellings and to provide some shelters, as far as they were able. Even then there was an equity issue. As the assistant chief engineer noted in a memo to a deputy chief engineer on August 29, 1940, "Logically, the occupants of domestic shelters should be given the same degree of protection as the people in public shelters, but in practice it will be difficult to carry this out owing to the small space available."[87] Equality of protection concerned civil servants and laypeople in different locations.

The main responsibility fell to Sir John Anderson, the home secretary. His job included air raid precautions from nonchemical weapons as well as gas before the war and during its early years. In July 1940, when Britain expected Germany to attempt an invasion imminently but before the Blitz had begun, Sir John had been part of the discussion about shelters in public. Oddly enough, the commitment to gasproof them had not been made earlier. In a House of Commons question session, Mr. Geoffrey Mander requested answers about anti-gas readiness, especially for shelters. Should there be "gas blankets" for "the entrance to public refuges which are not gas-proof?" Sir John allowed that now was the time to get them ready, but it would be local authorities who would decide what kind of fabric to use.[88] Following a common pattern, London would provide guidance, but the locals would execute any plans. Behind the scenes the discussion considered other proposals. Another solution included "trays of chloride of lime . . . at the entrances for the decontamination of people's boots before entering the shelter." World War I had taught the importance of neutralizing chemicals that landed on shoes and thus could be spread anywhere someone walked, yet the deputy chief engineer's office "doubt[ed] whether this would be possible" based on the structures of some of the shelters.[89] Additional suggestions ranged from putting a twelve- to eighteen-inch barrier of dirt on the roof of a shelter or simply plugging cracks with linoleum and other materials.[90]

Ultimately, the public gasproof shelter proved too difficult to manage. By January of 1941, London's citizens made it clear that they chose to sleep in their shelters to survive the Blitz; high explosive bombing had occurred and had to be faced. This meant that shelters had to be viable places for much longer stretches of time than originally envisioned. The result was that, as then home secretary and minister of security Herbert Morrison acknowledged, "Now that shelters are being used for sleeping, adequate ventilation is of the first importance. It is impracticable to reconcile this with efficient gas-proofing. Local authorities are therefore being informed that further steps to provide gas-proofing in naturally ventilated shelters should not be taken for the present and that reliance must be placed on the respirator as the first line of defence."[91]

Similar problems arose with regard to individual or family gas defense. The public had to be taught how to make its own shelters at home, and these were to be the primary lines of defense, with gas masks as backups.[92] Yet these, too, would not be enough. As part of its series of pamphlets on civil defense, the ministry of home security revised "Air Raids: What you Must Know, What you Must Do!" in 1941. It included sections on collective security, recommending everyday objects be utilized "to block up all openings through which air can enter," although even then a mask should be worn as a second means of protection. Brown paper, rolled newspapers, felt, mush ("made by soaking newspaper in water"), or cloth bags, as well as specially made "anti-gas plastic materials" could help fill gaps through which tainted air could winnow into a building. A room must be dedicated to being gasproof, but since that would make the room uninhabitable for ordinary living, the reality was that supplies had to be ready and last-minute finishing touches applied when gas was imminent.[93] The government strove for affordable self-empowerment while admitting that collective protection was not the sole solution, despite all of its detailed advice. As scholar Susan Grayzel has noted, though, the government's suggestions—not just gasproof rooms—assumed a level of prosperity that was not always present.[94] In this case, might a poor family have these materials or space in which to store them?

The government had to consider survival after a gas attack, too, especially the fact that civilians would need to eat and to decontaminate themselves and their spaces. As part of this campaign, the Air Raid Precautions Department prepared "The Protection of Foodstuffs against Poison Gas" in 1937. It reflected the government's attitude that gas measures had to be explained convincingly to the public; it was not enough to just issue orders. The eight-page booklet included sections on how gases contaminated food, types of packaging, and the "protective value" of items such as waxed cartons or greaseproof paper. It also explained the best ways to store, ventilate, and transport food.[95] Decontamination required expert help, though; the advice in a shorter leaflet, intended to fill the gap between editions of a more detailed book and for wider distribution, was simple and forceful: "notify an Air Raid Warden or the police immediately."[96]

For its part, with the planning beginning in the interwar period, the Ministry of Food tried to educate businesses through its own booklets and posters, with special versions to be issued periodically as well as to produce supplies needed for bulk food protection and to draft volunteers to help monitor the situation.[97]

Yet, as was apparent in a War Cabinet meeting, the government was frustrated that local preparations for food protection had not been completed a year and a half into the war. Furthermore, in April 1941, with Britain fighting

Germany almost alone and largely on the defensive, the risk of German invasion of the United Kingdom alive, and the Blitz on English cities continuing, a gas attack on London or even the beaches was still quite possible. Tarpaulins to cover food were not ready yet, and only 20 percent of local authorities had drafted (or at least forwarded to London) plans about their procedures for food protection.[98] It was time to ramp up the campaign through the distribution of more leaflets and through education broadcasts on the topic.[99] The detailed planning included decontamination measures, largely drawn up by the local governments. For example, the County Borough of Sunderland rounded up 105 volunteers who took anti-gas training to learn how to dispose of contaminated food, with others on call. The county assigned the volunteers to squads including butchers, bakers, retail shops, and wholesalers. Responsibility for moving foods was allocated to the businesses themselves, with the local and then national governments on call.[100]

## Individual Protection: Masks and the Main Tool

With all of these detailed plans developed and some implemented well before war broke out, why was Britain still unprepared in the late 1930s and even into the war years to defend its laypeople against gas comprehensively? One factor was the complexity of developing plans, protocols, and manufacturing equipment—especially when those change as the masks and protective gear did. Part of the answer was limited resources on the part of the government or local agencies; if Britain found it challenging to prepare to fight the enemy and defend the home front in a conventional war, then it is no surprise that the arrangements for protection against a novel, untried attack on the homeland could not be completed. Perhaps other factors, like cynicism that these techniques would work, played a role too. Looking at the debates over masks suggests reasons.

The most important means of protection were masks, the core defense equipment from World War I, and it is worth looking back over the interwar period at their development. It was critical at this time to protect civilians with them, and experts considered design, cost, longevity, distribution, training, and readiness. Participants in the political discussions of the mid-1930s wrestled with these core issues. One of the major factors was cost. If everyone needed a mask—and there was some debate about that—then who should provide the masks?[101] How much would the equipment cost, whether at the individual level or the governmental one? A more durable mask would cost more, but civilians might not need it. They would not need to labor in gas-filled environments; they needed to get to cover, even with the recognition that high explosive bombs might render that cover worthless. This issue had a political component, too. If civilians received fewer durable masks, was the government abandoning them? If people could not afford masks, did the government have to provide them? As one document noted, if people did not have respirators, "public alarm and resentment . . . might gravely embarrass the Government of the day in the prosecution of the war," regardless of which party or coalition formed the government.[102] Who would make the masks? And did the government need "to encourage the production of respirators by British firms in order to safeguard the position in time of emergency?"[103] In the end, politics, practicality, and morality combined to form a policy in which civilian model respirators (not as strong as military or air raid volunteer masks) would be provided for laymen.

Soon after the Nazis took power in Germany, discussions led to a commitment to produce seventy million respirators, distributed by early 1941, with approximately thirteen million more in reserve, more than enough for the entire population of Britain.[104] It was an impressive feat to do as much as they did, especially since masks have a life span, but it would be a daunting task to cover the entire population throughout the war years. They could incapacitate gases for several hours only before the neutralizing compounds failed. They would break from simple wear and tear, and they would disintegrate after sitting on the shelf because they were composed of substances like rubber.[105] Depending on what materials were used as neutralizers and how the mask was stored, it might survive for two to seven years.[106] Hence maintaining an adequate stock would be expensive. Masks might have to replaced, whether or not a war came, just to ensure readiness; that was not what any Treasury wanted to hear. Yet, as one representative from the Treasury Chambers wrote to Wing-Commander E. J. Hodsoll, G.B. of the Air Raids Precaution Department, on September 26, 1935, "It might be possible in the piping times of peace to say to the public 'Here is a good cheap respirator packed safely in a tin which you can buy for 2/- against any future emergency,'" but "No doubt the emergency issue would have to be free." The more sold, the less it would cost the government later. However, the Treasury, in this particular informal letter, ignored the shelf-life issue.[107]

Still, it seems that the idea that vulnerable people must have masks persisted, for humane and political reasons, and because Britain needed a functioning population to fight a future war. It was a political hot issue, even in the heart of the government, as illustrated by repeated debates in Parliament. For example, in 1936, MP William Gallacher wondered if the home secretary "is satisfied that this mask [that would be available to civilians] will afford genuine protection against possible gas attacks and not merely an illusion of protection?"[108] A few months earlier in the House of Lords, Lord Marley demanded to know just

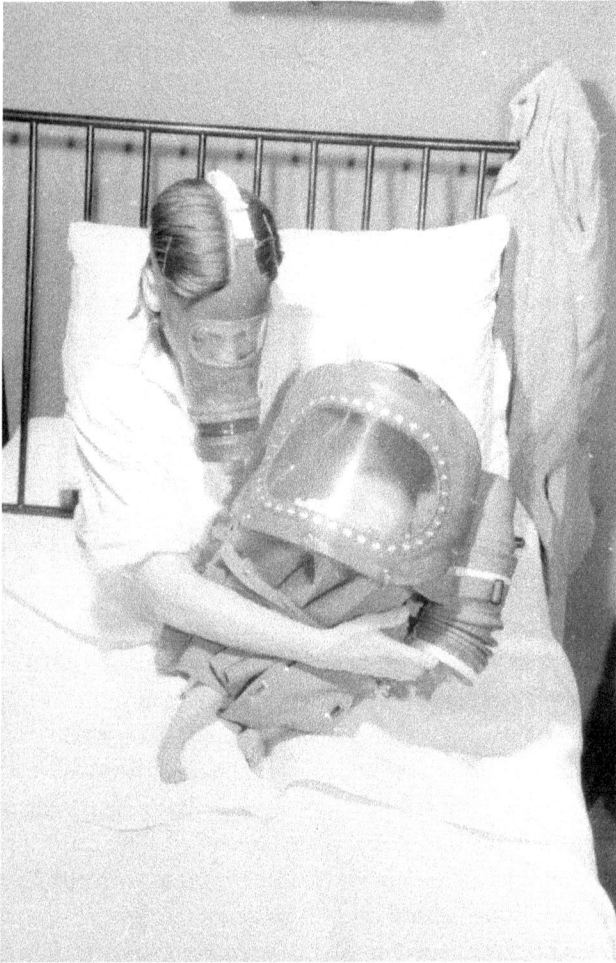

**FIGURE 5.** A gas mask had to create an air-tight seal around an individual's face. Because the British expected the enemy to deploy chemical weapons on their home front, the government had to develop gas masks for smaller faces, including babies. (Imperial War Museum, D3918)

how the government would protect the civilian population if a mask "cost . . . £2 7s. pd.," a price that would require "people who can live on nothing for five weeks" because of the expense.[109] As the accounts of the governmental discussions made clear, national security as well as politics were keys. This meant that the masks had to be ready when they were needed—whenever that might be. Unfortunately, this might put the financial burden on the government. As Sir Russell Scott, the permanent under-secretary for the Home Office, noted in a meeting on April 15, 1935, "only the Government could accumulate this supply [of masks], and once the Government had assumed responsibility for this, it was quite clear that no one else would be willing to pay." No decision was made then, but the writing was on the wall, although it was without "precedent" for the government to provide equipment or materials to laymen for their own use, even if that item—such as a respirator—was a necessity.[110] Therefore, there would have to be a "respirator, which is cheap to produce, simple, and could be worn by anybody, including women and children and aged persons." It would have limited use: "The idea of this respirator would be as an auxiliary to the gas-proof room in a house, and to enable the general public to undertake essential movement out of doors."[111] Regardless, politics and fairness demanded that it never looked like the rich could buy their way to better protection than the poor (although, of course, that was often true); there were concerns that "Communist elements are already engaged in spreading the story that air raid protection will be for the rich and not for the poor."[112]

All of these factors came together during in-depth debates about how to protect young children, namely those four and under who could not wear regular masks. Although the discussions and experiments supervised by the Home Office began in earnest in 1935, they continued for years. The major difficulty was how to design such respirators, since "there is no information available on which any attempt could be made to design a respirator or, in fact, any form of protection for babies," because "there is apparently no knowledge of the degree of resistance to inhalation which a baby could successfully survive."[113] Furthermore, the issue was not merely one of preventing suffocation, although that was the primary one, but also of minimizing psychological trauma in mothers and children. (Fathers were never mentioned.) It had to be easy to use since babies would not practice with the respirators the way adults could, and mothers would probably need to be able to support their infants, pump air into the containers holding the children, and perhaps be able to move to a new gas shelter—all at the same time. As the government's chemical warfare scientists wrote in a report: "individual protection" for mothers and infants "is required only for super-emergency conditions."[114] As important was consideration of the socioeconomic status and, thus, the resources parents had. While these masks might be free or low in cost, the issue was whether the government could or should develop a respirator that would fit over a baby carriage, or pram. On the one hand, this would make it easy to move the child and give him or her a place to rest. On the other hand, the family would have to have a specific buggy model on which to fit the respirator. The group involved was so concerned that it conducted informal surveys to see how many families in certain neighborhoods or particular medical clinics had a high-end pram; the results showed only 52 percent in Poplar, an area of East London, had the kind needed.[115]

In the end, by the time they were ready for trials in 1938, the air raid precaution experts decided to make two kinds of respirators, a small one for children aged two to four, who were too tiny for adult masks, and a bag respirator for babies under the age of two.[116] The idea was that a mother could carry a child tucked into a bag in one arm and, if the bag had a window, could see the child, making each feel better.[117] It had other benefits, such as room for a child to be "sick" without clogging a mask or tying the mother and child to one access point for air, as the Russians did when they linked the familial respirators.[118] All in all, the British took the production and testing of the infant gas mask seriously, considering its effectiveness, ease of use, and even psychological impact on the mother and child. Although the masks were not manufactured and distributed by the time the war started, the British were working to find an effective solution for even the youngest in the population, confident that gas was coming.

## And Then What Happened?

And then the war confounded expectations. The first months of fighting faded to a "phony war" in the winter of 1939; France and much of western Europe fell rapidly to the Nazis in the spring of 1940; and gas-laden bombers failed to drop CW on Britain, even after the Blitz began in the fall of 1940. The absence of gas was a boon, of course, but it led to unexpected consequences: British officials worried about how to keep the public alert and prepared for gas that might appear at any time. Since the United States and Canada were much less concerned about gas attacks on their soil, and since the United States had not joined the war until December of 1941, this inaction by the enemy did not impact them in the same way; they certainly did not need the kind of public messaging that Britain did to keep the population vigilant. As one famous British propaganda poster stated: "Hitler will send no warning—so always carry your gas mask."[119]

The situation was tricky, though. It is relatively simple if one can point to an exact date, or a narrow window, in which danger will occur because carrying a gas mask along with groceries, prams, attaché cases, and the like does not seem like such a burden if one believes that mask may save one's life in the next week. Apathy, laziness, and even fear of appearing "nervy," starts to gain the upper hand, though, if the vague—even if hideous—threat lingers for years without actually appearing. Yet, by September of 1939, soon after the war's start, reports filtered back to London that people had become slack in their behavior, with "children playing 'conkers' with their gas masks boxes," if indeed they had ever been enthusiastic.[120] That same month there was already a report that there was "a marked decline in the number of people . . . carrying gas-masks in the

**FIGURE 6.**  Countries that expected their cities to be bombarded by gas encouraged their populations to prepare for unexpected attacks. This British poster encouraged civilians to carry their gas masks everywhere they went, although not all laypeople heeded its advice. (Imperial War Museum, Art.IWM PST 13861)

streets . . . around Manchester."[121] The semiprofessional research organization Mass-Observation tracked gas mask carrying among the public during the early years of the war, noting its decline to as low as one one-thousandth in March of 1940, with a bump to one-fifth during the spring invasion of western Europe and up to only one-third after the Blitz began—at least in London.[122]

Even in a series of interviews of the man on the street the day after Home Secretary Herbert Morrison's speech about gas threats at the end of March, 1941, Mass-Observation correspondents asked whether interviewees carried masks. Answers included: "Well, I don't think it necessary. If there had been gas attacks, then I would. Not because I thought I might get caught, but because I would be afraid some warden chap would collar me about it." One rather lackluster citizen said: "[W]ell, being a warden, I suppose I have too [sic]." One man thought it was a burden and perhaps a bit childish: "I haven't carried anything around my neck since I was a schoolboy."[123] There was a common view that it was unnecessary, and thus carrying a mask was a "nuisance."[124] These adults were not taking gas attacks, or at least their masks, seriously. They were not angry about them, or afraid of them, either; they simply dismissed them.

The issue, at least once the war was imminent, was not necessarily distrust in science or technology. Probably, some people did believe implicitly, as Morrison stated, that "the civilian gas mask [. . .] when properly used gives full protection against any known war gas."[125] One Mass-Observation reporter, though, on March 29, 1941, thought that less than 50 percent of laymen had "unqualified faith" in their masks.[126] If a gas war was likely, then one had to rely on the mask. In terms of individual protection, it was the only possible defense. Shelters would not help you if you were on the street, after all, or if doors blew in because of high explosive blasts.

It may seem strange that civilians had to be reminded, especially after the public and emotional discussions leading up to the war. Perhaps they became desensitized to the warnings and the potential horror. As one reporter from Mass-Observation described a year after the war began, "There is clearly no excitement, no urgency, no sense of necessity associated with the gas mask."[127] Another survey in 1941 suggested that only 14 percent thought a gas attack was "very likely" or a "certainty."[128] Some may have decided gas was not coming after all. Other civilians thought it was simply a nuisance to carry a gas mask at all times; that might be why people did not tend to carry it shopping or to the garden allotments.[129] At least a portion did not want to look like cowards afraid of gas. As one man commented, he felt "somewhat ashamed of taking it [on a business trip] as my colleague did not."[130] There was no one answer; it was probably all of that and more.

Regardless, the government could not afford to have the population relax too much in case gas did come. An unprepared population might quickly become a panicked one, or worse, one with many preventable casualties. For those in the military, the situation was relatively easy: the government provided masks; the services provided training; military regulations demanded obedience. The soldiers, for the most part, would be ready. The government did not want to become authoritarian on the home front; this was total war in a parliamentary democracy.[131]

The scientists had done their part in developing effective masks, and the government had done its part in making them available; the civilians had to do their part to use them effectively. There was a third element of responsibility too. A population prepared to meet a gas attack could deter one: the government sent the message that civilians could influence the course of the war. In other words, while high home-front morale and dedicated physical work could continue the British war effort, defensive preparations could influence the enemy's choices. The British would not be victims, if they exerted themselves.

A mask, though, as World War I had taught, was only reliable if it were in good condition and the wearer could don it rapidly and properly. There was not much one could do about the former—masks would wear out, although the government largely tried to ignore that issue since it was hard to predict when it would happen.[132] More practically, the mask had to be fitted so that no gas could come between the face plate and the skin. That could be tricky if a person had not adjusted the straps and practiced "strapping it on." It would be even harder if an individual left the mask at home, or if the wearer ripped off the mask before the threat was over. These were not idle concerns—masks could feel suffocating even when they were working properly. Formal training or informal practice could help, but the government believed that if people stopped carrying respirators regularly, people would forget the details and procedures they needed to practice and remember.

No wonder there was a serious debate about using compulsion to gain compliance. Regulations, suggestions, and common sense at the start of the war all demanded that civilians carry their gas masks and know how to don them (as well as how to engage in other anti-gas measures such as seeking shelter or first aid). Legally requiring adherence to anti-gas policy might be effective, it could protect the government from condemnation for unpreparedness if gas casualties occurred, and it could ease the war effort by preventing the burden of mental or physical casualties.

The problem was that Ministry of Home Security officials involved in the discussion did not think compulsion would work. Enforcing it would be "an intolerable burden on the police . . . prosecutions would present too many opportunity [sic] to 'sea-lawyers' of all kinds, and . . . infliction of penalty would arouse resentment."[133] The negative consequences of wastage of limited resources, challenges to civilian morale, and scofflaws would not be worth it if the solution was unlikely to work. Imminent threats during the Blitz and the beginning of the war, speeches by the home secretary, distribution of gas masks, propaganda posters . . . all of those had not worked, after all. Would it really make sense to try to make those who still did not carry masks guilty of criminal behavior? Perhaps even worse, might laws inspire panic—the key emotion and behavior that the government had to avoid to maintain the war effort and civilian safety during an attack?

So where did this leave everyone? The government did not want to abandon the issue in case gas masks were needed. Eventually, officials decided to try more propaganda. They worried that such a campaign might send inadvertent and incorrect messages to Germany that Britain was preparing its civilians to defend against gas because it planned a first strike and then expected retaliatory gas attack from Germany. They doubted whether persuasive methods would be successful for any length of time on the home front. Still, if one kind of messaging did not work on civilians, maybe another would: if you could not compel people, perhaps you could cajole them.[134] The Home Office, the Ministry of Information, scientific experts, and even commercial advertisers joined together to form multimedia propaganda campaigns to achieve their goals. These ranged from posters to exhibitions in the London underground stations (Charing Cross was seen as a good locale) to leaflets.[135] Alliances with commercial enterprises led to friendly journalists writing articles castigating those who failed to wear masks and cinemas in certain regions agreeing to refuse patrons without them helped promote the issues, too.[136] The most enlightening campaign was the "Gas Quiz" series, published in newspapers courtesy of twenty advertising spots donated by Whitbread brewing company (now a much more diversified corporation) who turned over its weekly newspaper space to the government.[137]

This campaign was typical in that it demonstrated an effort to coax the public into believing that a gas threat is imminent and that, as a result, people had to take certain actions. It is also noteworthy because it was an educational campaign, prescribing specific behavior and not simply conveying a slogan. While a gas poster could, and did, remind one to carry a mask, such as the "Hitler will send no warning" poster mentioned above or the even simpler, "Take your Gas Mask Everywhere," these quizzes were much more detailed and serious.[138] They showed the efforts to which the government would go to train civilians: this was a total war. It also reflected a society at war: civilians are potential targets; everyone can protect oneself—do not rely upon others; everyone deserved to know the dangers that he or she faced. It sought to educate people about how to protect themselves as well as convince them to accept that effective anti-gas defense was a partnership. Of course, one could have gathered some of this information elsewhere, but the gas quiz campaign encapsulated it.

The weekly gas quizzes columns in the newspapers—complete with cartoons, simple pictures, and text —are a case study that illuminate the government's effort as well as commitment to trying persuasion and creating a culture in which masks were normal and necessary; the public had to buy into the need for making the effort. While peer pressure had discouraged some people from carrying masks according to Mass-Observation, the gas quizzes tried to generate a prevailing sentiment in favor of masks. While the same surveys reported that carrying masks was annoying, the quizzes attempted to ask people to rise above mild laziness and embrace responsibility. While the early years of the war had suggested that the gas threat had vanished, the newspaper campaign kept the existence of gas in the public eye. And, while some prewar fears had generated doubt that gas attacks could be survived, the quizzes argued that they could be managed.

The twenty gas quizzes in this campaign broke down into sixteen text-based ones, each one composed of three or four questions and answers. The instructions urged the reader to test himself or herself before reading the answer. The last four used drawings, each presenting a single question in a fun, or at least an easier, format to digest. Published in fifteen regional papers in 1941, from the *Daily Mail* to the *Cardiff Echo* and the *Glasgow Record*, the three main lessons conveyed to readers in the quizzes were: take responsibility for oneself, wear a mask responsibly, and gas is a threat that you can mitigate.[139]

The quizzes were a joint effort between the Public Relations Department representative, Mrs. Gertrude Williams; J. Walter Thompson Advertising's London office; some scientific-minded advisors (for accuracy), such as chemist Edward Armstrong; and the public. While the latter might not have realized it, some of the first questions chosen for the quiz series arose from what Williams called "Fan-Mail," letters written to her office.[140] The quizzes had to capture attention and fill gaps in public knowledge, clearly, but they did so by emphasizing the three themes mentioned above. Ostensibly, the messages were "Surprise is one of the enemy's strongest weapons" and "Have you got your mask with you," but the deeper messages were more revealing.[141]

The most obvious one was that every adult had to take responsibility for his or her own safety. One of the first questions, for example, was whether a man should give a woman his mask, if she forgot hers. Chivalry was not only dead, implied the answer, but unprepared women were a danger to the war effort. First it absolved servicemen by pointing out that they were forbidden to give up their masks. Then, women were chided directly for potentially killing someone else's husband or brother because of their own carelessness.[142] Later, in another quiz, it was clear that women had responsibility not only for themselves but for their children. A lesson was that even newborns a few days old could wear masks. Mothers must accustom them to donning respirators before a threat appeared. If necessary, one had to force a terrified child into a mask—but that should be unnecessary.[143] A good mother protected her child from fear as well as from physical danger.

By no means were women singled out. Other quiz questions offered advice on what to do if one was near-sighted (put the mask over the glasses) or far-sighted (tie them on with a string outside the mask).[144] Those more vulnerable, such as people with asthma or bronchitis, had to take extra care to learn to breathe through a mask.[145] As one might suspect, panic could prevent one from donning a respirator in a timely and effective manner. Panicked breathing could hurt someone with respiratory issues; self-control and practice were the keys then.

Branching out from situations specific to different kinds of individuals, the second theme explored how to handle situations in which one might find oneself during a gas attack. What should a person do if gas came while he or she was in a car, in a train, at home, upstairs, downstairs, at night . . . ?[146] How did one protect birds?[147] Would food have to be discarded (a true concern during rationing)?[148] In other words, how could someone go about daily life and react appropriately? When should the mask be put on, how long should it be worn, where should it be worn? Life—and the war effort—had to continue.

The last major theme confronted the fact that gas attacks had not yet occurred by late 1941. How much danger did the British people face, and could they affect the threat level? The questions and answers that fell into this category told a story that emphasized the government's basic line: gas was a real threat, even if it had not arrived yet. Behind the scenes, over the last couple of years, it had been clear that officials honestly believed that gas was a true danger; some, however, believed that the threat ebbed and flowed.[149] In the public quizzes, though, the message was much simpler. Distilled from the quizzes was the reminder that gas had been used after World War I in Ethiopia by the Italians, so it was not a weapon of the past.[150] Furthermore, Hitler was in charge in Germany, and it would be Hitler's decision to use gas. The best defense was to show Hitler that the British were ready for gas—and thus any gas attack (and even invasion) would be unlikely to benefit him most because people could defend against it.[151] Safety was their responsibility, and they could influence the enemy leadership.

As seen in the previous chapter, the Western Allies repeatedly tried to avoid a gas war through international diplomatic and legal efforts. As discussed in this chapter, they also engaged to varying extents in preparations to face gas attacks in the interwar period, if they could not prevent them. Canada generally embraced the same distaste of gas, but it felt less pressure and had less reason and opportunity to take action at home. The United States felt the least urgency of all. In the most vulnerable of the three Western Allies, Britain, domestic anti-gas preparations had to be adopted if there was a chance of surviving a gas war, yet there was a range of factors—from budgetary concerns involved in making masks for the entire population to fear of looking cowardly when carrying a mask—that delayed preparations and weakened enthusiasm for protective measures. Still, the government maintained its efforts to persuade its population to follow anti-gas protocols, especially once fighting began. These unique experiences shaped Britain's attitude toward war, and they are one reason it required so much effort for Britain, Canada, and the United States to develop an allied gas policy later in the war.

In the shorter term, though, once war broke out, the Western Allies chose a new path. To avert gas conflict, the Allies actually became increasingly belligerent—in tone—as will be seen in the next chapter. Internationally, the era of detached, unemotional legal wrangling had ended. With events, the immediacy of the gas threat grew, but so did the possibility of triggering a global gas war as a result of the very efforts of governments to prevent one.

# Chapter 3

# The Sole Exception to the Rule

There Will Be No Chemical Conflicts, but
Just in Case . . .

> While the probable repercussions must be fully realized[,] I consider that the military advantages to be gained are sufficient to justify us in taking this step [of using chemical weapons]. We must expect the Germans to spring one or more surprises on us as part of their invasion plan . . . At a time when our National [*sic*] existence is at stake, when we are threatened by an implacable enemy who himself recognizes no rules save those of expediency, we should not hesitate to adopt whatever means appear to offer the best chance of success.
>
> —Field Marshal Sr. John Dill, chief of the Imperial General Staff, June 15, 1940

One of Prime Minister Winston Churchill's most famous exhortations came on June 4, 1940, in a speech to the House of Commons. After the military and civilians worked together to evacuate thousands of British and French troops from Dunkirk, Churchill promised that, if the enemy did attempt to invade Britain, there would be a determined and desperate effort by the British people. He predicted that "we shall fight on the beaches, we shall fight on the landing grounds, we shall fight in the fields and in the streets, we shall fight in the hills."[1] He did not say so explicitly, but Churchill envisioned that the British would have used poison gas to defend those beaches, landing grounds, fields, streets, and hills.

Although Churchill was one of the stronger proponents of gas in the government, he was not alone in his views this time. Just eleven days after Churchill's speech, the chief of the Imperial General Staff, Field Marshal Sir John Dill, reached the dire conclusion quoted at the start of the chapter and expressed it explicitly, if in secret.[2] The British government had found the limits of its willingness to forego chemical weapons (CW); it would confront a war that included gas in a critical situation. And yet, even at this moment, it chose to play its CW cards close, not even hinting at a public policy that might suggest an imminent gas war. After all, throughout the interwar period and up to this point in the war, Britain's gas policy had been to pursue diplomatic agreement with belligerents that CW were taboo. Beneath the request to refrain from use lay the inherent threat to retaliate with gas if the Axis powers used it first. But as Britain lost its Allies to Nazi conquest and saw its very survival threatened in 1940 and 1941, it stepped closer to the brink of a first-use policy. Then, as the war turned back in the Allies' favor in 1942, Britain stepped back from the edge as demonstrated in its policy with Canada and the United States. Still, it had laid the groundwork for using CW if the circumstances were sufficiently serious, as they would become again late in 1945.

Britain's offensive first-use plans themselves did not violate international agreements. Executing them would have. A first strike might be preemptory or motivated by national survival, but that does not detract from the fact that such an action would still have been revolutionary for any of the Western Allies. This standard, national survival, demonstrated how dire the situation had to be before Britain's political and military leaders considered breaking the legal and moral ban against gas. Even then, it was a wrenching decision, one that required careful analysis and debate. Because Germany never invaded Britain, the discussion was moot. Regardless, Britain had a line in the sand; its gas restraint was not total.

Another problem, though, was that Britain was not alone; it was part of an Empire, a Commonwealth, and an alliance system, something that was a fountain of strength but also a basis of vulnerability. While the Empire and Commonwealth provided manpower, bases, and materials, they also housed millions of subjects, not all of whom could be protected by anti-gas measures. The most worrisome issue was that there were not enough respirators to protect the population of India, and the colony was a rich target close to Japan. Britain's need to avoid gas warfare, therefore, took into account its Empire and the Commonwealth.[3] This helps explain why, well before Britain inched toward a willingness to use gas in a dire situation such as an invasion, it had already begun to escalate the psychological battle with the enemy to deter a gas war.

Once the war began, and especially once Britain survived the lonely year between the fall of France and Operation Barbarossa, the psychological battles—and the verbal ones linked to them—became more aggressive. These began with British reminders that the enemy had promised in prewar years not to use gas and evolved to subtle and then increasingly explicit threats by Britain and the US leaders themselves that the Western Allies would retaliate if the foe released CW. While these measures could be seen as signs of desperation, merely a way to make it costly for the Axis to use gas but unlikely to guarantee stopping them, they could also be seen as thinly veiled threats too. Thus, as Britain and the United States gradually sharpened their verbal exchanges with the enemy over the first three years of the war, they eventually put themselves in a position in which they would have to use gas if the Axis called their bluff and used it first. The very British and US efforts to deter might spread a gas war, not avoid one, if one started. This change occurred despite the fact that actions and decisions up to the summer of 1945 suggest that Britain, Canada, and the United States did not want to wage a gas war and were not always prepared logistically to fight a sustained one; some actions by the enemy had to be resisted, ready or not. After that mental Rubicon had been crossed, the verbal warnings—implicit and explicit, mainly in diplomatic telegrams and political speeches—should be understood as allowing undeployed CW to shape behavior and perceptions.

Britain was more active than the United States and Canada in introducing CW as tools of psychological warfare that would unsettle and possibly demoralize or scare the enemy as well as moving down the road to potential physical deployment, but, since it had been involved in the war since its advent and was the nation that most expected to be a victim of CW, its motivation was high to take many of the leading steps to earn the reward of preventing one, even if those actions were accompanied by a greater risk of causing one. The United States also escalated the psychological pressure on the Axis, while Canada largely had relied on the British to take the lead on any chemical warfare efforts—offensive and defensive.

Even though the Allies—as it turned out—did not choose to or need to deploy gas as a weapon in the first half of the war, leaders invested resources in gauging Axis powers' plans, countries kept up with preparations for defensive war, and Allies worked among themselves to ensure a united front in case a gas war broke out. In doing so, even as they sought to reinforce a taboo, they inched toward risking a situation in which they would have to retaliate with gas, that is, a situation in which gas might be normalized in the long run.

Overall, then, regardless of national differences, poison gas shaped behavior even though it was not deployed, both as nations slid closer to using it and as they anticipated facing and then reacting to enemies' deployment of it. A gas war was a true possibility. The popular, international prewar conviction that gas warfare would come, destroying civilizations in its path, proved inaccurate, but some of the fears underlying that belief were rational. Physical chemical warfare, complete with the use of weapons on the battlefields and home front, nearly came to pass in the early years of the war in Europe. Psychological chemical warfare, wrapped up in diplomatic and political mind games and outright threats, was not only waged repeatedly but escalated during the same period.

## Preparedness: The First Steps

Chapter 1 looked at international negotiations between groups of nations, but one-on-one international preparations had foundations in the early interwar period too. In a report written in response to the 1922 Washington Naval Conference prohibition against gas, the British interpreted the French plan as an indication of their dubiousness about the power of the treaty. They noted that: "In accordance with the international engagements to which France has given her signature, the French Government will endeavour on the outbreak of war, and with the approval of the Allies, to obtain from the enemy government the guarantee that they will not use poison gas as a weapon of war. If this guarantee is not obtained, it reserves to itself the right to act in accordance with the circumstances."[4]

As mentioned in chapter 1, this position sufficiently impressed the British Committee of Imperial Defence that it recommended to the British government that "the French formula . . . be adopted." The cabinet approved it in 1925, establishing a national policy of preparations for deterrence and for retaliation.[5] This plan of action emphasized Britain's respect for law and, perhaps, it could function as an attempt to reassure the enemy that there was no need for a preemptive gas strike. It could be a way to emphasize that restraint could serve both sides well—if the enemy trusted Britain more than Britain trusted it.

Yet, it was a strange policy. How often do nations ask their peers, especially belligerents, if they will respect their signatures on agreements? Behind closed doors in the Committee of Imperial Defence meeting of December 15, 1938, Lord Halifax argued that one reason to make these requests was because "there was increasing evidence that enemy Governments seemed less likely to honour their word."[6] Perhaps a reminder would make a difference. Still, asking signatories to confirm their commitment to treaties carried risks. The telegraphic request could be perceived as a sign of weakness. Was Britain so worried about that it had to double-check its foes' promises?

Sending the messages was a clever diplomatic move, something that the British officials noted in their internal notes; they provided grounds to create a psychological weapon in the form of propaganda and implicit threats. The telegrams served to warn the recipients subtly that Britain was prepared to use gas in retaliation, although it would not introduce it. Although the British requests did not necessarily mention retaliation explicitly, the United Kingdom had inserted a reservation into the Geneva Gas Protocol that would allow it to respond with gas if attacked by it. This was a method, potentially, of reducing the likelihood that the enemy would use gas by warning that first strikes would have painful consequences. It also served to keep Britain's reputation as a law-abiding and civilized country intact.

For now, the telegrams were not shared with the public, but, within the government, the Air Raid Precautions department certainly expected to be kept up to date.[7] In the Foreign Office's view, the effort to send these challenges—as their purpose was to dare the enemy to acknowledge that it planned to use gas or to trap it into violating a promise to avoid it—was worth it; the telegrams could be publicized later in either case and used for "considerable propaganda value," for the benefit of Britain and detriment of the foe.[8] In that case, just sending the telegraphic query would show that Britain tried to keep gas off the battlefields and home fronts. In addition, if Germany or another country had given a guarantee and then used gas, it likely would be tarnished with the same kind of condemnation that it felt in World War I when it introduced gas, both for breaking legal and moral codes and for using CW. If Germany did not promise to abstain from CW, then it would be yet another black mark on its lengthy criminal record. Before the war started, then, there were plans to use gas as a retaliatory weapon in the war of public opinion, even if not a physical one.

The fears, and even conviction, that the Germans could and would use gas were reasonable. In World War I, Germany had unleashed CW, which the Allies perceived as breaking the Hague Conventions. Now, intelligence reports repeatedly forwarded news of German research, possession of gases, predictions about use, and other information that shaped British attitudes. Even before the war began, intelligence reports warned that Germany had "offensive gas units," had made "considerable development in the technique of spraying mustard gas from aeroplanes," and had an industrial giant, I.G. Farben, that could "manufacture an adequate wartime supply of toxic substance[s]." In other words, "[t]he conclusion to be drawn is that Germany is making the most thorough preparations for the employment of gas in war, and in this respect is very much ahead of this country [i.e., Britain]."[9]

Thus, when World War II began, the British government followed the plan. The Foreign Office sent the first request on September 3, 1939, the date Britain declared war:

The Under-Secretary of State for Foreign Affairs presents his compliments to the Under-Secretary of State for the Home Department and is directed by the Secretary of State for Foreign Affairs to state that His

Majesty's Representative at Berlin has been instructed to enquire of the German Government whether they are prepared to give an assurance to His Majesty's Government in the United Kingdom that they will observe the provisions of the Geneva Protocol . . .

The Swiss Minister as Representative in London of German interests, has been invited to address a similar request to the German Government, and all the remaining Missions in London have been informed of the action taken.[10]

Less than a week later, the response, via the Swiss, stated: "The German Government will observe for the duration for the war the prohibitions which form the subject of the Geneva Protocol. . . . It reserves full liberty of action in the event of the provisions of the protocol being infringed by the enemy."[11] Germany had signed the protocol; it reiterated that it would honor that agreement; and it, too, would retaliate if attacked with gas. It was a short, direct communication. Of course, because of Britain's lack of trust of the Germans, it did not settle the matter of whether there would be a gas attack. It may have helped, though. Beyond the possibility that the new promise's violation could be used to further blacken the Nazis' reputation for "frightfulness" for "use of a device which Germany pledged herself not to employ," as had occurred in World War I, there was the possibility that the telegram exchange could help deter a German attack.[12]

Even as British officials asked for such assurances, there was hope but not confidence that the telegrams would change Germany's expected behavior. At least some British officials associated with them did not think so, rejecting Germany's promise completely, commenting, "[p]resumably the answer is that no relaxation of this anti-gas precautions should be made on account of this undertaking."[13] The military, the Ministry of Home Security, and others had to continue their work, with all the expenses and energy involved.

While it was likely that this new diplomatic exchange was wishful thinking and would not change Axis behavior, it was one step toward escalating threats to Germany by implicitly reminding Germany that Britain would hold it to the terms of the Geneva Gas Protocol, including Britain's reservation to retaliate in kind if Germany used gas. This exchange was one nation speaking directly to another; it was a more directed communication than interwar discussions about gas restraint had been. After all, while some may still have held hope (or desperate faith) in the Geneva Protocol, that was simply an international treaty, and such agreements had not proved robust; the repeated German violations of the Treaty of Versailles had demonstrated that.

Britain requested guarantees from many nations, even though Germany was the most likely to wield gas. Throughout the early years of the war, the

British used neutral third parties to communicate with other Axis powers on this issue. For example, in June 1940, the British requested and received from the Italians, through the offices of the Brazilians, a promise to respect the Geneva Gas Protocol.[14]

# Invasion

In June 1940, the same month that Italy promised to respect the Geneva Gas Protocol, there was upheaval in Britain. The new prime minister, Winston Churchill, led a country that had just finished the Dunkirk evacuations and was facing a situation in which it would soon stand alone in Europe against the Axis. As noted at the beginning of the chapter, Churchill feared a German invasion would necessitate desperate measures—even on the beaches—to defend Britain's independent existence, and he was not the only one with this perspective that first use of gas might be necessary to do so.[15] This attitude was one that some other British leaders reluctantly came to support. As the quotation that opens the chapter makes clear, this dramatic change in the British policy to use gas only as in-kind retaliation would occur because of the ultimate crisis situation: Britain might have to break long-held moral and legal boundaries to defend its national identity.

As far back as May 1929, the British and French had considered that invasions in post–World War I European conflicts might involve gas. The minutes of the Anglo-French Chemical Warfare Conversations of that year warned that, "[t]he following types of attack are expected: . . . air spray or gas bomb . . . against home ports, bases, concentration areas and lines of communication generally. . . . Attacking troops may . . . be subjected to lethal gas . . ."[16] This scenario, or ones similar to it, underlay interwar efforts to ban gas and, failing that, to defend against it.

If the fact that gas did not become a regularly deployed weapon of World War II was unexpected, so was the fact that Germany did not invade the British Isles. With intelligence reports providing realistic warnings and even many civilians expressing fear, the British thought such an invasion was likely, sometimes more than others, until late in the war.[17] Although the most likely times for an invasion were in late 1940, the season when Hitler had planned to execute Operation Sea Lion, and the next spring, before Operation Barbarossa diverted so many German troops to the east, it was not until 1944 that Britain began to dismantle its defenses against invasion in any meaningful way.[18] The German threat to the home isles was not a danger that Britain could afford to underestimate. As a result, during this period the war leadership exerted energy, time, and resources developing policies for retaliation and defense behind closed doors and in public.[19]

Many expected the Germans to include gas during an invasion for many of the same reasons they anticipated the Germans would use gas at some point anyway: of course, Germany would break the law if it were convenient. But it was more than that; the stakes were some of the highest ones in the war. Regardless of why Germany planned to deploy gas, British policy had made it clear that the Empire would retaliate in kind.[20] At first glance, therefore, the interesting element in this situation is that the British were convinced until at least 1943, when worries about invasion faded, that they knew of at least one specific action—one they were confident would take place—that definitely would trigger a gas war.

What is more noteworthy is that Churchill and his colleagues planned to use gas to fend off the Germans, whether or not the Axis power deployed it.[21] Supporters of this policy started proposing first use shortly after Churchill became prime minister in May 1940. This idea was not the brainchild of one particularly tension-filled moment, nor did it arise only during the period when Britain stood alone and needed every weapon it could find to defend itself. In fact, over time, the proposal to introduce gas to the battlefield—in certain circumstances—gained more and stronger supporters. In addition, visions about how to use it broadened. Churchill had first proposed this policy after Dunkirk and during the last days of an independent France, but military and civilians repeated it and referred to it even after the United States and the USSR had joined the war.

As far as the British were concerned, the most dangerous time was from the spring of 1940 until the tide of the war changed for the Allies in Western Europe in 1944. Churchill was not the first one to raise the idea that Britain might want to deploy gas "irrespective of whether the enemy had first used it, in repelling an invasion." Less than two weeks after Dunkirk, and about the same amount of time before Churchill broached the topic, Field Marshal Sir John Dill, chief of the Imperial General Staff, considered this idea using military rationales. One key argument was that gas, specifically if it were sprayed from a plane, might be more effective and surprising than conventional high explosives at a crowded beach landing, especially if the Germans used low-quality anti-gas equipment. The contamination's lingering impact would slow the invading force, yet it should not harm civilians, presumably because they would have been evacuated from the landing zones.[22]

Dill recognized that there might be publicity blowback as well as the danger of "invit[ing] retaliation against our industry and civil population"; however, appropriate anti-gas training might negate the latter problems. As the most senior military man in Britain, Dill did not make this revolutionary proposal lightly. He was convinced that the invasion would occur, referring to it as a "when" not an "if." He thought it was likely that the Germans would use gas, and he thought it would be a critical point for Britain, one when "our National [*sic*] existence is at stake, when we are threatened by an implacable enemy who himself recognises no rules save those of expediency, [and thus] we should not hesitate to adopt whatever means appear to offer the best chance of success."[23] Using gas offensively as a first strike was not an easy line to cross, but national survival would make it worthwhile, whether the cost was a military one (although Dill did not think the immediate price would be high) or a moral one. This standard, one of national survival, demonstrated how extreme circumstances had to be before someone in Britain's leadership considered breaking the legal and moral ban against gas. Even then, it was not a simple equation for all the decision makers.

A vehement and almost immediate rejection of the proposal by Desmond F. Anderson, then assistant chief of the Imperial General Staff, to Dill stopped further circulation of this idea—until Churchill championed it anew. It was not that Anderson refuted the policy of retaliating in kind, but rather he thought that Britain might "throw away the incalculable moral strength we derive from keeping our pledged word for a tactical surprise, which may well produce immediate gains, but will in the long run rebound to our disadvantage" if the nation used gas first in defense against a conventional invasion. Beyond ethical losses, Britain would lose the public relations battle (with Germany fanning the propaganda flames) with the Axis powers, the United States, and neutral nations. He also worried about a drop in morale among British civilians and soldiers, a weakening of the British moral position with the United States and other neutrals, all for a military battle that Britain could well lose. Quite dramatically, Anderson ended his argument by saying that "Some of us would begin to wonder whether it really mattered which side won."[24] It is remarkable that someone in the Imperial General Staff, a veteran of the Western Front in World War I, would worry more about the process of survival and achieving victory after having weathered a prior war filled with gas, but for years Britain had been emphasizing a policy and culture that rejected first use of gas and condemned those who deployed it. Those restrictions had limited scientific research, stockpiling of equipment, and preparation of soldiers. While Anderson's view might seem strange when his country faced an *in extremis* situation, accepting that initiating gas—rather than retaliating—might be necessary required overturning the long-held policy not to be the first nation to deploy gas, something that might not have been easy to do, philosophically or emotionally.

Moreover, militarily there would be a cost. Anderson thought that German retaliation in a gas war might be more extensive than a German first strike since the enemy might want to keep the latter relatively quiet, unlike a response-in-kind that could be "directed deliberately on densely populated areas in the hope of causing the maximum suffering possible on women and children."[25]

Overall, Anderson had an elevated view of British honor and a very low one of the "Nazi mentality."[26] He was not the only one who critiqued gas use, but he was the most effective among core decision makers in making an extensive moral appeal.[27] Yet Churchill's interest kept the proposal alive.

Churchill wrote a memo to General Ismay at the end of June, demonstrating that he saw gas as a viable weapon in the last resort: "Supposing lodgment were effected on our coast, there could be no better points for application of mustard than these beaches and lodgment. In my view there would be no need to wait for the enemy to adopt such methods." The prime minister acknowledged that experts, such as the Home Defence, would have to weigh in and that the War Cabinet would make any final policy decisions, but now the idea was circulating.[28] In a less emotional but fairly similar response to Anderson's in that it focused on practicality as well as ethics, the commander-in-chief of the Home Defence, General Sir Edmund Ironside, rejected this idea because of current stock and promises, although he was in favor of preparing to retaliate in kind.[29] While offensive policy remained unsettled, the belief that Britain soon might face an invasion was real and inspired increasing offensive and defensive preparations of a chemical nature.[30]

It was not just the top war leaders who expected gas. MI14, a military intelligence branch, put it more dramatically early in 1941: "If Germany attempts to invade this country she will be undertaking a most hazardous operation for which the prize will be world domination. Into that operation she is certain to put all of her strength and if she considers that the use of gas will increase her chances of success she will not hesitate to use it."[31]

On the defensive side, the minister of Home Security reviewed the anti-gas practices and tried to reinvigorate civilian preparedness, as seen in the Gas Quiz campaign discussed in chapter 2.[32] Some were concerned about the state and effectiveness of citizen readiness, but others were not as concerned. One memo included the judgment that if Britain retaliated against German soldiers, and if civilians were far away or the amount were small, then the "[d]anger to civilians [would be] very slight."[33] Still, the experts took the matter seriously, considering multiple possible situations. Studies even included scientists examining "cloud gas attacks under inversion conditions," when air density is closer to the ground, while politicians and others set forth the procedure for investigating allegations of the Germans using gas and approving gas use when the time came.[34] It was clear that the War Cabinet would give the ultimate authorization to use gas, but then execution ought to pass to others, such as Bomber Command, to carry out those plans.[35]

Not all proponents of first use were enthusiastic. Sir Alan Brooke, a later chief of the Imperial General Staff, for example, thought deployment might be beneficial militarily. In January of 1941, he commented in a Chiefs of Staff meeting that "he would prefer not to initiate gas warfare, although we should get some local tactical benefit from using mustard gas on the beaches and on the early lodgments of an invasion," an argument stated previously by others, suggesting that such thinking was widespread.[36] That same month, the War Cabinet approved "retaliatory" gas use in the face of an invasion, motivated by some defensive war games to simulate Home Guard defense of Britain against invasions in Operation Victor.[37] The context makes it clear that retaliation was not strictly defined as being in kind; it could also simply be in response to an invasion itself.[38] Sir Alan Brooke's words indicated that the trigger for offensive gas use had been changed. Britain might initiate gas in dire circumstances instead of only retaliating. A policy line had been crossed.

## In North America

This British policy affected the other Western Allies, too, who were aware of Britain's increasing acceptance of first use of gas in certain circumstances. Behind closed doors, intelligence analysts in the United States "accepted the possibility" that Britain would respond to an invasion of its homeland with gas, although this action by a potential ally would seem to contradict Roosevelt's rejection of first use.[39] While the Western Allies would not finish developing a formal joint gas policy until 1944, the US reaction suggests that the foundation for chemical warfare cooperation in which offensive use was a possibility was laid even before the United States entered the war. Whether the private acknowledgement by the United States could be extrapolated to predict the responses of other neutral nations if Britain used gas offensively to defend its shores is unlikely. The United States was one of the few belligerents that had not signed the Geneva Gas Protocol. Presidential opinion was the strongest force underlying its own no-first-use policy, as Britain and other countries were aware. What would the dozens of other nations who had signed the protocol, many of whom were much more geographically vulnerable to the Axis, think? That remained unknown.

As for the United States itself, although Franklin Roosevelt may not have liked gas, he comprehended that the United States might be compelled to engage with it. If it did, it needed to be ready with respect to supplies and policy. When the United States did focus on gas readiness—eventually—it did so with determination. It would have been surprising if the military had been ready for chemical attacks in 1941; after all, it was not ready for a major war in most respects. Still, the Chemical Warfare Service (CWS) had begun to assist with relevant training, although not as smoothly as it later would.[40] As noted in an official history, "CWS personnel represented only four-tenths of one percent of the U.S. Army" by the end of 1941, weeks after Pearl Harbor, a number that was to grow dramatically.[41] Its budget increased to almost one billion dollars by 1942, from a prewar budget of two million.[42] In addition to personnel, preparation included production, and some of that was for Britain's benefit. Even before Pearl Harbor, the United States began to ramp up production of a range of chemicals, and Britain began to order US phosgene gas and anti-gas equipment as part of Lend-Lease.[43]

Further north, Canadian readiness to wage a gas war began a bit earlier, but, like the United States, it grew dramatically once the war began in 1939. Early scientific steps showed that Canada felt ties to Britain. For example, Canadian scientists Frederick Banting and Israel Rabinowitch asked for and received official sanction to travel to London to open a dialogue with the British chemical warfare effort, although Banting's requests had been denied the year before.[44] Although Banting was more interested in biological warfare, as befit the inventor of insulin, he and Rabinowitch did cooperate with Britain on chemical warfare. Banting engaged with British scientists about anti-gas ointment research, acknowledged that Canada would rely on the field station at Porton for some work on deployment, and encouraged scientists to serve at Porton. Later Rabinowitch used Porton's facilities to help prepare Canadian troops arriving in Europe.[45] In terms of domestic politics, it took longer to initiate activities to avert or fight a possible gas war. The Canadian War Cabinet waited until September 1940, over a year after the war began, even to address the issue.[46] Militarily, the Canadian Chemical Warfare Committee, with members from the armed services, began to meet that October, and General A. G. L. McNaughton, the commander of the First Division, had begun preparedness measures for the troops.[47]

Publicly, the Canadian government did not issue the warnings that Prime Minister Churchill and President Roosevelt would offer the Axis in 1942. Quietly, though, the leadership did discuss whether Canada would become involved in a gas war if Germany invaded Britain, especially if Canadian troops were in the United Kingdom at the time. By 1942 these conversations included consultations by the scientific and military experts at Suffield, the Allied experimental CW station in Alberta.[48] As one Canadian, probably a scientist, noted, "Amongst the numerous possible offensive uses of chemical warfare in retaliation, such as mining of beaches with solutions of mustard gas in oil, etc., many of . . . [which] have already been considered in detail, there is one possibility which might be mentioned—the emplacement of mines containing persistent vesicants for bulk contamination of airfields as a defence against parachute troops."[49]

One of his colleagues simply argued, "as soon as it is definitely established that the enemy is approaching our shores [in other words, even before it is known if Germany would be using gas in the United Kingdom], gas should be used by every available means."[50] This was dangerous, though, since gases could harm defenders and civilians as well as attacking forces.[51] Gas could linger, it could drift, and old or dud shells could be found by innocent people. There had to be a strong motivation to suggest these actions, incentives that seem to have been accepted. The tone in these discussions was matter of fact, and participants in them had thought carefully enough about the situation that they endorsed using it on the ground, not just the air, despite the fact that early retaliation plans focused on aerial deployment as well as a conclusion that "the first and most important task for the Canadian Army continued to be the defence of the British Isles."[52]

Attitudes in the United States and Canada demonstrate that key members of the Western Allies' war effort understood Britain's line in the sand and accepted it, or at least did not protest it. But why did Britain change its prewar gas policy so dramatically? It was not inevitable. After all, not everyone involved in decision-making suddenly became pro-gas converts. The Chiefs of Staff recognized that gas would not be released automatically but only if "it suited our book to do so" or in retaliation, yet this did not mean if it were expedient, but rather if it were crucial.[53] In addition, even if it were used in retaliation, it would have to be confirmed that gas had been used, the proper individuals notified (from the king on down), and then the War Cabinet could authorize it; that authority would not be delegated.[54] At least, as the war continued, Britain had more extensive stockpiles of gas to use, making the immediate military goals more feasible.[55] It would also make sense because the war had become more ruthless as it continued, including the damage incurred by bombing civilian targets on both sides. Perhaps the inventory, the new tone of the war, and the new countries involved helped maintain the more open policy regarding offensive gas use. National survival was the critical event that would lead Britain to change its long-held policy and cross its otherwise inviolate line; the British saw themselves as quite differ-ent from Germany, which was expected to use gas if it were merely expedient.

Of course, Operation Sea Lion, the invasion of Britain, never occurred, but in theory Britain showed that extreme events would make it imperil its reputation, risk global war, and change its behavior. Gas did not have to be deployed to change attitudes.

Germany expanded and then tightened its hold on western Europe. Between the threat of invasion for the first time in centuries and unprecedented aerial warfare, British leaders felt increasingly vulnerable and desperate—and they also were improving their capacity to wage chemical warfare. While of all the West-ern Allies Britain faced the most immediate dangers from gas on the home front, threats to global allies of Britain, Canada, and the United States led all three na-tions to rachet up or consider enhancing verbal warnings to the Axis. Those an-nouncements promised retaliation in kind, so they might increase deterrence but, if they failed, would also demand that the nations fight a gas war.

## Escalation: Warning the Axis

Although Britain entered World War II without either a stock of offensive weap-ons for sustained retaliation or a series of plants operating to fill the inventory quickly, by the end of 1940 both situations were changing rapidly.[56] Before then, Britain could have deployed gas by plane, but only in small amounts or for short bursts. Then the military would need to charge more bombs, produce more gas, create more weapon casings, and simply build inventories.[57] By 1941, though, the Royal Air Force could have shouldered the burden, even though the army was still readying itself, and both services continued to develop stockpiles.[58] The lack of the ideal level of preparedness did not stop the British from feeling com-mitted to a policy of retaliation in kind, however, from the early days of the war onward.[59]

Retaliation in kind was implicit in customary law and historical experience of chemical warfare; the Allies publicly had justified gas use in World War I on the grounds that they were retaliating against German use. For example, on July 7, 1915, Bernard Partridge published a cartoon in *Punch* depicting the Kaiser hud dling in his cape as he tried to escape from a billowing, dark cloud of gas labeled "retribution."[60] During the interwar period, several countries added reservations to the Geneva Gas Protocol when they signed it, including Britain, France, and Germany.[61] These extra clauses specifically permitted retaliation in kind as a way to bolster the law and discourage gas use. If the pure respect for the rule of law and a moral disgust of gas were not enough, then reluctance to face retaliatory gas attacks might discourage a first strike. Thus, retaliation, although motivated by fear and practicality, was part of the law and of expectations from the beginning of the Second World War. It was part of British and United States CW policies, and it was implicit in the telegrammed requests for guarantees sent to belligerents. It was most explicit in the warnings promulgated by Churchill and Roosevelt.

The telegrams were all well and good if they deterred a gas war, and at least they would be useful as propaganda even if they did not. But, was there a way to increase the chances of avoiding a gas war? As World War II continued and threats to the Allies escalated, British, and eventually US, rhetoric grew firmer. First Winston Churchill, then Franklin Roosevelt, warned Axis powers that their countries would retaliate with gas, presumably not just from home but, with time and logistics, from forward bases. While the core of the policy remained the same, what was noteworthy was that such warnings came from the top political leaders themselves, not just the diplomats. The warnings occurred publicly, they addressed particular Axis powers, they were very specific, and they spread protection over vulnerable allies, not just over the speakers' own nations. The announcements were the result of a long process of debate and evolving events.

## First Steps toward Public Warnings

There were frequent concerns that the Germans, Italians, or Japanese might use gas, but some threats influenced the Western Allies' positions, relationships, and policies more than others. In December, 1940, the British Joint Planning Staff (JPS) discussed a "telegram containing an unconfirmed report that the Italians contemplated using gas against the Ethiopians [again]" to "squash rebellion," something that the British did not want to see.[62] The JPS's task was "to consider the question of retaliation in such an eventuality."[63] At this point, the Allies had helped the court-in-exile return to Ethiopia (formerly Abyssinia) and struggle to expel the Italians as part of the ongoing East African campaign. Now there was concern that Italy would release CW as it had in 1935 and 1936 when it conquered Ethiopia. In the interwar period, the British had relied on scolding Italy with sanctions imposed by the League of Nations and with harsh words in the houses of Parliament. Britain had not even discussed releasing gas on Italy or even supplying Ethiopia with gas as a means of helping the African nation then. At that time, though, Britain did not face an immediate threat from Italy or its allies, just a vague danger because Italy's actions weakened the entire postwar system of collective security.

In 1940 the stakes were higher. The Blitz had started, so it was too late to avoid deliberate bombing of the home front. Britain was at war with Italy, too, by now, as Italy was an ally of Germany. If Italy used gas in Ethiopia, not only would that slow Britain's attempt to eject Italy from Africa, but perhaps it would increase the likelihood that one of the Axis powers would use gas on Britain. Furthermore, if Britain objected to Italy's gas use, or even helped Ethiopia in Africa, what kind of repercussion would arise? Would Britain itself be targeted? Finally, what choices did Britain actually have? The basic policy had been set by the cabinet: "we should be prepared to undertake the use of gas as a retaliatory measure if this weapon were to be used by our enemies."[64] The cabinet's phrasing, if interpreted liberally, implied that Britain could retaliate if the Axis targeted its allies, not just itself, but no specific promise had been made.

However, the Joint Planners were well aware that this situation might not remain localized as it had in the Western Front in World War I; there was the risk of widespread gas warfare. They noted that: "The practical issue which must govern our action in this case is the relative degree of preparedness for chemical warfare of the belligerents."[65] It was the defensive situation as well as the offensive one that caused concern at this point. The planners thought that the British Army was relatively safe.[66] However, there were people under the British Empire's protection who were not as prepared. For example, Egyptian civilians, part of the informal British Empire that protected the Suez Canal, lived in closer proximity to Italy than British laypeople and were "entirely unprotected against gas and, if the[y] . . . were to be subjected to this form of attack, our internal security problem would be vastly increased."[67] People would be hurt, and the Empire would wrestle with civil disruptions from the disorder and confusion.

The British did not want the tail to wag the dog, either. The War Office draft telegram to the commander-in-chief, Middle East, revealed that worry by noting that "there are disadvantages in giving [Ethiopian] . . . Chiefs a categorical promise to retaliate. You should temporise and say that our decision will depend on the form and scale of use of gas by the Italians."[68] Britain did not want any claims of gas—true or not—by the Ethiopians to force their hand or compel them to honor their promise. The use of gas had to be of a particular kind or amount, and that was not specified but was up to the British to determine.

And the dilemma did not end there. Allied considerations of gas warfare during World War II led to the conclusion that deployment would be more frequently aerial than ground based. This contradicted World War I, but it did match the interwar projections. Even in 1940, the Royal Air Force was ready to deploy some weapons, but the British Army in the Middle East, the one that would be most likely to retaliate against Italy for attacking Ethiopia, had "no means for offensive gas warfare by ground weapons."[69]

The implication was an unsatisfactory one. Britain might be able to punish Italy, and even deter it from wielding gas against Ethiopia, but the cost could be high: "our action against the Italians is likely to be far less effective than Italian action against the Abyssinians," presumably because the Italians, no matter how their soldiers might be equipped to withstand gas attacks (and the JPS thought their status was "poor"), would be better off than the Ethiopians who probably had not developed gear or effective shelters since the last time they suffered gas attacks.[70]

As a result, Britain was not about to squander the tools it did have in the current cold gas war. The Joint Planners recommended that Britain refrain from saying anything to Italy to avoid having to retaliate with its limited stores: "we should make no public mention of the use of gas by the Italians. To do so, and to fail to take retaliatory measures, might well lead the Germans to infer that we were actuated by fear of the consequences."[71] Fear about German actions was quite reasonable. Furthermore, while the planners thought a warning might deter Italy, "it might just tip the balance [the other way] if . . . [Germany] were hesitating."[72] Britain was so concerned about this that the planners wanted to impose censorship about news reports of localized gas use by Italy, if it occurred, and believed they should not make any public warnings threatening retaliation.[73]

In other words, the dilemma with Italy revolved around retaliation, but it also included the kind of calculations and assumptions that the Allies had to make when faced with future decisions about whether to use gas or even whether to threaten retaliation or to defend themselves openly against gas. Looking too ready or eager to face a gas attack might lead the enemy to think that a country was about to launch a gas attack, thus triggering a preemptive strike. Or, accusing the enemy of using gas if it had not done so might lure the foe into believing that a nation made allegations to establish a pretext for a so-called retaliatory strike. Often it was necessary to second-guess the meaning behind every piece of information and decision about gas to consider the obvious, and the potential, consequences.

Furthermore, even if Britain handled a threat in a relatively straightforward way by warning of retaliation, cautions about in-kind retribution would be effective only if they were believable. If the British bluff was called, either of two bad outcomes might occur. Either Britain would have to fulfill its obligation, and that could lead to a gas war that might lead to unrest in nearby British-controlled Egypt, if not chemical battles beyond Africa, or it might show the Germans that Britain had made an empty threat if Britain did not deploy gas or ran out of it. Any hope of deterring Germany—especially if it was wavering about whether to use gas—would be gone.

While some of the reports about gas threats could be ignored or down-graded, others could not.[74] The conviction helps explain why Britain issued blunt and strong warnings about its willingness to retaliate against direct German gas attacks, unlike its reaction to the threat of Italian gas use in Ethiopia. Although Churchill was already the face of a committed, fighting Britain, the Chiefs of Staff Committee and the War Cabinet discussed the idea of making an "explicit statement of policy" regarding retaliation. Exactly what that pronouncement should contain was debated, probably since any announcement would impact British subjects, the Axis, and the world.

Churchill, who had led the resistance to surrender in May 1940, separated a resolve to lead Britain in a gas-filled defense of the home islands, if necessary for national survival, from the proposition of fighting abroad with CW. Two months later, on Boxing Day in 1940 (what a Christmas he must have had), he wrote to General Ismay, the secretary of the Chiefs of Staff Committee. He let him know that "I am deeply anxious that gas warfare should not be adopted at the present time. For this very reason, I fear that the enemy may have it in mind, and perhaps it may be imminent. . . . every effort [must be] made to increase [our] retaliatory power."[75] If a gas war came, the British had to be able to meet it to minimize the advantages that the enemy would enjoy; Germany could not be allowed to deploy CW unopposed. But how could Britain maximize its efforts to avoid CW? Churchill's letter continues, "Sometimes I have wondered whether it would be any deterrent on the enemy if I were to say that we should never use gas ourselves unless it had first been used against us, but that we had actually in store many thousands of tons of various types of deadly gas with their necessary containers, and that we should immediately retaliate upon Germany."[76]

What is interesting is that Churchill was not suggesting a new policy, one that Germany did not know or could not figure out. After all, Britain had had this policy in place for years and had asked Germany for guarantees at the start of the war to ensure that it would honor the Geneva Gas Protocol. What was new was Churchill's aggressiveness and willingness to stretch the truth; he was wondering whether Britain should show (or tell) about its readiness and make explicit its willingness to use gas—it would not be mere token retaliation. One of the problems, though, was "there would be too much bluff in any such statement." Britain did not have enough weapons yet with which to retaliate around the world or extensively. Perhaps, even worse, such a warning might trigger the very actions he hoped to avoid. He, too, worried that it would serve as a "pretext" for Germany: "[t]hey would certainly say that we had threatened them with gas warfare. . . ."[77] After all, in World War I, the British thought that the Ottomans had claimed that the Allies had used gas first to pave the way for a pretext for guilt-free retaliation, so Britain was not being paranoid.[78] Perhaps it was better to wait before issuing a warning, at least until Britain had enough weapons to retaliate effectively over the long term.

In the end, at a March 1941 meeting, the War Cabinet chose to cover several bases in terms of its policy. The first was to reiterate its allegiance with the moral and legal taboos: "We regard the gas weapon with abhorrence and will in no circumstances be the first to make use of it." The next element would protect Britain's offensive preparations: "We cannot rely upon our enemy's undertakings not to use it as proof that he will not in fact do so." The government basically called the Germans liars and cheaters. A third element openly said that the result of these conclusions was that Britain had to prepare for a gas war. The one statement that the War Cabinet rejected, though, despite a recommendation by the home secretary and the minister of home security, was the blunt public warning that Churchill would give soon: "If he does [use gas], he may count upon powerful and immediate retaliation . . ."[79] The Chiefs of Staff thought that it was unnecessary to mention retaliation in an address aimed nominally at a domestic audience. Churchill was among the camp that thought otherwise, so much so that he asked the chiefs of staff to rethink the issue.[80] The results would have to wait three months; it was not until the Soviet Union became an ally that Churchill directly warned Germany about attacking other nations with gas.

## Japan: Escalating the War of the Words

In the meantime, even after the British committed to the concept of responding to an invasion with gas and developed procedures for that, and while they debated whether to issue new warnings—ones not tied to existing international treaties—they continued their policy of reinforcing the Geneva Gas Protocol. They used the United States to contact the Finns, Hungarians, and Romanians on December 8, 1941, both asking for promises and reminding them that the United Kingdom had signed Geneva itself.[81] The British were being thorough. The most interesting and extensive exchange of telegrams occurred between the British and the Japanese, though. Not only was Japan the Axis power able to threaten the Pacific and Asian British Empire, including India, but also Japan had not signed the Geneva Gas Protocol and was already thought to have used CW in China. Britain tried to pressure Japan into compliance with a treaty it had not signed, attempting to change Japan's presumed pro-gas behavior through a diplomatic exchange—couched as an implicit threat—in the midst of war.[82]

On December 21, 1941, in response to a British query about Japan's gas plans, the Japanese asked if the British would, in return, guarantee not to use gas.[83] Three days later London sent back the reply that it would.[84] But then the story changed from an interaction that looked like it would lead to a successful, simple exchange of equal promises to something more threatening and intense. A month later, on January 23, 1942, now that it had demonstrated its aggression against the Western powers at Pearl Harbor, Hong Kong, and other locales, the Japanese sent another telegram to London. The language suggested increased concern, a reasonable change considering recent Japanese successes in and near the British Empire in Asia. The translation read: "although they [the Japanese] have not yet ratified Geneva Protocol . . . they have so far abstained from employment of methods of warfare contrary to its terms as being opposed to the spirit of Bushido. They therefore see no reason to make an explicit declaration. [The] Japanese Government emphasize that their condition for renouncing these methods of warfare is the vigorous observance of Protocol by the enemy, and reserve their liberty of action in case of its violation."[85]

Japan seemed to be providing assurances that its own moral-military ethos held it back from first use of gas, but it was not that clear. Did Bushido, the code for aristocratic warriors, prohibit all gas use? Some? Why would the Japanese respect boundaries about gas, especially because the tying of Bushido's call for restraint to the Geneva Protocol hinted that if anyone else used gas, whether or not it was against Japan, that would remove barriers to gas use for Japan? More explicitly, the section about "reserving their liberty" certainly suggested Japan was willing to retaliate in kind if necessary. The British officials were confused.

One memo regarding the Japanese telegram summed this up: "Being unfamiliar with the Spirit of Bushido, am unable to suggest how far it is likely to restrain Japanese C.W. It has not apparently prevented the accumulation of considerable stock of gas and anti-gas equipment."[86] The distrust was not as deep as it was in the case of the Germans who had deployed gas against the British in the prior conflict, but in this case there was practical evidence that the Japanese themselves expected gas warfare, whether or not they started it. The fact that there was a likelihood that Japan had used gas in this war already, albeit against China and not Britain, was also worth considering. The British could not let the situation go.

The Army Council, the Admiralty, the Air Council, and Dominion Affairs, after consultations with the Army Council and the Foreign Office, ultimately agreed that the situation had to be clarified.[87] Yet there were some reasons for hesitation. A handwritten memo of January 29th from the Foreign Office argued, "it would be very weak to run after the Japanese . . . We have already intimated that we will play fair if they do, and they will certainly use gas if they see a chance of doing so with success."[88] Pressing the Japanese would not bind them in their own eyes any further than they felt they were already. It might even make the British look desperate, and thus weak.

In the end, though, the British response seemed to arise from a combination of suspicion that the Japanese statement about Bushido did not mean that gas would be foresworn except in retaliation and concern "that the Japanese Government will avail themselves of the use of poison gas in any circumstances where they consider that the advantage to be gained outweighs the risk of reprisals."[89] The government files did not contain any explicit reasons why Britain doubted Japan almost as much as it did Germany. It was unlikely to be pure racism, although scholars have long recognized that as an element in the Pacific War.[90] The years of Japanese brutality against China, and perhaps even the recent events at Pearl Harbor, most likely played a role. As Ashley Clarke, a high-ranking diplomat in the British embassy in Japan in the 1930s, and a representative at the World Disarmament Conference in the early 1930s, noted in a memo, "Bushido did not prevent the Japanese military from licensing the most ghastly excesses in China, notably in [the rape of] Nanking," when approximately three hundred thousand Chinese died, although he did agree that pushing the Japanese would not have much effect.[91] Clarke did not mention gas explicitly in his memo, nor did anyone else weighing in about how to interpret the Japanese communications.[92] However, there certainly had been articles in *The Times* that the Japanese had used gas in China recently.[93] Thus, during the core part of the debate in the Foreign Office about how to respond to Japan, it was logical to think Japan would use gas against Britain and the Commonwealth in the right circumstances.

Foreign Secretary Anthony Eden framed the British response. He wanted to restate the British gas policy "with a view to placing the blame for any subsequent occurrence fairly with the Japanese Government."[94] Whether he truly meant fairly, or rather squarely and clearly, was left open to interpretation. The other reason for pushing further had little to do with deterrence and more to do with the world stage. As he and his colleagues noted, publishing the exchange would provide greater justification for Britain to reserve the right to retaliate without a negative impact on its reputation.[95]

The draft reply made it clear that the British would be polite but also firm: "In view of the unsatisfactory and evasive attitude adopted by the Japanese Government . . . His Majesty's Government feel it incumbent upon them, while reiterating their determination to observe the [Geneva Gas] Protocol strictly so long as it continues to be observed by Japan, to reserve formally their full liberty of action in the event of any infringement thereof by Japanese forces."[96] The language about retaliation was quite formal, echoing terms used by Germany, and even Japan itself, and reiterating Britain's standard policy.

There was nothing new, but neither was there room for miscommunication here. Britain would not allow the Japanese to walk all over it, despite the Japanese victories in Singapore and other British possessions early in World War II; it was, in fact, a statement of will rather than a legal novelty. It did not really change Britain's position, but it revealed an effort to press Japan more emphatically than ever. The tone was tougher.

This was not enough, though. The law still played a prominent role in the version transmitted on March 21, 1942, reinforcing the rationale behind Britain's stance.[97] This message made it clear that Japan would not be granted any wiggle room, and Britain used international law to bind it firmly; the vague reference to the moral-military code of Bushido was not enough. Instead, the Foreign Office noted that:

> although the Japanese Government have not yet ratified the Geneva Protocol of 1925 . . . they are parties to Article 171 of the Treaty of Versailles, which expressly recognized that the use of asphyxiating, poisonous or other gases and all analogous liquids, materials or devices was prohibited. The Japanese Government also accepted Article V of the Treaty of Washington, 1922, [the Noxious Gases agreement], which stated that the use in war of asphyxiating . . . materials or devices has been justly condemned by the general opinion of the civilised world and prohibited in treaties to which a majority of the civilised Powers of the world were parties.[98]

The main purpose of the Treaty of Versailles, of course, had been to punish and hamstring Germany after World War I and to prevent it from endangering Europe again. Article 171 banned Germany from making, keeping, or deploying gas. However, as British officials had noted, the exact language of the clause— referring to "gases and all analogous liquids, materials, or devices, being prohibited" put limits on other countries, too, since it suggested that a customary ban on CW already existed.[99] It is a mark of how determined Britain was to restrain Japan that it included the reference to 171. The Air Council sent a letter to Eden questioning this: "it might at present [in 1942] be impolitic to make explicit reference to Article 171 . . . [but] Japan should not, without objection, be allowed to dispute the validity of a legal principle which it expressly recognized in 1919" when it was on the winning side that imposed the Treaty of Versailles on the Germans.[100]

How did the telegram come to include these terms? Eden had suggested adding a section to make sure that the Japanese and the world knew where everyone stood.[101] As the men in the Foreign Office considered the language to include in that final telegram to Japan, the legal sections of the specific treaties Britain should reference inspired the most debate.[102]

Eden had approved mentioning Versailles in the communiqué, and it became part of the telegram too.[103] Eden wanted to be clear; he chose to include language that "implicitly or explicitly forbids the use of poison gas."[104] The final version also included references to part of the Washington Naval Conference Noxious Gases agreement, which was not signed by as many countries but did firmly ban gas. The problem was that this treaty had never come into force (the French refused to ratify it because of clauses about submarines).

Interestingly, the telegram did not take advantage of the 1899 and 1907 Hague Convention clauses, the ones that governed during World War I. Those treaties banned gas as C. G. Caines, ex-representative for the Air Council, noted, and thus they would seem to be applicable to a legal warning to a nation that was a party to the conventions. The 1899 Convention explicitly banned gas, but it had been violated in World War I and might not seem to be the strongest bulwark against future CW use. A Foreign Office official noted that the 1907 Hague Convention seemed "too vague to be useful"; it mentioned that the treaty made it "especially forbidden . . . to employ poison or poisoned arms," but it did not mention gas explicitly.[105] If Britain rejected the reference to Bushido for the same reason, why include the Hague Conventions, even if the latter did suggest a ban that could be applied both to CW and biological weapons (BW)? If Britain really wanted to remove loopholes that Japan could use to justify using gas or even BW, the language in the Hague Conventions would not do that.

Furthermore, the British worked to clarify that Britain's reservation in the Geneva Protocol meant that retaliation would be limited to the theater in which the gas attack occurred. As one Foreign Office official wrote, "we must assume that we do not wish to introduce gas into the Eastern theatre ourselves until the enemy (ie., the Jap.se [sic]) do."[106] Considering that the United Kingdom was not ready for sustained gas warfare there, that made sense. A colleague responded: "It seems to follow from our general attitude that we w[oul]d not use gas in Libya or Norway because we had been forced to use it in retaliation in the F[ar].E[ast]. But of course we c[oul]d not guarantee to use gas only against Japse [sic] . . . as there might well be other Axis personnel serving with them. eg. [sic] technicians & staff missions."[107] It was risky to use gas in any arena since the chemical warfare might expand inadvertently.

The records do not indicate a Japanese response, but the message was certainly clear. While the exchange might not stop the Japanese from using CW against Britain, as Sir William Malkin, the legal advisor for the Foreign Office, affirmed: "the point is that the passages in these treaties make statements of existing fact which the Japanese accepted as accurate, and they can hardly get out of this now."[108] The Japanese would pay militarily and in reputation for using gas.

While the value of the latter might not have been much—Japan was already unpopular and feared by those they conquered and by the Allies—Britain explicitly and repeatedly tried to manipulate enemies into positions in which gas use would blacken their reputations. In addition, Japan was the country that confused the British the most, as seen by the debates behind the telegraphic exchanges. Since the Asian Axis power threatened the British Empire in India and Asia if it used gas, and appeared already willing to use gas in China, perhaps it makes sense that Britain spent so much time and effort reinforcing any power the legal treaties might have had and signaling to the Japanese that they were not out of the fight, despite the losses they suffered in the Empire on December 7/8, 1941. It could not do much else to strengthen its position via gas, at least not in late 1941 and early 1942.

The Japanese never did deploy gas as part of a centralized, consistent policy, although the Chinese government alleged that it continued to do so periodically.[109] The Japanese restraint about CW and BW when facing the Western Allies might not have been solely because of the telegrams, or even because of the telegrams at all. The fact that President Franklin Roosevelt warned the Japanese in June of 1942 that the United States would retaliate if the Axis power used gas along with the growing supplies and air power possessed by the Allies over the course of the war may well have played a role too. We just do not know. However, at the very least, they provided a firm foundation for deterrence that the US political and military might later reinforce, and it demonstrated that Britain did not yet feel obliged to consult its future gas policy allies about warnings to the enemy or CW policies in March of 1942.

Perhaps more interesting is that this is an example in which one of the Western Allies did use gas, just not physically. What this means is that Britain intended, even before the war, to adhere to the legal and moral policy it had adopted earlier. By pressuring Japan to reiterate or clarify its refusal to use gas, and reminding the country of its past—and still binding—promises not to use CW, Britain made gas both an enhanced and ready potential propaganda, legal, and diplomatic weapon. In other words, it waged a form of psychological warfare. This technique was stronger than negotiating the interwar treaties because it was based on direct exchanges between Britain and Japan during the conflict. In addition, Japan had already been tarred by the atrocities in Nanking and the surprise attack at Pearl Harbor, while Britain wrestled with the battle for the hearts and minds of Indians, so the struggle to blacken the reputation of the enemy continued on both sides throughout the war; propaganda served to motivate one's own people and allies and hopefully to weaken the same on the enemy side.

The search for reassurance by seeking guarantees also motivated some of the public, showing that, domestically at least, Britain was right to have taken the steps it had with the Axis powers. On December 10, 1941, during an early phase in the exchange of telegrams with Japan, a story in the national newspaper, the *Daily Telegraph*, reported Britain's efforts to gain assurances from Japan, Finland, Hungary, and Romania, noting that Britain had offered its own promises in return.[110] Despite that, in February of 1942, as the Foreign Office wrestled with its exchange with Japan, the International Committee of the Red Cross reached out to the government, explaining that it wanted to read the exchanges and publicize them further by releasing them in "The International Review of the Red Cross."[111] The Foreign Office was not thrilled; it wanted to release information on its own terms, including the communiqué about the Japanese negotiations.[112]

Another example showing that the government did not use the reassurances immediately came in May of 1942, when Gerald Bailey, director of the Executive Committee of the National Peace Council, wrote to Prime Minister Winston Churchill asking for the Allies jointly to renounce gas. In his proposal, Bailey referred to the obligations of the Geneva Gas Protocol. In return, he thought that Germany should be solicited to provide an equivalent promise.[113] It is interesting that not only was the National Peace Council ignorant of the British government's exchanges with Germany—probably they were being held in reserve until publication could have a galvanizing effect, such as when the Germans deployed gas—but it also suggested the same method and same legal rationale that Britain had indeed used.

Although Britain did not take advantage of probable lay interest and publicize exchanges with the Axis powers, waiting until they would have more impact if (or when, as was thought) the enemies released CW against Allied troops or civilians, these queries by the International Red Cross and the National Peace Council, along with the story in the newspaper, demonstrated the British officials were right. Gas could catch the public eye; it could be a "munition of the mind," as scholar Philip Taylor said about propaganda.[114] Gas caused psychological and emotional casualties, ones that generated fear of war and stress in individuals' efforts to prevent physical deployment or to protect oneself against it.

Furthermore, this was a first step in escalating the kind of gas war that did occur in World War II—one where the threat of gas was used to pressure enemies to refrain from releasing gas bombs, one where deterrence was attempted, even if there was not a lot of faith in it. Britain's telegrams implicitly made it clear that the Empire would hold the enemy to the standards of the Geneva Gas Protocol. By asking the Axis powers point blank about their intentions, the implication was that Britain was prepared to react in kind to those who used gas first. After all, Britain's official reservation to the Geneva Gas Protocol, when it signed the treaty, promised that response.

Already, therefore, by 1942 it was clear that gas could be used without being deployed. The Allies did not stop here; they continued to use gas as a tool in their efforts to shape the enemy's behavior regarding CW; in fact, now the United States joined the British, this time issuing explicit threats.

## The USSR Questions

And, if that was not enough to consider, Hitler attacked the Soviet Union in June 1941. This invasion changed the war in many ways, including adding complexity to the realm of CW diplomacy. Russia may have become a British ally after Germany broke the Nazi-Soviet Non-Aggression Pact in June 1941, but it was an uneasy alliance. It was not merely years of hostility and mutual ideological fear; there was simply a lack of trust that permeated the relationship between the two nations, including their interactions regarding chemical warfare. Would allying with the Soviet Union help or hurt the British pledges about CW? For example, even after Britain and the Soviets were military allies, and, more specifically, the former had offered some protection to the latter against gas attacks, when Soviet scientists came to Britain to consult on CW, the Joint Intelligence Sub-Committee received orders to figure out if there were "any secrets which should not be disclosed." This was not an alliance built on trust.[115]

Even worse was the uncertainty about whether the Soviets would refrain from introducing gas to the battlefield or otherwise acting in some way that might inspire the Germans to target them, perhaps obligating Britain to back up its new friend. These fears were rational. More than once, for example, British intelligence summaries reported that diplomatic rumors included a claim that Germany said Russia had used gas. While that might have been true, in the mind game that was an element of the cold gas war, British intelligence interpreted this as "the sort of report which the Germans are likely to spread before they themselves initiate gas warfare."[116]

The distrust was not new. A year earlier, before the British issued their warning to Germany about the danger of attacking the Soviets with gas, the news service Reuters had chimed in, with a Moscow correspondent sending a telegram in July 1941 to the British minister of information Duff Cooper "to the effect that the Germans intended using poison gas against the Russians." He further suggested that a British warning about retaliation "would prove an effective deterrent." Within the government, Cooper was a bit suspicious—he thought that the Russian government might have instigated this communication since a public warning would serve its interests, but he brought it to the attention of the War Cabinet all the same. For now, though, the War Cabinet declined to act, feeling that "it would be premature."[117]

Churchill was not precipitous either, especially considering his own long-term anti-Bolshevism and the recent Nazi-Soviet Non-Aggression pact that seemed to encourage Hitler at the cost of the West. Before Churchill made a public pronouncement, he and General Secretary Joseph Stalin had their own discussions, during which Churchill offered a private promise to retaliate against a German gas attack on the Soviets. The British prime minister waited for the right moment for a public warning, balancing several factors as he did so.[118] Was there really evidence that Germany might attack? Was everyone ready to defend against gas? Did the Allies have enough gas so that they could retaliate effectively?[119] The British did not want to be compelled to use the last arrow in their quiver, retaliation, if at all possible. Once it was played, it was played, and there would be no end to CW.

Besides, the British were always aware that the consequences had the potential to spread beyond Europe to the Pacific.[120] Once again, the War Cabinet did not put it past Japan to use the advent of chemical warfare in Europe now or even later (such as when D-Day finally occurred) as a pretext to starting gas war itself elsewhere. Therefore, it was important that the Russians looked beyond their immediate needs in Europe so that they tried to avoid CW as well.[121]

This underlying distrust of the Soviets and the wartime vulnerabilities of the British Empire to gas meant that the announcement had to be carefully framed to threaten, and hopefully influence, Germany, without binding Britain's hands any more than necessary. Specifically, Sir Charles Portal, the air chief marshal, argued that, "To prevent chemical warfare from being initiated over isolated cases of use by the Germans, it was thought that the public announcement to be made in this country should be so worded that it would make clear that we should only engage in chemical warfare if the enemy had used it on a large scale."[122] This echoed the War Office's ideas when the target of the warning was going to be Italy. Britain would need to keep its promise—for the sake of its credibility at home and abroad—but retaliating would have an immense military cost. How big an expense, especially since British adherence to the Geneva Gas Protocol and the Ten-Year rule in the 1930s left it unprepared for sustained warfare two years into a new conflict? The cost could be enormous, particularly in terms of a Japanese threat, if CW spread globally; this threat grew during the first half of the war as the Japanese "advance[d] to the Westward and [increased] the exposure of India to attack."[123]

Furthermore, it might even have a cost in terms of public opinion. Whether or not propaganda and public opinion were truly influential in all cases, perception, propaganda, and censorship played a major role during the war. Hence the Joint Planning Staff was concerned that a public announcement might backfire. Instead of deterring the Germans, it might "give her [*sic*] the opportunity to shift on to us the odium of an action from which our enemies alone would profit."[124] Even Churchill, who was usually among the most likely to risk gas or suggest using it, recommended that "it must also be remembered that if we made a declaration, and gas warfare ensued, we might be regarded as in some sense responsible for the start of gas warfare."[125] Best to leave loopholes about when to retaliate than to offer the Germans an opening to take action to which Britain would have to respond. The cost of having to fight a gas war, to defend against it, to face public pressure, to weigh legal bonds, and to parse diplomatic language all had to be considered.

A warning would also benefit Britain, of course. It reassured the Allies, suggesting that Britain was able to provide effective help in the fight against Germany, and this threat of retaliation in kind may also have helped deter the Axis from starting a gas war. After all, the Germans had not yet started a gas war, despite opportunity, but the British military and politicians were aware that Germany could: the foe had the materials to do so and, it was believed, the mental willingness to do so. A warning, if it was believable that Britain could retaliate, might keep Germany from launching gas.

However, no one knew how resistant Hitler and his cronies were to gas, but it was reasonable to believe that whatever obstacles to employing gas that existed so far could be overcome. Germany had proved willing to violate gas laws in the last war, and the Axis had proved itself capable of ruthless behavior in this one. Just looking at its violation of the Nazi-Soviet Non-Aggression Pact served as a reminder that the Nazi war machine was willing to flout diplomatic agreements. In fact, the Joint Planning Staff believed "it would be very wrong to make a public declaration, which would do nothing to prevent Germany initiating chemical warfare . . . but might give her the opportunity to shift on to us the odium of an action from which our enemies alone would profit." Somehow a warning might "provoke" Germany.[126] It was a difficult judgment call—what should Britain do, and how would Germany react to it?

There were other risks too. If the Germans could not be trusted, it was also true that it was quite unclear how far the Soviets could be trusted. In contrast to the alliance with Western Allies such as the United States and Canada, conversations among the British military leaders suggested that they were quite aware that the ties between Russia and Britain were based on expedience—a mutual dislike of Hitler—and not on any deeper sense of common goals. Participants in governmental discussions agonized over whether Russia might—deliberately or inadvertently—embroil Britain in a gas war.[127] Could the Russians be trusted to confirm accurately any reports of gas? Was there a diplomatic way to encourage the Soviets to let British representatives test alleged gas samples? Might the Soviets even lie about a gas attack just to compel Britain to honor its promise and fight Germany more intensely? British engagement in a gas war with Germany could not only cause misery to Germany—even if the latter could successfully defend against it—but it might also harm Britain. For the Soviet Union, which, as was well known, felt that the Western Allies let it bear the brunt of the fight against Hitler, any sort of reprieve from Germany's attacks might be worth it. Of course, false allegations of a gas war might embroil Russia in a gas war, too, but that did not seem to be a consideration to the British. As Noel Mason-Macfarlane, the head of the British Military Mission in Moscow, wrote privately to the chiefs of the Imperial General Staff, "Russia is not nearly so vulnerable to gas attack as Germany or England . . . It may well appear to the Soviet High Command that a really heavy gas attack by us on Western Germany is the best weapon at our disposal for relieving pressure on the Russian front . . . I am not suggesting that there is any strong probability at present that the Russians may be tempted to accuse the Germans of having used gas so as to bring our counter measures . . . into play. But they are very self centred [*sic*] and realist and should their position . . . deteriorate we ought not to exclude such a possibility" that they might lie.[128] The combination of a lack of real trust of the Russians and a message from the senior British military expert in Russia that practicality and self-interest might encourage them to drag Britain into a gas war—whether or not Germany started one—was definitely food for thought.

Just to make matters more complicated, Sir Charles Portal took the opposite position, and he, too, was influential. He told his fellow chiefs of staff: "that we could assume that the Russians did not really want to initiate chemical warfare . . . it was unlikely that the Russians would try and fake the use of gas on any larger scale. This would be a very dangerous game to play and if the Germans immediately denied it, it would undoubtedly lead to much ill-feeling between ourselves and the Russians . . . the Russians would be well aware of the possibilities in such a situation."[129] He did not necessarily trust the Russians outright, but he did trust them to see that they were much better off with Britain on their side. It is interesting that he thought Germany could be trusted at all—at least that is the implication if one might be willing to accept their denial. Perhaps it helped that he was convinced that any gas attack would be a major one; the British would be able to confirm it without any problems then, and trusting friend or foe would not be an issue.

What this debate really showed was that nothing was clear in the gas war, even when gas was not being used. It also showed just how tricky it was to "read" the players and to know what kind of pressure to apply to keep gas off the table. Would a warning deter Germany? Would the same announcement backfire and incite Russia, bringing about the very outcome—gas warfare—that Britain hoped to avoid? And, on top of this, what was Britain willing to promise a dubious ally?

The doubts helped explain why Britain wanted the public declaration to hinge on British "satisf[action]" that Germany had actually attacked Russia, and why the Western Allies later developed their own "United Nations" gas policy, one that really only included the British Empire and dominions as well as the United States, not Russia.[130] Furthermore, as Colonel W. G. Stirling of the War Cabinet Secretariat pointed out to a colleague, since the chiefs of staff "do not think it is to our advantage to start up gas warfare," policies should not require the British to help the Russians prove that gas had been used.[131] The burden was on their tenuous allies to convince Britain. That way, the British could refuse to believe that enough proof of gas existed if they chose, especially if the evidence was thin. (Interestingly, this was similar to the reaction of the United States vis-à-vis Chinese claims that the Japanese used CW and BW against them—and probably for the same reason, as will be discussed in the last chapter.) The other options considered were that the British should be "given facilities, including inspection by a medical officer, to satisfy ourselves that poison gas had in fact been used; or . . . to accept the position that we are, in fact, entirely in the hands of the Soviet authorities and to accept such circumstantial evidence as they may care to produce."[132] The Military Mission representative in Russia was doubtful about these options; he had little access to outside news and few facilities.[133] Thus, the safest option was a recommendation to let the stories about incidental gas attacks be ignored. The British would wait for "adequate proof" from the Soviets about a big attack.[134] This would lessen the chances that Britain would be drawn into an unwarranted gas war and would leave the burden on the Soviets to be convincing. It allowed some wiggle room for the British.

By the time Sir Charles had spoken up, though, Churchill had already made the promise, both privately to Stalin and aloud to the world. On May 10, 1942, just months after the British Foreign Office had ratcheted up pressure on Japan in the exchange of telegrams, Winston Churchill went even further in his public statement that "we shall treat the unprovoked use of poison gas against our Russian ally exactly as if it were used against ourselves, and if we are satisfied that this new outrage has been committed by Hitler we will use our great and growing air superiority in the West to carry gas warfare on the largest possible scale far and wide upon the towns and cities of Germany."[135]

This very long sentence had four key components to it. It was a direct and blunt threat, unlike the telegram the Foreign Office had sent at the beginning of the war. This was no gentle reminder of a promise to obey the law with the threat implied; this was taking protection and power into one's own hands. Furthermore, it was not suggesting that Britain itself would be a target, but rather Russia. Churchill's statement trumpeted that there was a strong alliance—Britain was willing to escalate a gas war for an ally if Germany started one. Third, Britain had to confirm that Germany had launched gas at Russia; it was Britain, not Russia, who had to "be satisfied." This might reassure Germany that Britain would not recklessly start a gas war, and it was a warning to Russia that Britain would not be pressured or tricked into starting one. Finally, it was a promulgation of the Allies' increasing strength: Britain's air power was growing, and it had the ability, Churchill claimed, to threaten the German homeland. The home front would pay for Hitler's attacks on Russia.

There was a caveat, too. Britain would respond to "unprovoked" attacks. Whether this meant simply that Britain would not be dragged into a gas war that Russia started or whether there might be situations that legitimized a first use of gas by Germany, there was no hint.

What is almost as interesting is what is missing. Russia is the only ally listed by name; Churchill ignored the countries and colonies threatened by Japan and other places in the world. Also, Britain did not consult or commit its Commonwealth. Furthermore, there was no mention of the United States, Britain's other major ally at this time. This was a warning focused on the situation in Europe.

Britain was right to be concerned about how the Germans would interpret the warning. A week after Churchill's announcement, the British obtained a copy of the Chilean ambassador in Berlin's telegram to his superiors reporting the German "official comments." He noted, "The English assertion is described as most suspicious and lends one to suppose that it is intended to use gas on GERMANY . . . if ENGLAND . . . gas attacks she will find GERMANY in a position to reply in a way suitable to—[sic] in the field of chemistry."[136] It seems that neither side was convinced that their warnings had prevented a gas war, but neither did a chemical war emerge.

## FDR's Broader Promise: Steps toward Allied Cooperation

Less than a month later, President Roosevelt matched, and even exceeded, Churchill's warning. On June 6, 1942, he spoke out, probably in response to

Chinese allegations of Japanese gas use as well as being inspired by Churchill's statement, but likely also inspired by the landing of the Japanese on the Aleutian Islands that day after attacking nearby bases earlier in the week. Perhaps the damage the US Navy inflicted during the Battle of Midway also motivated him. FDR's focus in this warning was on the Pacific theater: "If Japan persists in this inhuman form of warfare against China or against any other of the United Nations, such action will be regarded by this government as though taken against the United States and retaliation in kind and in full measure will be meted out."[137] In contrast to the British warning, FDR tried to protect all of the Allied nations. This substantially broadened the promise Churchill had made, and it certainly offered help to the British as well as its Empire and Commonwealth; British troops, Australians, New Zealanders, and others were realistic targets for Japan. The other point worth noting is that FDR spoke out although he may not have known yet that the recent battles of Midway and Coral Sea would change the momentum of the war in the Pacific. In other words, he threatened Japan just as their conflict intensified and as the United States demonstrated itself able to inflict substantial damage on the enemy navy, albeit at a substantial cost to itself.

Two days later he reinforced his message, this time starting by condemning CW dramatically, reinforcing his personal attitude and the national policy: "I have been loath to believe that any nation, even our present enemies, could or would be willing to loose upon mankind such terrible and inhumane weapons." This time, he announced explicitly: "We [the United States] promise to any perpetrators of such crimes full and swift retaliation in kind and I feel obliged now to warn the Axis armies and the Axis peoples in Europe and in Asia."[138] The United States warned against—and thus may have deterred or risked—a global gas war.[139]

FDR's bold statement could be seen as an early step in what would become a process of creating an Allied gas policy since it built on a promise that Churchill had recently made. The British did not take the opportunity to widen the prime minister's guarantee and match the US pledge. The British deemed themselves unable to carry through with a promise to retaliate against the Japanese, at least in 1942; limited gas warfare in the European theater, close to home, was all they could handle for the moment.[140]

In July, the Canadians discussed offering their own policy, based on Churchill's statement and FDR's warning. By June 1942, the Canadian minister of national defence, James Ralston, justified recommendations for increased CW production by alluding to both men's warnings. He had referred to FDR's language—retaliation if "any of the United Nations" were targeted—interpreting Roosevelt's more liberal one as governing without acknowledging that the two men's threats encompassed different terms.[141] It was as if FDR's actions, by broadening the commitments of the United States, dictated the behavior of some of the Allies too. Then, in a July 8, 1942, meeting of the Canadian Cabinet War Committee, Ralston went further suggesting that Canada adopt a statement equivalent to the one issued by the United States. He wanted his country to retaliate if an enemy—any Axis power—used it "against any of the United Nations."[142] The others at the Cabinet War Committee meeting argued that it would be better for Canada to follow the British and US leads; they did not want Canada to have the "terrible responsibility" of being the first actor, but they did want to "act in close connection with" their more powerful allies, and they accepted that "the use of gas should be on the same basis as that enunciated by" Churchill and Roosevelt.[143] Canada remained silent in public, but behind the scenes, it took another step toward setting out an allied wartime gas policy with Britain and the United States, despite the lack of explicit reference to that goal; that would come later. In addition, the outcome of the Cabinet War Committee meeting indicated that, like the other Western Allies, Canada adopted an attitude that increased the risk of gas warfare on behalf of its allies.

The ramifications of the leaders' warnings did not stop there. In April of 1943, after the battle of Kursk, seemingly prompted by the growing strength of the Allies in continental Europe in general and intelligence of renewed threats to Russia specifically, the British considered promising the Axis that retaliation would be launched against "the Nazi 'satellite' nations," if necessary.[144] Then, in September, when it was clear that Italy might become an Ally, or at least break away from Germany's side, the War Cabinet confronted intelligence that suggested that Hitler had threatened Italy with CW if it withdrew from the Axis.[145] The War Cabinet decided that it would retaliate no matter what, so it then debated whether to send a warning to the Germans.[146]

Interestingly, the War Cabinet also suggested that Canada should be given the opportunity to join in any warning because that nation's troops were fighting in southern Italy. The rest of the dominions could be kept in the dark until closer to the date of the warning; they could not be blindsided, but they were less involved and less powerful.[147] The British were becoming more entangled with their allies and aware of the need to manage relations with them.

In total, Churchill and FDR warned, or reiterated their warnings, six times by early September 1943.[148] Starting in 1942, though, the Allies transitioned to a combined gas policy, one that took two years to refine as the needs of the Western Allies and their relationship evolved over the middle phase of the war. The individual national warnings were indicators of desperation to avoid gas warfare as well as signs of allies protecting those who were weaker than they. Or, in the Soviet case, they were efforts to assist allies whom the British desperately needed to keep in the alliance to stand a chance of defeating Germany. While the warnings were generated for a variety of reasons, they gradually turned into coordinated policies that policed retaliation and established unified rules for starting a gas war. The bonds between the Western Allies grew, and their willingness to consider gas warfare while on the offensive broadened—a topic for a later chapter.

# CHAPTER 4

# The Limits of Friendship

## The Influence of Chemical Weapons on Alliances as World War II Expanded

> [Should] a single government be put into a position herein by an independent decision[,] it is enabled to embroil the whole world in gas warfare.
>
> —British Chiefs of Staff to the US Chiefs of Staff, January 1944

A gas war in one theater, even one launched by one Ally in retaliation against one Axis power, might spread chemical battles throughout the world, entangling all the belligerents. Combatants had to take seriously the possibility—at times the likelihood—of chemical warfare escalating. Despite recognizing that risk, as noted in the quotation at the start of the chapter, the Western Allies embarked on a combined chemical warfare policy. Because of this danger, gas changed behavior and affected relationships in World War II, even when it was not released on the battlefield.[1]

The Western Allies worked together scientifically, militarily, and politically from the top level downward, sharing trust, culture, and knowledge in ways none of them shared with the Soviet Union, the Free French, or China. Britain, the United States, and Canada were a subset of the greater group of Allies in World War II, especially in gas matters. Their relationship during World War II can be seen in the public warnings promulgated by Churchill and Roosevelt, and discussed by Canada, in chapter 3, although these were not coordinated. On the military side, an integral element of the relationship included US servicemen coming to Britain to see how the latter trained, tested, and equipped soldiers and airmen. At times, the British even loaned their anti-gas teachers to US air bases and units to help US forces establish their own procedures, leading to ones that mimicked those in Britain.[2] Certainly, scientists associated with the military shared information and worked together in Britain and North America, with Sir

Frederick Banting and Israel Rabinowitch, as was also discussed in chapter 3. These personal relationships were important, but a critical element on the road to preparedness, and one that illuminated the challenges of the impact of chemical weapons (CW) on the Western Allies' relationship, was creation of a combined gas policy between the United Kingdom, the United States, and Canada.

Having allies was critical for victory in World War II, but alliances were not trouble free. To wage an effective war, the Western Allies needed to cooperate despite some competing interests. Once the United States joined the conflict, developing a combined policy that governed when the Western Allies would use gas offensively or defensively became a new challenge.[3]

As with many situations in which nations have to relinquish some sovereignty to work together, critical questions included: how much independence would be lost, and what would be gained? How much do you trust your partners, especially if they have different vulnerabilities and priorities than you do? Might your collaborators endanger your troops or your civilians by focusing on their own needs? While it was relatively easy to see value in the general concept of a united allied policy, its success or failure during World War II would have global consequences, and managing the policy became more complicated as the military forces of the Allies became increasingly intertwined.[4]

From 1942, immediately after the United States entered the war, until V-E Day, there were several major challenges to the Western Allies working together. In this chapter, the focus will be on the ones that arose until just before D-Day, examining the Western Allies' preparation for retaliation, first in theory and then during a crisis, while the next chapter will examine the last year of the war in Europe. During the phases addressed in this chapter, there was escalation in the tests and trials of the gas alliance. The first challenge involved developing a unified Allied policy about gas, a process that stretched from 1942 until the cusp of D-Day. The next occurred in the middle of this period, in December 1943, when mustard gas from the United States spilled in Bari, Italy, sending the United States and Britain scrambling to contain the situation. Their first concern was to prevent the Germans from recognizing that the mustard gas was even present in the theater. Such knowledge might lead to a misunderstanding, willful or not, that would encourage Germany to open a hot gas war under the guise of retaliation or preemptive strike.

Creating and maintaining an effective cooperative relationship under these circumstances illustrates the energy the Allies dedicated to poison gas, even when it was not deployed: gas influenced the Allies' war. These events also demonstrated that chemical warfare required joint decision-making. Issues of international law, national sovereignty, and strategic vulnerability all played roles. Yet the three powers in question negotiated these hurdles successfully, managing to minimize risks that a gas war might explode and maintaining their relationship, both when the threats were theoretical and when there was an actual crisis. There was a price: sometimes compromising within an alliance came at a cost to their own citizens' well-being or the sovereign power of their own nations.

## Allied Gas Policy

After Pearl Harbor, Britain's gas policy was no longer its own. Its government had set a clear one: do not use gas first but be prepared to retaliate with it to defend the United Kingdom or some of its allies. As seen in chapter 3, though, there were temptations to violate that in the face of extreme national danger, namely invasion by Germany. Still, for the most part, Britain strove to adhere to its no-first-use policy. Partly this was out of a desire to obey the Geneva Gas Protocol, but it was also out of a political and military fear of gas warfare. Despite British governmental and military efforts from the interwar period onward to prepare offensively and defensively for gas war at home and in the field, there would be no way to avoid all casualties. Even in the best-case scenario in which Britain neutralized gas attacks through masks, saving many soldiers from injury or death, life would be miserable and expensive as decontamination units sprang into action, as food stores became damaged, and, in the worst case, if people panicked.

In addition, members of the Commonwealth had their own points of view and the legal independence to make some of their own decisions. While countries such as Canada willingly joined the British war effort in World War II and felt incredible loyalty to Britain, that did not mean that they allowed Britain to dictate all the policies governing Commonwealth and imperial behavior.[5] The gas dilemma illustrated this clearly, and the Canadian role is an excellent example. (Other parts of the Empire, such as India, had more complicated relationships. India contributed two million men to the war effort, but also it had widespread disaffection with the Empire.) Canada was the most active in gas policy formation with Britain and the United States.[6] The others were involved in gas-related activities, such as experiments in India, but when Canada spoke up, the more powerful countries listened.[7] Canada's geographical relationship with the United States, and the latter's willingness for Canada to participate in gas-related scientific as well as military exchanges, may also help explain Canada's special role. Informally, therefore, Canada proved to be the de facto leader of the independent-minded loyal Commonwealth countries, although its arguments spoke to its own concerns on this issue. Thus, it was not that it necessarily disagreed with British decisions—and in fact its own chemical warfare policy also rested on the Geneva Gas Protocol and permitted only retaliation—but rather its government did not want Britain to make decisions for it.[8] Canada also had to behave responsibly in light of its own international obligations and relationships. For example, Major-General Maurice Pope of the Canadian Joint Mission to London explicitly argued that "Canada [was] . . . a separate country having signed and ratified . . . [the Geneva Protocol]." Canada could not let another nation make decisions for it that might impact its treaty obligations, even if that other country was Britain.[9] As important, Canada's interests sometimes matched, but often contrasted, with those of the United States too. Canadian leaders sometimes had different interests from Britain, but more important, they sought recognition as a full partner in the Allied club, rather than just being seen as a leader among the Commonwealth states. Regardless, any role Canada won for itself had the potential to benefit its Commonwealth peers as well.

Canada's role in Allied chemical warfare had begun before the Western Allies considered creating a joint CW policy. In the early war years, Canada sought ways to help the British gas effort. In a move that might appall some of its citizens later, Canada worked hard to provide the land needed for a large-scale testing field for gases and their defenses. In the open spaces of Alberta, the Canadian government found land for the Suffield Experimental Station in 1941, a joint British and Canadian experimental chemical warfare base.[10] Canada and the United States exchanged chemical warfare liaison officers as well as observers.[11] In fact, historian Christopher Robin Paige argued that "[c]ollaboration between the United States of America, Britain and Canada on matters of chemical warfare probably surpassed that in any other field of defence during the war," and it included both "experiments and field tests."[12]

However, Canada also had its own concerns. Like Britain, Canada worried about attacks on its soil, whether conducted with gas or more conventional weapons, particularly in British Columbia.[13] Perhaps it was Japan's proximity to British Columbia (farther than the Maritimes to Germany, but with nothing but the sea in between) that raised alarms, especially once the Japanese occupied two of the Aleutian islands in 1942.[14] Certainly the rugged coastline was considered hard to defend.[15] While the United States faced similar vulnerabilities to Canada, it was not as concerned—or at least these geographical issues did not permeate the chemical warfare debates, despite attacks on US soil at Pearl Harbor and later on Kiska and Attu in Alaska. The occasional firing on Western targets from the sea or air with conventional weapons and incendiary balloons may have inspired newspaper headlines, but they were not

**FIGURE 7.** Preparations for offensive and defensive chemical warfare required extensive scientific research. The Western Allies engaged in some cooperative work, including outdoor experiments at Suffield near Medicine Hat, Alberta, in Canada. This sign stands at the entrance of the current base there. (Photo by M. Girard Dorsey.)

a key basis for the gas program in the United States, one that had begun growing before the first balloons in 1944 or even before Pearl Harbor.[16]

Canadians had another reason to be concerned. They had been the first victims of battlefield gas in World War I, along with the French Zouave, or Algerian, troops. The memory lingered.[17] Even in the heart of World War II, in 1943 the Toronto *Globe and Mail* reported that the "'Originals' of Ontario will Mark Ypres Battle," one of the many references over the years to anniversaries of the first gas attack on Canadian troops in April of 1915.[18]

In contrast, the United States was the five-hundred-pound gorilla in this story. Late to the war, it nonetheless made up for its tardiness by providing enormous resources of all kinds and fighting from a strong geographical base. The United States faced neither invasion nor shortages in the same way that Britain did, so it did not feel the same vulnerabilities. Yet, it was not until 1944 that it had enough gas to retaliate effectively in Europe.[19] Still, it did not feel the same vulnerabilities.

Even so, in general, the US chemical warfare policy established after Pearl Harbor mirrored Britain's: no first use, but it reserved the right of retaliation. There were two critical differences, however. The first was that the United States had not ratified the Geneva Gas Protocol. Thus, it was not bound by international law to refrain from initiating gas warfare—and the major powers were well aware of this. It is true that it had signed the Hague Conventions of 1899 and 1907, but those were weak restraints, ones that were nearly meaningless after Germany's initiation of gas during World War I. Except for rare instances, Britain, the United States, and Canada did not refer to the Hague Conventions, but rather to the Geneva Gas Protocol when discussing legal bans. The same seemed to be true of other nations who conversed with these major Allies. Thus, what bound the United States was its own restraint, as expressed through Franklin Roosevelt's presidential proclamation of policy, and possibly public opinion, but not laws.

And that led to the second difference in the three countries' gas policies. The United States, through Roosevelt, warned the Axis that it would retaliate in kind to gas attacks against itself and its Allies. At first glance this seems similar to Churchill's declaration, but the US proclamation was much broader than the British one. The United States promised protection to any Ally against any Axis power, not just Russia (and later a liberated Italy) against Germany. To make matters even more complicated, as noted in chapter 3, Canada had not warned the enemies through a similar public proclamation, but then its own retaliation-based policy focused on keeping gas in one theater or defending the homeland.[20] Even this could be ambiguous, though. Would the retaliation policy be triggered if a few Canadians attached to a multinational Allied force suffered in a gas attack? Or, would it be activated only if Canadians at home were the main targets?[21] Where did the limits of diplomatic friendship, military strategy, and national sovereignty lie?

The practical, if frightening, implications for Canada and Britain—particularly the latter—was that they could get caught in a global gas war that they adamantly did not want. For instance, if the United States decided to retaliate against Japan for a gas attack in China, Britain would almost certainly be dragged into the fray. Britain, after all, had its own troops in the China-India-Burma theater, and there was no guarantee that Japan would respect the uniforms of one Ally versus another. In World War I, after all, use of gas by the Germans at the Second Battle of Ypres had led to gas use by most of the belligerents on the Western Front within months. Although regular gas use had not spread to other fronts at that time, there was no guarantee that gas use would be limited to one theater this time; the numbers of soldiers, the scale of bombing, and the scale of theaters had all expanded in this war. Why would gas be different? Britain might even find itself in a chemical conflict in Europe, all because its Ally had a different stance on gas. Finally, in general, a close alliance with the United States logically suggested that Britain (and its Empire and Commonwealth) should integrate policy—and later troops—with the United States. This made the dangers more acute; if a US commander, for example, became involved in a gas exchange, so would the British soldiers tied to him. Since gas was different in kind than other weapons, these concerns about its spread between theaters and to other Allies was an issue that would be unique to CW.

Yet, no effective, unified policy existed in 1942, even months after the United States entered the war; as could be seen with the gradual deepening of air war cooperation regarding targets and techniques, it could take time to integrate Allies' values and approaches.[22] What may have made the development of a gas policy harder was that the protocols had to be developed without the benefit of experience deploying CW. Its necessity was clear to the Western Allies, but the process of negotiating an Allied policy took months of work on the part of all the parties: it was relatively easy to agree that the core gas allies needed a shared policy to respond to CW threats efficiently, but they found it challenging to create one that also protected their individual interests and national defense as much as possible.

## Acting as One? Creating an Allied Policy on Chemical Warfare

### The First Draft

What is not surprising is that the three nations began to discuss coordination in March of 1942, mere months after Pearl Harbor. What is surprising is that the negotiations took two years, given Paige's conclusion that the alliance was closer in terms of CW policy than anything else.

The formulation of an Allied policy could have been simple—but only to a point. The three parties shared a core value: there was a loose foundation for a restraining common policy of no-first-use based on the Geneva Protocol and, in the case of the United States, presidential preference. In fact, ever since World War I there had been a practical response to enemy gas use: retaliate in kind. Using gas first in 1915 had generated international outrage against Germany in that conflict; would the same happen if it were used first in World War II? Uproars could influence the endless struggle to undermine the enemy's morale, to tighten bonds with one's allies or neutrals, and to strengthen the spirit of one's own citizens.

Avoiding those tensions meant that agreement on the foundational no-first-use basis for a policy was not enough to create a solid working arrangement. The separate national warnings and strategic interests regarding gas meant that there was doubt about the depth of the commitment to the shared outlook. For example, each country might differ about which type of authority could authorize the use of gas. At least as contentious was the decision about what would trigger retaliation. The leaders' consensus opinion seemed to be that use of gas by the enemy had to be met with a forceful and immediate retaliation in kind. Yet, it was critical not to make a mistake in determining when gas had been used. In most countries, this meant establishing a chain of command to communicate about possible enemy gas use and reserving the final decision to release retaliatory gas to the political authorities, such as the War Cabinet in Britain.[23] Would each country be as careful as the others when assessing evidence?

Furthermore, although the discussions focused on the issue of retaliation, they also addressed the precarious matter of first use. Despite their inclination and previous legal, diplomatic, and public promises, the Allies understood that they might feel compelled to launch the first attack. While retaliation might make one's Ally vulnerable to a gas war, at least the actor would have been impelled to release CW. In an offensive campaign, the actor might be deliberately endangering an Ally because of its own priorities. A common policy might or might not be able to inhibit each of the Western Allies more than their current promises or legal obligations, but it could be framed to slow down the actor and to allow the other Allies to prepare for a gas war to be unleashed.

Even if they agreed about why gas could be released, and who could approve its deployment, how much warning did one's allies need before taking these actions? A thorough, effective policy that accounted for not only the current needs of each of the Allies, but also their changing needs as the war evolved, could be critical for the survival of huge numbers of troops and civilians who might suffer or perish in a global gas war. For example, it might be necessary to relinquish elements of one's own sovereignty to encourage a more proactive ally to do the same, thus increasing the opportunity to stop or slow down a nation that wanted to launch gas. That braking system had to be matched with the potential need to let a nation react quickly and independently, so as not to put its own soldiers at risk by being unable to respond to an attack. Achieving that balance required the military negotiators to weigh the diplomatic factors as well as strategic ones—it was a painstaking process.

Thus, the focus was on creating a policy of retaliation after proven enemy gas use, but there was more to it. In particular, there was room for legal obligations; there were spaces for independent national action; there were concerns about regions vulnerable to attack; there were problems about how to acknowledge commands for multinational forces; and the issue arose of which nations could have input in decisions. This was a policy about using gas, but it was also about exerting power and sovereignty while maintaining alliances.[24]

With the British instigating the discussions, the major policy decisions were made by British and US military leaders in the Joint Chiefs of Staff and Chiefs of Staff Committee and approved by the Combined Chiefs of Staff. The first British note on the subject reverberated with urgency. Lt. Col. C. S. Sugden of the War Office wrote to Colonel W. G. Stirling of the War Cabinet Secretariat about a week after Churchill's public warning in May 1942 (described in chapter 3). He lamented: "Nothing has been done so far towards producing a co-ordinated United Nations Policy for chemical warfare and I am anxious to get matters moving as soon as possible."[25] (Whether or not Sugden envisioned the inclusion of allies such as Russia, there was no real discussion among the negotiators about including so many countries.). It would be a major endeavor; not only was he proposing an allied CW policy that might include the United States, but it would need to incorporate parts of the Empire and Commonwealth that had been excluded.[26] Leaders from the United States considered the discussions necessary, but the issues were complex enough that six months later the policy still was not finished.[27]

The British Combined Chiefs of Staff proposed a policy for the United States and the British Commonwealth to adopt, stating it in two succinct paragraphs:

(a) Gas warfare will be undertaken by both the United States and British Commonwealth forces on the order of the Combined Chiefs of Staff after approval by the appropriate governmental authorities; or independently by any such Nation in retaliation, on the decision of a representative designated for that purpose by its highest governmental authority.

(b) The United States and British Commonwealth forces will provide evidence of the enemy's use of gas warfare and make prompt confirmed transmittal of the information to the Combined Chiefs of Staff. When the decision to retaliate is made independently by any such Nation, it will give immediate confirmed advice to the Combined Chiefs of Staff.[28]

Adding gas to the war would change the conflict dramatically; it was a weapon that was different in kind, not just scale. In the eyes of the drafters of this version of the policy, introducing gas required political decisions at the "highest governmental authority" to instigate it; no mere general should have the power to change the war so radically on his own, even when retaliating. At this point in late 1942, Roosevelt's warnings, the British leadership's actions, and Canada's sovereignty interests meant that each nation seemed to desire retaining some freedom to decide to respond on its own, for both political and military reasons. This kept independent authority largely intact and permitted a more rapid response in the field. However, Britain set itself up as the speaker for itself and the whole Commonwealth, leaving only the United Kingdom and the United States as the Western Allied actors who had a say in releasing gas. This proposed agreement highlighted the limitations that remained in the integrated gas policy, even between two allies—this was a political decision between the most powerful countries.

## What about Me? Which Nations Get a Say?

To complicate matters, Canada spoke up, and in doing so enlarged and lengthened the debate. It argued that its own safety and sovereignty were at risk and that it should have an explicit role in any decisions.

The Canadians recognized that the Combined Chiefs' original proposal allowed leaders from Britain and the United States to dominate the decision-making, essentially overriding the national identity and independence that the Canadians had strived to establish. From the first day of the war, Canada had repeatedly emphasized and exercised its sovereign power. Unlike in World War I, it insisted upon declaring war on its own (and did so on September 10, 1939), in contrast to the colony of India, rather than let Britain sweep it into the conflict with its own declaration. Canada had demonstrated its individual value when it offered to help Britain. One example was the willingness to lend the vast spaces of Alberta to the chemical warfare research experts by establishing the Suffield testing ground. Canada had and would make many other contributions to the British and Allied war effort—supplying human and material resources including over one million service personnel and ten kinds of planes as well as other vehicles—but as if to emphasize it was not just Britain's acolyte in gas matters, Canada undertook efforts to establish its own relationship with the US military and scientific experts in this area.[29]

Canada objected to the first draft of the allied policy. Striving to keep power in his own hands while maintaining alignment with FDR and Churchill, Canadian prime minister Mackenzie King wrote in his diary that, "we should not allow the military authorities to take any action on their own; that the War Committee itself would have to be 'satisfied' in the first instance that we were acting in accord with the United States in any resort to the use of gas and that we were in agreement with both the President and Churchill about its use in the right way at the right time if that became necessary."[30]

Canada proposed the insertion of a clause in the policy that "other Commonwealth Governments concerned" would have to give "approval," along with the United States and United Kingdom, before gas warfare could be initiated.[31] While Canada did not request a special status for itself by name, choosing instead to represent its fellow Commonwealth countries, it was the one who argued for the change, and it was the only one who took part in the debates over the policy, probably because of its more active role in other parts of the gas research and trial process.

In making its request, Canada followed an interesting strategy: it proposed it in Washington where the US Chiefs of Staff, the ones who hammered out the details of the US policy, approved that proposal before the British discussed it.[32] In this situation, the British were relatively sympathetic and seemed to support some alterations, perhaps because Britain did not envision using gas as a first strike except in such dire circumstances that would seem difficult to quibble over. As one secretary to the Combined Chiefs of Staff, British Brigadier Harold Redman, wrote to US Navy Captain Forrest B. Royal, "It is morally certain that the Commonwealths concerned would most certainly see eye to eye with the U.S. and British Governments as to the necessity in any given set of circumstances of resorting to gas warfare." Yet, he also feared that neither the United States nor the United Kingdom could compel Commonwealth troops to act; only their governments could.[33] With Canada placated by the change in language about responsibility, the discussion moved to the more difficult issue of retaliation; here the United States was the outlier.[34]

## Who Is the Boss? Who Makes the Decision for a Nation?

In formulating the retaliation policy, there were two main problems. The first concern was about who had the power to make the decisions within each country that retaliation was necessary. It was one thing to accept another member in the club, such as Canada, but it was another to delegate authority to approve gas warfare to an individual or group that the others did not trust or to allow it to use a procedure that might not accurately investigate reports of gas attacks by the enemy. Britain itself was adamant that its War Cabinet would approve any use of gas by that country.[35] However, upon examination in December of 1942, some of its experts, particularly those in the British Chiefs of Staff Committee, recognized that the language that had been suggested by the Combined Chiefs of Staff, namely that retaliation could be authorized "on the decision of a representative especially designated for that purpose," allowed a loophole in which it seemed like the authority could be delegated, perhaps even to US general Douglas MacArthur (the only individual listed by name in the minutes), who was a purely military authority.[36] To ensure that other countries did not interpret the policy that way—because Britain itself did not intend to exploit loopholes and make it too easy to approve gas use—another amendment arose. Could the term "evidence" be substituted to ensure the call to use gas to be made in the highest levels of government, the War Cabinet in Britain's case, to clarify matters and ensure the procedure Britain preferred?[37] In other words, a military commander could offer evidence of enemy gas use to his government, but he could not make a decision to deploy his armed force's CW. This made sense; after all, the evidence that gas has been used by the enemy most likely would be provided by local authorities in the attacked area, so it would be firsthand and thus as reliable as possible. The authority to respond would remain in the hands of the highest political authorities of a country, and definitely not in the hands or any one military leader, no matter how exalted, who might not see the whole picture. A telegram to the United States seemed to settle the issue within weeks. Gas remained too important to be left to underlings.[38]

With relief, on January 11, 1944, the British Chiefs of Staff Committee perused a copy of the orders given to US commanders that specified how gas attacks had to be reported and to whom. Specifically, "When the use of poison gas by the enemy has been reported and verified by the theater commanders, the Joint Chiefs of Staff will submit for the approval of the President a recommendation on the decision to be made."[39] At least three steps were set out for verification, and a reiteration that "no retaliation by using gas will be made" until the White House had approved.[40] It also clarified that permission to use gas came from the president himself, although it would be reasonable that he would be guided by the Joint Chiefs of Staff.[41] This was so important that this information—that the War Cabinets in Britain and Canada and the president in the United States are the ultimate authorities—appears again in the discussions. It bore repeating that launching gas was a political decision informed by military evidence.[42]

## Are You the Boss of Me? Can One Nation Restrain Another?

The negotiations continued. The next problem was that the original policy permitted nations to act "independently in retaliation." The British Chiefs of Staff worked on finessing this term repeatedly, facing rejection from the Chiefs of

Staff and even their own prime minister, but they kept trying.[43] By February of 1944, the situation on the battlefield had become trickier because Allied troop integration had increased. A commander from one country might find himself in charge of troops from the United States, United Kingdom, and a Commonwealth country. Should his government "be put into a position herein by an independent decision it is enabled to embroil the whole world in gas warfare[?]" as the British Chiefs of Staff told the Chiefs of Staff bluntly?[44] If so, a decision by one country could generate a gas war that would involve one's own soldiers under an Ally's command. In the worst case, a gas war could spread to another theater, incorporating even more Allied soldiers without their governments ever having a say. That kind of erosion of sovereignty did not sit well with the British and Canadians. They seemed to sense that they were more reluctant to use gas in any circumstances, perhaps because of their greater vulnerability to gas and because the United States faced fewer legal restraints regarding chemicals, and thus they were more in favor of abrogating the ability for any one country to retaliate on its own. The fact that the head of the multinational Operations Torch, Husky, and Overlord was from the United States may have made a difference too. The British Vice-Chiefs of Staff concluded that the practical organization of Allied soldiers "makes the independent action by any one Government . . . inappropriate and in effect invalidates the arrangements for independent retaliation."[45] Usually, actions by one commander or one country, no matter how exalted, did not have those kinds of repercussions.

That was Britain and Canada's perspective. The United States was even more reluctant to give up any national power, though, mainly because it feared that an individual country could make decisions—and thus retaliate more effectively—than could a committee of belligerents. The United States would not want to abandon the power of individual sovereignty; it did not want to give up the right to respond independently, leaving itself at the mercy of acquiring others' approval before retaliating against an attack, especially when it would be contributing most of the effort to end the Pacific War. The US Chiefs of Staff argued, "In the event of any enemy using gas, the situation may well demand prompt retaliation to the fullest possible extent. Any inability to take such action might well have the gravest military consequences; and the disapproval of any Government, no matter how little concerned, would prevent effective action."[46] While outright refusal of approval by other Allies was a concern, as the negotiations about retaliation policy continued, it was clear that the United States mainly feared communication delays. A firm believer that immediate retaliation would have the most impact, it feared that consultation would inhibit that.

The British were sympathetic to the US desire to honor their president's proclamation without delay, probably out of the need to ensure credibility as much as out of loyalty.[47] After all, Churchill had committed the British to retaliating against Germany immediately if the foe used gas against Russia. Still, as the Vice-Chiefs of Staff noted, "it is inconceivable that we should do so without first consulting the United States, or for that matter, the Dominions, and we feel that in practice consultations should be necessary."[48] It was not merely diplomatic protocol or alliance loyalty but also necessity that motivated them. Executing offensive and defensive retaliatory measures required cooperation. Moreover, it probably would not slow down reaction time since rapid retaliation still had to wait for confirmation that gas use occurred, communication of the news to the commander's government, and discussion by that government; then, finally, the conclusion reached could be implemented. So, during this period "some time will be available for consultation between governments," and Britain did not just mean a United States-United Kingdom discussion but also one that involved the dominions.[49] That might even be an advantage. After all, "the necessity for consultation is in itself a safeguard against over-precipitate action by an individual authority."[50] Gas warfare could be a nightmare; there could be no chance of starting it by mistake. The dilemma, in some ways, was the story of fighting one's own ally so that it did not become a danger to you because of its aggressive decision-making; the United States could not be allowed to drag Britain into a gas war inappropriately. The United States worried that Britain's caution would slow down a response.

Even a compromise solution was a hard sell, and the British tried multiple times for a change that would, effectively, make "the same rules apply for retaliation with gas as now apply to the initiation of gas warfare by any member of the Allies." In other words, the British wanted any player—especially the United States—to act after approval by the three major Western Allies and preferred a decision to be approved by the Combined Chiefs of Staff, if possible. As late as January 18, 1944, the United States was not convinced.[51] In trying to find a mutually agreeable compromise, the British Vice-Chiefs decided that the key element was that all the Allies needed notice; they could not be caught by surprise when a gas war exploded. With this in mind, they proposed that a country that decided to retaliate should "give immediate confirmed advice to the Combined Chiefs of Staff of its intention before taking any such action [underline in original]."[52] This suggestion just required consultation or notice, not approval, before retaliation. It also permitted the other Allies to prepare to be hit by an expanding gas war, as Sir John Dill, the lead British representative in the Joint Staff Mission to the United States and former chief of the Imperial General Staff, noted, with India, Britain's most vulnerable possession, in mind.[53]

On the other hand, the United States read the spirit of the words behind this and thought that morally it obligated the acting nation to get approval or at least that "the government making the decision . . . [would] not act until the other governments concerned present their view."[54] In US eyes, the compromise did not really change the rules. An interservice committee, the Joint Staff Planners, also argued that Roosevelt's proclamation promising "full and swift retaliation in kind" meant that the decision was a political one, outside the realm of even the top military men in the Joint Chiefs.[55] In the eyes of the Joint Staff Planners, there were other reasons why speed was important, too, namely "the psychological and moral effect of such immediate action on our enemies and on our forces . . . and, of even greater importance, . . . for immediate counteraction in order to neutralize at once the enemy's ability to inflict further damage on Allied forces and populations."[56] Gas threats and attacks offered psychological challenges and were withstood by keeping panic in abeyance, not just by physical anti-gas measures. So, a massive and instantaneous response was a message to Allied civilians and soldiers, not just a way to protect troops and laymen physically.

It is not surprising, then, that the Chiefs of Staff rejected the compromise, as did Churchill.[57] Churchill's refusal fit his personality as well, perhaps, as the bonds he felt being an ally of the United States. (He was not the only one. Air Marshal Sir Douglas Evill and Vice-Chief of the Imperial General Staff Lt. General Archibald Nye had both expressed the opinion to their peers at the Chiefs of Staff Committee meeting on October 15, 1943, that consultation with the dominions "might not be acceptable in every instance," and even if political needs meant that they had to be included in the discussion, the military "operations should not be prejudiced." Speed was of the essence.)[58]

The dominions were not ignored, though. Even in February of 1944, the War Office reassured the British authorities in Australia that it was "inconceivable that Dominions would not (repeat not) be consulted regarding alteration of policy."[59] By the middle of March, though, it seems that the Chiefs of Staff pressed forward, informing the British representatives in Washington that the changes about initiating gas had been approved as had amendments requiring "confirmed advice" before retaliation.[60] The British kept pushing along this avenue, wanting complete clarification, partially because they felt the need to protect the dominions.[61] It was quite a balancing act, both within England and between its Allies.

Luck was with Britain and Canada, as was persistence. General George Marshall, the chief of staff, became personally involved, championing the British interpretation just as Churchill backed the one from the United States. By April 1944, just before D-Day, the more limited sovereignty language was approved.[62] The United States finally recognized that gas warfare might spread, and, even worse, they "fully appreciate[d] risk that precipatory retaliatory action by one Government might be followed by further enemy attacks on allied areas particularly exposed to gas attack." The United States would try to allow allies time to prepare, if the United States led a retaliatory strike, by giving "confirmed advice" to its allies.[63] Technically, the United States did not have its promises regarding retaliation constrained by having to ask others for approval, but it still gave some preparation time to its allies.[64]

However, this might draw Allied troops into waging gas warfare simply because they might be under US command (or someone else's command) if a retaliatory order were given in a specific theater, an increasingly likely problem as the war continued and more multinational forces developed.[65] This dilemma led to discussions in the Commonwealth. For instance, in New Zealand, the Chiefs of Staff, and later the deputy chief of air staff, had considered what New Zealand's troops should do if they were part of a multinational force led by an commander from the United States who ordered gas use; should the troops follow their commander or wait for approval from Auckland, or even London? Eventually, the New Zealanders decided to follow their commander's lead in terms of retaliation, no matter his nationality.[66] It would have been interesting to see how a combined gas policy played out in practice, if that occurred. The Western Allies did not give a lot of thought to what the smaller Allies might do.

## Agreement

In the end, the Western Allies agreed to a policy that addressed initiation as well as retaliation, one that balanced individual action and ceding sovereignty. The US Chiefs of Staff agreed that "Gas warfare will be undertaken by both the US and British Commonwealth forces on the order of the Combined Chiefs of Staff after approval of the United States and United Kingdom and other Commonwealth Governments concerned" before a Western Ally initiates gas warfare—and this meant that authority must come from the top, that is, the supreme military-political leaders of the British War Cabinet, US president Roosevelt, and the Canadian Cabinet War Committee.[67]

Secondly, retaliation had to follow a careful path. The countries had to set up reporting protocols, a coordinating procedure that they did not do for any other weapon. There would be some delay—full approval by all participants was not required as it was for initiating gas. Britain thought that was enough—"a very successful termination of long drawn-out negotiations"—it could make its concerns known if necessary.[68] This seemed to satisfy Canada's original concerns as well.[69]

There was fair warning to all participants that a government might act "in fulfillment of commitments" when retaliating—that could mean honoring reservations submitted with the Geneva Gas Protocol or Churchill's and FDR's warnings, despite the fact that this meant different nations technically had varying obligations, such as Britain's focus on Europe unlike Roosevelt's wider umbrella.[70] Finally, the United States (or any actor) would tell the Allies of its plans before it retaliated.[71] Deployment would not be as easy or fast as originally intended, but all the Western Allies would be on the same page.

Independent exercise of national power was limited; restraint was enhanced. Britain made it clear repeatedly that it was not worried about an internal loose cannon (its reporting procedures, lack of delegation of authority, and dislike of gas war ensured this), but it was worried about its powerful ally, the United States. Once again, Britain was in a weak position with regard to gas—much as it was when it faced Germany at the start of the war, and it had to use its weakness to protect itself by sending telegrams to try to pressure Germany into gas restraint. Britain now gave up sovereignty to act by allowing its Commonwealth to have a say, too, in order to force its US ally to do the same; with both bound equivalently, chemical warfare would be even more likely to be prevented. And there was a second point. Yes, bringing in Canada and the other Commonwealth members helped slow down the United States, if it were to act rashly, but it was also done out of honest loyalty to the dominion Allies and awareness of their vulnerabilities.

Finally, although the biggest arguments were over retaliation protocols, the most likely reason that the Allies would start a gas war, the very fact that the first section of the joint policy focused on initiation, meant that throughout the war there was recognition that there might come a time when an Ally needed to make a first strike with gas, no matter what Churchill and Roosevelt said publicly now, no matter what the Canadian prime minister, Mackenzie King, wrote in his diary, and no matter who had signed the Geneva Gas Protocol. No doubt British leaders remembered how close they had come to starting a gas war in 1940, and perhaps US leaders were already looking for ways to reduce the fearsome toll of island-hopping across the Pacific to Tokyo.

Yet, the first gas crisis that arose because of physical injuries from gas in the field was not one any of them had envisioned.

## Bari

It was one thing to negotiate an Allied chemical warfare policy and prepare for retaliation in the abstract; it was another to face a crisis in which poison gas had been released. In December of 1943, Britain and the United States faced a dire situation in Bari, Italy, where they both had troops and bases. A store of gas from the United States injured and killed soldiers and civilians, providing the only extensive theater gas casualties of the war among the Western Allies. The incident also offered a chance for Britain and the United States to work together to manage a gas crisis in which gas was both released and had the potential to be deployed by the enemy.[72] This was not the threat they expected—after all the gas was Allied, not Axis. However, the episode did demonstrate that Britain and the United States were willing to sacrifice the health of their own people— in this case by concealing the cause of their injuries, thus inhibiting proper medical care. Working together, they kept the presence of gas in the theater a secret from the Germans, thus withholding a possible pretext for their own gas attack. How did such a convoluted situation occur?

A core part of each country's gas policy required it to be prepared to retaliate with CW immediately—or at least as fast as possible. Earlier in the war this plan made Britain's leaders nervous because it required the nation to step up production of poison gas without delay to be ready to execute their plans; it would be difficult to retaliate instantly without weapons to deploy. If it did come to the point of launching gas weapons, then immediacy would be critical because the common opinion was that a surprise attack stood the best chance of breaking through anti-gas defenses. Even more important, it would also make the threat of retaliation more serious—and a likely more effective deterrent—if the responder possessed weapons and its enemy knew it. Likewise, in the United States, there was both strong popular and political resistance to chemical warfare, as well as recognition of the need to prepare to retaliate to make FDR's warnings credible.

By the middle of the war, in 1943, the Allies were ready to store gas weapons in forward areas. So that the troops would be ready, fifteen days' worth should be stored as far forward as Italy by February 1, 1944. According to an October 1943 plan, two months before the attack at Bari, ships had to start carrying the weapon that fall to get enough to the target port in Italy by the target date of March 1944.[73]

Planners, though, understood that transporting such weapons close to the front was very risky. On the one hand, if the enemy knew about the presence of nearby gas, that could act as a deterrent to an Axis first strike with CW. On the other, if the enemy found out about the presence of gas in the theater, it might interpret—sincerely or for public relations reasons—the situation in a way that could hurt the Allies: the presence of gas in a war theater could mean an Ally was preparing to initiate a gas war, rather than just preparing to defend against one started by the other side. Perhaps such an interpretation would lead the Axis to launch a preemptive first strike with CW. So, the Allies felt they had to move gas to continental Europe but decided to do so secretly.

Then, on the night of December 1, the US ship, *John Harvey*, docked in Bari, Italy, carrying mustard.[74] The harbor was at "utmost capacity," which, as investigators later acknowledged was "a heavy risk to take for a small port within easy reach of the enemy," making it a rich and "vulnerable target" for an air raid.[75] That evening German planes attacked Bari, and, among other targets, hit the ship laden with "540 tons of mustard gas bombs," although they did so without knowing about the special cargo.[76] The Final Report of Bari Mustard Gas Casualties, undated, but clearly written within a few months of the incident, captured the dramatic nature of the attack and its impact on land as well as on the ships in the port. It recalled that "The explosions in the harbor that evening were of tremendous violence. Window glass seven miles distant was shattered, and considerable other damage done in Bari." In all, sixteen ships sank, with more damaged. Some suffered direct hits, like the *John Harvey*, and total casualties. Gas leaked into the harbor and into the air, with few noticing anything unusual about the smell and no one reporting gas. Perhaps the burning fuels, the multiple explosions, the casualties coated in oil, and the fear of exposure on a cold night distracted the wounded, the medical workers, and the local civilians alike.[77] To exacerbate matters further, the gas spread as tainted ships moved to other ports

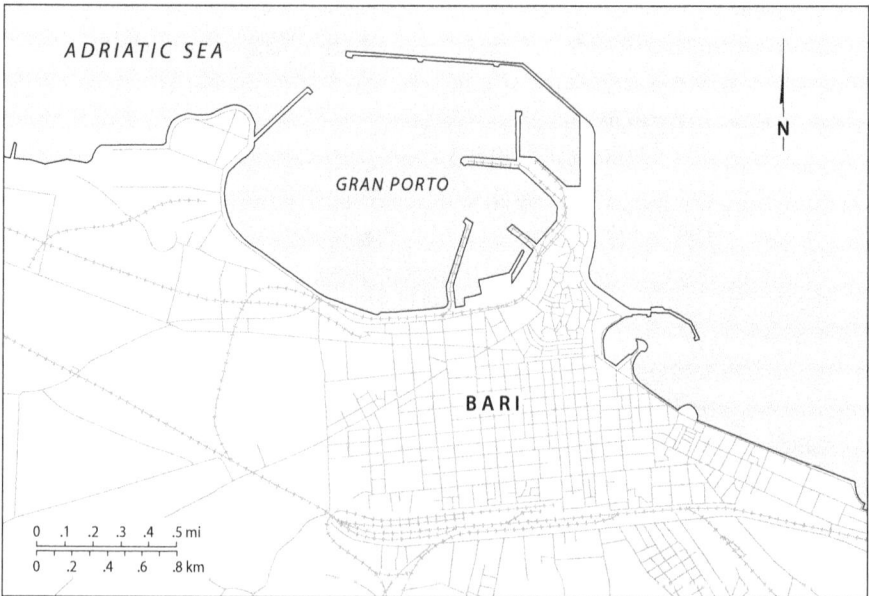

**MAP 1.** On the night of December 2/3, 1943, the Germans attacked Allied ships in the harbor of Bari, Italy, leading to mustard gas contamination of the port and nearby town when a ship carrying stores exploded. (Map by Bill Nelson.)

in Italy because of the "fires raging" in Bari harbor.[78] Of the air raid's eight hundred plus casualties, 688 were from gas and, of those, seventy died; some of the gas fatalities never received life-saving treatment because of the secrecy surrounding the presence of the CW.[79]

Despite those numbers, very few anywhere knew about the gas on board, and everyone on the *John Harvey* died so they were unable to tell anyone.[80] As gas leaked into the harbor and spread into the town, civilian personnel (including Allied ones) were effectively gassed by their own side, with no chance or reason to avail themselves of anti-gas respirators, clothing, or decontamination units.[81] These casualties combined with exposure, explosive burns, and all the more traditional results of an air raid on a port. As an example, "one section of the outer harbor wall, covering an area approximately fifty . . . yards was found to be contaminated. In this area, approximately 35 . . . [mustard] bombs were located, a number of which had been ruptured by the force of the explosion . . . more of these bombs were exploded in mid-air . . . [and were the cause] of many of the survivors being contaminated."[82] The damage from gas occurred not just at the moment of the air raid but also as its repercussions spread to the surrounding areas.

In the aftermath, both before and after symptoms of mustard gas exposure could be seen, the overburdened hospitals and first aid stations failed to offer appropriate treatment because medical personnel had no idea that they faced gas wounds.[83] Because many of the victims had been burned by mustard gas diluted with oil and water from the harbor, the wounds did not look like traditional burns, making them even more difficult to diagnose. They were unrecognizable until Stewart Alexander, a physician and consultant to the Chemical Warfare Service called to the site, made the connection days later.[84]

Even worse, as one report noted, treatment was "actually favourable to the absorption of the mustard" because it allowed the gas to keep in contact with skin and continue to burn it.[85] Mustard continues to burn as long as skin is in contact with it, whether through clothes saturated with it, blankets that absorb some, or simply because the skin has not been washed. Thus, victims kept suffering even after they saw medical personnel. The doctors, nurses, and medics focused on shock and exposure, which they knew the patients suffered and which would be treated by wrapping wet individuals up rather than washing them off. Furthermore, even if the first responders had known about the gas, there was no protocol for treating burns made from mustard mixed with water and oil.[86]

As the caregivers sought to treat the wounded and ascertain why so many had strange wounds or failed to heal, military leaders all the way back to London responded with ire and fear. What if the enemy found out that the Allies had gas in the forward theater? What would it do? Would it use the gas release as a pretext to claim that the Allies had started, or were about to start, a gas war, thus justifying any use of gas itself as retaliation? Would the Axis simply use it as a public relations weapon and claim that the Allies disdained the law and the moral taboo? Secret discussion explicitly referred to concerns that the presence of gas would become fodder for "'enemy propaganda.'"[87] That sort of information could rile up the enemy's war effort, offend allies, and lead to domestic unrest by those who despised gas.[88] How could this be prevented?

Basically, the cover-up began. Traditional censorship was the first step, of course. Although the word was probably out in Bari itself, perhaps it could be contained there. Both British and US military postal censors as well as civilian ones received their orders.[89] Britain would tap the Political Warfare Executive, one of its intelligence organizations, to counter any enemy propaganda that might develop.[90] Mainly, though, the Allies held their breath. As the British propaganda ministry representative wrote in a memo, the war correspondents had left Bari on the morning after the raid and so had not gathered much of the news nor reported it. In fact, "None of the many stories which they filed with the M[inistry] of I[nformation] . . . had any mention of this particular incident . . . I agree it is best to let sleeping dogs lie."[91] If possible.

The next phase showed how serious the Allies were. After a brief debate, and a period in which some authorities were told that wounds should be reported honestly, that is, a gassed eye would be listed in casualty reports and soldiers' records as a gassed eye, this changed.[92] In a decision made at the Chief of Staff level in the theater, but passed up to the Combined Chiefs of Staff and British Chiefs of Staff, the wounded did receive the acknowledgment that these were battle casualties of sorts: "enemy action" became the generic label given to anything from burns to eye damage to bronchitis and would be used for the assignment of pensions, disabilities, and other official purposes.[93] The cover-up became quite elaborate and long-lasting. For example, since Indian soldiers and merchant navy sailors had been wounded and killed, the British India Office's compliance had to be secured.[94] All avenues that might allow leaks about what really happened at Bari had to be blocked even from casualties' future medical providers, even if that resulted in care that failed to prevent or treat ailments that emerged later because of the gas exposure. This reticence even robbed soldiers of their proper disability payments decades in the future.[95]

Finally, there was a Board of Inquiry—one stacked to keep the true story as quiet as possible. This was not, by any stretch of the imagination, an independent investigation, but it was filled with military expertise. Instead, although the Allies wanted to figure out what happened, where the dangers lay, and how to prevent them from recurring, they needed to keep it quiet. So, the very board members who would investigate and analyze the situation were ones who came to the inquiry with the most information about it.[96]

By May of 1944, just weeks before D-Day, there was an exception to the policy of "keep it quiet at all costs." Since Britain was "constantly" transporting CW, there was a policy to keep a few key people informed, ones who comprised a so-called "Nursemaid Squad" and accompanied dangerous cargo, as well as local medical and naval authorities in locales wherever gas was transported.[97] While the purpose of this policy was to have people in place who could handle problems if they arose, perhaps this was as much of a way of maintaining secrecy as ensuring that the needless casualties at Bari did not recur.

Britain and the United States, the main Allies involved, were incredibly lucky overall. Bari was a personal disaster for those caught in the backlash of the attack, but this was not an Allied military disaster. Word did not get out that gas had been present and had been the problem. And, perhaps, there was a benefit to the whole event. The British and the US officials worked together well to handle the situation, which offered hope, even if they did not explicitly note that, for mutual management of gas problems in the rest of the war. But this episode also shows how stressful and dangerous the gas war was, even when it was a cold one. Just as World War I had shown, the threat of gas could be tension-filled and demoralizing for soldiers; the danger that the enemy would misread defensive efforts—such as plans to be prepared for retaliation—as offensive ones, was rife. Casualties could occur from accidents. A lot of energy had to be expended to make sure plans to prevent gas war did not become reasons to cause or expand it. Predictions, and sometimes personal suffering, were a key part of avoiding the gas conflict during World War II.

The Western Allies grew closer with regard to gas policy once the United States officially joined the war. The core of the gas alliance revolved around shared needs and values: the countries needed to work in tandem to wage conventional war in multiple theaters successfully, to restrain each other from starting a gas war, and to protect their citizens from gas attacks on the home front. Negotiations to achieve these goals and responding to crises proved that the Allies could compromise and find common ground—eventually, and sometimes at the cost of sovereignty, as in a joint chemical warfare policy. Other times it was at the cost of men, as at Bari. The real test to avert a gas war and maintain the alliance was to come, but Bari illustrated the actual dangers of inadvertent gas release as well as the extensive effort necessary to protect secrecy of gas preparations. Those costs and threats would continue, if not escalate.

The risk of gas warfare in Europe was at an apogee on the cusp of D-Day. Intelligence estimates had repeatedly concluded that Germany might resort to gas out of desperation and might be on edge about signs of imminent Allied gas use. A successful invasion of Fortress Europe could certainly be a critical moment, and the Allies held their breath to see what the summer of 1944 would bring.

# CHAPTER 5

# Rolling the Dice

## Risking Gas Warfare in Europe

> It is absurd to consider morality on this topic when everybody used . . . [gas] in the last war without a word of complaint from the moralists or the Church. On the other hand, in the last war the bombing of open cities was regarded as forbidden. Now everybody does it as a matter of course. It is simply a question of fashion changing as she does between long and short skirts for women.
>
> —Winston Churchill, July 6, 1944

Winston Churchill's analysis of poison gas, just a month after D-Day and three weeks after Germany began to drop Vengeance weapons, that is, the V-1 flying bombs and V-2 rockets, on England, presented a much more open attitude about chemical weapons (CW) than what most Allied laymen or leadership, whether military or civilian, had expressed earlier in World War II.[1] While Churchill's perspective was shaped by the fact that he himself had always been more accepting of gas than the majority of people who spoke out about it, and while he did have a dramatic turn of phrase, his comment contains accurate elements. Gas did become an accepted, if not condoned, weapon in World War I. And belligerents violated rules of behavior, such as targeting civilians, more often in World War II than during the previous global conflict. However, a month to the day after D-Day, when Churchill shared the views stated in the epigraph, he captured a new willingness to consider gas as a practical weapon, not just as a last resort in a desperate situation. At this point in the war the Western Allies' attitudes toward gas and behavior toward a potential gas war began to shift away from a fairly rigid rejection of it for moral and diplomatic reasons, although they did not accept it freely.

D-Day is seen as a milestone in the Western Allies' road to victory in Europe, and it was also a turning point in their struggle to manage poison gas. Planning for the invasion of Normandy, and for the months after it, required that the Allies repeatedly reconsider the threat of German gas use and what that meant for their own actions. It also led to a reassessment of the long-published Allied philosophy that gas would be used solely in retaliation. Overall, the Allies still did not want a gas war, but at times they started to show a willingness to take increased risks that could lead to its advent, if that was the price of defeating Germany.

At the same time, as the British and their Allies drove toward Berlin after D-Day, the temptation to find excuses to initiate gas warfare arose. Gas could bring benefits including terrifying the enemy, injuring and killing foes, and exhausting soldiers who had to follow gas protocols constantly. Resorting to gas was not easy, though, and potential justifications were still couched in defensive terms, such as retaliation for atrocities (even if the atrocity was not a gas attack), but they did reveal a somewhat malleable perspective on gas warfare. In late 1944 and 1945, the Allies could not bear to make a first strike—for military and other reasons—but they were not as afraid as earlier of considering the issue of using gas or becoming involved in a gas war.

US, Canadian, and British attitudes toward such things as white phosphorus (WP) and botulism helped shape the discussions and decisions about how to balance risk and reward from using CW during this period. It is worth noting that these two examples involved materials that were not always considered CW, yet, for the purposes of the intra-Allied negotiations, they were CW.

During the eleven months between D-Day and V-E Day, the United States took the most risk-tolerant attitude of the three Western Allies regarding CW in its efforts to win the war as quickly as possible by championing the use of WP. The British leadership, as a whole, was more risk-averse in its efforts to win the war without facing or deploying poison gas, even when it faced devastating threats at home from German V-1/V-2 attacks. Canada struggled to balance threats to its soldiers' safety against jeopardy to the alliance as it decided to withhold a botulism vaccine from its own soldiers during the D-Day invasion preparations and follow-up; protecting its citizens in this case could endanger the Allied units. Contrasting objectives required chemical warfare-related alliance politics to evolve; the result was that the United States gradually increased its power in the alliance, much as it took the lead on many policy issues in the war. Allied actions demonstrated that all of them agreed that the alliance's survival had to be the first goal.

Depending on the threat faced during this period, the danger to each of the three nations varied, and thus, so did their interactions. At times the alliance members worked together and at times independently, but repeatedly they tried to limit friends and foes from inciting or chancing a gas war when one or another felt less risk tolerant than its partners. The price was a probable, and likely physical, cost to their soldiers and civilians. They rolled the dice on the alliance, testing the bonds of their relationship and its ability to prevent a gas war compared to their willingness to pay for that success in the blood of their men.

## Exchanging Rockets for Gas? A New Weapon, a New Response

As if the Blitz of 1940–1941 and its smaller-scaled follow-up, the little Blitz on London from January to May 1944, were not enough, Germany targeted British civilians with the Vengeance weapons from the aftermath of D-Day almost until the end of the war.[2] While the Allies had hints of a German secret weapon program, they struggled to recognize that there were two Vengeance weapons, not just one, for a long time.[3] Operation Bodyline, begun in 1943, morphed into Operation Crossbow as the Britain and the United States sought to combat these new weapons. This effort involved hundreds of Allied specialists, including intelligence, reconnaissance, and scientific experts, who gathered information, examined photographs, and studied remnants to determine the nature and potential of these weapons. What the weapons were and what they could do, not to mention how to respond, were topics for the political and military leadership over the course of the operation, parts of which occurred in the year before D-Day and other parts in the months afterward.

Well before the Allies recognized that the German long-range secret weapons were actually two weapons, they recognized that British civilians might be the targets; both sides had hit their opponents' civilians for years. The Allies could not retaliate in kind with unmanned rockets or flying bombs like those the Germans developed, though. The method they had been using, manned bombers, was notorious for the risk to the crews' lives. Probably because of that, as well as fear about the casualties the V-weapons could cause, dread of weapons of mass destruction (WMD) in the long-range weapons, and concern about war weariness, in October 1943, even before the German rockets had been deployed against Britain, Chief of the Imperial General Staff Sir Alan Brooke told the Chiefs of Staff Committee that the British war leadership needed to think about whether to initiate gas warfare in two circumstances: against German civilians in retaliation for long-range weapons (regardless of what sort of payload they carried) or, more directly, against the rocket-launching sites. Of course, this was a military problem on one level: would gas make a difference against sites, and how would gas missions impact the bomber fleet?[4]

However, the dilemma transformed into a complex diplomatic and political one as the Vice-Chiefs of Staff, the deputies to the Chiefs of Staff and head of operations for their services, rejected the claim that gas was permissible even though using such rockets was "an act of indiscriminate warfare against the civilian population," and thus an atrocity worthy of otherwise-banned retaliation, one presumably worse than conventional bombing.[5] The Chiefs of Staff punted the issue to the British Joint Intelligence Committee for research. Would Germany respond to these actions with CW? How did the Joint Intelligence Committee assess the anticipated responses of the German satellite and neutral nations to Allied CW use? What would happen on the Eastern Front if the Western Allies changed their policy, especially if Allied gas use provoked a wider gas war in a tit-for-tat escalation? Would Russia release gas then, too?

Gas was not the first weapon that the Chiefs of Staff had considered. The group, as one might expect, originally discussed responding to the long-range weapons with more traditional means. In September 1943, they debated whether conventional weapons, such as "long range guns," specifically "the three 13.5 inch and the two 14 inch guns belonging to the Royal Marine Siege Regiment," could damage or ruin the rocket sites. It turned out that this was not an option because of the limited range of the guns and prior commitments for them.[6]

So British leaders turned reluctantly to gas as a possible tool of retaliation and rocket destruction. Could words alone be enough? Might warning the Germans that they would use gas in retaliation serve as a sufficient deterrent, much as Churchill and Roosevelt had warned Axis powers that gas attacks would be met by Allied gas attacks? In this case, the Vice-Chiefs of Staff did not think it would stop the Germans altogether. However, maybe the warning at least would delay deployment until the rockets reached the stage of being "highly effective" rather than probably operational.[7] For the Allies, who were anxious about new German weapons and determined to launch D-Day in 1944, even a delay might lessen the impact of the V-weapons.[8]

Of course, threats could backfire. If the Allies were not ready—militarily or mentally—to use gas, then the Germans could call their bluff, leading to "some embarrassing political repercussions in this country." Then Britain would look weaker among its own people, its Allies, the enemy, and the neutral powers. Its threats, such as the earlier ones about using CW at all, would lose force as well. This was a real issue; the Vice-Chiefs thought the word would get out, even if the warnings had been communicated "only through black and unacknowledgeable channels."[9] The consequences of using threats of gas as a deterrent, therefore, ranged from potential temporary effectiveness to undermining domestic (and presumably international) credibility.

Furthermore, even if the Allies were willing to carry through and use gas against German civilians in retaliation, British analysis concluded that the results would not benefit the Allies. Although this calculus began because of fears that the German rockets would target British civilians, this was not the main factor in the overall analysis. (Actually, the Allies underestimated the danger because they did not know that the Germans had new gases—nerve gases—available until late in the war.[10]) The Vice-Chiefs thought that rockets filled with gas against prepared British civilians would not cause much more damage than conventionally armed rockets, so the biggest impact would be on the battlefronts. But, if the British actions opened a phase when both sides used gas, the advantage the Western Allies would have against the Germans on the continent would be outweighed by the drawbacks of German gas attacks against less-prepared Russia.[11] Using CW was not worthwhile militarily, especially since the Allies would not be able to eliminate rockets with their own use of gas.

In addition, conventional weapons would be more useful than gas against the rocket sites; the latter would probably not "bring about unconditional surrender."[12] In other words, the short- and long-term results from an Allied gas attack would not be worth it if the goals were stopping the rockets and winning the war in Europe more easily. There was also a chance that chemical bombardments of the British home front might be more serious than anticipated; the physical cost of using gas might be higher than was tolerable, too.

Politically, while the British government might lose credibility among its own people for failing to live up to its warnings, it would definitely lose credibility at home and abroad for not adhering to promises it made in the Geneva Protocol—if the V-weapon did not have chemical and biological weapons (CBW) in it and if the Germans were not the first users of CBW. The Vice-Chiefs of Staff explicitly reported that they saw the treaty, as flawed as it was, as a chain restricting their actions, one that would "condemn our action as unjustified [and] would diminish the sympathy that most of [the neutrals] . . . have for us."[13] Neutral powers in World War II could still be swayed to one side or another. Even if they remained officially neutral, they provided arenas for diplomatic conduits, such as Sweden, and valuable supplies or services, such as shipping by Spain.[14] Even worse, CW would spread onto all the Allies and undermine their stance as the side that used "humane" fighting. That result would cause tension within the Allies as well.[15] Another way to see how resistant the British attitude was toward gas is to recognize that the Vice-Chiefs of Staff were worried about Britain's global reputation if it used gas on Germans two months after it firebombed Hamburg, an operation so destructive that one reviewer of Keith Lowe's book on the bombed city calls it "'Germany's Nagasaki.'"[16]

The Geneva Protocol was not the only factor inhibiting the British. The gas policy the Western Allies were developing was also an element, and the British noted that they would need US and dominion permission to wage gas warfare against the Germans offensively in retaliation for conventionally armed rocket attacks. In addition, less formally, the Vice-Chiefs expressed concern that the Soviets, who, in British eyes, focused on their own needs rather than those of the whole Allied war effort, "would be resentful," if the British acted "without consulting them or contrary to their express wishes."[17] After all, a gas war that spread throughout the European theater would involve the Russians deeply; they would be justifiably upset if their ally ensnared them in one without their permission.

During 1943, the debate focused on whether Britain would use gas against Germany to retaliate for the forthcoming rockets, even if the new weapons did not have WMDs onboard. The conclusions did not lead to a widespread acceptance of CW. Even with devastating conventional bombers already the dominant weapon, it would have required another step down the road of brutalizing warfare to adopt gas bombs.

In 1944, that would change. First, though, in the immediate run up to D-Day and the summer after it, the Western Allies struggled with how much to risk provoking a chemical war as well as how much damage they might be willing to absorb if one broke out and they had not prepared for it fully, as they struggled to set policies for WP use and anti-botulism vaccines. These negotiations took place after the first round of decisions rejecting CW retaliation for the V-weapons and before the core of the second round, and they demonstrate that the weaker Allies, Britain in the case of WP and Canada in the vaccine situation, still preferred their relationship with each other over their individual values and gas safety. They also demonstrated that the alliance as a whole was showing a greater willingness to risk chemical warfare and its consequences by establishing policies that allowed for broad use of WP and narrow ones for protection against botulism.

## White Phosphorus

One question was whether the double-edged sword of WP could be used against Germany. On the one hand, it is an incendiary that could be used to burn items or flush people out of safe havens. It could locate or screen something on the battlefield as well. On the other hand, it could be used as an antipersonnel weapon when deployed "as a casualty producing agent against troops in the open" by burning human targets directly or by reacting with moisture, whether in the air or "in people's lungs, to form phosphoric acid."[18] The first purposes were legal, according to international agreements at the time.[19] Antipersonnel attacks caused by chemicals, whether or not they were less humane, were not. Instead, using WP in that way transformed it into CW because it targeted people with toxic chemicals to harm them with those particles, and thus it was banned by law and ostracized by morality. The complex nature of WP meant that labels describing its use as "antipersonnel" did not identify it as CW or not. Instead, intent made the difference—but it was not just intent about the target but also how an actor meant to use the weapon against the target.

The US military identified WP as "antipersonnel," yet it categorized the substance as a smoke or incendiary, not CW. The main goal of a smoke weapon was not necessarily harm—or at least it was not to cause harm intentionally through the chemicals in WP. It was developed to screen troops or to smoke out people from bunkers and other hiding places. Explicit harm resulted from releasing WP as a purely incendiary weapon; throughout World War II, bombers dropped incendiaries, including WP. There are numerous open references to using WP against the enemy, especially in the United States, despite the fact that the chemical warfare units often deployed WP.[20] In a *Time* magazine article on November 29, 1943, the author wrote, "Originally used to cloak troops or positions with harmless white clouds, WP (white phosphorus) has become one of the great anti-personnel weapons of the war. When a WP shell busts in a spectacular flower of smoke . . . it scatters flaming phosphorus particles over a wide area. The rain of fire sticks to clothing, cannot be brushed off. Larger particles burn through to produce burns particularly painful and hard to heal."[21]

However, other Western Allies, particularly some of the British leadership, feared that WP—at least when it was intended and labeled as "anti-personnel" would be seen as chemical warfare by the enemy. The fear that the Axis powers would see it that way too at some point—even if they had not during its past deployments—led back to the mind games the Allies sometimes played when they guessed and double-guessed what the enemy thought or would claim. At first glance, this may seem to be an overreaction, but, in actuality, the debate about how to perceive WP led to tensions in the Western alliance too.

The United States, particularly General Dwight David Eisenhower, wanted to deploy WP once the Allies invaded France. While Eisenhower was not its only proponent, as supreme Allied commander, his authority counted in this situation—at least in terms of overall Allied policy. The troops needed help landing at and breaking out of Normandy; WP might make the difference. Eisenhower argued that a precedent had been set and that there were no legal or military difficulties using WP, despite risks that the enemy might misunderstand how the Allies meant to deploy it. The month before D-Day, he told Air Chief Marshal Sir Trafford Leigh-Mallory, the air commander-in-chief of the Allied Expeditionary Air Force, that using WP "as an incendiary agent" despite the side effect of harming people nearby was "normal procedure in other theatres" and had not led to claims that the users had started a chemical war.[22] The British themselves had acquired the chemical compound from the United States courtesy of lend-lease, so it would be hard to object to Eisenhower's point about WP's use in specific circumstances.[23] Furthermore, as General Bedell Smith, Eisenhower's chief of staff, reminded the secretary to the British Chiefs of Staff Committee after D-Day, WP "has been frequently used by the Allied Armies in Italy and by the U.S[.] forces in the Pacific as a screening and an incendiary agent with its inevitable consequent effects on personnel." He was well aware that WP could not distinguish between inanimate and human targets, no matter why it was deployed.[24]

If that was not enough, Smith shared intelligence reports that noted that Germany had been using WP smoke for screening and "harassing" purposes since the spring of 1944 in ever-increasing amounts at Anzio, Italy.[25] Finally, he wrote what everyone already knew: the law did not ban the United States from using gas. He also shared something that no one else ever pointed out or thought was valid: the British were not bound because "the necessary ratifications were never deposited in Washington."[26] While the last point seems to have been incorrect, it may have helped, along with the rest of the factors, to explain why Eisenhower decided in favor of using WP in ways that risked escalating its use from screening to antipersonnel deployment, no matter the British reluctance.

Perhaps Eisenhower's desire to finish the war conflicted with the United Kingdom's wariness about starting a gas war at this late date, but, regardless of WP's use in the past, the British war leaders, at least the ones who dreaded chemical warfare and violating international law, disliked WP no matter what Eisenhower or Smith said. While they could not stop Eisenhower's pronouncements, they could drag their feet about British employment and try to prevent flagrant usage, even if that meant engaging in subterfuges.

It was true that, at this point, Eisenhower did not intend it to be used overtly or primarily as an antipersonnel weapon that damaged the lungs because of toxic chemicals. Intent, though, as any lawyer will tell you, can be difficult to prove. Even worse, Britain and the other belligerents were not acting in courts of law, but rather courts of public opinion and of their own consciences. The other audience was the enemy's political and military leaders, ones who might or might not have the same perspective or even want to give Britain and its Allies the benefit of the doubt that any deployment of WP was legitimate. Sincere, or even deliberate, misreading of a situation that led to a conclusion that the Allies used CW would give an enemy an excuse to justify deployment of poison gas as retaliation legal under Geneva Protocol reservations. Just because other Axis powers had not already claimed that the Allies used CW after deploying WP in other theaters did not mean that the Germans would behave the same way in France, especially during or after a major invasion.

Finally, the fact that the Germans used WP smoke did not guarantee that they would treat WP incendiaries as acceptable armaments, too, especially at such a pivotal moment in the war.

The issue arose at the highest levels in Britain on June 1, 1944, days before the invasion of Normandy. The stakes were clear: the Allies had to take the beaches for the Second Front to succeed. Perhaps it is not surprising, then, that the air commander-in-chief of the Allied Expeditionary Air Force looked for the added advantage that WP might give his men. Specifically, he wanted British permission to use it as an antipersonnel weapon. Leigh-Mallory was British, so he began by consulting the United Kingdom's Air Ministry. It equivocated: "in view of the importance of avoiding any action which would give the enemy a reasonable pretext for initiating gas warfare against our forces in OVERLORD [the code name for the invasion of Normandy]," the Air Ministry "could not authorize the use of white phosphorus as a casualty producing agent against personnel"—but it did not ban it either.[27] White phosphorus might make the difference for the landing, but the Allies would be most vulnerable to gas attacks themselves at that time too. Clearly the Air Ministry was uncomfortable, but it seemed to recognize both the costs and benefits of the weapons as well as the locus of the real authority here because it punted the final decision up to Eisenhower rather than rejecting Leigh-Mallory's request outright.[28]

The air commander-in-chief turned to Eisenhower who, on his own authority, then made a different decision and publicized it. He did not quite explicitly condone WP as an antipersonnel weapon, but the implication was that it could be used that way. Specifically, this announcement made it more obvious than previously that he tolerated the unintended costs of WP; he proclaimed that WP had been used elsewhere "as a screening agent and as an incendiary agent against material with consequent effects on its accompanying personnel." Thus, troops could and "should . . . plan on the use of white phosphorus whenever it will assist your operational plans in support of" D-Day.[29] In other words, collateral or incidental effects almost certainly would include casualties from WP's components, even if the intent to cause toxic harm directly had not been present, but that was acceptable. Eisenhower seemed less concerned about interpreting international law conservatively or about risking gas war by using WP than about winning the war quickly.

Eisenhower's announcement did not end the discussion, though, at least for the British. The British Foreign Office and Chiefs of Staff had made their own assessments of WP use, including moral or legal, considerations. Brigadier Leslie Hollis, the senior assistant secretary to the War Cabinet, summed up discussions in a memo to Winston Churchill. Hollis thought that "[t]he legal position was not entirely clear" about using WP as an antipersonnel weapon; the British, after all, had signed the Geneva Gas Protocol and were bound by it, but the United States was not.[30] While it might seem odd that Britain raised this question considering how confidently the United States held the opposing view, it is worth remember that in the 1920s, as discussed in chapter one, Britain had been very concerned about whether the 1925 treaty prevented defensive research and planning; this was not the first time, in other words, that the British questioned whether it should interpret international law as restrictively as possible. More practically, Hollis also was aware that Britain was "more concerned than the U.S.A. . . . [about] the effects of any initiation of chemical warfare," implying that the British Isles were more likely to bear the brunt of enemy attacks on civilians during a gas war.[31] Legally and practically, Britain was more vulnerable to a retaliatory German aerial gas war on its cities and needed to be more cautious than did the United States.

How could Britain solve this situation without clashing with Eisenhower, violating its own legal principles, or making its people more susceptible to gas? Interestingly, the British decision makers did not raise the dilemma that WP in any form might make the difference between successful and failed landings on D-Day. Instead, the Chiefs of Staff developed a three-part plan of action. Eisenhower would not be "overrid[den]," but he would be "asked to make certain that no orders should be given for the specific use of white phosphorus as an anti-personnel weapon."[32] In other words, Ike should clarify his earlier remarks. This ought to remove some of the temptation, and all the approval, of using WP illegally while allowing Eisenhower to save face. In fact, when sending their message to Eisenhower, the British noted that the Geneva Gas Protocol banned its use in antipersonnel weapons—not specifying whether that meant causing incendiary and/or toxic damage—despite the fact that the earlier internal British memo had been less certain about that issue.[33]

The British went to further lengths to protect themselves from anyone misunderstanding or manipulating the situation, as is clear from another decision to make sure no WP weapons "should be labelled or known as 'anti-personnel' weapons."[34] There was concern that simply possessing contraband weapons, especially close to the front, was tantamount to saying that the owner would use them soon, whether or not that was the case. They decided that "no reference to its use as such [to WP as anti-personnel weapons] should be made in any documents, training pamphlets or orders liable to fall into the hands of the enemy."[35] The message was really that no one should let on that Britain was even aware of the possibility of using WP illegally. This requirement was also a statement about the lack of trust in Germany's "honor" and an awareness that perception or publicity of any action could be manipulated in the war. A more charitable interpretation might be that the Chiefs of Staff recognized that in a war of the scale and depth of World War II, one never really knew what the enemy might do if pushed to the wall. Britain knew that using WP as an antipersonnel weapon might only introduce or reinforce German fears about what it might do—and thus what actions Germany might need to take to defend itself.

Even as the British debated among themselves, Eisenhower reinforced his original decision and perhaps moved even further away from the British position in some ways. Addressing Leigh-Mallory the day before the invasion, Eisenhower said, "no restrictions are placed on the employment of this agent, no orders will be given for the specific use of WP as an anti-personnel weapon." So, he specifically made it clear that he would not forbid its use in any way—the bluntest Eisenhower came to endorsing its use in all manners—but he would not explicitly encourage its use as an antipersonnel weapon. He did echo the British requirement that nothing be labeled to indicate that WP could be an antipersonnel weapon, a request that the British Chiefs of Staff asked Churchill to communicate to Eisenhower, but that did not take away from the freedom and permission he now gave Leigh-Mallory, a relatively gas-positive British commander.[36]

The day after the invasion, however, Foreign Secretary Anthony Eden sent his own memo to the prime minister, reinforcing his office's stance and the primacy of the law in decision-making. Eden believed the case was clear: "if these bombs are used primarily against personnel, their use is certainly illegal" under the Hague Land Warfare Regulations, the international agreement from 1899 that originally banned poison gas use as well as other weapons. He quoted Article 23(a), which banned arms that generated needless casualties and harm. Perhaps Eden was focusing more on whether other weapons, ones that did not cause such injuries, were available? Regardless, he was not simply wondering whether a weapon without incendiary properties had to be used. Eden also explained, "it is understood that this phosphorus is poisonous" and thus against the Geneva Gas Protocol, too. Eden, perhaps unnecessarily, emphasized that "on the 4th September 1939, His Majesty's Government reaffirmed their intention to abide by the terms of that Protocol, so long as the enemy Governments did so."[37] Whether or not Eden understood the law correctly, his position, and thus his interpretation, was powerful: the law, and Britain's promise, bound the nation. Eden did not even allude to military considerations. Of course, by the time Eden sent his note, it was clear that the Allies had established solid beach-heads, and the critical step in the invasion of Europe was completed. This communication did offer a way to protest the US stance without adding tension to the alliance relationship, as well as to reinforce Britain's position and reputation, if that were ever needed. It is possible that Britain thought it could influence the United States, too.

Churchill, who, as prime minister and minister for defence, had a strong voice, did not let it go, even though D-Day was over. He held that the Chiefs of Staff had rejected WP on military grounds to avoid retaliation and were dubious about its legal legitimacy, and that the Foreign Office condemned antipersonnel use of WP firmly on legal grounds. Churchill consulted again with his Chiefs of Staff who, days later on June 21, reported that they amended their opinion to conform with Eden's: antipersonnel use henceforth would be viewed as absolutely illegal. The Chiefs of Staff still disagreed with the Foreign Office slightly: "although a case might be made for the legality of White Phosphorus as an antipersonnel weapon, it would be a weak one," but they were not willing to push the issue in theory, just as they had not been willing in practice.[38] Edging toward the more legally conservative stance may have been easier because the Chiefs of Staff remained focused on Overlord, not the entire liberation of Europe; they noted that the critical time for using WP as an antipersonnel weapon had passed; the policy had been decided and the issue was moot—for now.

Still, the issue was not as resolved as the Chiefs of Staff had thought. In October 1944, when the march to Berlin was on its way, and, in the intelligence analysts' eyes it was extremely doubtful that Germany would resort to gas, the British 2nd Tactical Air Force asked for "a precision incendiary weapon to dislodge the enemy from strong points which were" inaccessible to other weapons, presumably not directly using it to injure people even if it exposed them to danger by making their defensive positions untenable.[39] Specifically, the unit ask permission to deploy "white or liquid phosphorus or thickened fuel."[40] This request rose to the Chiefs of Staff Committee, who parsed out the true nature of the request. Sir Charles Portal, chief of the air staff, concluded that there was clear and explicit evidence that the Air Force desired to use WP legally "as a normal incendiary weapon" since it had suggested "'thickened fuel' [in other words, a substance like napalm] . . . as an alternative filling." This relieved the committee who "took note with approval."[41] The legal niceties—since CW targeted people, not things—and the messages sent to the enemy as well as the world (if they decided to broadcast this matter), still counted, even though, practically speaking, the Allies might have been able to use the weapon against the Germans with increasing military impunity.

The WP debate may not have created Allied tensions as far as the United States was concerned, but it was a problem for the British. There was no real debate about resisting the US commander's decision, but there were deep discussions about how to meet Britain's interests—especially its legal obligations—while not resisting US leadership in this part of the war. The United States was a dominant ally in this situation, but the British refused to abandon their principles completely. The result was that, although the Allies were willing to risk misinterpretation of WP use, they were not willing to embrace CW use outright. It is also likely that their need to make sure that the Germans could not use their actions as a pretext for retaliation was lessened; as the war wound down, the British knew that Hitler might resort to CW, but they thought it was less likely. This was quite a difference from the situation after the Bari attack, and it showed the changed momentum in the war in Europe.

# Do You Want a Shot?

## Substance X, the Botulism Threat

If the logistics of planning D-Day while keeping it a secret, the incredible gamble of an amphibious landing on the coast of Fortress Europe; the challenges of keeping a multinational, multilingual Allied force united; and the concerns about Nazi desperation provoking a potential gas war were not enough, the specter of chemical and biological warfare raised its ghastly head high during the spring preparation for the invasion of Normandy. As some scientists noted, "it could be used very effectively in the forthcoming invasion."[42]

One specific threat was botulism, an example not only of chemical warfare—as defined at the time—but one that illustrates the tension CW could cause among the Allies. What made botulism a particularly complex challenge was the nature of the disease. Botulism is caused by bacteria that produces a toxic chemical. As a result, while it is generally labeled a biological weapon (BW), it can be considered a CW in many ways, unlike some other diseases. Just as WP was a CW when it targeted humans, botulism (or rather the toxin) has properties of a CW because it is a chemical that attacks humans. It was often biologists who considered whether botulism was a viable threat, and how it could be combated if it were, because the toxin arose from bacteria as opposed to a manmade chemical.[43] However, the government committees set up to wrestle with this issue were not always specialized biological warfare committees. The Canadian biological warfare committee meetings were categorized as chemical warfare policy documents in the files.[44] Henry Stimson, the US secretary of war, thought chemical and biological weapons were closely related, and since a specific biological warfare committee did not exist in the United States as late as the early spring of 1944, he requested both that the chief of the Chemical Warfare

Service take charge of offensive BW issues and that the US CW liaison to Britain have a seat on the British biological warfare committee. Work on "X," otherwise known as botulism, along with several other diseases, transferred to the auspices of the US Chemical Warfare Service.[45] As a result, the story of botulism has a role in the chemical warfare history of World War II.

Why did BW have such a marginal role even in the run up to D-Day, despite all the scientific advances in other areas? Until this point, biologically influenced weapons had been a theoretical threat, but a much lesser one that that of pure chemical ones. Scientists and others had realized since the days of World War I that it ought to be possible to deploy germs in modern weaponry, just as they had recognized that poison gas could be employed that way long before the latter was used in 1915.[46] However, weaponizing germs effectively was much more challenging than doing the same for gases; one could spread germs, but starting an actual epidemic was more difficult. That did not stop the scientists in various countries from trying, of course, nor did it stop government concerns or allegations that biological warfare had been attempted, such as the Chinese reports of Japanese efforts to release the bubonic plague in 1940.[47] It did not stop efforts to develop defensive tools either. The extent of the effort varied. In the early phase of the war, Britain "concluded that there was little immediate practical danger and nothing much was being done," although experts considered the threat. But in Canada, the specialist opinion was that "the dangers . . . from German use of bacteria in warfare were quite real."[48]

However, although there was enough fear of CBW and enough awareness of the possibility of making these novel armaments to inspire a clause in the interwar Geneva Gas Protocol explicitly prohibiting biological warfare (although it was called bacteriological in that document) in international law for the first time, the British did not even start an inter-services biological warfare committee until the middle of World War II. In the earlier years of the war, the British had a bacteriological warfare committee, largely under the auspices of the chemical warfare committee, until June of 1944 because of its small size and the relative triviality of the topic.[49] After the botulism debate between the Canada, Britain, and the United States, its importance changed.

What is amazing is that it was Canada who inspired this heightened vigilance in 1944, not Britain, the powerful United States, or the menacing Germany. It was not even the recurrent Chinese allegations about Japan's use of CBW. Canadian scientific advances in botulism research, combined with D-Day's approach, seems to have triggered the events discussed here. As a result, the most extensive Allied debate during World War II about the combination of CW and BW had ramifications not just for the mid-century understanding of WMD, but it also added complexity to the planning for D-Day and demonstrated the commitment of the Western Allies to one another. Canada was the least powerful of the big three, but in this situation, it made the decision to prioritize the alliance over the safety of its citizens and demonstrated the commitment one Western Ally could show another.

By early 1944, scientists had developed an inoculation, known as Esoid, that protected against some of the major strains of botulism. Botulism is not an esoteric germ, of course. Even today, most people are aware of it at some level and look askance at dented and bulging cans of food and poorly preserved jars of produce for fear of food poisoning caused by botulism. It is sickening and even fatal. But can it be induced on a wide scale into an army, depleting and debilitating that force? Three years of Canadian experiments found that it was "about 1500 times [more toxic] than phosgene" gas, and it could be weaponized through a "bursting bomb" such that it had killed animals, infecting victims "by mouth, by inhalations, by eye, nose, or in the tissues as introduced on a projectile."[50] The Canadians noted that the British had managed to weaponize it through "coated projectiles" and that it was "effective" that way, too, theoretically. Since symptoms did not manifest for "6 to 24 hours" after infection, warning or full-time protection was necessary.[51]

On the chance that it could be used on the battlefield this way or in some other manner, the Canadian and US scientific chemical war effort ran experiments and conducted research about how to best protect servicemen while maintaining their ability to fight effectively. In the Canadians' eyes, the results offered two options. The first was simple: rely on gas masks. They would impede the spread of botulism, especially if some adjustments were made to the respirators, but even those changes would fail to make this option "sufficient due to the fact that no means of detection [of botulism] . . . are known."[52] How would everyone know when to put on the masks?

The second was better: inoculate the troops with Esoid. This process required two injections, three weeks apart, before a man should be well protected.[53] An inoculated man would not be hampered by wearing the uncomfortable mask or even wear it out by using up the limited lifespan of the neutralizing chemicals in the respirators.

But inoculation came with its own risks. As conversations between the Canadian liaisons in London, the military commanders in Ottawa, and the scientists in North America developed, it became clear that there were two types of problems. The first were military-medical ones: was there enough Esoid to inoculate, and was it safe? The second was whether inoculation was politically wise. Or, more simply: could it be done, and should it be done?

The Canadian argument was that its scientists had made a critical breakthrough: the serum was ready for use now, and it could be manufactured on a large scale.[54] Working with the United States, they had not only created a vaccine but also tested it sufficiently so that they could endorse it. Perhaps as important, the two countries had produced a stockpile of it; if the United States shared its vaccines, there would be enough for Britain too.[55] There was about a month and a half left until the invasion, so there was time to transport the serum to Britain, inoculate the Allied troops, and proceed with the invasion with a bit more protection than earlier.

It was not just Operation Overlord that provoked the consideration of Esoid at this time. It was also the intelligence reports that the Allies studied. While intelligence experts considered everything from rumors to reliable reports, stories about WMD had to be considered. In March, the Joint Intelligence Sub-Committee addressed motivations and concluded that "[i]t is so vitally necessary for the Germans to defeat OVERLORD that they would have a strong incentive to initiate gas warfare if circumstances arose in which they appreciated that its use might be decisive." At the same time, the committee noted that there were a lot of factors to consider to which they did not have access.[56] Analysts in April acknowledged Nazi CBW capabilities.[57] Releasing every and any weapon, including CBW, to repel an invasion of continental Europe both fit with the long-standing Allied predictions about Nazi behavior and ability and also may have seemed likely because Britain had been willing to defend itself with gas if Germany had invaded its islands. One report concluded that although German use of CBW to combat Overlord was "improbable," there was still a fair amount of confidence that the Nazis "would certainly retaliate" in kind against Allied gas use.[58] Cleary, the rumors about CBW had to be taken seriously because there ranged a possibility, if not a probability, that the Germans might use CW, although less was known about BW.[59]

The availability of the vaccine, the momentousness of the D-Day invasion, and the possibilities of German BW attacks convinced the Canadians that the inoculations should be administered. They raised the issue of using it now with Britain, and later the United States. Since they were involved in an alliance and the invasion force was multinational, it makes sense that the dominion would expect any medical defenses against BW to be part of a concerted Allied action.

The Canadians introduced the possibility informally in a conversation between Lt. Gen. Ken Stuart, the chief of staff of the Canadian Military Headquarters in London, and Lt. Gen. Bedell Smith, the chief of staff to Eisenhower, on April 24, 1944. The highest level of the Supreme Headquarters Allied Expeditionary Force (SHAEF) seemed predisposed to inoculating.[60]

The situation rapidly became more complicated, though, and a series of fears had to be considered that weighed against protecting the Allied forces. The first was that there were mixed opinions about the intelligence reports and what they meant. The Canadian position was that the Germans had been investigating botulism in particular since 1936; it was a danger.[61] On the other hand, a British expert, Dr. Vines, accessed a contemporary Office of Strategic Services intelligence report. He argued that the Germans could not weaponize botulism, and he was not the only one who thought that X was a future weapon, but not a current one.[62] There was a middle ground, too, at least compared to the main Canadian position; Professor G. S. Wilson, an eminent Canadian scientist, was "on the border line" about the level of the threat, but thought that "X would be a surprise weapon," so vaccination must take place "now, otherwise it would be too late."[63] Intelligence is notoriously difficult to evaluate, and it is challenging to decide when it is reliable enough to shape actions. In this situation, there was not a lot of weighing or assessment done by the decision-makers; Britain and the United States took the intelligence experts' opinions as offered.[64] On the other hand, Ottawa was never fully convinced that a *lack* of intelligence confirming the threat should be the basis for a decision.[65]

Still, that alone did not stop the inoculations. The next issue was one of safety; if Esoid was supposed to protect, it should not actually cause harm. Here there was some debate among the three Allies. The Canadians were convinced it worked; yes, there were occasional side effects, but that was inherent in any vaccination. In contrast, the United States argued that the verdict was not in on Esoid because not enough work had been done on it, although Stuart did note to Lt. General John Carl Murchie, the chief of the Canadian General Staff, that if Canadians were inoculated, that would provide further proof that the vaccine worked. Such a step would help remove the "experimental" label.[66] However, Dr. Boles, affiliated with the War Department, told Murchie that the United States had conducted tests resulting in very high rates of negative reactions. They also thought the dosage, the period before coverage from the immunization, and the extent of coverage "has not yet been definitely determined."[67] The Canadians were puzzled and quite annoyed at the implied slur on their work. McGill University's professor E. G. D. Murray noted that no one had reported deaths. He also did not understand how, if there was a reaction from a tainted or dangerous vaccine, the death toll would be so low; would not any contamination in a serum have been spread to everyone who received that batch? Murray proposed instead that the US death might have been from some other causes or from getting botulism before the inoculation had time to take effect.[68]

Murray pushed even further in making his case. Only four hundred US subjects had been vaccinated during the clinical testing, and only one hundred Canadians. However, he argued that "experimental" vaccines, such as tetanus, had been used successfully before.[69] The precedent had been set. Certainly, he thought the vaccination might provide some protection, and he did not think it dangerous. Today we might question using a vaccine after so few trials, but this was an emergency, and Murray, a respected microbiologist, had a different professional opinion than the US scientists.[70]

In the end, the puzzled Canadians decided that the US stance resulted from a typographical error about the number of problem reactions and from the legacy of faulty US inoculations in the past. In particular, a yellow fever scare had scarred the US perspective. Earlier in the war—so it was still in recent memory—contaminated yellow fever vaccines had sickened soldiers. It turned out that the problem was not the vaccine per se, but that the serum for some batches had come from a soldier who had hepatitis, resulting in "over 50,000 cases of jaundice."[71] As Canadians discussed, at the time the US army calculated the cost to be "nearly 4000 deaths and a couple of divisions rendered incapable of operation for a considerable period," and "[t]hey are finding these deaths difficult to explain."[72] (A 2013 article reviewing scientific literature suggests that the death rate was closer to two dozen.[73]) Murray dismissed the yellow fever analogy; he argued that many people globally had been inoculated with yellow fever serum successfully and, besides, it was a very different kind of vaccine. There was no point in comparing Esoid with that one.[74]

The United States dismissed the vaccine on the grounds of effectiveness, too, and not just because they believed it was still "in experimental stage only;" it provided coverage against two of the five strains of botulism only. It might be that protecting against two strains was worth the risk, if those strains were the most likely to be weaponized or were the most dangerous, but there was neither medical nor intelligence proof of that.[75] On the other hand, most people who suffered from botulism fell ill with strains A and B, the very kinds that the vaccine covered.[76] The Canadians dismissed all three concerns: they had confidence in the vaccine, did not think lack of intelligence that the Germans were intending to use botulism was a reason to skip protection, and they trusted their science.

The insurmountable hurdle, though, was an eminently practical one: after all the arguing, enough time had lapsed that sufficient doses of Esoid to protect all three forces would not reach Britain until August, well after D-Day. This reinforced the argument about the doubtful intelligence reports enough that the War Office and SHAEF decided against inoculation, surprising Lt. Gen. Stuart with this news on May 17, 1944, at a point when it was too late to get full vaccination coverage before D-Day anyway.[77] The next day, the British set out their reasons: it was not just availability, and the rejection of the latest intelligence, it was a general belief that "whilst B.W. in general might well be a menace,

X-Toxin is a comparatively minor part," and it would be sufficient to train medical officers about how to prevent botulism. They felt so strongly that even if the supply problem had been solved, they would not act now, although they would take the precaution of beginning to build up a stockpile in Britain so action could be taken relatively quickly in the future; Germany might use BW as the Allies moved closer to the Fatherland even if it did not release it at Normandy.[78]

Yet there was one more twist, and one that explains the opposing viewpoints more clearly. Historian David Avery posits that the United States misled Canada, blaming the imaginary medical woes for its decision not to use Esoid as a way to hide the fact that the United States and British did not share intelligence from Ultra (presumably hinting that the likelihood of Nazi CBW attacks were negligible) with Canada, and that information played a role in the other Western Allies' decision not to vaccinate against botulism after all.[79] Widening knowledge of Ultra to Canadians would lessen the security around the United States' and United Kingdom's ability to break some German codes; that information was too important to risk, even if it assuaged Canadian about the risks of botulism.[80] Thus, in the Canadians' eyes, Britain resisted inoculating because of supply shortages and intelligence while the United States was swayed by medical reasoning. In reality, different pieces of intelligence played a major role for both the United States/United Kingdom and Canada, the former to resist and the latter to encourage inoculation.

## Go It Alone?

This would seem to present a simple end to the debate, but instead it is where the situation becomes more illuminating from the historians' perspective. Canada firmly believed in the danger, it had confidence in Esoid's safety and effectiveness (although it admitted that it was still, technically, experimental), there was enough of the serum to protect its own troops, and there was enough time before the scheduled invasion to inoculate its own soldiers and ready their immune systems.[81] Should it act unilaterally in this situation? Canada was vocally frustrated with the decision made by the United States and Britain. Not only had the other two changed their minds 180 degrees about inoculating, but also they seemed to do so in conversations that excluded Canada. They presented their new opinion once it was set. Still, the three countries were a team. Did Canada have the authority to act on its own in this matter, and, if it did, should it? The answer depended on the SHAEF (or, more accurately, British and US) permission as well as the Canadian decision. Thus, the question switched from the military-medical dilemma all three Allies pondered to a political one for Canada: "Should we use Esoid?" Canada's perspective that the other Allies had weak reasons for refusing to vaccinate makes it even more clear that the Canadians valued the alliance over their own soldiers' safety, especially if this situation made them think twice about whether to use the available vaccine on their own men.

The alliance was a partnership, not a dictatorship, and Canada did possess stores of the inoculation, so the military and political response was that Canada could act on its own. The Canadian decision makers were too aware of the ramifications of the decision to make it an easy one. As the debate continued through May, the three weeks needed before the Esoid would protect the men bound for the invasion dwindled and vanished. Yet the telegrams and notes recording the discussion weighing the pros and cons of the decision did not emphasize that point.

The simplest case was in favor of inoculation: Canada had Esoid, and the troops could be protected, so use it. This was a rationale that was supported by humane reasoning as well as some political and military thoughts. Why risk losing more soldiers than necessary if you were about to launch a second front? How would you explain it to your constituents if you failed to protect their husbands and sons? The Canadian War Committee pressed Stuart to work with Britain and the United States to find an acceptable cover story, clearly wanting to inoculate and believing that it could be done. They were "anxious to avoid anything which would prejudice [the] situation with respect to other troops and civilian population."[82]

The argument against protection was more complex and required weighing various wartime priorities. First was the prerequisite that Britain and the United States demanded that Canada meet before using Esoid. Instead of deciding whether all the Allies should use the goal, this time the key purpose was to develop a "cover plan." Furthermore, "our action" cannot "impair their [the British and US] position, either with their own t[roo]ps or civilians" nor alert the enemy that the Canadians were preparing to confront CBW.[83] A simple solution was to present the inoculation as a booster or to hide it by mixing it with a standard immunization.[84] This seemed an unnecessarily elaborate cover-up, and back in the days when Canada thought all the Allies would be using Esoid, there had been a proposal to "merely say that this inoculation is against 'X' disease and go on with it."[85]

But that solution was flawed too. The Allies had used deterrence repeatedly in the war to warn the Axis powers away from poison gas use. When Roosevelt and Churchill, for example, announced that they would retaliate in kind if the enemy used poison gas, it was clear that their countries had to prepare for that eventuality.[86] When Britain conducted public education campaigns about and mass distributions of gas masks, it was clear that its leaders expected that a gas attack was a true threat. In this case it was different, probably because the Allies were still concerned about giving Germany a pretext either for thinking that it could use WMD itself as a preemptive strike or for seizing on the Allied preparations as the basis for propaganda spun to suggest that the Allies were inoculating themselves only because they intended to use CBW soon. Remembering the previous debates the British had about engaging in actions that the Germans might misinterpret aggressively, such as the Bari incident, this made sense. Experiences from World War I had taught the British that such manipulations occurred; the Central Powers had publicized allegations of Allied gas use in preparation for using gas themselves.[87]

One might also wonder if the Allies wanted to hold a trump card, that is, whether they wanted to hide from the Germans that they could defend against botulism so as to surprise the enemy with their ability to resist if an attack ever came. And there was another concern. The Canadians formed a fraction of the Allied forces heading to France; if they alone were protected against a particular attack, could they prosecute the offensive drive across France by themselves? No.[88] If that was the case, aside from humanitarian reasons, did it matter if the Canadians were protected? They could not save the day.

And how much of a secret should—or could—the inoculations be? While tight security might benefit the Allies vis-à-vis the enemy, it might inflict some injuries on their own side as well.[89] First of all, it is easy to imagine the blow to the morale and cohesion of an Allied force if it became known that only some men had received protection from the threat; the reverberations of this kind of inequity might "have disastrous effects on allied preparations and intentions for the approaching invasion . . . and on the outlook of the British and US troops."[90] It was General Harry Crerar, commander of the First Canadian Army, a unit soon to fight in Normandy, who raised these questions. If he, the one directly in charge of the Canadians who would fight in Normandy, was willing to risk his men's lives by omitting the vaccination, it suggests how deeply a key senior Canadian valued the alliance. Not all armies treated their men equally in terms of pay, uniforms, and even toilet paper rations, as scholar Paul Fussell notes, but those are not core issues of defense, unlike physical protection from new weapons.[91]

Secondly, there was the physical damage to consider. Inoculations can produce side effects, and after Bari, the Allies had learned the lesson that if the medical corps was ignorant of the presence of CBW, then treatments might not only fail to help the injured but also hurt them. The treatment for mustard gas victims is very different from shock or other burn victims, for instance. So, while a cover story could say vaguely that Canadian soldiers needed one more compulsory jab as a booster, the doctors and medics themselves needed to know that the shots protected against X so that they could look for side effects.[92] Another reason to tell the doctors had more to do with human nature than medical science: if the medical officers did not know why they were administering a new inoculation, they would probably wonder and gossip about it, which would be "equally dangerous to security."[93]

Despite the very real problems that could arise if the enemy found out about the inoculations, or just finding out that there had been an extra inoculation—however that was explained—there was anxiety about what would happen if people recognized or heard hints about the purpose of Esoid. One way in which CBW could cause damage was by inciting fear in potential victims. As described in chapter 2, for instance, the British worked hard to prepare the civilian population to face gas attacks without panic. As one late May report noted: "The psychological potentialities are tremendous. Any public knowledge or even suspicion or rumour of the existence of this threat would be likely to cause widespread alarm and distraction." In this case, the Canadian report ignored how soldiers might feel; instead it noted that "fear of causing civilian alarm" might have been one reason not to give inoculations to soldiers.[94]

The details of a proposed cover plan inspired a lot of discussion over the last weeks in May and the first weeks in June. One suggestion noted that D-Day would generate refugees whose health had already been compromised during Nazi rule, a situation that would be ripe for encouraging disease. Ailments would not respect the civilian-troop barrier, thus endangering the invading force. The inoculations therefore would be preventative.[95] One version of this story went so far as to mislabel Esoid as "an Influenzal type of toxoid as a means of partial protection amongst civilians . . ." which would be "given subcutaneously in two doses of 1cc each, 3 weeks apart."[96] That was tricky, though. The US Army had started administering the new flu vaccine in 1943, and soldiers received only one dose, unlike the booster needed for Esoid.[97] Canada might have been able to manage the subterfuge because it began producing the influenza vaccine after D-Day, or the plan might have generated more rumors.[98]

Sheer realism led to doubt that secrecy could be maintained. As Stuart telegraphed, "What about RCAF [Royal Canadian Air Force] and RCN [Royal Canadian Navy] personnel particularly RCN men who are manning landing craft[?] What about Canadian Army officers serving with British Army[?] How can cover possibly be maintained in such cases[?]"[99]

In the end, though, the most persuasive arguments were ones that looked at the long term. The decision makers agreed that in the short term Canada, and possibly the war effort, would be served best by inoculation if its soldiers were safe and maintained effectiveness. That was the military assessment, and there was even a political one: unilateral immunization "would serve as a very clear example of our independent national responsibility and status."[100] That could be quite tempting for Canada, which continually tried to assert its sovereignty and its right to be regarded as an equal ally.

In the long term, the drawbacks, potential or actual, would outweigh the benefits. What if Canada's inoculation program inspired "general alarm," which could be a problem among friend or foe?[101] Canada still had to work with the other Allies, and thus it decided that loyalty to them outweighed protecting its own men. If there was fear, or if Germany felt provoked into trying CBW, would the number of immune Canadians be able to compensate for "interruption to the normal civil processes of port and transport ops [which] would be fatal to the success of the invasion" and thus lengthen World War II?[102]

Another prediction was that there would be "catastrophic" panic if word seeped out. The same analysis pointed out that the Canadians were outnumbered ten to one by their Allies, and this did not even count the civilians in the critical ports.[103] In a worst-case scenario the Canadians would look "selfish" if they protected themselves and somehow "left comrades in arms and English civilians exposed." This was not a rational argument since one might wonder how the Canadians were supposed to protect everyone themselves, but the author of this idea was a pessimist. The note continued with the idea that "Brit[ish] and US Governments might be loath to admit having had stocks [of Esoid]." But perhaps the worst case imagined was that British and US public outcry "would be so serious as to impair their ability to continue aggressive prosecution of the war."[104] This might be unrealistic speculation, but it was taken seriously enough to be raised at the headquarters of the First Canadian Army.

On the other hand, the cynical view was that if the Germans deployed CBW against unprotected Allies, that act could be turned to a propaganda advantage—as long as no one knew that there had been the potential to protect Allied soldiers with Esoid's existence. The public would think that the enemy had broken one more moral and legal taboo by introducing CBW.[105]

Canada's decision, because of the political and military ramifications, had to be made at the highest level, but eventually the arguments against inoculating convinced Stuart, and he told Murchie that.[106] Ottawa was not ready to give up, though, and replied to Stuart six days later raising a new issue in the debate. Had Stuart considered that the "enemy would be justified in claiming X as CW not BW agent?"[107] Why raise this now? The records did not elaborate on this argument, but one possible explanation is that Ottawa was cryptically referring to the belief that the Germans would lie about using WMD, claiming they were only retaliating. Germany had CW, too, so an in-kind response would require CW. If one takes that one step further, it would make sense that there might be some advocates of the idea that the Germans might claim to be using

CW rather than BW at any particular time because the former, while illegal and unpopular, had been used before; there might be more tolerance for CW than BW.

Ottawa did raise a good question though. If Germany believed, or was willing to argue, that botulism was a CW, would it be more likely to use it? As the Canadian telegram stated bluntly, "if available [it] would be selected because of greatly superior effect impossibility of detection . . ." This then changed the question: "We provide protection again other CW agents now and it is difficult to see what valid reason may be given for omitting protection against this."[108] If this line of reasoning were accepted, it would be the United States and Britain who would bear a larger burden for justifying refusal of Esoid.

Still, all three Allies decided not to vaccinate against X during the summer of 1944 while fighting in France.[109] Canada retained the right to decide on unilateral action, at least technically, which Britain's War Office acknowledged. Perhaps London gave it even more freedom than the combined CW policy did, at least theoretically. In the latter there were administrative limits: the Combined Chiefs of Staff had to give the order to act offensively, and the Allies had be to informed about retaliatory actions.[110] Yet the chains on Canada's decision-making about toxoid were unwritten, but still strong; the decision had wider ramifications than whether or not Canada should protect its troops with an inoculation.[111] Canada proved in this situation that it would not risk the stability of the alliance, or the war effort, to protect its own men in a situation in which there was not a clear military advantage; the humanitarian benefit was not enough to overcome the political costs. Canada had a seat at the decision-making table, but, at least in this case, the respect granted to a second-tier ally. As the War Office wrote to Stuart announcing that Britain would finally form an Inter-Service Sub-Committee on Biological Warfare—a formal unit to study BW issues—it noted that the new committee would be told that "The contribution of Canada to BW is next in importance to that of the U.S.A. and U.K."[112] The announcement was both a reassurance that Canada had a role but simultaneously a reminder of its junior status.

For all concerned, it is fortunate that the invasion and following advance through France occurred without any CBW. While it would be interesting to speculate about why Germany did not attempt it—whether it was limited by ability or policy—it is still enlightening to see what the Allies predicted and how they prioritized their needs. The Allies had long convinced themselves that Germany would use CBW if it suited them, and they themselves did not really want to open that caldron during the invasion. Practicality played a role: was there enough Esoid, and would it work? Prediction played a role: intelligence concluded that the Germans were unlikely to use BW now, so the usual reasons for considering violation of the CBW taboo—namely national survival at some level—did not hold. It was alliance politics that proved the most unstable element at the beginning of this episode, but they proved to be firm by the end because Canada was willing to absorb the payment for a united front.

The Western alliance was not equitable, but it was one in which there was a role for the Canadians—at least in research, development, and even exercise of sovereignty, if not always in policy. It is also one more example when the British had to weather a situation in which its Allies might take bolder steps than it could or wanted to take. Just as Roosevelt had threatened retaliation for a wider range of attacks than Churchill had, thus increasing the likelihood that an Axis attack somewhere would lead to global gas warfare, and just as Britain feared that the United States, free from the constraints of the Geneva Gas Protocol and even domestic populations vulnerable to gas attacks, might initiate gas attacks or worry less about receiving them, so too Canada and the United States could have protected themselves through vaccination, a move that the Germans probably would have discovered at some point. Britain was dependent on its allies not only for supplies and strength but also for restraint. And as in the examples with the United States, Britain could not order Canada to toe its own line, although it could push harder than it could with the United States. This it did by requesting a leak-proof cover story for any Canadian vaccination scheme.

At the same time, Canada was a loyal and productive ally. Britain's championing of Canada and the other dominions' requests to be consulted in policy decisions about retaliation in the face of a gas attack (as seen in chapter 3) demonstrated Canada's position. This desire to see the Allies follow their own gas policy, and the need to make the alliance work without US domination of it everywhere, led to some careful maneuvering and breath holding.

## Vengeance, Again

When V-weapons reappeared on the horizon in 1944, the threat was more of a challenge to the barriers against a gas war than to the alliance. First in anticipation of WMDs in the months before and after D-Day, and then in discussions about retaliation once the V-weapons began landing, Winston Churchill led discussions within Britain about the possibility of deterring or responding to the new threats with poison gas, whether or not the German armaments carried unconventional weapons. The US Joint Committee on New Weapons and Equipment also started to process information and possibilities; it began to take seriously the potential for the rockets to carry chemical and/or biological warfare toxins. In the end, Allied leaders chose not to use CW, but their discussions show that they had moved beyond seeing gas as a weapon of last resort against invasion and to maintain national independence; the line that indicated threats severe enough to trigger a gas response seemed to be moving toward serious, but lesser, threats.

## A New Year, a New Country

In the first week of 1944, the US Joint Chiefs of Staff received a report mulling over the CBW question, emphasizing its critical nature and potential widespread ramifications. Despite the fact that months later the United States would minimize the threat of German use of botulism against the Normandy landings, Dr. Vannevar Bush's Joint Committee on New Weapons and Equipment took on the question of what would happen if German rockets and planes contained "biological toxins" instead of just high explosives because "[t]here is a strong indication" that the Germans would release such a weapon and would do so "imminent[ly]." They might contain other BW substances, but the focus in this meeting was the likelihood of toxins.[113] (The distinction between the biological toxins and bacteriologicals, i.e., bacteria that cause contagious diseases, is subtle. For example, a biological toxin can be poison distilled from a plant that can inhibit the nervous system without being communicable to other humans. Botulism fits into this category, as does ricin, a compound that receives attention today as a likely bioweapon.)[114] While the Committee spent more space analyzing the BW possibilities—the newest and thus probably least well-known weapon to consider—they did not ignore a range of possible payloads for the rockets, including "conventional gas" and "possibly other materials." With respect to BW, the biggest deterrent might be its novelty: Who knew if it would work?

If it did, though, they concluded that the effects could be "devastating" on British targets, knowing that the German weapon sites put London and Bristol in danger. The group was more pessimistic about the results than the British had been. The United States predicted that civilians were not fully prepared because they had not been carrying or using masks regularly. A surprise gas attack would be powerful, and so would a biological attack. The good news was that the British government knew how to defend against a gas attack, but the bad news was that its "[d]efenses against biological toxin are believed to be undeveloped and inadequate." Even worse, perhaps, the impact "may conceivably affect the entire plan for the European theater," although those details were not explained. Presumably this meant that once gas or BW appeared, a full-fledged gas war would soon start.[115] While the Committee members discussed plans for defensive measures, they did not sound confident about current preparedness.

The other step would be retaliation. The Committee was blunt and unanimous in its recommendation: "If gases, toxins, or bacteriologicals are used, prompt retaliation by gas warfare methods is indicated" en masse and from the air. The authors made it clear that there was not a lot of knowledge about how to react to BW threats. Gas should be the all-purpose answer to a German attack.[116]

That, at least, was the US view at the time. It was not the last word. Later in the month and into the spring, the Committee discussed CW: What if Germany used V-weapons to deliver gas? The men emphasized the likely efforts to interdict supplies to the D-Day invasion and Allied soldiers as well as impacting British civilians.[117] The danger here was that persistent gases, such as mustard, could wound soldiers or make their work less efficient if they had to labor while wearing anti-gas equipment. There were costs for inanimate objects too; persistent gases could contaminate the ground and equipment, either destroying it or requiring cleaning before use.

In this case, too, the Committee expected any Allied reaction to be with gas, although exactly how extensive a retaliation effort and when it could be mounted had to be considered. The Joint Staff Planners summed up their multipage recommendations: the Allies needed to keep bombing and "place ourselves in a greater state of readiness to retaliate by the use of gas in overwhelming power, and if we develop the methods and means for detection of these agents and protection against their effects, we can remove the prospect of any such advantage [that would incite the Germans to use rockets with WMDs]." Of course, the problem with reiterating this policy of retaliation to the Germans was that they might assume it was a bluff and call it, starting a CBW war whether or not the Allies were ready. Or, they might twist the Allies' words, claiming that they hinted at offensive preparations and thus the Germans had to strike first in self-defense.[118] In other words, the same concerns the Allies had in the past appeared here as well.

The other problem was on the Allied side. At this point, March of 1944, the final version of the combined gas policy had not yet been approved, leaving confusion about whether a commander of multinational forces had to get permission just from his government or from all the governments from which he drew soldiers if he wanted to use gas.[119] The Allies now could "reach a position to retaliate with toxic gases in overwhelming force . . . with some diversion of effort and resources," although the United States was ready to "retaliate with prompt gas attack," presumably, for now, generating a swift but short attack versus a sustained one.[120] How intensively or how long could the Allies retaliate at this point? Detailed US plans showed that at least some of the military took this option seriously as early as January. The United States would work with the British to drop gas by air for fifteen days, using both persistent gases like mustard, and nonpersistent gases, such as phosgene. The report by Brigadier General Alden Waitt, assistant chief of the Chemical Warfare Service for Field Operations, was detailed, listing quantities of bombs filled with different kinds of gases in the European theaters, weather considerations, target characteristics, and other details. Theoretically, the CWS was ready to go.[121]

The questions raised and the proposals made continued to circulate to SHAEF and then to the Joint Staff Planners so that the latter could comment on how these dilemmas would change their strategies; the answer was almost none. Rockets with high explosives or gas would have "tactical rather than strategical significance," with meaningful but not game-changing impacts. There was less confidence if the Germans used BW, but the Allied leadership concluded that work on such weapons was not far enough along to be relevant.[122] For now, the United States thought CW, and perhaps BW, were threats that could be answered with gas, although using gas was never a foolproof response.

## Winston Churchill's Questions

While the United States developed a plan that satisfied it for now, the British renewed their debates about using CW once Hitler began ordering Vengeance weapon attacks against British cities and civilians in June 1944. In the United States, the committees who studied the subject of responding to V-weapons with CW had had just two clear triggers: a German use of gas on British civilians or on the battlefront. Neither happened, and the United States seemed satisfied with detailing a policy for gas use but going no further than that yet. And yet a month after D-Day, the British discussion about using gas in retaliation to the Vengeance weapons—and by now they knew that there were flying bombs as well as rockets—took on new life. There were domestic and international consequences to consider, ones related to morale, the military, and the alliances. Winston Churchill, one of the most gas-tolerant of the British leaders, was intimately involved. His frustration with the inability to stop or adequately respond to the V-1 and V-2 attacks seeped through his memos to the Chiefs of Staff. While his military leadership never adopted the proposal to respond in kind, Churchill merely tabled the issue rather than abandoning it. If the war had continued, if Germany had hit UK urban centers harder, what might have happened?

On July 4, 1944, the home secretary and minister of home security, Herbert Morrison, the head of civil defense and thus a holder of a broad portfolio including anti-gas work in the United Kingdom, wrote to Winston Churchill. He responded to a question that had seemed to arise out of the debate about rocket sites: "Would it be wise to saturate and resaturate [*sic*] the Pas de Calais area concerned with gas?" Morrison particularly focused on foreign and domestic civilian casualties. He addressed a question that had not arisen in earlier discussions about collateral damage. If the launch sites were targeted, might innocent French be hurt? In Morrison's eyes, "they ought not be there," a rather callous view, perhaps.[123]

What he could add was that he did not think that "the [British] people" were in "a good temper."[124] Fighting a gas war was more than a matter of training and using defensive equipment; it was also a matter of keeping up morale, and that was a concern. The domestic challenge was that British civilians, unlike those in a totalitarian or occupied country, had the ability to speak out, to protest.[125] The Chiefs of Staff, later in July, reinforced Morrison's view. They believed that civilians might "be resentful of being subjected to gas attack if it was felt that this could have been avoided," although any "shock" they felt at first would decrease once they saw "the efficacy of protective and remedial measures." What might not be as easy to reconcile in the laymen's minds would be the "grave concern" if the Germans retaliated on prisoners of war.[126]

Some of the other assumptions and topics for consideration by the Chiefs of Staff recall the issues raised in the fall of 1943, with a few added nuances and changes in attitude. They sided with the United States about preparedness but were more concerned about morale than physical readiness. The assumption remained that once gas warfare opened it would spread across the theater, if not beyond. Thus, diplomatically, the Chiefs of Staff recognized that the decision for "initiation of the use of gas" to combat the Vengeance weapons, required not just consultation but full "agreement" from the Western Allies as well as Russia. While Russia was not part of the combined chemical warfare policy, it was an ally who would be deeply involved in a European gas war.[127] If gas use could be justified as retaliation for CW deployed via the V-weapons, that approval might come quickly. If it was retaliation for the weapons laden with conventional armaments, that might not be the case.

The military debates that arose in this iteration of the discussion were broader than they had been previously, addressing German production targets as well as rocket sites. Based on what the British knew about the V-1 and V-2 sites, they still concluded that Allied gas attacks would be "negligible" in effect. This conclusion rested on several factors, including ones that were hard to calculate. For instance, the Allies could not identify all the sites, especially since some were mobile. While they did not know if the morale of the V-program personnel would break under gas, the analysts were fairly certain about their disappointing conclusion.[128]

The potential effect of CW on the German manufacturing effort was unknown, though. While there seemed to be more confidence in using CW than BW, in general, in this case the British Chiefs of Staff had even more faith in high explosives. After all, the Allies had been bombing the Axis with high explosives for years, and they felt they were making progress; they knew that they could continue to pressure Germany with the current approach. Who knew if CW would work as planned? If it did, the Allies—perhaps with US manufacturing might in mind—would survive a mutual gas war better than the Germans.[129] The Chiefs of Staff, though, also looked at the wider picture: German retaliation probably also would hit the Allies hard on the European battlefield by slowing down the transport of supplies to and around Normandy and the Russian push toward Germany.[130] Perhaps even worse, in the long term other theaters, namely the Far East, were not ready for gas wars.[131] So, aside from any concerns about escalating the war, there was the question of whether gas would do any good in the wider scheme of things.

The Chiefs of Staff had shifted their position a bit since the fall of 1943, although they were still generally against CW use for military, domestic, and diplomatic reasons. Of course, Winston Churchill was still more open-minded toward gas; by this time, he was almost eager to use it. The day after the Chiefs of Staff's July 6 report discouraging the use of gas for now, the prime minister told the House of Commons that he thought the "damage . . . done by [the flying bomb's] blast effect has been extensive," although not as widespread as the fire and other bombing the Allies deployed against Germany. Later in the speech he suggested that the Allied defenses had done well, destroying many bombs and limiting the casualties to approximately "one person per bomb."[132] In public, he was confident.

In private, the same day, Churchill made it clear that his willingness to use gas still existed, and he wanted the Chiefs of Staff Committee to reexamine the issue and make a "cold-blooded calculation."[133] He was well aware that Britain could not act on its own—he would "have to square Uncle Joe [Stalin] and the President [Roosevelt]"—but he felt that that was his problem; the Chiefs should not worry about diplomatic matters.[134] (Clearly he did not think that the dominions were an issue either since he did not even mention them.)

Part of this was because Churchill saw the conventional attacks from the V-weapons as sufficiently destructive and inhumane to inspire an attack with a new weapon that might make a difference and certainly would catch attention. He also did not think that gas was as deadly or appalling as others did. As he wrote in a memo, "Although one sees how unpleasant it is to receive poison gas attacks, from which nearly everyone recovers. . . . One really must not be bound within silly conventions of the mind."[135] Churchill was not governed by fears that gas was inhumane, a common perception of the time. He ignored the fact that people died from gas attacks and that disabled men populated Britain, but, in his defense, he was not alone. Some interwar experts had argued that gas was less deadly than conventional weapons.[136]

What did concern him were the British civilians and the war effort on the home front. Churchill had demonstrated earlier in the conflict that he would lead Britain into gas warfare if it was necessary for national survival, perhaps after a German invasion. Churchill feared the consequences might be "life or death" for Britain; he later worried that the V-weapons could create "far-ranging and devasting effect . . . on many centres of Government and labour." Passionately, he proclaimed that "I should be prepared to do anything that would hit the enemy in a murderous place [emphasis in original]." To do that, he would "drench" the urban centers of Germany to keep the citizens "requiring constant medical attention." He would aim at military targets, too, envisioning—likely unrealistically—to "stop all work at the flying bomb sites."[137]

Yet, Churchill did not require a crisis of that magnitude to turn to gas. He also declared that he would "use it . . . if it could be shown . . . that it would shorten the war by a year."[138] This was not a matter of national survival, per se, although Britain was weary and a shorter war would save lives and money. Churchill was much further along the spectrum toward acceptance of a gas war than the Chiefs of Staff; he was decisive, but he also viewed the consequences of a gas war as less serious and the moral restraints as weaker.

The Chiefs of Staff delayed responding for three weeks until Churchill pushed them again; then they recommended restraint.[139] They essentially repeated their earlier concerns but also addressed Churchill's two named issues. Their predictions were that the impact would be "negligible" on the V-weapon sites and gas would not win the war for the Allies.[140] They did not give Churchill any new support.

The Chiefs of Staff did leave the door open to using CW, even if Britain itself were not under attack or fighting for its very survival. While the long-term effects of a gas war probably would not provide actual benefit to Britain's war effort, a surprise attack might provide forward momentum against the Germans, but "[o]nly in the event of a situation . . . when no other means of forcing the German lines in Normandy can be found."[141] This was a limited situation, but it did offer the possibility of gas warfare.

His disgusted response to the Chiefs of Staff report was as dramatic and blunt as the prime minister could be: "I am not at all convinced by the negative report. But clearly I cannot make head against the parsons and the warriors at the same time." He gave in, for now, reserving the right to raise the issue again "when things get worse." He was not particularly optimistic at that moment, but then the Vengeance campaign was at its most effective that month. Hundreds of V-2s had landed in the United Kingdom, and while the numbers are hard to determine exactly, they killed thousands.[142] While the rocket and flying bombs continued to land in southern England through March of 1945, July proved to be the month with the greatest number of casualties, but their devastation never reached the numbers that the Blitz had produced. While the Blitz caused approximately 43,000 deaths, the V-weapons generated close to 8,800.[143] The rockets and flying bombs were terrifying and destructive, but they did not become a matter of "life or death" with regard to national survival.

In addition, the Allies did manage to break out of Normandy and push toward Berlin. The Battle of the Bulge may have provided the largest obstacle in the drive toward Berlin, but the movement suggested that conventional methods of war were enough and that gas, even if it proved helpful, would not "shorten the war by a year or two."[144]

It was not a radical shift in outlook to consider using CW against the Germans in retaliation for WMD targeted against the Allies; that was the policy from the opening of the war. There were some new factors, though, in the discussions associated with Operations Bodyline and Crossbow, the projects to combat the V-weapons. One was consideration of making enemy civilians, not just soldiers, primary targets. Another is that the British, at least, seemed to be inching closer to considering gas use, whether or not it was in retaliation. While Churchill was at the forefront of this drive, the Chiefs of Staff, the Joint Intelligence Committee, and others mulled seriously over what it would mean to use gas at other times, such as just to push the Normandy advance forward. That openness to discussing gas use would be taken further as the war between Japan and the Western Allies raged.

In the meantime, the Western Allied relationship continued to evolve. Decisions about gas demonstrated that the participants were not equal in strength, but they were committed to the relationship and to each other, whether the United States assessed the impact of gas retaliation for V-weapons on British civilians, the Canadians bowed to British and US willingness to risk CBW casualties in the face of potential CBW attacks by the Germans, or the British tolerated Eisenhower's refusal to let the British interpretation of the Geneva Gas Protocol bind Allied efforts to finish the war.

In the Pacific theater, the United States had a larger role and say, but not the only one. The challenges the Japanese provided the Allies, and the Westerners' perception of their enemy there, all made it much more likely that the war in that theater would have ended with chemical weapons.

# CHAPTER 6

# Critical Timing

## The Increasing Likelihood of Chemical Warfare in the Pacific

> Gas is a decisive weapon. Properly used it can shorten the war and save many lives.
>
> —Major General William N. Porter, chief of the Chemical Warfare Service

World War II marks the dawn of the nuclear age, but it could have been the war that cemented poison gas's place in the panoply of acceptable weapons. World War II ended with a bloody but conventional defeat in Europe and with a shocking new weapon in the Pacific. Secrecy had surrounded the Manhattan Project; even Harry Truman did not know about the nuclear quest until two weeks after he became president, a few months before the *Enola Gay* dropped the first atomic bomb on Hiroshima. Thus, in the months leading up to the bombs' use, Allied leaders could not count on a nuclear ending. Nuclear weapons were new—there was no experience with them and no general fear and worry built up about them in the wider population and military as opposed to those who knew about the Manhattan Project. Instead, they had other visions for ending the war.

One option was increased conventional aerial bombing, which had escalated over the course of the war. That had not been enough to defeat Japan yet, but it could continue, along with a naval blockade. The other obvious option was an amphibious invasion, with its attendant high casualties but quicker resolution. Given the high cost of previous campaigns against the Japanese, Allied planners were open to considering any option to shorten the war and reduce Allied casualties. Gas was one of these options.[1]

Instead of a conflict that demonstrated that nations could refrain from using dreaded and devastating weapons like chemical weapons (CW), the war almost ended with a demonstration that the Allies would use gas when it suited their interests—something that would have been difficult for many to contemplate seriously before 1945. General William Porter, chief of the American Chemical Warfare Service, for one, envisioned gas-drenched Japanese beaches and towns filled with civilians and soldiers blinded with mustard; asphyxiated by phosgene; or wounded by open sores, redness, and other ailments in the final efforts to end the war. As noted in the quotation at the beginning of the chapter, he essentially argued that gas could be humane, lessening the casualties that war demanded.[2] Whether or not one agrees with Porter's assessment of the nature of gas, the Allies came very close to trying CW. The Allies' resistance to using gas gradually eroded over the course of the war, and the last years of the war included not just varied discussions but also detailed plans about using chemicals against the Japanese. While the United States' restraints regarding CW had always been weaker than those of the other Western Allies, key British planners joined the United States in considering seriously the benefits of launching gas in the Pacific. The Canadians would have embraced the change as part of combined Allied invasions of the home islands of Japan.[3]

This increasing openness to deploying gas was a result not just of changes in Western attitudes, although that was crucial, but also of repeated allegations of Japanese biological and chemical attacks on the Chinese. In addition, it was a result of prohibitions against gas that left room for its use in retaliation, including FDR and Churchill's warnings to the Axis powers as well as reservations to the Geneva Gas Protocol's language that restricted parties from first use of gas but not retaliation.[4] The transition was a slow and complex process, though. It was not just experiential, legal, or moral motivations that shifted attitudes. There were also practical issues: Would gas end the war sooner? Would gas lessen the number of Allied casualties? Would gas combat the problem of Allied war weariness? By mid-war, especially 1943, the Western Allies could see that they were gaining strength against Japan and eventually would win. Now gas could be an offensive tool, used not only as a means of national survival as it was envisioned by the British in Europe but also a way to win the war sooner and at a lower cost with less war weariness—if popular opinion accepted the tradeoff.

Even into 1945, while the atomic bomb was just a dream, many British and US leaders saw gas as the weapon of last resort. They did not want to risk a gas war, either by seizing on any possible chance to retaliate or by giving Axis powers a pretext for launching CW preemptively, such as by claiming that mere forward theater storage of CW showed that the Allies were about to start using gas.[5] During the early portion of the war with Japan, international treaties and public promises by President Roosevelt and Prime Minister Churchill prevented the Allies from introducing gas to the battlefield. In addition, World War I had demonstrated that CW would increase the misery on the battlefield. Thus, while the Allies remained worried about enemy gas attacks, the self-restraining promises also provided relief to a certain degree because the Western Allies were not completely ready logistically or mentally to fight a gas war at the beginning of the conflict.

These issues did not mean that Britain and the United States ignored the issue of gas in the Pacific theater throughout the war. They conducted meaningful debates about whether Japan had used gas or whether the Allies should use it in the Pacific; Canada lacked the gas or manpower to play a role in executing an attack in that theater and hence played a lesser role than in Europe.[6] Despite superficial appearances that the no-first-use policy was clear cut, it was not. For instance, Prime Minister Churchill and President Roosevelt had stated clearly and repeatedly during the war that their nations would not start a gas war, but that they would retaliate in kind for their own countries as well as their Allies if the Axis powers released CW. In the case of the United States, not just gas but any "inhumane devices" would trigger a response. While the definition of those "inhumane devices" was not specified in the public warnings, internal US memos indicated that some in the State Department and military thought biological weapons (BW) would qualify, while others were not sure.[7] Furthermore, without a combined BW policy, and having just completed a drawn-out negotiation to create a combined CW policy, retaliating in kind might mean using CW in response to BW and CW attacks.[8] There were other ambiguities; Churchill's warnings focused on threats to the European Axis powers, but by the later years of the war, pro-gas officers in Britain entertained the idea of using gas against Japan as if there were no barriers—not even the Geneva Gas Protocol—to doing so.

There was another factor at play, although the official discussions about gas planning did not mention it explicitly. This was the fact that the target was Japan, not Germany. As historian John Dower has discussed thoroughly, the Pacific war had a pronounced racial component; each side perceived the other in terms that permitted brutal behavior at times and demeaning opinions often.[9] The military and diplomatic officials in Britain and the United States did not say that they were more willing to use gas on Japan because racism motivated them or that its people were more barbaric than the Germans. There probably was some of that behind the changing attitudes toward gas in the Pacific war. However, there were many other motivations to use CW in Japan, and, because a lot of the World War II racism was so open, there was no reason to hide it in debates if it was a dominant and conscious rationale for including gas in attack plans. For one thing, some gas proponents did not find gas inhumane; they would have been willing to use it—if it made sense politically and militarily—on any target. The leaders of the Chemical Warfare Service (CWS), such as General William Porter, were of this ilk. He wrote expectantly about possible gas attacks both in Europe and in Japan.[10] Even in 1944, when Gallup asked US civilians about the possibility of dropping CW on Axis cities, they varied little in their responses when asked about urban areas in Germany as opposed to Japan, although Japan was a slightly more popular target.[11]

Among the war leadership, some willingness to target Japan instead of Germany was purely practical. By 1944, General George Marshall, the United States chief of staff, feared, for example, that a gas war in Europe would be costly to the Allies, especially those in Britain who were within easy reach of German retaliatory weaponry that could carry gas.[12] (Note that the British colonies and dominions, such as heavily bombarded Malta, were not considered in this rationale.) When Allied CW stock was limited, using it also meant that waging a widespread gas war (not just a retaliatory strike) in two theaters would be challenging; as one official feared, an attack on Japan before V-E Day might incline the Germans to use gas too.[13] There were other reasons it was more logical to attack Japan, not Germany, with gas. The British Chiefs of Staff representatives conveyed to the Combined Chiefs of Staff that the German nerve gases discovered at the end of the European war might be saved for use in Japan because there was "no evidence that the Japanese have any knowledge of these gases." It could be a "valuable weapon for tactical surprise."[14]

Yet the new phase in the Allied military attitude toward gas began well before 1945. It started as the tide began to turn in the Allies' favor in the Pacific, and it became clear how much time and blood it would take to defeat the Japanese. The idea of using gas offensively became more attractive—even if many involved in these discussions referred to US use of gas as retaliatory, no matter when or why they planned to release it. For example, General Porter argued that the Japanese had used gas against the Chinese, even after Roosevelt warned them of the consequences, so the United States had carte blanche to use gas in retaliation any time it chose.[15] Unlike how the British had in Europe or the way some US military experts did in the Pacific, Porter did not believe that retaliation had to be an immediate and direct response to an enemy's action. Thus, while the Allies did discuss retaliatory use of gas, most detailed plans involving gas were, frankly, purely offensive in nature—offensive in terms of being part of an attack on the enemy (rather than fighting them off) and offensive in terms of initiating and regularizing gas use. Chemical warfare did not have to be a one and done deployment justified as a response to a recent action by the enemy.[16]

As the war continued, the combination of all these factors meant that leadership circles from both the United States and Britain contained powerful men who not only favored using gas but also developed detailed plans about how it could be used. The Lethbridge Mission, led by the British but accompanied by some US advisers, toured the Pacific theater and concluded that gas should be used against Japan. Other discussions reached the highest levels in the military, including the Chiefs of Staff in the United States, and there were proposals to talk to the president—first Roosevelt and then Truman—about priorities and permissions with regard to gas war preparation and planning. Momentum was building to use gas in the invasion of Japan, until the use of the atom bomb rendered the planning moot.

## Avoid a Gas War with Japan

From the start of World War II, the Western Allies believed Japan would use gas without regard for the Geneva Protocol or any ideas of international law. Wanting to avoid such an attack, they themselves did not plan to start a gas war, at least at first, but the threat of gas in the Pacific region began well before the attacks on December 7/8, 1941, brought the United States and British Empire into the Pacific war. The Japanese appear to have used CW and BW in the 1937 Rape of Nanking, which now symbolizes the brutal and destructive Japanese war in China during the 1930s, according to a British Military Intelligence report.[17] During the conflict, the League of Nations had sided, ineffectually but repeatedly, with China against Japanese aggression, including warning Japan about "the reprobation of the civilised world" if it "resort[ed]" to the banned gas warfare and a plea to other nations to report such behavior to the League.[18] The resolutions did not promise more forceful action if Japan broke the law.

As war continued, China repeatedly reported that Japan used chemical and biological weapons (CBW) in its attacks.[19] In international, official circles at the time, it was well-accepted that Japan used chemical warfare in China before Pearl Harbor. A combination of detailed, repeated allegations by the Chinese combined with reports substantiated by Westerners in China helped to bolster the Chinese claims. The British air attaché, Wing Commander James Warburton, reported to the Air Ministry that he had seen a Japanese "gas filled bomb stated [by his Chinese hosts] to have been dropped by the Japanese air forces in December 1939 at Shahsien, Shansi."[20] Japan's cruel behavior, including mass rape and mass beheadings, in China made it easy to believe that it would engage in other forms of uncivilized behavior, such as using CBW. Japan's wartime behavior and the absence of its signature on the Geneva Gas

Protocol formed the foundation for this distrust. The British Army Council shared its conviction with the Foreign Office in February of 1942: we "agree with the view that the Japanese Government will avail themselves of the use of poison gas in any circumstances where they consider that the advantage to be gained outweighs the risk of reprisals."[21] The irony is that by 1945, the United States was moving to the same perspective on gas, although proponents claimed humanitarian and diplomatic, not just military, justifications.

Despite Japan's refusal to be limited by the Geneva Gas Protocol, throughout the war it tried to avoid international condemnation for using gas. A desire to keep CBW use in the shadows made it hard for its victims and for observers to collect evidence about Japan's gas attacks. This dilemma was one that obstructed Chinese officials during the war as the nation struggled to find proof that outsiders would accept officially. But almost immediately after widespread attacks on December 7/8, 1941, Western sources began listing charges of Japanese gas use. The Foreign Office files on "Enemy Breaches of the Rules of Warfare, &c [sic]" from November 1941 to January 1942 included evidence of varying degrees of reliability of lethal and nonlethal gas use in China. In one instance, a Japanese prisoner of war provided a confession. In another, General John Magruder, the head of the United States military mission at Chungking, on Boxing Day in 1941 said that mustard gas and lewisite "had been confirmed," although the report cautioned, "It is, however, not clear how it has been confirmed." How trustworthy was that proof? A third report simply listed matter-of-factly that "The Japanese are reported to have used mild tear gas against Australian troops in Malaya." This sounded definite, but should Britain protest against tear gas use? US police had used it for years during domestic crises, after all. Although the use of gas by the military in war was prohibited by law, Britain eventually had decided it was acceptable for police to use tear gas in the colonies in the 1930s. Thus, to some it was humane in contrast to using bullets, yet not all gas use was the same. Police use was not the same as military use in war; that, in fact, was the premise of Britain's decision that it could use gas in the Empire without breaking the Geneva Gas Protocol.[22]

These nuances made claims of Japanese gas use complicated. The care the British authors of the report took was so important. They were careful to distinguish between trustworthy information based on their own knowledge as compared to information passed on by a US general who could not attest to how it had been confirmed: they agreed that some Japanese soldiers in Malaya had gas, probably "prussic acid for use against tanks," likely to winnow into the largely impenetrable vehicles. (Prussic acid had been thought to be one of the deadliest gases developed during World War I—at least until detailed experiments showed that it was not always as fatal as it had been thought.) The authors of the report cautioned that it could cause death when used in quantities, but small amounts would "at the most" cause "loss of consciousness."[23] Thus, it was reasonable to conclude that Japan used some gas, but not that there was reliable proof of consistent, lethal use.

Meanwhile, intelligence from other sources reinforced the uneasiness about gas. The day after Pearl Harbor, the Free French warned the Chinese, who passed it on to the British, that Germany had given Japan "several kinds of newly invented poison gases to be tried out in CHINA so that their efficacy might be tested in preparation for their use in EUROPE."[24] Whether or not this or any other rumor was true, it is clear that CW posed a constant threat.

Even when the proof that Japan was prepared to use gas was present, determining whether blowing the whistle on the Japanese would do anything useful for the Allies proved to be a problem. Condemnation in the court of public opinion was one thing, but for a long time the Allies could not physically punish Japan. In July of 1942, a British agent in Washington sent a message to the Admiralty. He noted that the United States debated announcing that it had found Japanese CW "flasks." The Joint Staff Mission and the US Chiefs of Staff thought that publicizing the fact that Japan had CW equipment might encourage it to refrain from using gas "until an extreme emergency arises;" it might buy time. However, "If the matter is suppressed the Psychological [sic] re-action of the Japanese will be to say to themselves [that the Allies] . . . are so dumb that they do not understand what [the] flask . . . is, and in consequence use gas at the first available opportunity."[25] The report did not say what action the United States took in the end, but it did mention that the Joint Chiefs hoped that Britain would take the lead.

The United States took a similar approach to gathering and sharing allegations, such as the proof that soldiers carried CW in Malaya, if not elsewhere. News of these finds even reached the top echelons in the United States and Britain, but it received cautious responses. George Marshall, the US chief of staff, explained to Field Marshal Sir John Dill on January 15, 1942, that, "I do not think that harm can result from publication of the factual data pertaining to the Japanese chemical grenades found in Malay [sic]. It is possible that such publication may have a deterrent effect on the use of this type of weapon. Furthermore, if these facts are to be made public, it should be done by British authorities, and without hint of reprisals."[26] In this short note, Marshall reflected a methodology that both nations used repeatedly: deterrence. In this case, though, unlike the later statements by the political leaders Churchill and Roosevelt, he did not recommend using a warning. He simply wanted the enemy to know that the Allies were aware that Japan had gas on the front lines. It seems that he did not want to escalate tensions, but rather he sought to make the Japanese think carefully about future actions. What could the West do, after all, in the weeks immediately following Pearl Harbor?

They did wield words. It was during the following months that Churchill and Roosevelt each issued their public warnings, against Germany in the case of the former and against anyone who used gas against an ally in the latter.[27] (See chapter 3 for a more detailed discussion.) A combination of deterrents and moral statements against gas, they were as far as Britain and the United States were able and willing to go on this front.

Likewise the Canadians considered the Chinese reports and their implications.[28] The Canadian General Staff took the stories seriously enough to report to Prime Minister Mackenzie King that "[r]ecent developments] in the war situation [presumably the December 7/8th attacks] have enhanced the operational importance of Chemical Warfare generally, and particularly in respect of offensive and defensive weapons and supplies related to vesicant gases," alleging that Japan had used them in China and had the ability to make some, like mustard.[29] While Canada did not accuse or challenge Japan directly, it was sufficiently concerned that the Canadian Chemical Warfare program was "designed" with the danger of a Japanese invasion of Canada in mind.[30]

Still, this did not mean that the United States, or even Britain, was any more interested than it had been in becoming involved in a gas war that launched CW rather than simply threats about retaliation and propaganda. The reports make it clear that the British and US experts took the rumors of gas use seriously. They also make the experts' frustration clear: claims of CBW still were not enough, even detritus of CBW still was not enough. There needed to be documented, thorough investigations linking Japanese actions to injuries generated by CBW before any firm conclusions could be made.

In dismissing evidence of Japanese gas use, at this point in the war Canadians noted that the Japanese had not used gas against whites, and Canada was the one Western Ally that discussed this idea openly and extensively. The unstated message was that there was firm belief that the armies of the Empire of the Rising Sun did release CBW on the Chinese, which research confirms today, but that that was of limited significance.[31] The potential victims about whom the Western Allies cared most, namely their own soldiers and civilians, were safe so far. It also hinted at a suspicion that attacking the Chinese with gas was of a different caliber than attacking great powers, probably for racial reasons. As Major H. A. Delcellier noted in an assessment of a report on Canadian CW policy, "Would you consider that the isolated case of gas being used against Chinese troops does not change the situation 'radically,' but it might be considered that the use against white troops would increase the charges of 'abrogation' very materially?"[32] At the same time, one Canadian expert thought it was unlikely that Japan would use gas against Westerners for quite some time, thus reducing the need for Canada to make gas for the purpose of retaliating against the Japanese. The rationale was that "it is inconceivable that the enemy would inaugurate the use of gas against the whites for small raids," and Japan would not be ready for large-scale attacks "against the whites" until Russia can no longer threaten "retaliation against Japanese cities."[33] Again, a month later in May of 1942, the Canadians noted that "Gas has not been used in this war against white troops or civilian populations."[34]

For their part, the US experts suggested that the Japanese practice was partly because of "fear of retaliation" because the Chinese had given no indication that they could use gas against the Japanese.[35] While this interpretation may not have been accurate, as is suggested by the Allied reluctance to confirm Japanese gas use officially, despite the available evidence and number of allegations, it was a palatable conclusion. This fits with interwar gas use in which the targets were colonial, non-Western subjects, such as in Morocco.[36] Most famous was the use of mustard gas by the Italians in Ethiopia, which did inspire a large outcry, especially in Britain, but the protestors' tone implied they were concerned mainly because Italy's successful use meant that gas could also be a threat to European countries.[37] Still, it seems likely that the theory that gas would be less objectionable politically and militarily against nonwhite, non-Western targets has some validity. However, it fails to explain fully the reluctance of the Western Allies either to find enough proof that Japan used gas against China to trigger retaliation or the greater willingness to contemplate using gas against Japan rather than Germany. Race, status, or habit were probably in the minds of analysts who explicitly referenced the limits of Japan's gas use, but it did not indicate greater willingness to open a gas war against the Japanese at that point.

It was not just once or twice but rather hundreds of times that the Western Allies dismissed Chinese allegations of Japanese gas use. While midwar US intelligence reports list pages of unconfirmed rumors of Japanese gas attacks, detailed down to the date, location, and type of gas, for the most part, there are only a few that are specified as "confirmed."[38] Even this seems unreliable, though. A 1944 report by US Military Intelligence states that the Japanese used some gas, while the same year the US Joint Logistics Committee said the opposite—neither referring to the other's report.[39] Was this the result of a lack of sharing or perhaps the product of terminology? Did the reports get lost, or were they ignored by those who might have to act on confirmed gas use? Did report readers dismiss the isolated, confirmed gas attacks as unworthy of official notice because they were rare, rather than products of a systematically employed policy? There is no commentary about this in the files, but since one was an intelligence report, it could be a matter of seeing different information.

Britain and the United States, the two Western Allies who analyzed the allegations, were on the same page in terms of caution. The Allies were well aware that the Japanese had the resources to engage in chemical warfare, they knew that its army had specially designated chemical warfare troops, and they recognized that some soldiers carried gas. Furthermore, according to a British War Office report, by 1942 the Allies had found Japanese instructions that demanded:

> before using weapons[,] the character 'Aka[,]' which signified poison-gas[,] was to be removed from them, and 'tubes' and other traces destroyed after use; all enemy found suffering from gas were to be killed; special care taken of orders for the use of gas; practices were to be kept secret by posting patrols round the area; and gas was not to be used where neutrals were living. . . . These instructions appear to have been faithfully followed, as evidence of Japanese use of gas against the Chinese—perhaps also against the British in Malaya—has been very difficult to get and especially to confirm.[40]

Thus, between the rumors and the facts that the Allies did know, there was ample reason to believe that the Japanese used CBW sometimes, even if the Western Allies did not want it to be common knowledge. Still, they resisted certifying evidence as confirmation a policy of widespread, Japanese gas use.

Even when their ally China brought pressure to bear, the Western Allies proved reluctant to undertake a physical response. During the war, the Chinese repeatedly sought to convince the Western Allies, the League of Nations, and the Pacific War Council (PWC) that Japan had continued to used gas more than eight hundred times since invading their country.[41] An illustrative example occurred in July of 1942, less than a month after FDR's first warning to Japan not to use gas. China had, through its ambassador to Britain, Wellington Koo, once again sent allegations of Japanese gas use to Britain.[42] This time the Asian ally hoped that Britain would expand its promise to retaliate on behalf of an ally to the Pacific theater; earlier, Churchill had suggested that "he would have the position considered." Koo also wanted Churchill and the Allies to take up China's cause in another venue; he suggested raising the issue of gas use at the PWC, a body that, when meeting in London to discuss management of the war with Japan, did so under British auspices.[43] This was something that the British prime minister had suggested he might do, if the occasion demanded.[44] Inside the British government, diplomatic and military opinions clashed. Hastings Ismay, the prime minister's chief military adviser, told Churchill that Foreign Secretary Anthony Eden believed "it would be impossible to refuse," and thus sought permission on July 9 to put the allegations on the PWC agenda.[45] Churchill generally approved.[46] However, Ismay seemed to have second thoughts and to look for alternative action. He consulted Sir Edward Bridges, the secretary to the cabinet, who reminded him that the War Cabinet had looked at Britain's global readiness and noted that "we are not in a position to wage chemical warfare in any oversea[s] theatre."[47] As a result, Ismay told Sir Alexander Cadogan, the permanent under-secretary at the Foreign Office, that "From the military point of view, I think it is fairly clear . . . that we ought not to take any action which is likely to increase the chances of gas warfare being started in any oversea[s] theatre." Because the War Cabinet thought Japan would use gas if it helped them, "This seems to imply . . . that while a declaration giving a warning of retaliation [the job of the prime minister or the Foreign Office] was likely to have some deterrent effect on the Germans, it was unlikely to have a deterrent effect on the Japanese."[48] Worse, it would not only be ineffective at preventing a gas attack; instead, a warning or condemnation in the PWC might provide that pretext for deploying gas. (The Allies had expressed a similar fear regarding Germany.) Or, perhaps denunciation would remove any inhibition Japan felt about using gas in ways that would inspire official international notice, leaving Japan open to using CW more widely.

With that in mind, Ismay wondered if a diplomatic conversation with the Chinese would help reduce the pressure from Koo and be a better way of handling the situation, although "Clearly there are important issues of principle involved." Ismay ended with a plea: "[C]an you think of a better way of dealing with this rather tiresome question?"[49] On August 19 the Foreign Office communicated with Ismay on the topic again. Foreign Secretary Anthony Eden had concluded that considering the issue in the relatively confidential confines of the PWC was acceptable, but he did not want the British government to raise the issue more publicly, at least not without more (and perhaps officially confirmed) Chinese allegations.[50] Britain's real concern seemed to be about public commitments to retaliate with gas on China's behalf, whether made by Churchill or FDR. The Foreign Office was more interested, at this point, in making sure that the United States did not start a gas war—even on the grounds of retaliation—without consulting the United Kingdom, than in protecting China.[51]

More commonly, the Western Allies dismissed the allegations as rare attacks, and they blamed any actual use on local commanders who used gas out of fear or desperation. In April 1943, the Combined Intelligence Committee reported to the Combined Chiefs of Staff that "The dispersed character of her [Japanese] operations and the relative autonomy of her task force commanders might result in the unconcerted use of gas by a commander acting on his own initiative. Some instances of this character have already been reported."[52] A year earlier, an even more explicit example of unwillingness to take action appeared in a British Military Intelligence community report that dismissed some examples as trials: since "the Japanese must share the now universal opinion that gas, to be effective as a weapon, must be used on a large scale, the only conclusion that can be drawn from these isolated cases in China is that they were 'experimental' only."[53] The War Office agreed at another time: "Most of the cases seem to indicate sporadic use, not fully co-ordinated with higher policy."[54] This was all likely to be true, but the danger was that Japan might be testing gas to see when it would be useful . . . and to see if the Allies would react.

In 1943, the United States had the perfect opportunity to condemn Japan for gas use but instead reiterated the British conclusion that any gas use was not part of Japanese policy. The Military Intelligence Service Research Unit report "confirmed" that Japan even used some gases in battles with the Western Allies, such as choking gas on February 19, 1943, on Guadalcanal, and "poison gas in the form of toxic smoke," which was ". . . used twice (23 January and 28 January 1943) by hard pressed individual Japanese soldiers."[55] Yet, something held the US military back from proclaiming this widely or acting on it. As late as September 30, 1943, the more august Combined Intelligence Committee had not thought that Japan has used gas in Guadalcanal.[56] Part of the problem seems to have been finding proof that was acceptable to everyone or shared with everyone in authority in the United States.[57] Hence in 1944, the Joint Logistics Committee wrote a report assessing Japan's CW capabilities and proclivities and repeated the Combined Intelligence Committee's conclusion that Japan had not used gas in Guadalcanal or other tight spots.[58] What explains this interpretation? The standards of proof for the Military Intelligence Research Unit probably were more lax than those for the Combined and Joint Logistics Committees, but it is also reasonable to think that information from the first group had not been communicated to the latter.

Japan probably did not want a full-fledged gas war at this point. If CW were deployed on both sides, it would be hard on everyone, not to mention demand a lot of resources, but no one knew for sure what Japan intended. So, to avoid living up to the letter of Roosevelt and Churchill's promises to China and other allies without harming their own reputations or military standing, Britain and the United States had to find pretexts for ignoring confirmed gas attacks. Part of that came from the way they interpreted the prime minister's and the president's warnings. Since neither stated how much gas had to be released by a foe before the United States would retaliate in kind, the military implicitly interpreted it as a warning against a proven regular policy of gas use or a major deployment of CW, based on the dismissals listed and reasons for ignoring specific instances. Thus, individual uses of CW confirmed by some person or group did not rise to the level of gas use that had to be acknowledged officially or that would trigger Roosevelt's promise to retaliate. In fact, a sustained Allied CW campaign would not have been possible even at the end of 1943, although General Porter thought the United States could be ready in early 1944, but a symbolic attack probably would have been possible much earlier. That topic did not come up in the discussions about Guadalcanal, and it is likely because the commanders did not like gas and did not default to considering it; it had its detractors and supporters, as was apparent from the World War I and interwar discussion.[59] The Allies dreaded chemical warfare for multiple reasons that varied over time, many of them listed earlier, including communication, inventory, regional vulnerabilities, and general dislike of gas. If one combined this perspective with the conviction that the Japanese would use gas as soon as it proved advantageous, then the repeated failure to accept many allegations of gas use as true as well as a pattern of ignoring the confirmed instances suggests that the Allies really did not *want* to find gas warfare—or to have to use it—at least not during most of the war.

Complicating matters was US general Albert Wedemeyer's promise to help China with defensive measures and to give notice before the United States launched any gas attacks.[60] It is unclear why, but Wedemeyer had also struck a deal with Chiang Kai Shek (now Jiang Jieshi) that restricted the former's use of gas to tactical, not strategic, purposes.[61] This would not inhibit all use of gas in the Pacific theater, but it did add restraints.

There were also logistical concerns. No matter what, a gas war was onerous for everyone, even if offensive use led to a great victory. A nation had to transport and store bulky or fragile weapons to the front lines. (The catastrophe in Bari, discussed in chapter 3, when Germany conducted an air raid that hit a ship carrying mustard gas, is a good example of such challenges.) It was not only the nature of the munitions, but also the need to find shipping space for a new weapon that posed a dilemma.[62] Since the Western Allies anticipated deploying gas mainly from the air, planning required determining how to ensure that there were enough planes available and, considering the limited number of aircraft, how much of the cargo should be gas and how much should be high explosives. Whether or not it was deployed by air, the military had to consider defensive issues, including the amount of protective equipment soldiers and nearby civilians should have. Both had to be ready for retaliatory attacks by the enemy. The fact that there were never enough masks for all the vulnerable populations in the Pacific theater was one factor (although this became less of an issue once Japan lost much of its ability to deploy gas far from home later in the war).[63] The other problems included making sure defensive gear was up to date, since masks, especially, had a shelf life. Wearing and carrying gear, from respirators to capes, not only burdened soldiers with extra weight but it also wearied them in a tropical climate where additional layers could cause misery. It was also an issue if, for instance, British plans scheduled front-line soldiers in Europe to attack on D-Day without personal anti-gas equipment (although everyone else would have it), or if soldiers universally left behind equipment that seemed burdensome and unnecessary; it is easy to see why requiring soldiers to don or pack too much defensive gear had little appeal.[64] Thus, the best scenario included avoiding the escalation of threats that led to the necessity of distributing offensive and defensive CW equipment, not just avoiding a hot chemical war.

Psychological concerns, too, could erode civilian and military morale. Gas caused more casualties when targets were unprepared and did not or could not get masks on in time. Since gases injured in seconds, and since neutralizing chemicals in masks wear out if they are used too long, how long should a soldier wear a mask? No one wanted to don it too soon or have to wear it too long. An added challenge was that masks were uncomfortable; as one World War I soldier said it felt like being smothered trying to breathe through it.[65]

Regardless of whether it could cause emotional or psychological harm, could gas cause physical casualties? In World War I, gas had been launched against relatively static targets, the trenches. There had been efforts to develop bombs that could be deployed by airplanes in the interwar period, and the Italian use of mustard gas proved that that this could work. Contemporary planners dismissed these concerns.[66] Air-dropped gases could chase the moving targets "on the march," for instance.[67] In particular, gas could be used in new ways: that is, it could be a unique weapon in its ability to clear caves or similar hideouts of stubborn Japanese soldiers. As the commanding general of the CWS summarized, "it is expected to solve the tactical problem which has been so acute in this area . . . wiping out Japanese suicide resistance when it is concentrated in pockets, at a cost of heavy casualties to the United Nations forces often after the military decision has been conclusively won." After conquering some of the Pacific islands gradually and at great cost, this became a particularly attractive idea. Gas could seep into crevices in "dugouts, bunkers and pillboxes," even if shelters were solid enough to withstand a lot of shelling or explosives.[68] Gas did not require soldiers to get close enough to deploy flamethrowers or satchel charges. Thus, gas could be used to speed clearance of island fortifications as the armed forces worked their way toward the home islands, it could be used to weaken Japanese resistance during amphibious landings, and it could be used purely in retaliation.

If gas were used in the first two instances, it would look like an offensive use of gas—even if it could be argued that it was merely a delayed retaliation against the Japanese (just as the British responded to the German introduction of gas in World War I five months after the attack) rather than the immediate response in kind to the very units that broke the gas truce.[69] Most of the planners did not even pay lip service to the idea that certain plans—such as clearing caves or beaches—could be retaliation of any sort; they did not discuss justifications at all but instead acted as if gas were simply another weapon to consider on its military merits. That approach makes sense considering it was their job to decide how to wield gas, not to set policy. Thus, the experts discussed whether gas could be used effectively enough to warrant the risk of Japanese retaliation. Once the hot gas war opened, there would be no going back. This meant that the first use of gas by the Allies had to be worth all of the frustration and dangers inherent in facing increased likelihood of future attacks by the Japanese. This had to be sensible not only militarily but also politically. The United States and Britain, after all, had promised publicly and repeatedly not to use gas in a first offensive strike. Changing policy would be tricky to justify and might be costly politically. Yet this reluctance to use gas would soon be eroded.

## From "Don't Launch" to "Well, Maybe . . ."

If the war in the Pacific opened with the Allies concerned about the Japanese launching gas warfare, the middle phase of the war was a transition period as the Allies built the capacity to sustain CW and began to change their minds about using gas themselves from 1943 onward. This was not simply a matter of the Allies overcoming their reluctance toward releasing CW and gaining confidence in their ability to deploy gas; it was paralleled by Japan becoming more vulnerable physically.

The change in British and US attitudes is clear if one looks at events before and after 1943. In the former period, Allies looked for hints that Japan was preparing for gas use. They viewed any allegations by the Japanese that Britain or the United States used gas as a sign that Japan wanted to establish a pretext for using gas itself while calling it "retaliation" rather than "first strike." In a 1942 War Office telegram to the commander-in-chief in India, London reported that Tokyo had sent a "telegram to Italian paper Messagero" containing allegations that the British and Chinese used gas and poisoned water in Burma. More worrisome than the accusation, as seen by London's transmittal of it to imperial outposts, was the Japanese statement that "'military circles

declare they can no longer observe their traditionally chivalrous methods'."
Did this mean that Japan was paving the way for using gas—or for something
else? And who was the target? Was it the Chinese, or any of the Allies? The
War Office concluded that this was "[p]robably usual Axis technique but the
possibility of Japs [sic] seeking excuses for using gas cannot be ignored."[70]

But for a year beginning in spring 1943, the US State Department and the
army wrestled with Japan's fears that the Allies might use gas. Simultaneously,
they protected themselves from creating a pretext that Japan could exploit to
launch its own attack or to blacken the United States' reputation with its allies
or neutrals. During this time, even as the Allies maintained a healthy fear of
the Axis power's future actions, Japan began to express concern about the
Allies, putting the United States, at least, on the defensive. The United States
had to tread carefully. Kendrick Lee's contribution, "Gas Warfare," on May 16,
1943, in *Editorial Research Reports*, the forerunner to *CQ Researcher*, a publication
created to inform editors with reports to help them write about current events,
shared that Japan had broadcast a charge that the United States had used gas
in retaking Attu. The US Navy denied the report, explaining that the service
had used "nonpoisonous smoke screens" as a cover, not gas.[71] The United
States did not let this allegation go unchecked, but it did not make a dramatic
statement either. In addition, there were signs that could be read to mean that
seeming Japanese vulnerability may have been pretexts for "retaliating" with
gas such as when the *Domei* news agency of Tokyo claimed for the first time
that the Japanese army found gas in the possession of the Chinese. The US
assessment "thought that the charge may be significant." This could be a ploy,
or simply another move in the propaganda war.[72] What is more interesting is
that a couple of months later, General Porter announced that smoke screens
had been used in the amphibious landing in Sicily.[73] This seemed to be an effort
to preempt any German or Italian claims of gas use there.

Perhaps more noteworthy, Lee also wrote that just a few months earlier,
weeks after Pearl Harbor, on January 23, 1942, a Tokyo radio broadcast had
claimed that US and Filipino soldiers used "gas shells in the Battle of Bataan."
General Douglas MacArthur took this seriously and saw it as a slur. He "advises
that there is absolutely no truth in this statement . . . [and] however foully the
enemy may act . . . he will abide by decent concepts of humanity and civilization" [brackets in original].[74] The fact that the US War Department released Mac-
Arthur's statement suggests that the United States understood that a chemical
war had started, but in the press, not on the battlefield. The United States could
not afford to be tarred by the brush that it used gas, even if the United States was
not legally banned by the General Gas Protocol from doing so. The use of gas

would risk membership in the club of "humanity and civilization." The United States wanted to assure the world that it would not forfeit its position there, while simultaneously suggesting that Japan might.

Reports later in the war indicated that Japan increasingly feared the Allied gas threat and took more pains to avoid the enemy deploying it. By October of 1943, it was thought that "[r]ecent evidence indicates an intention on the part of Japan to restrict her gas warfare activities to defense, except in retaliation." Proof included fewer gas units in the Japanese army.[75] Allied wariness about the Japanese could not be laid to rest. Local Japanese commanders retained the ability and authority to wield gas. Also, as with Germany at the end of the war, the analysts noted, there was the potential for Japan to start using gas on a wide scale out of desperation. On November 29, 1943, US ambassador Clarence Gauss, in Chungking, offered his opinion that, even now, the Japanese, if they "suddenly launched [gas] on a large scale . . . [could] over-run Kunming and Chungking and could probably take Changsha."[76] Whether he was correct or not, his report was worth considering and became part of intelligence analysis.

A few weeks earlier, the gas war had reached a kind of standoff. The worst of the threat of Japanese-originated gas deployment was over. Likewise, the British and the US intelligence staff agreed that "it would be most disadvantageous to initiate chemical warfare against Japan at this time." The situation and attitude toward gas had not reversed completely, although it was starting to change.[77]

Even as the United States defended itself against the Japanese to win public opinion, there were also signs in public and private that the nation might be warming to the idea of using CW, an attitude that had international repercussions. For example, on January 30, 1944, the New York Times published "A War Without Quarter Forecast in the Pacific," explicitly suggesting that recent atrocity stories coming out of the Pacific meant that US public opinion might be more open to gas, if not fully supportive of gas use.[78] On February 15, 1944, Cordell Hull, the secretary of state, received a letter from Amleto Giovanni Cicognani, the archbishop of Laodicea in Turkey, writing on behalf of the Vatican. It conveyed that the Japanese ambassador to the church had been worried about the implications of that newspaper story and thought that it suggested the US military would use CW in the near future. It also said that the Japanese proclaimed their innocence in any charges of using gas in China and that the nation promised not to use gas if the United States did not. That the Japanese raised the idea that the United States might use gas and raised it through an institution that could wield moral power suggested a level of desperation.[79]

When both bodies approached the United States, US leaders debated about what to say, to whom, and when. The Department of State consulted the Joint

Chiefs of Staff and considered the secretary of war and secretary of the navy's earlier 1942 rejections of gas.[80] Officials mulled over FDR's policy and the United States' official position.[81] While the Joint Staff Planners recommended responding to Cicognani with a brief letter from Admiral Leahy, chief of staff to the president, reminding him of FDR's 1943 warning, it also suggested ignoring the *New York Times* article.[82] The journalist's article was "the expression of an individual citizen and has no official standing."[83] The Joint Chiefs of Staff agreed.[84] There the matter ended, after taking up the attention of several high-level groups over the course of two months. The next month, only weeks before the scheduled invasion date for Normandy, the matter raised its head again. This time, Dr. Marc Peter, of the International Committee of the Red Cross (ICRC), another neutral, globally-recognized institution, wrote directly to the US secretary of state Cordell Hull, expressing the same concerns that Japan had shared with the Holy See.[85] The Joint Chiefs opted to respond as they had to the previous letter.[86] It is likely that the Joint Chiefs wanted to keep this conversation as quiet as possible, hesitating to give more fodder to the propaganda war and to the idea that the United States might use gas—at least until the United States was ready to deploy it.

Japan probably did doubt the sincerity of the Allied promises not to start a gas war; the Allies felt the same way about theirs, and the United States' refusal to sign the Geneva Gas Protocol meant that it would be relatively easy for the United States to change its gas policy unilaterally and instantaneously. Furthermore, Japan's gas policy had little to do with its own allies, as the Combined Intelligence Committee had noted, so it was unlikely that Japan would believe that the United States felt firmly bound by its allies' restrictions.[87]

The United States was not the only one mulling over the gas threats and use in Asia. In June of 1943, the British Chiefs of Staff sent a group of men from the different services under Major-General John Sydney Lethbridge, accompanied by advisers from the United States and Canada selected by the Combined Chiefs of Staff, around the Pacific and Indian theaters. The committee examined the situation and consulted with allies from various countries, "with the duty of investigating at first-hand what types and scales of equipment, and what organisation of units would be required for the most effective and economic prosecution of the war against JAPAN."[88] The Lethbridge Mission brief allowed them to "go where they pleased," and required them to consider various issues, including chemical warfare.[89]

Although CW was not particularly popular among the Chiefs of Staff in London, the Lethbridge Mission firmly supported the possibility of using gas. Consulting locally stationed experts from the United States and Australia, the mission concluded that chemical warfare could be used "effectively" against Japan "to secure decisive strategic and tactical advantages," partly because tropical climates increased the persistence of gas and because Japan was losing its ability to "retaliate."[90] More emphatically, in his Interim Report on Chemical Warfare, Lethbridge concluded: "I am of the opinion that the Jap[anese] forces in the field will not be able to survive C.W. attack. This attack, however, must be administered with complete ruthlessness and on a vast scale, employing a mixture of chemical agents that will not only cause mutilation and death, but by their very diversity of effect create terror and panic in the minds of the victims."[91]

The debate had opened, and some influential experts who had been in the field were in favor of using gas. Other experts expressed some doubts. As Major-General Gerald Brunskill, of the British Directorate of Special Weapons and Vehicles, wrote, "the recommendation for ruthless chemical attack is not supported by any quantitative appreciation of the scale on which it must be carried out to be effective."[92]

Winston Churchill pushed his advisers to report about the possibility to him.[93] The Inter-Services Committee on Chemical Warfare prepared a report for the Chiefs of Staff Committee in late July 1944.[94] The firm conclusion was that Britain was not ready to wage a gas war against Japan, either now, while Germany was still a threat, or for some time after victory had been achieved in Europe, for some of the same reasons that the United States had mentioned. There were also some factors that were specific to Britain's position. The United Kingdom had stored the majority of its poison gas at home, ready to retaliate against Germany if it attacked. To fight Japan, the United Kingdom would need to expand production greatly or to transfer its stock to the Pacific. The latter would be possible after the United Kingdom was no longer at risk from Germany, but this would take time.[95] Furthermore, the United States did not have enough variety of gases ready itself; it had only mustard, not nonpersistent gases, ready to be air dropped, and even then, "stocks of gas weapons are inadequate" for a sustained campaign.[96] There would be enough weapons for ground deployment, but that was because the army did not have a large role in an envisioned gas war, unlike the air forces.[97] In addition, the British did not think their men would be prepared to face the enemy's response in kind for six months to a year; they knew from research that defensive gear required adjustments for tropical climates. It would take at least half a year to reequip the men properly, not to mention adding six and a half pounds of gear to each person and eighty tons to each division. The methods of supply and communication would have to change too. The concern was not just for the European troops; "native[s]" did not have defensive gear, and thus supplies would have to be delivered without their help.[98]

During this same phase in the war, General Porter recognized that non-military issues demanded consideration. In one memo, Porter stated his conviction that the United States had legality as well as justification on its side since Japan used gas against China even after FDR's warning, neither Japan nor the United States had signed Geneva, and the British had reserved the right of retaliation when they ratified the Geneva Gas Protocol.[99] He thought that the United States would be in the right if it used gas; it could call its actions retaliation, and the US public might even "force the issue" if "shocked at large casualties and Japanese barbarities."[100] More practically, he believed that if the United States waited until Germany had been defeated, then neither of the main Axis powers would be in a position to use gas against the Allies "decisively." He even assumed that Britain, the United States' wariest ally when it came to using gas, would agree, so there would be no diplomatic or strategic repercussions if the United States began using CW.[101]

The Army's most enthusiastic supporter of gas warfare did not necessarily want to wait until the European conflict ended, so he went a step further. At the end of 1943, Porter wrote to Lt. General Joseph McNarney, the deputy chief of staff, opening his letter with a prediction that "gas warfare appears imminent within the next few weeks" in Europe or the Pacific. As a result, and because he saw his role as including serving as a "technical" adviser to General Marshall, Porter drafted a plan for using gas in the Pacific theater, a plan that he hoped Marshall would study.[102] Porter made a strong case, opening his memorandum with a reminder about how many US casualties, how many supplies, and how much time it cost to take Betio, part of Tarawa, from the Japanese: "Over 3,000 tons of high explosive munitions were used against the island of Betio, which is less than one square mile in area and which was defended by about 4,000 Japanese marines. . . . the island was taken only after a four-day battle by landing forces and at the expense of nearly 4,000 American casualties."[103]

He then offered a vision of the conquest of Tarawa, if only gas had been used. It would have taken just nine hundred tons of mustard gas and a four-day wait while the Japanese were incapacitated by the gas. No "material loss" to US forces would have resulted because US anti-gas equipment was quite strong (especially compared to that available to the Japanese).[104] Porter also recognized that the Japanese could not target US civilians since they did not have the airpower or the gas inventory to do so; he did admit that US military and Chinese targets would have to weather some retaliation. Although the Chinese were not as well protected by masks and other gear, he thought their low density of soldiers and increased Allied air protection would help minimize any Japanese retaliation.[105] Porter ignored the possibility that Japan might strike out against Chinese civilians, Indians, and prisoners of war; he was too focused on military targets and may have assumed Japan would be too.

Porter made his point that gas could be a great advantage militarily when used on the offensive in the right situation. He was firm and confident: "Gas is a decisive weapon. Properly used it can shorten the war and save many lives."[106] While that had not been the case in World War I, this was a different war, and Porter planned to use his weapons for a new purpose against a different foe in a dissimilar climate. One of the characteristics of mustard gas is that it could harm on contact and via vapors over the course of several days. Research had shown that it emanated for up to three days after being deployed in the tropics. For these reasons it would be particularly effective during missions to kill or wound Japanese in jungle bunkers, and it would limit their mobility in areas where the liquid mustard gas fell.[107] (In World War I mustard sometimes burned through the soles of boots creating a temporary no man's land where it fell.)

The CWS had researched other gases, using Florida, Panama, and areas of the Pacific as testing zones in some rough locales, hoping to get accurate information about the effects of gas in rain, mud, and humidity.[108] The locales were often unpleasant. As Colonel George Unmacht of the CWS wrote to his superior, General Alden Waitt, the location in Makua on Oahu in Hawaii was so rough that he nicknamed it Makuacanal because it reminded him of living situations on Guadalcanal.[109] The results suggested that gases such as CC, a nonpersistent but lethal compound, could be dropped by planes and "penetrate bunkers, dugouts, and pillboxes" as well.[110] This would allow for a more rapid follow-up by Allied forces, since they would not have to wait as long for the chemicals to clear.

With some effort, Porter predicted that the United States could be ready to launch a "large-scale use of our gas within sixty days" for deployment from the air and 120 days for launching from land, if enough weapons reached the Pacific and with sufficient chemical experts dedicated to the tasks.[111] Over the next two years, US assessments suggested that by the beginning of 1944 there was enough mustard gas—but not phosgene—in the theater for "routine chemical warfare" although not intense "retaliation."[112] One goal of retaliation was to produce a psychologically overwhelming attack that would make the enemy regret using gas because it would punish the aggressors severely; it contrasted with more efficient, smaller military launches with specific tactical goals.[113] Still, common sense suggests that once a belligerent released CW through either approach, each side was likely to use gas repeatedly and widely.

Thus, despite Porter's careful arguments, General Thomas Handy, the assistant chief of staff, argued that the Operations Division (OPD) failed to endorse offensive gas use as soon as possible in the Pacific partly because chemical warfare might not be contained.[114] The United States could find itself fighting a global gas war, and at the end of 1943, the Allies did not want a gas war erupting in Europe, especially because of any action they took in the Pacific. With D-Day approaching, no one wanted to give the Germans "an excuse to use a potent weapon such as gas, which could cause the failure of OVERLORD-ANVIL."[115] Amphibious landings were challenging in the best of circumstances, and gas would only increase the level of difficulty. It was tricky to synchronize all the other elements, even before adding gas to the mix. In addition, gas benefited the defender, the Axis, and the Axis would use gas to push the Allies away in the future, in the OPD's eyes.[116] Still, Handy noted that the United States might well face gas warfare "on all active fronts" started by someone else, and it should be ready.[117]

It is interesting that Handy's other argument against opening a gas war in the near future had to do with an issue that Porter ignored, namely the vulnerability of the British, Australians, Russians, and Chinese. (The New Zealanders were not listed, but presumably they were included.) While North America was out of reach for the Japanese, as Handy noted, thus protecting the Canadian and US civilians, the same was not true of the other Allies. Furthermore, it seems clear the OPD, for one, was not convinced that Japan (or even Germany) would limit any gas targets to the military. The US allies' vulnerability should be a reason for the United States to limit its own actions.[118]

Handy's memo did not rule out offensive gas use ever, though, despite FDR's policies. Porter had made some good arguments, but the timing was not right, nor was it solely a US decision. Six months made a difference in this war, though. In 1944, the Allied military began reconsidering the idea of using CBW for the final defeat of Japan in a serious way.[119] In February, General Brehon Somervell, the commanding general of the Army Service Forces, the section of the Army that supervised the CWS, asked for a full-scale study to assess preparedness of the United States as well as the Chinese.[120] The US general Alden M. Waitt demonstrated that some of the mental groundwork for Allied use of gas existed when he reminded, and perhaps tried to persuade, the Canadian Chemical Warfare Inter-Service Board that the Japanese had used gas often enough that the Allies could use it themselves, claiming they were using it on the legitimate grounds of retaliation.[121] No decisions were made yet, but the Western Allies took another step closer to unleashing CW on Japan.

## Looking ahead to Formosa

As the war continued, there were new incentives for the Allies to become more proactive with gas; it was not simply that former obstacles had lessened. Now there were political reasons to use CW. As the war dragged on, there was widespread concern that the US public was becoming increasingly war weary. For instance, journalists, enabled by a change in military and propaganda policy approved by FDR and the secretary of state, Henry Stimson, had begun showing dead US soldiers to the home front in an effort to remind them that even though the tide had turned in favor of the Allies, the war still needed to be fought and at a high cost.[122] With regard to CW, this meant that there was a suspicion that the war needed to be won in as timely a manner as possible, and gas might be the key to that. Some in the US leadership thought public opinion in the United States would "demand" gas against the Japanese at some point; civilians would see CW as a way to end the war as quickly as possible and with as few US casualties as possible.[123] After all, even Roosevelt, the holdout against gas up until this point, had, as historian David Reynolds argued, become "the pioneer of technowar: massive firepower [in this case bombers and the atomic bomb program] applied with the intent of minimizing US casualties."[124] Gas might well be next, even for him.

The British also began to consider offensive gas use more widely in 1944. General George Giffard, the commander-in-chief of the 11th Army Group, South East Asia Command, wrote to Lieutenant-General Sir Edwin Morris, the chief of the general staff, General Headquarters in India, in February of 1944 about chemical warfare, musing that offensive gas use against the Japanese might shorten the war (by winnowing into bunkers, for instance) while the Japanese were less prepared for such a conflict. However, there were concerns specific to Britain, such as India's vulnerability as well as more general concerns about the "stigma" of using gas in the global eye, in addition to practical issues such as supplying and decontaminating soldiers or Japanese retaliation against POWs.[125] It was not an easy choice.

As both the war in Europe came closer to ending and the Japanese became weaker, yet no closer to surrendering, deploying gas increasingly seemed like an appealing option for reasons of morale, politics, and resources. The Chiefs of Staff Committee directed the Inter-Services Committee on Chemical Warfare to utilize investigations the Allies conducted on poison gas and to assess CW use in the tropics.[126] The Allies considered whether to use it in an assault on Formosa (now Taiwan), planned for February of 1945 at the earliest; by then the Allies could move more of their equipment and manpower to the Pacific.[127] Formosa seemed a likely candidate because of its importance in setting the foundation for Operation Downfall, the invasion of Japan. Also, as the British Inter-Services Committee on Chemical Warfare reported to the Chiefs of Staff Committee in January of 1945, an attack on Formosa could be a model for other amphibious attacks, and "we were advised that the operation might be a critical one, on the success or failure of which a rapid conclusion or prolongation of the war against Japan might depend."[128] In particular, gas might allow the Allies to achieve quicker victories, with fewer conventional and chemical casualties than they would have anticipated the previous year.[129] To do this, the first aim would be "directed towards securing the maximum panic and confusion and fatal [enemy] casualties."[130] At the same time, the British Inter-Services Committee on Chemical Warfare, in an examination of the impact of a potential gas attack on Japan, stated that "So far as is known the state of anti-gas training of Japanese forces is good and any shortcomings are likely to be quickly remedied after the first shock."[131] Victory by gas would not be automatic.

However, the plan set out by the Inter-Services Committee on Chemical Warfare did not mention the civilians on Formosa; either the planners ignored them, they did not care, or they assumed that the gas attacks would be able to target the Japanese defenders and not catch the civilians up in the backlash or as collateral damage. Considering the British were the ones who worried most about its own civilians becoming targets, whether at home or in the Empire, this is quite interesting. The committee did caution that it was not considering "the political effects" or the ripple effects of using gas on Formosa and how that might impact other operations or theaters, so it seems it was punting that issue.[132]

The proposed benefits were much like the ones Porter suggested when he sent his report to Marshall: Gas bombing in advance of the invasion could remove the Japanese ability to defend the island.[133] Also, if a CW attack went as planned, the takeover of Formosa could be faster and much less costly than a conventional attack.[134] Of course, predicting what would actually happen was challenging since, as the report authors noted, "At the present time there is no indication when the operation will be carried out and what forces will be employed. Nor is it certain whether the objective will be the capture of the whole or only part of the island."[135] There were numerous other factors that the committee considered, including weather, climate, and topography.[136] It also incorporated information available from the United States, specifically the Combined Operations Headquarters and the CWS's list of targets and the types and amount of gases needed to hit them.[137] Clearly any attack would be a combined effort in terms of knowledge and resources; the UK authors noted that neither the United States nor the United Kingdom had enough gas on hand right now for such a massive deployment, but they were confident the United States had the production capability to rectify that.[138]

Japan had sufficient quantities of gas for retaliation, but the Allies expected their naval-based air superiority to cut into the enemy's ability to respond by air, if not by land, in a limited fashion.[139] Thus, besides preparing for launching gas, organizers noted that Allied soldiers would have to wear anti-gas gear to face the remnants of Allied gas that might linger and any Japanese gas launched in retaliation. All the necessary gear would decrease soldiers' freedom of movement.[140] The men would be uncomfortable wearing capes and respirators, both because the gear was bulky and because of the temperature. Added to that would be the increased anxiety soldiers would feel, facing such a weapon for the first time. These burdens would continue too; once gas was introduced in the war, soldiers would have to be prepared to face it thereafter; one side or the other would be likely to keep it in play. On the logistics end, additional equipment would strain the Allied supply lines further since they would have to find transport space for anti-gas equipment and decontamination materials.[141]

If gas did not work as planned, "the consequences may be serious, or even disastrous, to the success of this critical operation," and there were a lot of complex factors to balance.[142] One of the biggest problems was timing: How quickly could the Japanese decontaminate a site? How effective were the Japanese anti-gas measures? Even harder to predict was the weather, a factor that could influence the effectiveness of gas, and that could not be predicted months ahead of time. Would the planes needed to carry gas be available? Overall, as the planners recognized: "the launching of the assault at the correct moment would be more a matter of luck than the result of careful timing."[143] Gas use might devastate the enemy, but it was a military gamble.

The fact that there were other options, namely using high explosives, made the risks of using gas even less attractive. And, in fact, even if the Allies planned to use gas, if CW failed to bring victory, the attackers would have to resort to high explosives as well as face retaliatory gas attacks, making it all the harder to continue the assault.[144] High explosives might lead to a bloody fight—of the sort the Allies had experienced on the Pacific islands already—but they were more predictable and easier to use. For example, the timing of CW used for "drenching beach defences" would have to be coordinated with the landing because the effect of gas might be delayed; with high explosives, the bombardment could continue up to the moment of the landing. Gas was also more of a weapon against men than machines, whereas high explosives could target both. That meant that any guns that high explosives destroyed would be unavailable, whereas a gassed crew might be able to use those batteries for a time while injured, or they might be replaced.[145]

The report was strewn with doubts, which made the overall recommendation against gas warfare unsurprising: The Inter-Services Committee was too risk-averse to support the plan. It did not reject it because of a dislike of gas, however, but rather because there were too many uncertainties about whether the Allies could launch the attack so successfully that the Japanese would not fight back with gas. This might be possible logistically, but the British Chiefs of Staff were not convinced because it was hard to predict the weather, challenging to ensure the necessary split-second timing in an amphibious attack even without gas, and bothersome to stockpile all of the needed supplies.[146] The Chiefs of Staff had some valid concerns, but these were practical, not the emotional ones based on fear or legalistic ones that were widespread a decade earlier.

And in fact, the committee ended its report on a more far-reaching negative note. Looking beyond Formosa, it concluded that "Gas is not a suitable weapon for employment in support of an amphibious operation."[147] That was quite a statement, since the military conditions in favor of gas use were unlikely to become any better as the war went on. Still, this was just one opinion. Moreover, technically it rejected gas in one kind of operation, not all missions. The door for gas use was still open, and other British factions continued to support it.

Porter's argument that gas would have saved time and manpower on Tarawa may have helped open his colleagues' minds to the idea of gas, but it was the plans to invade Formosa that demonstrated that the Allies began to seriously consider using CW in future battles. Perhaps these never would have come to pass, even if the Joint Chiefs had not decided for other reasons to invade Luzon and later target Okinawa instead of Formosa.[148] However, the significance of this was critical; now even British planners openly calculated how and whether to incorporate gas in future attacks. This was a dramatic change in attitude and approach.

## Crop Destruction: Getting Closer to Deploying Gas

Britain and the United States also mulled deploying chemicals to defeat the foe in a nontraditional way. Even during World War I, when nations were focused largely on the global conflict, countries experimented with pesticides to help their own agricultural production.[149] That was a forerunner of British research into chemicals that became known as 1313 and 1414, developed in late 1942 by Imperial Chemical Industries (ICI) and the Agricultural Research Council respectively.[150] British scientists categorized these two compounds as crop destroyers since they targeted the plants, like rice, on which the Japanese depended. (1313, code-named LN.33, destroyed cereals and rice, while 1414, code-named LN.32, did the same for root crops.)[151] These seemed to be an attractive method for weakening the Japanese resistance.

However, the scientists trod a very fine line here. They did not want to be involved in anything that was technically chemical or biological weaponry.

Crop destroyers did not produce illness, so they were not BW, even though they targeted living organisms and, if effective, could induce starvation. According to the Foreign Office legal counsel, they were also not CW because they did not harm humans or animals directly, even if humans or animals ate tainted plants. This was important because the Geneva Gas Protocol viewed CBW as weapons that hurt or killed humans. The scientists were so aware of this that they even calculated whether the crop destroyers could kill people if they were ingested.[152] The prediction was that one would have to consume a field full, more or less, of any of the crop-destruction products before it would be problematic.[153]

Still, the scientists viewed crop destroyers as CBW effectively, but perhaps without the moral taint; the notes and reports about them are located in the CBW files. Yet the British refrained from deploying them because it would take at least two years to produce enough to use effectively. They also planned to offer research about them to the United States.[154] The United States had been undertaking its own research into crop destruction with a compound similar to 1414, but, as far as the British knew, did not have a version of 1313. Since ICI thought that the United States might be able to expand field testing on rice for 1313, if it knew about it, the company was willing to share the information.[155] As Lord Cherwell, one of Churchill's scientific advisers recommended, and as the prime minister agreed, the United States "could probably make the material much more quickly [and] . . . might wish to use it against the Japanese."[156] That did not mean that the British should abdicate all participation in crop destruction research. It is worth noting that Cherwell thought Britain ought to keep track of the new knowledge since "use of such material might be valuable after the war for keeping order in the world."[157] Churchill, himself, simply thought that Britain should be able to defend against similar weapons, if necessary.[158]

The US experts conducted their own balancing act between the spirit and the letter of the law, using scientific nuances to find their equilibrium. When George W. Merck, of Merck & Co. and a World War II consultant to Secretary of War Henry Stimson, weighed in on crop destruction, he pointed out that 1313 and 1414 were "Not Classed as Poisons" for the same reasons the British Foreign Office exonerated them.[159] Major General Myron C. Cramer, the judge advocate general, generated a detailed brief that gave the United States legal permission to use crop-destroying chemicals, having surveyed both treaties and customary law. As he pointed out, not only did those laws not prohibit crop destruction chemicals with these particular characteristics but also, according to several legal sources, "a belligerent is entitled to deprive the enemy of food and water, and to destroy his sources of supply whether in depots, in transit on land, or growing in his fields."[160] There was some concern about the public perception of these chemicals, though. The secretary of war, for example, wanted a "study . . . of the possible U.S. public reaction."[161]

Perhaps more relevant to the debate were the questions of what would happen in the field if it were used. The United States considered plans to use it on islands skipped during island hopping and later on crops in the home islands themselves as part of Operation Downfall, the plan to invade the Japanese home islands—assuming the United States would be capable of deploying it in 1946.[162] Would Japan perceive crop-destruction chemicals—even if they were not true CW in Allied eyes—as an excuse to deploy CW?[163] Once again, Allies worried about pretexts for Axis first strikes with CW, especially since they believed the Japanese might use gas if they thought it would benefit them. In February 1945, the Joint Intelligence Committee noted "in the final defence of Japan" the enemy might deploy CW "as a last desperate resort and at whatever cost to their civilian population," duplicating the extremes to which they went during the island-hopping portions of the war.[164] There was some awareness, therefore, that the Japanese might react much as the British had planned to respond if they had been invaded.

The deciding factor was quite different, though. While the Joint Planning Staff-Joint Logistics Committee Subcommittee approved the general policy of using crop destruction, it was concerned about the burden of its effects during occupation. Once the United States defeated Japan and occupied it, the United States would be responsible for feeding the former Axis power.[165] Ruining the rice crop would make occupation even more onerous than it would be anyway.[166] There were humanitarian elements here—the United States did not want to starve people in peacetime and recognized a responsibility to care for an occupied nation. This was matched by self-interest, though, and a hesitance to do something so close to the line, at least without more incentive.

Not everyone in power agreed, especially the navy. As General George Lincoln, described by the New York Times as "Marshall's principal planner for . . . the projected invasion of Japan," wrote to the army's Policy Section: the navy "do[es] not want the Chiefs of Staff to go on record in writing in this matter and consider that the chemical agent [i.e, the crop destroyer] can be used in bypassed areas without any action by the Chiefs of Staff," a comment implying that the other branch did not want the United States tainted by the topic, even behind closed doors, whether with an eye to history or to leaks is unclear.[167] Yet, it seemed that the navy not only demonstrated a willingness to use crop destruction agents but also did not require the highest levels of approval for it.

Thus, even if 1313 and 1414 were not, technically, CBW, they had the ability to trigger the same revulsion. As with poison gas, we do not know if the Allies would have used crop destroyers in 1946 to defeat Japan, although General

Lincoln explicitly expressed willingness to consider that option if the war continued.[168] Any extensive plans for the United States to use them would have involved the war continuing beyond 1945, and longer for the British by the time they produced substances in sufficient quantities.[169] The war ended before a final decision had to be made, although by the time that happened, there existed detailed plans to use full-fledged poison gas offensively.

## Ending the War: Olympic

History, prejudice, fear, and predictions all led to the idea that gas would make an appearance during World War II, whether courtesy of the Allies or Axis. Unlike during the interwar period, by 1945 the Allies were no longer convinced that chemical warfare would break out, but both logic and fear led them to think the threat was still present. As one report suggested, even late in the war the Japanese, perhaps just locally, even if there were no hope of survival, might use gas in an effort to make the invader pay.[170] Now the focus was on whether—and how—to use gas against Japan in offensive attacks to end the war sooner and with fewer Western casualties.

The only possibly legitimate gas target now that Formosa had been dismissed, according to the Joint Logistics Committee, was "Japan Proper," presumably the home islands. Japanese troops could be found in China, the Philippines, and Korea, too, but US gas policy required that gas be used against an enemy in retaliation, not initiated against an enemy in an allied or victim's land.[171] It also thought that justifying gas use on the grounds of retaliation required some sort of substantial use by the Japanese. Exactly what that would be was never made clear, but alleged "[s]mall scale use of chemical agents," and "local use," which had been reported from China and the Pacific, "[s]o far . . . have been considered as insufficient for the Allies to accuse the Japanese of gas warfare."[172] The "so far" meant that the judgment about what was acceptable for retaliation might change, but for the moment, it seems that FDR's ultimatum required a Japanese policy condoning gas use on a widespread basis before Allied retaliation would be triggered. If the purpose of his warning was to deter gas use by the Japanese when they were at their zenith and could really inflict harm on Allied soldiers and all civilians, then it makes sense, as the Axis power retreated in July of 1945, not to launch gas warfare unless and until the Allies really wanted to do so. They did not need to use Japanese small scale use as a pretext.

To be prepared, the CWS developed detailed plans about how to deploy gas during attacks on Japan. These attacks on the home islands would be part of

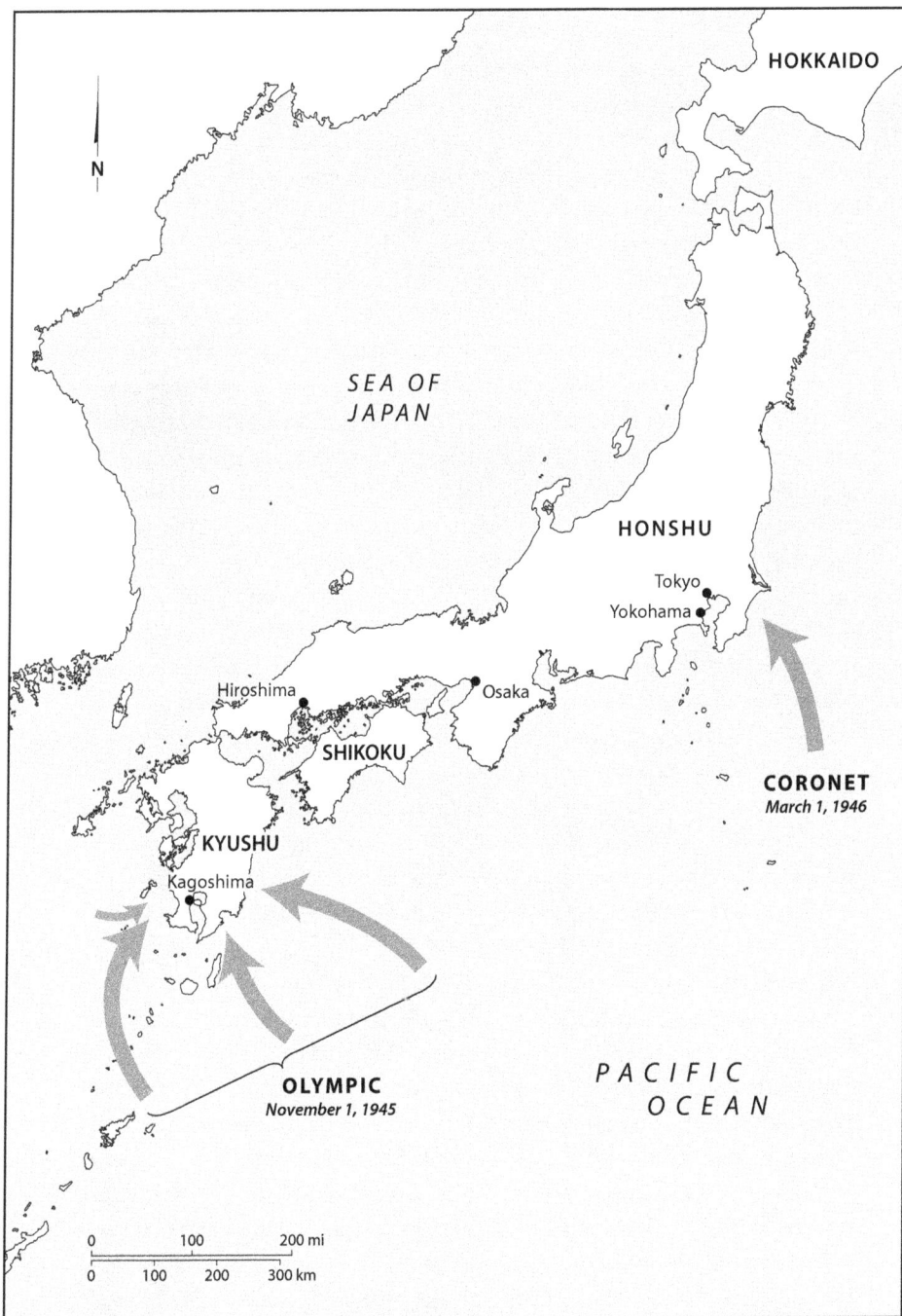

**MAP 2.** Operation Downfall, the plan to invade the home islands of Japan, included two major components, Olympic and Coronet. As part of the preparation process, the American military had engaged in detailed discussions about including poison gas to weaken the Japanese defenses. (Map by Bill Nelson.)

Operation Downfall, an attack that would be divided into Operation Olympic, expected to start on November 1, 1945 (X-Day), and followed up by Coronet on March 1, 1946 (Y-Day).[173]

Plans carefully distinguished between using gas tactically (i.e., in support of other fighting efforts) and strategically (i.e., in unlimited amounts, much like it would be released during a retaliatory attack). The latter was "attack . . . against centers of war production, transportation and communication to disorganize the enemy's national life and break his will to resist . . . with overwhelming strikes against vital target areas carried out in such rapid succession that the enemy does not have time to recover his poise and replace losses before a decisive blow by the invading forces is struck." According to the CWS, the benefit of gas was its multipronged effectiveness: it could reduce casualties substantially, perhaps even 30–50 percent, while leading to a quicker end to the war. More immediately, it could hinder Japanese defenses, and it could "break . . . [its] will."[174] Breaking Japan's will required targeting cities, a technique that previously had mixed success in World War II using conventional air power. Rotterdam had fallen quickly, but London, for example, had withstood months of assaults. Even dropping gas might not lead to inevitable success. Still, the CWS thought that planes from ground bases could drop a combination of gas and high explosives that would target more than seventeen million people in the first fifteen days of Coronet by breaking windows with the high explosives that would allow phosgene to overwhelm the poor Japanese military and civilian defenses, creating casualties and, it hoped, not just fear but outright "panic."[175] Then, once US troops had landed, gas could be deployed against entrenched Japanese troops in caves and other challenging locales.[176] Testing in caves and bunkers in Utah backed up the feasibility of this proposal.[177]

Despite all of the potential benefits, the CWS recommended delaying gas use until Coronet; they wanted to avoid giving the Japanese several months between Olympic and Coronet to prepare for gas attacks.[178] Yet, there were reasons to use it in Olympic: the Army could follow up instantly on the advantages provided by hitting the Japanese with gas; Japan would not have had a chance to prepare responses. By Coronet, Japan would be less capable of launching retaliation, even with gas.[179] To achieve advantages in either operation, the military had to develop detailed gas plans, and it did. The United States considered the specific units that would be available, the cities to be targeted, the date to be selected, the ordnance to deploy, and other details.[180] The report advised, for example,

On the basis of CWS [Chemical War Service] estimates that persistent chemicals remain effective for 7 to 10 days under average conditions it would appear than an area of approximately 250 sq[uare] mi[les] could be kept contaminated and made less useful or denied altogether to the enemy. Roads and railways might be blocked at vulnerable points in central Kyushu, where the Kyushu-Sammyaku range restricts passage to narrow coastal corridors. The Simonoseki area and the base areas of Yawata and Fukuoka in northern Kyushu and airfields in Kyushu appear to be critical points which are suitable as objectives for chemical bombardment . . . [181]

The British gas experts still had more doubts about using gas during an amphibious landing (as opposed to after it). General Porter responded emphatically by arguing that US soldiers would carry defensive equipment anyway, so withholding gas during the landing would not save them from any burdens. More importantly, gas would hamstring the Japanese when used appropriately. US air superiority and the plentiful use of gas would overcome any challenges inherent in trying to synchronize gas deployment with the rest of the landing, according to his calculations.[182]

By July of 1945, almost exactly a month before the *Enola Gay* dropped a nuclear bomb on Hiroshima, the detailed gas plan was ready for execution, even if it had not yet been approved by all of the relevant authorities. At the grassroots level, the United States would have to make sure the public was behind it. The War Department doubted that the public would endorse it, but some military experts thought that could be changed. As a memo to General Lincoln in early June of 1945 argued, "Roosevelt damned it pretty thoroughly as 'desperate and barbarous,' . . . Before we use it, therefore, we should certainly consider the reaction of our own population at home, the soldiers engaged, who will be subject of retaliatory action by the Japanese, the reaction of the Japanese, our Allies, and the rest of the world." The author thought that public opinion, if it could not be changed, might outweigh the benefits of gas. However, another report thought that the government could "sell the idea" of using gas.[183]

Although these reports and comments did not refer to opinion polls, Gallup did survey the US public repeatedly during the war. Starting in September of 1944 and ending in mid-June of 1945, the organization asked several questions seeking to find out why and when the United States might be ready to use gas. The questions varied with respect to the targets (Japanese soldiers or cities), the motivation for gas use (to "shorten the war," if Japan "execute[s] any American bomber pilots," and to save soldiers' lives), and the dates when the survey occurred.[184] While there was never a majority that approved of gas use, the numbers of supporters grew—although not in a straight line—over the nine months to approximately 40 percent. Those who objected decreased, and those with no opinion increased.[185] If the war had continued, it seems likely that this trend would have persisted as war-weariness increased and if, as the War Department suggested, the government promulgated pro-CW propaganda, especially if it were tied to the already increasing revelations about the bloody costs of the Pacific War.

As scholar Michael Sherry pointed out, US morale was such a concern late in the war that General Marshall "wondered if the nation would even stay the course."[186] Despite the lack of enthusiastic popular support for gas, it is reasonable to believe that the military, and perhaps even the United States government, would have promoted and perhaps engaged in gas use against Japan to win the war quickly, save US lives, and maintain the United States's will to fight.

More immediately, the decision makers in the JCS mulled it over, and it became fodder for political discussion in the United States. General Marshall had been raising the question of using gas after discussing the bomb in a meeting with Secretary of War Stimson at the end of May 1945, although the way he phrased it was more substantial than that. As Assistant Secretary of War John J. McCloy's record of the conversation stated, Marshall proposed "new weapons and tactics to cope with the care and last ditch defense tactics of the suicidal Japanese. He sought to avoid the attrition we were suffering from such fanatical but hopeless defense methods." He suggested gas, specifically, as well as unnamed weapons: use it "on the outlying islands where operations were now going on or were about to take place. He spoke of the type of gas that might be employed. It did not need to be our newest and most potent—just drench them and sicken them so that the fight would be taken out of them—saturate an area, possibly with mustard, and just stand off."[187] Marshall recognized the physical and emotional cost of the island campaigns the United States had faced as it slogged toward the heart of the Japanese empire.

John McCloy, who does not seem to have been privy to those in the military who had already considered offensive plans, followed up on Marshall's comments. He wrote to Marshall in mid-June of 1945 to ask whether completely offensive (as opposed to retaliatory) gas use should be studied in detail. He justified this by arguing that "Such a study will enable us to appraise our policy with greater certainty in the face of the public pressure for the use of gas, which may develop as our casualties rise due to the Okinawa cave type of Japanese defense."[188] He, too, was worried about war weariness, as was the chief of staff's staff, who reported that the US people have "been conditioned against the use of chemical warfare," but they might have to "balance" that "against the additional cost in American youth, American resources and the length of this war."[189]

Marshall's support of gas use continued into July. The leading generals and admirals discussed the subject, some supporting the use of gas and some not.[190] Admiral Ernest King, chief of naval operations, did not want to rush into any decisions; he was more worried about shipping space, as were some of his fellow commanders.[191] One problem with launching an extensive gas war—whether for retaliatory or offensive purposes—was that space shortages required CW to get shipping prioritization, and that would be at the price of limiting transport for some other critical supplies. Although the Joint Chiefs of Staff did approve of logistical plans to ensure "minimum stocks of 75 days supply for the Pacific theater and of 90 days supply for the India-Burma and China Theater" of "chemical munitions" by Olympic's start date, it did not direct how this would occur.[192] However, as General Marshall wrote in a 1945 memo, as the Allies gained on the Japanese homeland they now had the potential to deploy more gas and to drop it on new destinations.[193] Ability to use gas, and the feasibility to use it in different ways, could change over time.

At the top, there was even a plan for General Marshall to raise the issue with President Truman, to see if he were willing to reverse President Roosevelt's policy. As one general pointed out, that really would not be the end of the decision-making process, though, even if Truman endorsed gas. The United States was not truly an independent actor; it was part of an alliance. Politically, the United States would have to gain approval from Britain and Canada because of the combined chemical warfare policy the nations had developed earlier in the war. One tactic would be to point out that "the cost of the Pacific War, particularly the cost in lives, is being borne by the United States and not by Great Britain." Presumably, though, the price would be assessed in Chinese lives, too; General Albert Wedemeyer, assigned to work closely with Chiang Kai-Shek, had made CW policy promises to China, which, as a chief of staff's staff report noted, "will be the nation most affected by Japanese [gas] retaliation." The authors also recommended that the United States's proposed plan "should be taken up with Marshal Stalin." While no promises or formal agreement had been made to the Soviet Union yet, there was a very practical reason: "If Russia Later [sic] comes into the war [as promised at Yalta], Marshal Stalin will have a greater interest than the Prime Minister [of Britain] in this matter [fighting in the Pacific]."[194] That was at the international level and was something that the president (Roosevelt at the time the report was written) could take on if he approved the gas plans.[195]

Despite the difficulty of making the decision to use gas, the evidence shows that the pro-gas lobby in the US military was growing in power and argument. It also suggested that the decision makers feared the public's war weariness and thought that United States citizens would embrace gassing the enemy, as unpalatable as that idea had been for years, if that saved US lives. However, Marshall's consultation with Truman never came to pass because the bomb reached fruition.[196] It is worth remembering, though, that Truman was particularly concerned about saving US lives—and that was something gas might have been able to do.[197]

Despite all the wrangling, gas was not used and nuclear weapons, almost immediately after they were created, were. Unlike gas, there was no experience with nuclear weapons. It took dropping the bombs to comprehend the long-lasting damage that atomic armaments could yield. What advisers did know was that dropping a nuclear bomb was an escalation of air power—a bigger bomb. In addition, planners knew the addition of gas might help the Allies dramatically, but it was also clear that CW would be part of a time-consuming, conventional amphibious invasion. In contrast, those who recommended that Truman use the bomb thought it would end the war quickly with as few US casualties as possible, which was FDR's, and later Truman's, goal.[198] At the time, it seemed like an almost miraculous end to a drawn-out war. Finally, because of these and other reasons, there was little debate over the decision to bomb Hiroshima, and there had been decades of extended arguments about the use of gas.[199] There was a different calculus involved in using the atomic bomb rather than gas. All of that helped make it possible to use the new atomic bomb even while gas, a weapon that existed, was harder to approve.

But gas was almost used. What led to these shifts and this effort? It was not a lessened respect for the law on the Allied side, since neither the United States nor Japan had signed the Geneva Gas Protocol. There were some military factors, such as a greater ability to actually launch CW because of an anticipated greater number of planes that would be in the Pacific theater once the war in Europe ended. The supplies shipped from Europe, though, could have been dedicated to high explosives and fire bombing, just as they were in Europe. The number of enemy nations that might have released gas decreased after V-E Day, but the militaries began considering offensive gas use before then. Those factors alone were not enough.

FDR's policy against first use was an issue, but at least some of the experts thought that his mind could be changed. After April 1945, once Truman became president, perhaps he would be willing to reverse US policy. Some even thought that public opinion, rather than condemning gas use, might compel gas use as the war continued. And this is one of the most important reasons for the greater interest in CBW: the war had continued, and the fear of US casualties had grown. Just as Churchill had been willing to use gas as a last resort to defend Britain, if the Germans invaded the United Kingdom; just as intelligence analysts for the British and United States feared that the Axis would use gas out of desperation when they faced defeat; now the United States saw the war weariness as an important threat to maintaining the vigor of the war effort, one that might be worth using gas war to avoid or at least to minimize. The US effort was not about to collapse just yet, of course, but how long could it sustain morale and the sacrifices required to fight the Japanese? It was a danger to consider, at least in the mind of some of the most influential war leaders. The United States did not face the desperation of invasion, but there were other factors that lowered the bar against use enough to make the threats that the United States did face seem enough to justify gas.

The other important reasons had to do with the stage of the war as well as the opponent. Japan was weaker than the Allies who viewed it as a vicious, non-Western opponent. Since World War I, gas had been used or discussed in colonial episodes such as the Italians in Ethiopia or against the Rif, Berbers in Morocco who fought against colonialism in the early 1920s in North Africa. Or, it had been released in situations in which the stronger power, the one who had gas, launched it against a weaker one that was seen as less civilized and perhaps a lower "other," that is, racially or developmentally different as in the Sino-Japanese war of the 1930s. The Japanese, those responsible in US eyes for the Rape of Nanking, the Bataan Death March, the beheading of Doolittle's men, and regular suicidal attacks, were less civilized in the eyes of some and yet sufficiently formidable that a powerful weapon would be helpful. Propaganda had encouraged this view by depicting the Japanese as hordes of pests or insects to be squashed; as less than human. Racism was not overtly discussed, but it is hard to believe it was not a factor that made considering gas easier.

There were a lot of reasons why Japan looked like a potential target. The United States had always had a looser attitude toward gas than the British or many others. It was the United States' insistence on encouraging police forces in the United States to use tear gas in riots and other criminal situations that compelled negotiators of the Geneva Gas Protocol to exclude police use of tear gas from the ban. The United States, therefore, had always had an easier attitude toward some gases, and had shown a willingness to target its own people. Also, historian Edmund Russell has suggested that insecticides and gas have some parallels or connections; this connection may have provided an alternative and less extreme way for some to view gas.[200] Perhaps that helped make it easier to think about aiming it at the Japanese.

The British considered gas seriously, and even planned for a Formosan attack, but they would have needed US help to launch gas there. Also, Britain never embraced it quite as extensively as the United States, and there is no evidence that Churchill or his Chiefs of Staff would have agitated for gas attacks in the Pacific, despite some enthusiasm for it by the Lethbridge Mission. If Churchill, the strongest high-ranking gas proponent in Britain did not agitate for chemical use in Japan, it is unlikely that his successor Clement Attlee would have either. However, there is no reason to think that Britain or Canada would have resisted the United States if the latter had strongly argued for gas, especially since many of the same arguments in favor of gas could be made by the British as well as the United States: the war was dragging on, the threat to the colonies and dominions by a Japanese gas attack was gone, and the United States was more powerful in the Pacific.

Overall, then, the decision about whether to use gas against Japan would have been mainly a US decision, with Britain and, as noted earlier, Canada, participating or experiencing the results, reluctantly or enthusiastically. It might well have been too hard a line to cross. Still, without nuclear weapons, instead of a successful step in the effort to ban widespread use of gas in the future, the legacy of World War I chemical warfare, the Treaty of Versailles, and the Geneva Gas protocol might have been wiped out by a decision by the world's greatest power to launch a CW attack to shorten the war.

# Epilogue

## "I Am Fear": Legacies of Silent Chemical Warfare

Transport for London covers the walls of the subway stations with advertisements, poems, and announcements of all kinds. In the summer of 2014, while I was traveling on the tube in London, one ad caught my eye. It was part of a campaign to generate interest in the First World War Galleries at the Imperial War Museum during the centennial commemoration of the conflict. This poster had a picture of an early gas mask, specifically a tube helmet model. It was not one of the ones common today with snouts and ribbed tubing, but rather it was an early one with what looked more like a canvas bag for the head with a straw projecting from the middle of the face. On the left-hand side of the poster was a story about phosgene gas, a bane of World War I, and the gas mask's relationship to it. Told from the perspective of the helmet, the poster explained the mask's use as well as the costs and benefits of wearing it. The mask was presented as a hero for "saving lives." Yet, the title of the poster was "I am Fear," referring to gas more than to the gas mask. Although the helmet was almost one hundred years old at the time, more than three-quarters of a century after World War II, and even decades after the signing of the most recent anti-gas treaty, the combination of gas and fear resonates.[1] Gas is still alive. One of the messages of this book is that gas, even when not deployed, has been an active weapon that shapes attitudes and actions within and between countries, during times of peace and times of war. The events of the interwar period and World War II demonstrated that. It is still true today.

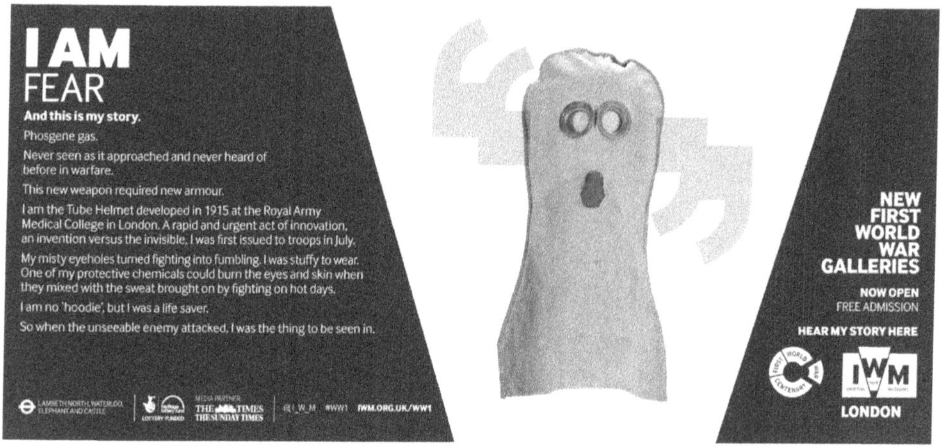
I AM
FEAR
And this is my story.
Phosgene gas.
Never seen as it approached and never heard of before in warfare.
This new weapon required new armour.
I am the Tube Helmet developed in 1915 at the Royal Army Medical College in London. A rapid and urgent act of innovation, an invention versus the invisible, I was first issued to troops in July.
My misty eyeholes turned fighting into fumbling. I was stuffy to wear. One of my protective chemicals could burn the eyes and skin when they mixed with the sweat brought on by fighting on hot days.
I am no 'hoodie', but I was a life saver.
So when the unseeable enemy attacked, I was the thing to be seen in.
LAMBETH NORTH, WATERLOO, ELEPHANT AND CASTLE
LOTTERY FUNDED
MEDIA PARTNER
THE TIMES
THE SUNDAY TIMES
#WW1
IWM.ORG.UK/WW1
NEW
FIRST
WORLD
WAR
GALLERIES
NOW OPEN
FREE ADMISSION
HEAR MY STORY HERE
FIRST WORLD WAR CENTENARY
IWM
LONDON

**FIGURE 8.** This 2014 poster created by Paul Domenet was part of the one-hundred-year commemoration of World War I in Britain. The visual and verbal descriptions of a gas mask, an item intimately connected with chemical weapons, focused on fear. This is the very emotion that many countries, and individuals, felt in the interwar period and World War II when they considered poison gas. (Courtesy of Paul Domenet.)

And it is worth considering what did not happen but could have. In 1940 the Germans bombed the city of Coventry so intensely that the British created a new word to describe it; "blitz" was not enough. To be thoroughly obliterated now was to be "coventrated." Even today the rubble of the cathedral litters the ground as a reminder. Yet Coventry was only one victim of intense conventional aerial bombing. Think of the images of Dresden and Tokyo. These cities were nearly flattened, requiring years to rebuild. How much worse would the damage have been if the World War II bombers had used poison gas in conjunction with high explosives and fire bombs? What if the Germans had used the newer class of chemical weapons (CW), nerve gases, that they had developed?

Certainly, if gas had been widely deployed, the suffering and destruction would not have been evenly distributed. Among the Western Allies, the Canadian and US home fronts would have emerged largely unscathed. Their soldiers, while targets, would have been much better prepared with anti-gas equipment than the soldiers or civilians in nations like China and the Soviet Union, as long as the Germans had not introduced nerve gas to the Allies, who would have been completely surprised and unready for it. The British Empire would have experienced a variety of effects; some, if not most, of the United Kingdom might well have faced gas from invaders, airplanes, and V-weapons at some point in the conflict, while subjects in India largely would have been unprepared. Countries farther from the battlefronts, like New Zealand, did not prepare extensively for CW attacks, predicting that, if they came, they would target sites of military importance like airports. Thus, only emergency personnel in specific areas had gas masks.[2] It was a risky gamble.

World War II did not see gas released widely and regularly, nor have the decades since then, so the legacy of World War II CW is quite different than it might have been. Gas still influenced the Western Allies' behavior, emotions, and outlook, and preparing to use it cost resources and energy. Weapons do not have to be used on battlefields, in other words, to make a difference.

Gas had a personal and physical impact; it led to individual tragedies because of the long-term injuries it caused as well as the frustration toward authority it inspired. The munitions workers, of course, suffered from accidents and from the hazards of working next to toxic chemicals. Lois Moore was a civilian who earned $1 a day and had the opportunity "for also . . . helping our country" at the Huntsville Arsenal in Alabama when she started work in a factory that made napalm, white phosphorus, tear gas, and mustard gas, among other substances. Despite some protections, she remembered blisters from mustard gas and said "breathing [it] caused lots of people to have cancers."[3] She knew it was dangerous at the time, although she was not aware about the long-term effects.

There is a growing body of literature today about CW experimentation on nations' own citizens and subjects during World War II and afterwards in efforts to ensure that offensive gases and defensive equipment worked.[4] That is further support of the argument in this book that a weapon can be used without being deployed. Bertram Stevens, a British soldier, was gassed at Bari, Italy, in 1943 when a German air raid destroyed a US ship carrying mustard gas. Stevens did not know he had been gassed until decades later. In the meantime, he developed ailments, struggled with the pension system, and eventually became a cause célèbre in the 1980s. Disseminated via newspapers and radio, his story reached Prime Minister Margaret Thatcher's office and even led to changes in pension policy.[5]

Gas changed mental, emotional, and physical actions globally and locally; CW policy and practice were not simply military issues. The 1925 Geneva Gas Protocol, although it was an untrusted ban, was honored in the end. That was quite impressive, considering its flaws and the public doubt leaders in various countries expressed even during the treaty negotiations. This outcome reminds us that a prohibition, especially a dubious one, does not eliminate fear, resources, or strategies focused on that weapon, but it can still be quite valuable. Even when gases were not deployed, they shaped diplomatic negotiations, political debates, and grassroots behavior. They impacted preparations for war, whether at home or abroad. They influenced Allied relationships internationally and government-lay interactions domestically.

Belligerents did not deploy gas as a common weapon of war during World War II, despite repeated temptations to do so. If the war had continued or if there had been more challenges to the national survival of the Western Allies, it is unlikely that the Geneva Gas Protocol would have emerged unscathed, regardless of the United States, Canada, and Britain's firm policies and proclamations against offensive gas use. The red line against gas confronted challenges from 1940 onward, and especially after V-E Day. These trials included threats to national existence and occasions when the cost of victory through conventional means seemed too high, whether those arose because of dangers of invasion to Britain, destructiveness from V-weapons, or perceptions of US war weariness and revulsion toward casualties in the Pacific theater.[6] As the war continued and the result of Axis retaliation in kind decreased, the direness of the Western Allies' situation lessened. So did the degree of motivation needed to consider offensive gas use seriously, at least for some in power. No one who contemplated the German execution of Operation Sea Lion could have expected Britain to persist as a separate, independent country if Germany triumphed. Facing such a desperate situation, the British leadership in 1940 recognized that drastic measures, including offensive gas use, might be necessary to ward off the enemy. It would be a lesser evil to use gas than to lose the nation. However, in 1945, when some US leaders feared the United States would not maintain high enough morale to continue to fight the Japanese for a year or more while absorbing the heavy casualties that the island-hopping campaigns demanded, they did not fear for the United States' future survival. Still, they contemplated a role for gas in Operation Downfall.

As we know, V-E and V-J Days ended World War II without the release of gas, but those people involved in staving off and yet preparing for the next chemical conflict continued their work. In the winter of 1945, before the defeat of Japan, the British were already considering how to restructure the future chemical warfare efforts, especially temporarily decreasing gas production while maintaining the ability to ramp it up again.[7] There was no repeat of the years immediately after World War I, though. While gas remained banned by international law, the tight alliance Britain, the United States, and Canada had developed during World War II continued in the postwar chemical plans and actions in the first decades of the Cold War, particularly in the realm of shared research.[8] There were discussions about sharing production and supply. The British were particularly interested in this. Production was expensive—it might be less expensive if the United States would foot the bill to build factories.[9] That did not mean that the three nations worked totally in concert; for instance, the United States did not ratify the Geneva Gas Protocol until 1975. Even after the success of a common combined gas policy during World War II and a long-term cooperative postwar CW relationship, the United States maintained an independent legal stance.

It would be hard to believe that the Allies' 1945 discovery of sarin and tabun in the German arsenal did not have something to do with the concern that gas remained a threat. Once the atomic bomb dropped on Hiroshima and Nagasaki, it may well have seemed that restraints against weapons of mass destruction had weakened further too. The advent of the Cold War, especially the USSR as a powerful enemy, raised the general threat level. With all of those developments, the Allies must have been even more relieved that chemical warfare had been avoided and even more determined not to be shocked again.

Yet, despite the behind-the-scenes work on chemical and biological weapons by the Western Allies, the rejection of gas use remained—at least among the powers most concerned about their public images and particularly among the countries who could wield conventional and perhaps nuclear power. All of this is relevant to an ongoing discussion about whether there is a taboo against gas, or simply a norm against gas use, or something else. For the most part CW use in the post–World War II era was ignored and occurred outside of the great power circle. The vast majority took place outside of the industrialized world or in civil conflicts.[10] These events did not catch attention the way World War I gas use on the Western Front did nor did they seem to endanger great powers. It was the former that started global outcries about gas in 1915 and the latter, in the form of Italy's release of mustard gas in Ethiopia in 1935–1936, that cemented the conviction that gas would be used in future wars. Of course, hot wars did not occur among the world's largest powers after World War II either. Thus, the general rejection of gas, and the de facto restriction of it from direct great power hostilities, reappeared after World War II.

Some actions taken to diminish the risk of CW have developed outside of treaties. The United States took an enormous unilateral step in 1969 when President Richard Nixon proclaimed that it would eradicate its arsenal of biological weapons as well as offensive CW.[11] This led to President George H. W. Bush's proclamation during the First Gulf War implying US retaliation in kind to nuclear, biological, or chemical weapons would have to be with nuclear weapons.[12] Thus, while the expectation was that gas and even biological warfare would not touch the great powers, worry about it remained.

Although there was a general perception that gas was taboo among most countries, some nations were not perceived as law-abiding, and, as everyone knew, taboos and laws could be broken in the realm of CW—and had been in World War I. There were years of negotiations to replace the Geneva Gas Protocol with a stronger treaty, one that could inspire more trust.[13] The Chemical Weapons Convention (CWC) came into force in 1997, negotiations having been concluded in 1992 after twenty years of debate.[14] With 193 parties as of 2022, it is a complex and ever-evolving treaty that bans not only CW use but also the "development, production, acquisition, stockpiling, retention, transfer or use of chemical weapons." It has concrete and detailed procedures to prevent future gas use, including requirements for nations to destroy CW arsenals and for verification protocols not just for weapons but also for components.[15] There are mechanisms and organizations, such as the Scientific Advisory Board, to provide ongoing efforts to ensure that regulation of CW evolves with science and technology, unlike in earlier treaties.[16] This is a much more complex effort to ban gas than has existed previously. The result superficially looks like there is an effective barrier against gas, although a deeper look makes it clear that the status of CW is not that simple.

In many ways, the CWC has been successful. Nations have destroyed 98 percent of their CW, and, according to the Organisation for the Prohibition of Chemical Weapons (OPCW), the body that governs and administers the CWC, 98 percent of the world's people live in states that are part of the CWC. All but three countries are parties, although one signatory, Israel, had not ratified it by 2022.[17] The ramifications may stretch farther. It is impossible to prove the exact impact, but perhaps the ability to prevent major CW use since 1918 has had a restraining influence on nuclear-weapon states.[18] Perhaps some actors, once the initial fascination with nuclear weapons passed and as the potential for mutually assured destruction grew, recognized the history of legal restraint of gas could be applied to other WMDs.

Those benefits of the CWC are balanced by weaknesses; as the events in Syria since 2012 have shown, gas still may be released in wars.[19] Reports from reputable news organizations declare that Russian security forces have used nerve gases against their domestic opponents—not battlefield use, perhaps, but deployment against a political enemy in the case of Alexei Navalny and an intelligence enemy in the case of Sergei Skirpal.[20]

As the Inter-Services Committee on Chemical Warfare wrote in 1945 after the defeat of Germany: just because gas was not used to defeat the Axis power, "we do not consider that this provides any grounds for regarding gas as an obsolete weapon . . . chemical warfare will remain a weapon of great potentialities."[21] Those potentialities were enough to shape the CW policies of the three Western Allies during the war, and they remain with us today. Even the sporadic use of CW since 1945 should remind us of the horrors that Allied leaders feared during the war. And yet studying the intersection of social, political, diplomatic, scientific, military, and legal perspectives on the Allies' gas policies should make us wary of any promise of an absolute taboo on the use of any weapon in a time of war. In the spring of 2022, political and military experts warned that Russia might use chemical weapons in Ukraine.[22]

Whether or not CW are used in Eastern Europe despite the CWC, repeated gas use in wars such as that in Syria and acts of terrorism in Japan and Britain show that the Inter-Services Committee on Chemical Warfare is correct. Gas war is possible. World War II shows that it can be contained, even under strained circumstances, but its very existence still shapes the way we look at the world. Whether or not it is deployed, gas is still a weapon that demands attention if we want to avoid the human suffering of Wilfred Owen's men in the front lines, Lois Moore in Huntsville, Bertram Stevens in Bari, and even Syrians in a civil war today. More than one hundred years after the Second Battle of Ypres, the mere existence of gas and gas masks can still provoke fear.

# Notes

## Intoduction

1. Wilfred Owen, "Dulce et Decorum Est," *Poems* (Viking Press, 1921), posted on Poetry Foundation, https://www.poetryfoundation.org/poems/46560/dulce-et-deco rum-est.

2. Claire Langhamer, Lucy Noakes, and Claudia Siebrecht, eds., *Total War: An Emotional History* (Oxford: Oxford University Press, 2020); and Joanna Bourke, *Fear: A Cultural History* (Emeryville, CA: Shoemaker & Hoard, 2006) offer just two examples of recent scholarship on the power and pervasiveness of emotions. Fear requires energy and should be counted as a cost for a defender and as a psychological resource for the attacker, whether or not the dreaded action occurred.

3. *The Papers of George Catlett Marshall*, ed. Larry I. Bland and Sharon Ritenour Stevens (Lexington, VA: The George C. Marshall Foundation, 1981). Electronic version based on *The Papers of George Catlett Marshall*, vol. 5, *"The Finest Soldier," January 1, 1945–January 7, 1947* (Baltimore and London: The Johns Hopkins University Press, 2003), 205–7.

4. For example, the Germans bombed British towns multiple times, beginning in 1914 in Scarborough, moving to other communities and hitting greater London the next year. For more details, see Susan R. Grayzel, *At Home and Under Fire: Air Raids and Culture in Britain from the Great War to the Blitz* (New York: Cambridge University Press, 2013), 23–27.

5. "Protocol for the Prohibition of the Use in War of Asphyxiating, Poisonous, or Other Gases, and of Bacteriological Methods of Warfare (Geneva Protocol)," June 17, 1925, https://www.state.gov/t/isn/4784.htm, hereinafter "Geneva Gas Protocol"; and Earl of Halsbury, *1944* (London: Thornton Butterworth, 1926). Scholars of emotions in total war accept that "emotions are what people say they are feeling." Langhamer, *Total War*, ix. As demonstrated in this book, especially in chapter 2, numerous speeches, interviews, and novels express fear about gas, as do actions.

6. As part of her work about fear, Joanna Bourke states that "[w]ar domesticated terror." *Fear*, 195. Peter Stansky, in his book about the Blitz, repeatedly uses the word "terror" to describe the bombing. See, for example, Peter Stansky, *The First Day of the Blitz: September 7, 1940* (New Haven: Yale University Press, 2007), 3 and 5.

7. Note that these years included dates before the start of World War II, particularly before the attack on Pearl Harbor. Once President Franklin Roosevelt warned the Axis powers that that United States would retaliate in kind if belligerents used CW against its Allies, there were no officially and publicly confirmed cases.

8. For example, one of the initial gas commanders in World War I Britain and a chemist writing late in the interwar period both agree that gas was not the weapon that produced the most wartime casualties. Charles H. Foulkes, *Gas!: The Story of the Special Brigade* (Edinburgh: William Blackwood, 1934), 338; Austin M. Prentiss, *Chemicals in War: A Treatise on Chemical Warfare* (New York: McGraw-Hill, 1937), 671. Modern scholars question the accuracy of past statistics. It would be hard to calculate them precisely. Robert Harris and Jeremy Paxman, *A Higher Form of Killing: The Secret Story of Gas and Germ Warfare* (London: Chatto & Windus, 1982), 34. Was a victim gassed before he was shot? Shot because he was distracted by gas? Did a pulmonary patient die of gas or the flu?

9. Barton J. Bernstein, "Why We Didn't Use Poison Gas in World War II," *American Heritage* 36, no. 5 (1985): 42 provides a concise discussion of the warnings issued by Churchill and Roosevelt to the Axis powers. The common consensus is that Hitler did not like gas because he himself had been gassed in World War I. However, Germany did have nerve gases, and at least one historian says that Hitler was willing to use gas against the Russians, thinking them inferior to the Western Europeans. The Western Allies were wary of Hitler's restraint too. Jonathan B. Tucker, *War of Nerves: Chemical Warfare from World War I to al-Qaeda* (New York: Pantheon Books, 2006), 44 and 56.

10. A useful source looking at the deterrence argument, especially its relationship to unpreparedness during World War II, is John Ellis van Courtland Moon, "Chemical Weapons and Deterrence: The World War II Experience," *International Security* 8, no. 4 (Spring 1984), 3–35.

11. Shortages must be viewed on a global level. In early 1942, Britain, for example, had sufficient resources and production capability to bomb Europe in a "sustained" fashion with gas, but New Zealand did not have any such weapons nor a plan to supply them. N. H. Bottomley, "Memorandum by the Chairman of the Inter-Service Committee on Chemical Warfare," in War Cabinet, Chiefs of Staff Committee, "Preparedness to Engage in Chemical Warfare," COS (42) 81 (0), March 31, 1942, CAB 80/62, The National Archives [hereinafter TNA]. Julian Perry Robinson, *The Rise of CB Weapons*, vol. 1, *The Problem of Chemical and Biological Warfare* (Stockholm: Almqvist and Wiksell, 1971), 302–13 contains a scholarly discussion of shortages and perceptions of plenty.

12. See chapters two and three in Marion Girard, *A Strange and Formidable Weapon: British Responses to World War I Poison Gas* (Lincoln: University of Nebraska Press, 2008) for more details about these activities.

13. "Geneva Gas Protocol."

14. For a brief discussion of transnational history, see *1914–1918 Online: International Encyclopedia of the First World War*, s.v. "Historiography, 1918-Today," by Jay Winter, last updated November 11, 2014, https://encyclopedia.1914-1918-online.net/article/historiography_1918-today. As he notes, "Transnational history does not start with one state and move on to others, but takes multiple levels of historical experience as given, levels which are both below and above the national level . . . [For example,] the history of mutiny is transnational, in that it happened in different armies for different reasons, some of which are strikingly similar to the sources of protest and refusal in other armies."

15. The text of the treaty and a link to the signatories (and the dates when they ratified the document) can be found in "Geneva Gas Protocol."

16. Valerie Adams, *Chemical Warfare, Chemical Disarmament* (Bloomington: Indiana University Press, 1990), 5.

17. There are other ways to classify gases too. See Adams, *Chemical Warfare*, 7–10.

18. More accurately, tear gases are not intended to produce lasting harm or death. However, in close quarters, their effects may be more pronounced than when they are deployed outdoors. The effects may vary depending on the sensitivity of the gassed individual or how directly the gas sprayed the victim's face. In addition, scientific research indicates that effects can last for months. Y. G. Karagama, J. R. Newton, and C. J. R. Newbegin, "Short-Term and Long-Term Physical Effects of Exposure to CS Spray," *Journal of the Royal Society of Medicine*, 96, no. 4 (April 2003): 172–74, https://www.ncbi.nlm.nih.gov/pmc/articles/PMC539444/; Anna Feigenbaum, *Tear Gas: From the Battlefields of World War I to the Streets of Today* (London: Verso, 2017), 8–10; and Daniel Yetman, "How Does Tear Gas Affect the Human Body?" *Healthline*, May 28, 2020, https://www.healthline.com/health/tear-gas-effects.

19. Julia Masterson and Leanne Quinn, updaters, "Timeline of Syrian Chemical Weapons Activity, 2012–2018," *Arms Control Association*, May 2021, https://www.armscontrol.org/factsheets/Timeline-of-Syrian-Chemical-Weapons-Activity.

20. Donald H. Avery, *The Science of War: Canadian Scientists and Allied Military Technology during the Second World War* (Toronto: University of Toronto Press, 1998), 146.

21. "Facts about Sarin," Emergency Preparedness and Response, Centers for Disease Control, April 4, 2018, https://emergency.cdc.gov/agent/sarin/basics/facts.asp.

22. Tucker, *War of Nerves*, 86.

23. Organisation for the Prohibition of Chemical Weapons, "The Sarin Gas Attack in Japan and the Related Forensic Investigation," *Synthesis*, June 1, 2001, https://www.opcw.org/media-centre/news/2001/06/sarin-gas-attack-japan-and-related-forensic-investigation; Organisation for the Prohibition of Chemical Weapons, "OPCW Fact-Finding Mission Confirms Use of Chemical Weapons in Khan Shaykhun on 4 April 2017," OPCW Press Release, June 30, 2017, https://www.opcw.org/news/article/opcw-fact-finding-mission-confirms-use-of-chemical-weapons-in-khan-shaykhun-on-4-april-2017. Skirpal's daughter, Yulia, was poisoned at the same time. Another woman, Dawn Sturgess, incidentally came into contact with the nerve agent later and died. Investigations have linked a Novichok CW to the poisoning of Alexei Navalny by the Russians in 2018 as well. Lesley Wroughton, "U.S. Imposes Sanctions on Russia for Nerve Agent Attack in UK," Reuters, August 8, 2018, https://www.reuters.com/article/us-britain-poison-skripal-usa/u-s-imposes-sanctions-on-russia-for-nerve-agent-attack-in-uk-idUSKBN1KT2FC; Tim Lister, "Bellingcat: Russian Scientists Secretly Developing Novichok Nerve Agent, and Working with Military Intelligence," CNN, October 23, 2020, https://www.cnn.com/2020/10/23/europe/bellingcat-russia-novichok-report-intl/index.html. There have been occasional, but less well-known and localized, gas attacks at other times. See, for example, Asher Orkaby, "Forgotten Gas Attacks in Yemen Haunt Syria Crisis," Bloomberg, 2013, http://www.tinyurl.com/y39wt8uq at Weatherhead Center for International Affairs, Harvard University, https://wcfia.harvard.edu/publications/forgotten-gas-attacks-yemen-haunt-syria-crisis, accessed January 15, 2022.

24. In an article, Tim Cook focuses on the interwar period but also discusses the distinction between gas and other weapons. See the comparison with high explosives in Tim Cook, "'Against God-Inspired Conscience': The Perception of Gas Warfare as a Weapon of Mass Destruction, 1915–1939," *War & Society*, 18, no. 1 (May 2000), 47.

25. See, for example, Tim Cook, *No Place to Run: The Canadian Corps and Gas Warfare in the First World War* (Vancouver: UBC Press, 1999); and George H. Cassar, *Trial by Gas: The British Army at the Second Battle of Ypres* (n.p.: Potomac Books, 2014) for accounts of early gas attacks and their impacts on different armies.

26. Captain H. H. MacMahon, *Memorandum*, October 13, 1918, Folder DGS/ M92, WO 142/109, TNA.

27. A. T. Sloggett, *SS 452: Memorandum on Gas Poisoning in Warfare with Notes on Its Pathology and Treatment* (General Headquarters, Second Echelon, July 20, 1916), 15, 16.

28. Susan L. Smith, *Toxic Exposures: Mustard Gas and the Health Consequences of World War II in the United States* (New Brunswick, NJ: Rutgers University Press, 2017), 122–23.

29. *SS 136: Defensive Measures against Gas Attacks* (London: Harrison and Sons for HMSO, 1916); and Smith, *Toxic Exposures*, 29.

30. Major H. B. McCance to Controller, Chemical Warfare Department, Minute, September 14, 1918, WO 142/120, Box CWD/144, TNA; and Anonymous (illegible signature), "Babies' Devices," Meeting Notes, March 3, 1938, HO 45/17620, TNA.

31. Leo P. Brophy, Wyndham D. Miles, and Rexmond C. Cochrane, *The Chemical Warfare Service: From Laboratory to Field* (Washington, DC: Office of the Chief of Military History, Department of the Army, 1959), 78–79.

32. Article 21, "Laws and Customs of War on Land (Hague II)," July 29, 1899, The Avalon Project, https://avalon.law.yale.edu/19th_century/hague02.asp#art1; and "Declaration on the Use of Bullets Which Expand or Flatten Easily in the Human Body, July 29, 1899," The Avalon Project, http://avalon.law.yale.edu/19th_century/dec99-03.asp.

33. "Declaration on the Use of Projectiles the Object of Which is the Diffusion of Asphyxiating or Deleterious Gases, July 29, 1899," The Avalon Project at Yale Law School, https://avalon.law.yale.edu/19th_century/dec99-02.asp, offers one translation of the French, but Alfred Mahan makes it clear that the ban prohibited weapons whose "sole purpose" was deadly. Captain Alfred Mahan, "Peace Conference at The Hague 1899: Report of Captain Mahan to the American Commission to the International Conference to the Hague, on Disarmament, etc., with Reference to Navies," The Avalon Project at Yale Law School, July 31, 1899, https://avalon.law.yale.edu/19th_century/hag99-06.asp.

34. Captain Mahan quoted in James Scott, "The Hague Peace Conference of 1899," *The Proceedings of The Hague Peace Conferences, Translation of Official Texts, Conference of 1899* (New York: Oxford University Press, 1920), 283.

35. Ulrich Trumpeter, "The Road to Ypres: The Beginnings of Gas Warfare in World War I," *The Journal of Modern History* 47 (September 1975): 462–63 and 469.

36. Asquith to King George V, April 27, 1915, CAB 37/127/40, also listed as CAB 41/36/18, TNA.

37. 18 Parl. Deb. H.L. (5th series) (May 18, 1915) cols. 1017–18; and 71 Parl. Deb. H.C. (5th series) (May 5, 1915) col. 1205.

38. The intangibles of gas—such as the threat that it will come, the contamination of those who wield it, and the inherent immorality of it—are part of what make it an unusual and powerful weapon. See the discussion of the psychological associations of it, for example, in Cook, "Against God-Inspired Conscience," 55; and Girard, *A Strange and Formidable Weapon*, 132–34.

39. See Cook, *No Place to Run* for a detailed account of the Canadian experience with CW in World War I.

40. 18 Parl. Deb. H.L. (5th series) (May 18, 1915), cols. 1017–18.

41. Thomas I. Faith, *Behind the Gas Mask: The U.S. Chemical Warfare Service in War and Peace* (Urbana: University of Illinois Press, 2014), 13–15 discusses the early months. Theo Emery also provides a detailed description of the US World War I chemical warfare efforts in Theo Emery, *Hellfire Boys: The Birth of the U.S. Chemical Warfare Service and the Race for the World's Deadliest Weapons* (New York: Little, Brown, 2017).

42. Faith, *Behind the Gas Mask*, 47.

43. Winston Churchill, "GT [Cabinet Memorandum] 3835: Munitions Programme, 1919," March 5, 1919, CAB 24/44, TNA; and "Minutes of Proceedings at a Conference to consider the supply of Gas for 1919 as affected by the Policy of the General Staff," March 19, 1918, MUN 5/198/1650/29, TNA.

44. There were some investigations into biological warfare in World War I. See the description of the efforts by a few Germans to infect horses in the United States with glanders to interfere with the war effort. Note, however, Blum's subtitle indicates that he sees the effort as terrorism—perhaps state-sponsored—rather than a full-scale military mission. Howard Blum, *Dark Invasion: 1915: Germany's Secret War and the Hunt for the First Terrorist Cell in America* (New York: HarperCollins, 2014), 265–72.

45. H. F. Downie to Williams and McSeeney, December 7, 1933, CO 323/1248/18, TNA.

46. Andrew Iarocci, "'A Unique Art': Canadian Anti-Gas Respirator Production in the Second World War," *Canadian Military History*, 18, 4 (2009), 51–64 details Canada's interwar and wartime efforts to develop a national respirator industry separate from Britain's.

## 1. Chain, Tool, Shield

1. Lord Edward Grey, *Twenty-Five Years*, quoted in Committee of Imperial Defence, Extract from the Minutes of the 217th Meeting, November 11, 1926, in M. P. Hankey, "Ratification of Protocol for Prohibition of Use of Poisonous Gases," CP -97(29), 25, March 25, 1929, CAB 24/202, TNA.

2. Thomas I. Faith, *Behind the Gas Mask: The U.S. Chemical Warfare Service in War and Peace* (Urbana: University of Illinois Press, 2014), 83; and Kevin Takashi Fujitani, "The United States and Chemical Warfare: The 1925 Geneva Gas Protocol and Its Legacy," University of Hawaii, 1991, MA Thesis, 69.

3. Herbert Hoover, "President Hoover's Proposals to the World Disarmament Conference. June 22, 1932," and Franklin Roosevelt, "Message Sent by President Roosevelt to 54 Heads of State, May 16, 1933," in "President Roosevelt's Message to 54 Nations. May 16, 1933," in *A Documentary History of Arms Control and Disarmament*, Trevor N Dupuy and Gay M. Hammerman, eds., (New York: R. R. Bowker Company, 1973), 191, 252–54.

4. C. F. Lambe, G. M. Stewart, and W. Elliot, *Report by the Joint Planning Staff*, J.P. (48) 382, April 10, 1942, CAB 84/44/75, TNA.

5. Edward M. Spiers, *Chemical Warfare* (Urbana: University of Illinois Press, 1986), 34–61.

6. Canada signed and ratified the protocol separately from Britain. Dupuy and Hammerman, *A Documentary History of Arms Control and Disarmament*, 125.

7. "Pershing Backs Poison Gas Ban: Expresses Strong Views in Favor of the Protocol Adopted at Geneva," *The New York Times,* June 11, 1925, ProQuest Historical Newspapers. It is worth noting that Pershing's anti-gas pronouncements took place after World War I; he accepted the presence of CW in the wartime arsenal.

8. Faith, *Behind the Gas Mask*, 58–59.

9. Jeffrey T. Richelson, *A Century of Spies: Intelligence in the Twentieth Century* (New York: Oxford University Press, 1995, 1997), 71. The MI8, also known as The Black Chamber, received support from the State Department and Military Intelligence in the War Department.

10. Allison Sobek, Karen Anderson, and Melissa Doak, "How Did the Women's International League for Peace and Freedom Campaign against Chemical Warfare, 1915–1930?" (Binghamton: State University of New York, 2001), https://documents.alexanderstreet.com/d/1000682890. Cecilia Lynch notes that the WILPF was one of many international and national groups "stretching across the political spectrum" and ranging from pacifists to more flexible groups who supported disarmament of some sort, not just with regards to gas. Cecelia Lynch, "A Matter of Controversy: The Peace Movement and British Arms Policy in the Interwar Period," in *Arms Limitation and Disarmament: Restraints on War, 1899–1939*, ed. B. J. C. McKercher (Westport, CT: Praeger, 1992), 65.

11. Faith, *Behind the Gas Mask*, 62.

12. "Upholds Gas Warfare," *The New York Times*, February 17, 1919, ProQuest Historical Newspapers.

13. "Poison Gas Uses in Peace," *The New York Times*, April 4, 1923, ProQuest Historical Newspapers.

14. Faith, *Behind the Gas Mask*, 69–70; and Theo Emery, *Hellfire Boys: The Birth of the U.S. Chemical Warfare Service and the Race for the World's Deadliest Weapons* (New York: Little, Brown, 2017), 420–21.

15. Emery, *Hellfire Boys*, 404.

16. Will Irwin, "Wilbur and the Next War: Will Irwin Replies to the Naval Secretary's Attack on 'the Writers Who Seek to Terrorize the People,'" *The New York Times*, February 4, 1925, ProQuest Historical Newspapers.

17. Faith, *Behind the Gas Mask*, 100–101; and Anna Feigenbaum, "100 Years of Tear Gas," *Atlantic*, August 16, 2014, https://www.theatlantic.com/international/archive/2014/08/100-years-of-tear-gas/378632.

18. A. H. Ulm, "Senate to Debate Warfare with Gas," *The New York Times*, October 31, 1926, ProQuest Historical Newspapers.

19. For a more detailed discussion about the public gas debate in interwar Britain, see Marion Girard, *A Strange and Formidable Weapon: British Responses to World War I Poison Gas* (Lincoln: University of Nebraska Press: 2008), 157–90.

20. Popular novelist H. G. Wells wrote a science fiction "history" of the future in which gas war proved catastrophic. H. G. Wells, *The Shape of Things to Come* (New York: Macmillan, 1933). Lord Halsbury, who served in World War I, became an outspoken critic of gas and a proponent of the idea that future chemical warfare would destroy society. His work can be seen in the Earl of Halsbury, "Gas!" *British Legion Journal*, January 1933: 238–39. There is a growing body of scholarship on interwar and wartime fiction about future wars. Many focus on works about the impact of planes,

but some specifically examine books in which gas dropped from planes devastates civilization. For example, Paul Saint-Amour has a section about the future "terror" of a gas war; Susan Grayzel emphasizes the impact of World War I air war experiences; Brett Holman, among other points, notes that novelists made experts' theories about threats—whether or not about gas itself—accessible to the public; and Girard notes that the question about whether gas is a humane weapon was addressed by novels. Paul K. Saint Amour, *Tense Future: Modernism, Total War, Encyclopedic Form* (Oxford: Oxford University Press, 2015), 143–52; Susan Grayzel, *At Home and Under Fire: Air Raids and Culture in Britain from the Great War to the Blitz* (New York: Cambridge University Press, 2012), 93–120; Brett Holman, *The Next War in the Air: Britain's Fear of the Bomber, 1908–1941* (London: Routledge, 2014) https://ebookcentral.proquest.com/lib/unh/detail.action?docID=4414984, 13; and Girard, *A Strange and Formidable Weapon*, 173–175.

21. Special Cable to *The New York Times*, "More Deadly Gases Made for the Next War Can Wipe Out Cities, Says Lord Halsbury," *The New York Times*, January 1, 1933, ProQuest Historical Newspapers.

22. See, for example, Union of Democratic Control, *Poison Gas*, (London: Farleigh Press, 1935).

23. Louis Jackson, "Gas Precautions," *The Times* (London), October 14, 1935, *The Times* Digital Archive.

24. J. B. S. Haldane, *Callinicus: A Defence of Chemical Warfare* (New York: E. P. Dutton, 1925); Major General Charles H. Foulkes, *"Gas!": The Story of the Special Brigade* (Edinburgh: William Blackwood, 1934).

25. Winston S. Churchill, Memo, May 22, 1919, WO 32/5185, TNA.

26. Major General Sir Henry F. Thuillier, *Gas in the Next War* (London: Geoffrey Bles, 1939).

27. Spiers, *Chemical Warfare*, 49.

28. "War Use of Aircraft," *The Times* (London), August 23, 1922, *The Times* Digital Archives.

29. "Aeronautics: Anaesthetic Warfare" *Time*, June 25, 1923, https://content.time.com/time/subscriber/article/0,33009,715936,00.html.

30. "British Air Policy," *The Times* (London), March 21, 1922, *The Times* Digital Archive, vividly describes the damage to military and civilian targets that are possible with advances in airpower and the use of gas bombs. See also "Chemical Warfare: Effect of Poison Gas from Aeroplanes," *The Times* (London), February 9, 1928, *The Times* Digital Archive, about Lefebure and other gas-military experts' views.

31. Letter to the Editor, "Poison Gas in War," *Globe and Mail* (Toronto), August 24, 1925, ProQuest Historical Newspapers.

32. See, for example, "Canada Lends Help in Paving Pathway to Peace of the World," *Globe and Mail* (Toronto), June 18, 1925, ProQuest Historical Newspapers, which reports on the signing of the Geneva Gas Protocol. Another story recounts a US chemist's opinion about the United States's readiness to face a gas war, "Poison-Gas Expert Has Little Faith in Nations' Pacts," *Globe and Mail* (Toronto), August 20, 1928, ProQuest Historical Newspapers.

33. The British branch of the organization, the Women's International League, had more diverse interests, including socialism. Cecilia Lynch, *Beyond Appeasement:*

*Interpreting Interwar Peace Movements in World Politics* (Ithaca, NY: Cornell University Press, 1999), 32–33.

34. *Document 20: Can We Outlaw Poison Gas? (Washington, D.C.: Women's International League for Peace and Freedom [1927]). The Records of the Women's International League for Peace and Freedom, U.S. Section, 1919–1959, Swarthmore College Peace Collection (Microfilm, reel 33, frames 281–84),* by Women's International League for Peace and Freedom, 1915-. Included in *How Did the Women's International League for Peace and Freedom Campaign against Chemical Warfare, 1915–1930?,* by Allison Sobek. (Binghamton: State University of New York at Binghamton, 2001), at https://documents.alexanderstreet.com/d/1000679974.

35. "Medicine: War Gas Protection," *Time,* October 26, 1931, http://www.time.com/time/magazine/article/0,9171,742510,00.html.

36. "The Versailles Treaty," June 28, 1919, Avalon Project, https://avalon.law.yale.edu/subject_menus/versailles_menu.asp. The Treaty of Versailles also banned or limited German use and possession of other tools of war, such as planes and submarines.

37. "Laws of War: Laws and Customs of War on Land (Hague IV), October 18, 1907," The Avalon Project, http://avalon.law.yale.edu/20th_century/hague04.asp.

38. See, for example, Churchill, Minute 8, May 22, 1919, WO 32/5185, TNA. Note that he also said that "Gas is a more merciful weapon than high explosive shell"; it had dual attractiveness, therefore.

39. Churchill, Minute 8, May 22, 1919, WO 32/5185, TNA.

40. Geoff Simons, *Iraq: From Sumer to Post-Saddam*, 3rd ed. (Houndsmill, Basingstoke, Hampshire: Palgrave Macmillan, 2004), 213. More recent scholarship rejects this assertion, noting that at times there was willingness to use tear gas, but it was not released. R. M. Douglas, "Did the British Use Gas in Mandatory Iraq?" *Journal of Modern History* 81 (December 2009): 887.

41. Elihu Root, "International Law at the Arms Conference," *Proceedings of the American Society of International Law at its Sixteenth Annual Meeting, Washington D.C., April 27–29, 1922* (Washington, DC: American Society of International Law; Concord, NH: The Rumford Press, 1922), 11, HathiTrust.org.

42. The secretary of state [Charles E. Hughes] to the French chargé (Beam), telegram, 500.A41a/12, Document 87, Washington, DC, September 20, 1921 in *Papers Relating to the Foreign Relations of the United States,* 1921, vol. 1, https://history.state.gov/historicaldocuments/frus1921v01/d87; and Sir Laming Worthington-Evans in Committee of Imperial Defence, "Chemical Warfare Policy," 723-B in Cabinet, "Chemical Warfare Policy, CP 344 (2), October 8, 1926, p. 5, CAB 24/181, TNA.

43. League of Nations, *Report of the Temporary Mixed Commission for the Reduction of Armaments* (Extract), pp. 2–3, WO 188/144, TNA; League of Nations, *Report,* C.P. 3245, September 7, 1922, CAB 24/139, TNA.

44. League of Nations, *Report,* WO 188/144, 12.

45. League of Nations, *Report,* WO 188/144, 12.

46. Leo P. Brophy and George J. B. Fisher, *United States Army in World War II: The Technical Services. The Chemical Warfare Service: Organizing for War,* 2004 ed. (Washington, DC: Center of Military History, United States Army, 1959), 24.

47. Brophy and Fisher, *Organizing for War,* 24 and 32.

48. Faith, *Behind the Gas Mask,* 95; and Brophy and Fisher, *Organizing,* 31.

49. Nations ratified the Chemical Warfare Convention of the 1990s at various times; Britain did so in 1997. "Evolution of the Status of Participation in the Convention," Organisation for the Prohibition of Chemical Weapons, https://www.opcw.org/evolution-status-participation-convention.

50. The Geneva Gas Protocol was an annex to the Convention for the Supervision of Trade in Arms and War Munitions of 1925, a treaty that the United States and other great powers signed, but "many of the principal arms-producing Powers, including the United States" did not ratify it. The United States did not even send it to the Senate for consideration. "Convention for the Supervision of Trade in Arms and War Munitions," *The American Journal of International Law* 20, no. 1 (January, 1926): 151–54, https://www.jstor.org/stable/2188821.

51. Later the Geneva Gas Protocol states "Whereas the prohibition of such [gas] use has been declared in Treaties to which the majority of Powers of the world are Parties; and To [sic] the end that this prohibition shall be universally accepted as a part of International Law, binding alike the conscience and the practice of nations . . ." "Protocol for the Prohibition of the Use in War of Asphyxiating, Poisonous, or Other Gases, and of Bacteriological Methods of Warfare (Geneva Protocol)," June 17, 1925, https://www.state.gov/t/isn/4784.htm, hereinafter "Geneva Gas Protocol."

52. "Geneva Gas Protocol."

53. "Geneva Gas Protocol."

54. Air Staff, "Chemical Warfare Policy" in Cabinet "Chemical Warfare Policy," October 15, 1926, CP 352 (26), pp. 1–2, CAB 26/181, TNA.

55. H. J. Creedy, letter from the War Office to the secretary, Committee of Imperial Defence, October 13, 1926, in Committee of Imperial Defence, "Chemical Warfare Policy," 725-B, in Cabinet, "Chemical Warfare Policy," October 14, 1926, CP 346 (26), CAB 24/181, TNA; and Sir Laming Worthington-Evans in Committee of Imperial Defence, "Chemical Warfare Policy," 723-B in Cabinet, "Chemical Warfare Policy," CP 344 (26), October 8, 1926, pp. 2–3, CAB 24/181, TNA.

56. "Geneva Gas Protocol."

57. For example, the Kellogg-Briand Pact outlawed war, but it lacked assurances and deterrence. "Kellogg-Briand Pact, 1928," The Avalon Project, https://avalon.law.yale.edu/20th_century/kbpact.asp.

58. Adam Roberts, "Land Warfare: From Hague to Nuremberg," Michael Howard, George J. Andreopoulos, and Mark R. Shulman, eds., *The Laws of War: Constraints on Warfare in the Western World* (New Haven, CT: Yale, 1994), 127.

59. Laming Worthington-Evans, CP 344 (26), p. 3, CAB 24/181, TNA; and Laming Worthington-Evans in Committee of Imperial Defence, "Chemical Warfare Policy," 709-B, p. 2, CAB 4/15, TNA.

60. Lord Onslow, October 10, 1926, in October 18, 1926, CP 353 (26), p. 5 CAB 24/181, TNA.

61. Committee of Imperial Defence, "Chemical Warfare Policy," 708-B, p. 3, CAB 4/15, TNA; and H. J. Creedy, Letter from the War Office to the Secretary, October 13, 1926, in Committee of Imperial Defence, "Chemical Warfare Policy," 725-B, in Cabinet, "Chemical Warfare Policy," October 14, 1926, CP 346 (26) CAB 24/181, TNA.

62. Cabinet, February 18, 1925, CAB 9(25), p. 262, CAB 23/49/18, TNA.

63. French Field Service Regulations quoted in Cabinet 9(25), February 18, 1925, CAB 23/49/18, TNA.

64. French Field Service Regulations quoted in Cabinet 9(25), February 18, 1925, CAB 23/49/18; and Cabinet 50(26), August 3, 1926, pp. 298–99, CAB 23/53, TNA.

65. "Chemical Warfare Policy," Cabinet 53(26), October 18, 1926, p. 5, CAB 23/53/23, TNA.

66. "Cabinet Warfare Policy," Cabinet 14(27), March 3, 1927, p. 7, CAB 23/54/14, TNA.

67. See, for example, Committee of Imperial Defence, "Chemical Warfare Policy," 723-B, in Cabinet, "Chemical Warfare Policy," CP 344 (26), October 12, 1926, pp. 1 and 2, CAB 24/81, TNA; and Committee of Imperial Defence, Extract from the Minutes of the 217th Meeting, November 11, 1926, in Cabinet, "Ratification of Protocol for Prohibition of Use of Poisonous Gases," March 25, 1929, C.P. 97(29), p. 1, CAB 24/202/47, TNA.

68. Cabinet 14(27), p. 8, CAB 23/54/14.

69. Cabinet 14(27), p. 8, CAB 23/54/14.

70. Cabinet 18(29), April 22, 1929, p. 6, CAB 23/60/18, TNA. The cabinet conclusions indicate that the British decided to ratify in 1929, but a table lists the deposits of the ratifications in France as 1930. "The Geneva Protocol."

71. Hugh Trenchard, in appendix, March 25, 1929, in Cabinet, "Chemical Warfare Policy: Ratification of Protocol for Prohibition of Use of Poisonous Gases," CP 128 (29), April 29, 1929, p. 2, CAB 24/203/28, TNA.

72. Sir Austen Chamberlain, Committee of Imperial Defence, extract from the minutes of the 241st meeting, held on April 23, 1929, "Chemical Warfare Policy," in Cabinet, "Chemical Warfare Policy: Ratification of Protocol for Prohibition of Use of Poisonous Gases," CP 128 (29), April 29, 1929, p. 1, CAB 24/203/28, TNA. It was clear from the preliminary meetings that chemical warfare would be discussed.

73. Foreign Office to His Majesty's Consul, Geneva, No. 41, "Chemical Warfare Policy," CP 128(29), April 23, 1929, p. 1, CAB 24/203/28, TNA.

74. 16 Can. Parl. Deb. (3rd session, HC) (1929), vol. 3, 2631.

75. 16 Can. Parl. Deb. (3rd session, Sen.) (1929), vol. 1, 271.

76. 16 Can. Parl. Deb. (3rd session, HC) (1929), vol. 3, 2631.

77. 16 Can. Parl. Deb. (3rd session, HC) (1929), vol. 3, 2631 and 2632.

78. 16 Can. Parl. Deb. (3rd session, HC) (1929), vol. 3, 2633.

79. "Cabinet Portraits—Hon. R. J. Manion," Maclean's, October 1, 1930, https://archive.macleans.ca/article/1930/10/1/cabinet-portraits-2.

80. 16 Can. Parl. Deb. (3rd session, HC) (1929), vol. 3, 2634.

81. 16 Can. Parl. Deb. (3rd session, Sen.) (1929), vol. 1, 272.

82. 16 Can. Parl. Deb. (3rd session, HC) (1929), vol. 3, 2631.

83. 16 Can. Parl. Deb. (3rd session, Sen.) (1929), vol. 1, 273.

84. 16 Can. Parl. Deb. (3rd session, HC) (1929), vol. 3, 2631.

85. 16 Can. Parl. Deb. (3rd session, Sen.) (1929), vol. 1, 272.

86. See, for example, A. H. Ulm, "Senate to Debate Warfare with Gas"; and Lynch, Beyond Appeasement, 71.

87. Ulm, "Senate to Debate Warfare with Gas."

88. Ulm, "Senate to Debate Warfare with Gas."

89. "Pershing Backs Poison Gas Ban."

90. Special to *The New York Times*. "Chemists Protest Poison Gas Ban," *New York Times,* December 10, 1926, ProQuest Historical Newspapers.

91. Special to *The New York Times*. "Ban on Poison Gas Opposed by Legion," *New York Times,* October 11, 1926, ProQuest Historical Newspapers.

92. 69 Cong. Rec. S153–154 (December 9, 1926), HeinOnline; and 71 Cong. Rec. H1825 (May 23, 1929), HeinOnline.

93. See, for example, "Pershing Backs Poison Gas Ban"; and Special to *The New York Times*, "Our Position on Poison Gas." *New York Times,* January 31, 1927, ProQuest Historical Newspapers.

94. 69 Cong. Rec. S151 (December 9, 1926), HeinOnline.

95. 69 Cong. Rec. S146 (December 9, 1926), HeinOnline.

96. 69 Cong. Rec. S146 and S363 (December 9, 1926), HeinOnline.

97. 71 Cong. Rec. H1824 (May 23, 1929), HeinOnline.

98. Fujitani, "The 1925 Geneva Gas Protocol," 108–9.

99. See the extensive discussion in Cabinet, "Material for Deciding British Policy in View of Germany's Withdrawal from the Disarmament Conference," CP 240(33), October 1933, CAB 24/243/39, TNA.

100. Cabinet 28(34), July 11, 1934, pp. 9–11, CAB 23/79/13, TNA.

101. Committee of Imperial Defence, "Extract from the Minutes of the 341st Meeting," December 15, 1938, p. 1, CAB 104/146, TNA.

102. H. M. Knatchbull Hugessen, "Copy of a Letter from the Foreign Office to the Secretary, Committee of Imperial Defence, November 29, 1938," in Committee of Imperial Defence, "The Use of Gas in War," 1489B, p. 1, CAB 104/146, TNA.

## 2. Is There Any Hope?

1. For example, see Mr. Boothy and Viscount Cranborne's reactions expressed in the epigraphs at the beginning of the chapter. 310 Parl. Deb. H.C. (5th ser.) (April 9, 1936), cols. 3040–66; and 310 Parl. Deb. H.C. (5th ser.) (April 9, 1936), cols. 3060 and 3062.

2. As scholars of the history of emotion note, "[b]y the middle of the 20th century . . . fear was so central to understandings of morale, and thus of how to win a war, that a range of discursive devices emerged to control and contain its expression." Claire Langhamer, Lucy Noakes, and Claudia Siebrecht, eds., "Introduction," *Total War: An Emotional History* (Oxford: Oxford University Press, 2020), 17. While they focused on World War II, their statement fits the attitudes, especially in Britain, in the years leading up to that conflict. Furthermore, it was actions, like the bombing in Ethiopia, as well as thoughts, such as beliefs that gas would appear in future wars, and words, such as the apocalyptic stories discussed in this chapter, that led to fear in Britain. There were actions (such as development of gas masks, discussed later in this chapter) as well as discursive devices (such as government air raid instructions) to help manage it.

3. One scholar noted that military expert Basil Liddell Hart believed Italy tried to keep its gas use quiet to avoid public outcry. It failed. Brett Holman, *The Next War in the Air: Britain's Fear of the Bomber, 1908–1941* (Farnham, Surrey, England: Ashgate, 2014), 141. For additional details about the gas use itself, see Rainer Baudendistel, *Between Bombs and Good Intentions: The International Committee of the Red Cross (ICRC) and the Italo-Ethiopian War, 1935–1936* (New York: Berghahn Books, 2006), 264–70.

4. "Mustard Gas in Abyssinia," *The Times* (London), March 25, 1936, *The Times* Digital Archive.

5. "The Collapse of Ethiopia," *Los Angeles Times,* May 5, 1936, ProQuest Historical Newspapers.

6. *Toronto Star Weekly,* August 1, 1936, quoted in John Bryden, *Deadly Allies: Canada's Secret War, 1937–1947* (Toronto: McClelland & Stewart Inc, 1989), 14. The outrage in these stories was matched by the tone of articles about Italian bombing "of the British Red Cross Ambulance [*sic*] . . . deliberately bombed at mid-day on 4th March while situated in the open on Korem Plain, two miles from the nearest troops" and identified by flags. 309 Parl. Deb. H.C. (5th ser.) (March 9, 1936), col. 1781. Gas, therefore, was unusual because the anger at its use was not connected to immediate damage to Britain, and it was similar to rage at violations of other norms of expected behavior.

7. Lina Grip and John Hart, "The Use of Chemical Weapons in the 1935–1936 Italo-Ethiopian War," *SIPRI Arms Control and Non-Proliferation Programme,* October 2009, 2, https://www.sipri.org/sites/default/files/Italo-Ethiopian-war.pdf.

8. Baudendistel, *Between Bombs and Good Intentions,* 265. Note that Spain used gas in Morocco against rebels in the Rif War, but this received almost no notice. The fact that this took place so soon after World War I, before the Geneva Gas Protocol, and was an internal colonial war probably made a difference. It was listed in one *New York Times* article during the core conflict, and even then it was a brief and matter-of-fact reference. See "Fierce Battle at Alhucemas," *New York Times,* August 25, 1923, ProQuest Historical Newspapers. The French later joined the war, and in this case General Hure was praised for not using gas, even though it might have enabled an easy victory. "Foreign News: Lion Trap," *Time,* August 14, 1933, www.time.com.

9. Both Italy and Ethiopia had ratified the Geneva Gas Protocol. "Protocol for the Prohibition of the Use in War of Asphyxiating, Poisonous, or Other Gases, and of Bacteriological Methods of Warfare (Geneva Protocol)," June 17, 1925, https://www.state.gov/t/isn/4784.htm, hereinafter "Geneva Gas Protocol." Also, while the focus of this section is Britain's reaction, that country was not alone in seeing widespread implications of the events in Africa. The International Committee of the Red Cross thought they "threatened the[international] legal system itself." Baudendistel, *Between Bombs and Good Intentions,* 291.

10. 100 Parl. Deb. H.L., (5th ser.) (March 30, 1936), col. 340; and "Geneva Gas Protocol." Ethiopia ratified the treaty on October 7, 1935, nearly three months before Italy used gas on it. Italy had ratified several years earlier in 1928.

11. Baudendistel, *Between Bombs and Good Intentions,* 267.

12. Baudendistel, *Between Bombs and Good Intentions,* 265.

13. Kim A. Wagner, "Savage Warfare: Violence and the Rule of Colonial Difference in Early British Counterinsurgency," *History Workshop Journal* 85 (January 3, 2018): 222, 225, https://doi.org/10.1093/hwj/dbx053.

This is a debated issue; see Huw Bennett, Michael Finch, Andrei Mamolea, and David Morgan-Owen, "Studying Mars and Clio: Or How Not to Write about the Ethics of Military Conduct and Military History," *History Workshop Journal* 88 (August 16, 2019): 274–80, https://doi.org/10.1093/hwj/dbz034; and Kim A. Wagner, "Expanding Bullets and Savage Warfare," *History Workshop Journal* 88 (August 14, 2019): 281–87, https://doi.org/10.1093/hwj/dbz044.

14. A week and a half later, Viscount Cranborne made a similar statement in the House of Commons: "if it turns out as a result of examination that they have used this gas, then it is clear that there has been a breach of a solemn undertaking, not only against the Abyssinian Government but against all the other signatories to the Protocol." 310 Parl. Deb. H.C. (5th ser.) (April 9, 1936), col 3061.

15. 100 Parl. Deb. H.L. (5th ser.) (March 30, 1936), cols. 343–44.

16. 100 Parl. Deb. H.L. (5th ser.) (March 30, 1936), cols. 347.

17. 310 Parl. Deb. H.C. (5th ser.) (April 9, 1936), cols. 3062. Lord Cranborne did not sit in the House of Lords until 1941; he was elected to represent South Dorset, while Viscount Cranborne, before that.

18. 310 Parl. Deb. H.C. (5th ser.) (April 9, 1936), cols. 3062. Another scholar argued that "Sections of the British press and Parliament were outraged by this gross violation of international law, but the government remained unmoved." Steven Morewood, "'This Silly African Business': The Military Dimension of Britain's Response to the Abyssinian Crisis," in G. Bruce Strang, *Collision of Empires: Italy's Invasion of Ethiopia and its International Impact* (Surrey: Ashgate, 2013), 90. However, what is relevant to this chapter is that there was public outcry.

19. This was an era of film, too, but the focus here will be on the novels, a rich art form.

20. See, for example, I. F. Clarke, *Voices Prophesying War: Future Wars, 1963–3749*, 2nd ed. (Oxford: Clarendon Press, 1992) and note 20 in chapter 1 for other scholarship on the topic.

21. Maroula Joannou, "(Mary) Cicely Hamilton [née Hammill]," *Oxford Dictionary of National Biography*, September 23, 2004, https://doi-org.unh.idm.oclc.org/10.1093/ref:odnb/38633.

22. "New Novels. A Tale of Time." *The Times* (London), May 3, 1922, *The Times Digital Archive*.

23. It is worth noting that the fascination with gas and its dangers played out differently in Weimar Germany. A play titled *Poison Gas*, written by Lampel, faced partial, if not total, censorship because it loosely reprised a true story of a gas disaster that occurred in a German town when toxins leaked and killed locals. "Poison Gas Play in Berlin: Censorship Controversy," *The Times* (London), March 4, 1929, Times Digital Archive.

24. Joannou, "Hamilton."

25. Earl of Halsbury, *1944* (London: Thornton Butterworth, 1926).

26. Earl of Halsbury, "Gas!" *British Legion Journal*, January 1933, 238–39.

27. H. G. Wells, *The Shape of Things to Come* (New York: Macmillan, 1933), 46–47, 148, and 156. *The Shape of Things to Come* became a film in 1936 as *Things to Come* and was later remade, at least once, in 1979, although the story changed in the transformation. *Things to Come* and *The Shape of Things to Come*, Imdb.com, https://www.imdb.com/title/tt0028358 and https://www.imdb.com/title/tt0079894.

28. Wells, *Things to Come*, 61.

29. "Campion, Sarah," *The Encyclopedia of Science Fiction*, http://www.sf-encyclopedia.com/entry/campion_sarah; and Sarah Campion, *Thirty Million Gas Masks* (Manchester: Peter Davies, Limited, 1937).

30. Clipping of *News Chronicle* Special, "Gas-Proof Cases Save the Babies," *News Chronicle*, December 10, 1935, HO 45/17620, TNA.

31. Hubert Phillips, *News Chronicle*, quoted in Campion, *Thirty Million Gas Masks*, 9.

32. Campion, *Thirty Million Gas Masks*, 313.

33. "'Idiot's Delight' at the Apollo," *Illustrated London News*, April 2, 1938, 600.

34. "Town-Planning against Air Attack: A Project from Soviet Russia," *Illustrated London News*, July 23, 1927, 146. One benefit of using the *ILN* as the illustration of a widely read magazine to show the public's view of gas and its threats is that articles contain both text and visuals, thus creating a rich source for analysis.

35. "Medicine: War Gas Protection," *Time*, October 26, 1931, http://www.time.com /time/magazine/article/0,9171,742510,00.html.

36. "Germany's Idea of Future Warfare: Gas-Bomb Attacks Predicted" and "When Everyone Would Be in the Front Line: Chemical Warfare," *Illustrated London News*, February 1, 1930, 162–63.

37. C. E. Bower, "The Menace of Gas Warfare: Home Precautions the Citizen Should Take," *Illustrated London News*, May 2, 1936, 752.

38. "Poison Gas Protection," *Maclean's*, May 15, 1937, https://archive.macleans.ca /article/1937/5/15/poison-gas-protection; and "Population of France from 1700– 2020," Statista 2022, https://www.statista.com/statistics/1009279/total-population -france-1700–2020.

39. "Poison Gas Protection," *Maclean's*, May 15, 1937, https://archive.macleans.ca /article/1937/5/15/poison-gas-protection.

40. The symbolic and emotional value of gas masks has been discussed in, for example, a catalog by Ana Carden-Coyne about art and an article by Susan Grayzel. Ana Carden Coyne, David Morris, and Tim Wilcox, eds., "The Sensory War: Bodies, Minds, and Environments," in *The Sensory War, 1914–2014* (Manchester: Manchester Art Gallery, 2014), 10–31; and Susan Grayzel, "'Macabre and Hilarious' The Emotional Life of the Civilian Gas Mask in France during and after the First World War," 40–58, in *Total War: An Emotional History*, ed. Claire Langhamer, Lucy Noakes, and Claudia Siebrecht.

41. "Civilians Gas-Masked: Precautions Geneva May Render Superfluous," *Illustrated London News*, February 20, 1932, 280.

42. "Foreign Precautions against Gas Attack: What Is Britain Doing? Gas-Mask Making, for Defence in War, as a German Peace-Time Industry," *Illustrated London News*, July 9, 1932, 46.

43. "Everyone's Doing It but Us! Civilians and Officials Training against Gas-Attack and Aerial Bombing," *Illustrated London News*, October 8, 1932, 531; and see also "Anti-Gas Defence Training in Germany: A Realistic 'Air Raid,'" *Illustrated London News*, July 9, 1932, 47.

44. "Science: Mars in White Smock," *Time*, March 9, 1937, http://www.time.com /time/magazine/article/0,9171,930911,00.html.

45. "Mars in White Smock." Note that the United States had developed a new weapon, lewisite, near the end of the war, but although this had not been used, it was known and was not radically different from the others used in World War I.

46. "Mars in White Smock."

47. "What to Do when Enemy Bombers Attack You," *Life*, March 14, 1938, 4–5.

48. "What to Do when Enemy Bombers Attack You," 5.

49. Aerial attacks on civilians occurred during World War I, although not to the same extent as during World War II. Susan Grayzel, *At Home and Under Fire: Air Raids*

*and Culture in Britain from the Great War to the Blitz* (New York: Cambridge University Press, 2012), 22–25.

50. D. J. C. Wiseman, *Gas Warfare*, vol. 1, *The Second World War, 1939–1945, Army: Special Weapons and Types of Warfare* (n.p.: The War Office, 1951), 294–295, 296–97. Most of the gear falls into the categories of masks, items of clothing with chemical protection, and alarms of various sorts.

51. Wiseman, *Gas Warfare*, 192.

52. "Medicine: War Gas Protection." Interestingly, although the very practice of encouraging extensive anti-gas measures means that the writers of the magazine did not have faith in international treaties banning gas, the recommended "safety zones" were to be "protected like Red Cross stations by international agreement."

53. James H. Powers, "Military Madness of the World," *Boston Globe*, April 26, 1936, ProQuest Historical Newspapers.

54. Bryden, *Deadly Allies*, 14.

55. Andrew Iarocci, "'A Unique Art' Canadian Anti-Gas Respirator Production in the Second World War," *Canadian Military History* 18, 4 (2009), 55–61.

56. "Anti-Gas Classes to Be Started in Winnipeg," *Globe and Mail* (Toronto), March 18, 1937, ProQuest Historical Newspapers.

57. Faith, *Behind the Gas Mask*, 110.

58. Faith, *Behind the Gas Mask*, 71 citing US Senate Committee on Military Affairs, Reorganization of the Army, August 8, 1919, part 2, p. 93.

59. See chapter 3 in Faith, *Behind the Gas Mask* for an in-depth discussion.

60. For a detailed account of the interwar and wartime production, see Leo P. Brophy, Wyndham D. Miles, and Rexmond C. Cochrane, *The Chemical Warfare Service: From Laboratory to Field* (Washington, DC: Office of the Chief of Military History, Department of the Army, 1959), 314–41.

61. Leo P. Brophy and George J. B. Fisher, *United States Army in World War II: The Technical Services. The Chemical Warfare Service: Organizing for War* (Washington, DC, Center of Military History, United States Army, 2004, 1959), 32.

62. Brophy and Fisher, *Organizing for War*, 229.

63. Brophy, Miles, and Cochrane, *From Laboratory to Field*, 85–86 and 318.

64. Brophy and Fisher, *Organizing for War*, 231 32.

65. Brophy and Fisher, *Organizing for War*, 232–45.

66. The "emergency period" was the phase between President Franklin Roosevelt's Executive Order 8244, which "authorized an increase in the strength of the Army" and thus signaled serious preparation for war on many military fronts—including CW—between September 8, 1939, and the attack on Pearl Harbor on December 7, 1941. Brophy and Fisher, *Organizing for War*, 199.

67. "The Poison Gas Peril: Search for Antidote," *The Times* (London), January 4, 1929, *The Times* Digital Archive.

68. "The Poison Gas Peril."

69. Terence O'Brien, *Civil Defence* (London: Her Majesty's Stationery Office and Longmans, Green, 1955), 14–15.

70. O'Brien, *Civil Defence*, 60, 62–63, 166–67, and 300.

71. O'Brien, *Civil Defence*, 15, 25–26, 31, and 166–67, for example. R. R. Scott, Chairman, Air Raid Precautions (Policy) Sub-Committee, Committee of Imperial Defence,"

report in "Policy with Regard to Respirators," A.R.P. 42 [also paper No. A.R.P. (O) 514], October 14, 1935, HO 45/16428, TNA.

72. Even during the war, this probably did not reach 100 percent anywhere. See, for example, Mass-Observation, *Supplementary Report on Gas Mask Posters, M-O 5.8.41*, MO Online File Report 814, 3, Mass-Observation Archives (hereinafter MO) in which it is clear that even after a poster education campaign and during the war, in July 1941 less than half of the people surveyed would put on a gas mask or even knew what to do if they heard a gas rattle (an alarm).

73. Lt. Col. Kenneth H. Cousland, "The Great War. 1914–1918: A Former 'Gunner' of the First World War Looks Back," 56, Liddell Hart Centre for Military Archives, King's College (hereinafter LHCMA), London.

74. "Memorandum prepared by the War Office and the Air Ministry," in Committee of Imperial Defence, "The Manufacture of Toxic Gas for Use in War," 1465-B, August 1938, p. 2, CAB 104/106, TNA.

75. L.C.Hollis (?) (illegible) to General Hastings Ismay, letter, June 13, 1939, p. 1, CAB 104/146, TNA.

76. Home Office, "Home Office Memorandum, Position at April 1939," 1 May 1939, Annex 4 to Illeg. To Ismay letter, June 13, 1939, p. 15, CAB 104/146, TNA.

77. S.R. Bennett to Whitely, "Modification of Babies' Helmets for Adults," November 11, 1939, p. 1, HO 186/220, TNA.

78. "Under London's First Gasproof [*sic*] Office: Shelter for Ten," *Illustrated London News*, October 17, 1936, 663.

79. "The A.G.P. Co. Ltd," *Illustrated London News*, May 7, 1938. Also see the A.G.P. ad in "Gas Protection," *Illustrated London News* July 16, 1938, 37.

80. "Horrible but Possible," ad, *Illustrated London News*, July 16, 1938, 137.

81. "Train Them to Wear Them First," Newspaper clipping from the *Star*, November 16, 1932, SxMOA1/2/55/1/A/17, MO.

82. "Our History," PDSA, https://www.pdsa.org.uk/what-we-do/why-were-special; and "A.R.P. Needs," *The Times* (London), September 28, 1938, *The Times* Digital Archive.

83. Coe, Local Defence Division, Naval Staff, to P [?] M Osmond, Ministry of Home Security, August 18, 1940, "Shelters: Gas Proofing," HO 197/5, TNA.

84. "Under London's First Gasproof Office," *Illustrated London News*. According to the National Archives historic currency calculator, 40 shillings, the cost of the office, in 1935 would be approximately £101 in value today and in 1940 would be equal to about £80, both equivalent to a skilled tradesman's daily pay. The National Archives, https://www.nationalarchives.gov.uk/currency-converter/#. In Oanda's currency calculator, that is equivalent to $137 or $109 in 2022. Oanda, https://www.oanda.com/currency/converter/.

85. There is excellent scholarship on this topic for some debates, criticism, and proposals. See, for example, Peter Stanksy, *The First Day of the Blitz: September 7, 1940* (New Haven, CT: Yale University Press, 2007); and Grayzel, 271–73.

86. Undated (probably 1941), untitled memo of discussion with the Ministers of Home Security and Health, p. 3, CAB 118/26, TNA.

87. Assistant chief engineer to deputy chief engineer, "Gas Proofing Public Shelters," Memo, August 29, 1940, "Shelters: Gas-Proofing," HO 197/5, TNA.

88. Sir John Anderson and Mr. Mander, extract from Hansard, July 16, 1940, HO 197/5, TNA; and R.C. Cox, deputy chief engineer to senior regional technical officers and assistant chief engineers, "Gasproofing Public Shelters," August 8, 1940, "Shelters: Gas-Proofing," HO 197/5, TNA.

89. Correspondence between assistant chief engineer and deputy chief engineer, August 10, 1940, "Public Shelters: Gas-Proofing," HO 197/5, TNA.

90. "Gas Proofing Public Shelters," HO 197/5.

91. Herbert Morrison, "'Anti-Gas Precautions,' Memo by Home Secretary and Minister of Home Security," War Cabinet, W.P. (41) 15, January 24, 1941, folder 1, p. 4, HO 186/1498, TNA.

92. J. A. Sadd, Superintendent, Defensive Munitions Dept., Porton, "Summary of Methods of Protecting Small Children," Porton Report Number 1657, February 1, 1937, p. 2, HO 45/17620, TNA.

93. Ministry of Home Security, "Air Raids: What You Must Know, What You Must Do," revised edition, 1941. London: H.M. Stationery Office, "Instruction of the Public—Suggestions for Training," table of contents and p. 45, HO 186/962, TNA.

94. Grayzel, *At Home and Under Fire*, 235.

95. Air Raid Precautions Department, Home Office, "The Protection of Foodstuffs against Poison Gas," London: His Majesty's Stationery Office, 1937, p. 5, HO 186/166, TNA.

96. Draft, "Public Information Leaflet No. 6: Poison Gas and Food in Your Home," 1939, p. 2, HO 186/166, TNA.

97. War Cabinet, 2/1/38, April 25, 1941, p. 2, CAB 118/26, TNA; and Anti-Gas Precautions "Memorandum Prepared by the Home Secretary with the Other Civil Departments Concerned," pp. 3–4, CAB 118/26, TNA.

98. War Cabinet, p. 2, CAB 118/26.

99. War Cabinet, p. 5, CAB 118/26.

100. ARP Headquarters, County Borough of Sunderland, "Treatment and Disposal of Foodstuffs Contaminated by Gas," October 18, 1941, HO 186/1883, TNA; and ARP Headquarters, County Borough of Sunderland, "Food Decontamination Arrangements," June 15, 1942, HO 186/1883, TNA.

101. One report "submit[ted] to the Policy Committee the following questions: (a) Is it necessary to ensure that at the outbreak of war cheap respirators shall be available in all parts of the country liable to air attack for all persons not in possession of higher-grade respirators? If so (b) Should this object be achieved by the accumulation of the necessary stocks to the cost of the Government and by the Government? (c) Should such stocks be issued free of charge when the emergency arises or on payment? Or (d) Can the object be achieved by encouraging strictly controlled private production, the general public being required to buy its own respirators?" R. R. Scott, *Report by Organisation Sub-Committee*, in Committee of Imperial Defence, Air Raids Precautions (Policy) Sub-Committee. Policy with Regard to Respirators. A.R.P. (P) 42 (Also Paper No. A.R.P. (O) 514), October 14, 1935, p. 4, HO 45/16428, TNA.

102. Scott, "Report by Organisation Sub-Committee," 9, HO 45/16248.

103. H. L. Pritchard, A.T. Sumner, E.H. Hodgson, R.D. Fennelly, and E.J. Hodsoll, Air Raid Precautions (Organisation) Sub-Committee, "Sub-Committee on Policy with

Regard to Respirators," Report, Committee of Imperial Defence, A.R.P. (O) 328, March 6, 1934, HO 45/16248, TNA.

104. L.T.D. Williams, "Summary of Main Conclusions Reached," February 3, 1941, p. 2, HO 186/1498, TNA; and Herbert Morrison, "Memorandum by Home Secretary and Minister of Home Security," January 24, 1941, p. 1, Anti-Gas Precautions, War Cabinet, W.P. 41 (15), HO 186/1498, TNA. The population of Britain was approximately 48 million at the time; thus, if these masks worked and did not become obsolete, most adult Britons who used respirators would find some protection. The Empire had approximately 389 million in India alone; there was no way to protect them. "UK Population Change," archived on January 5, 2016, The National Archives, https://webarchive .nationalarchives.gov.uk/ukgwa/20160105160709/http://www.ons.gov.uk/ons /resources/figure2s_tcm77-292368.png; and "Population of India," Advocate (Burnie, Tas.), March 31, 1943, Trove, https://trove.nla.gov.au/newspaper/article/68804483.

105. Chairman, Air Raid Precautions (Organsation) Sub-Committee, "Policy with Regard to Respirators," Committee of Imperial Defence, July 1935, p. 4, HO 45/16428, TNA.

106. Major Summer, in extract from minutes of meeting of Air Raid Precautions (Organisation), April 15, 1935, p. 2, HO 45/16428, TNA.

107. Illeg. to Wing-Commander E.J. Hodsoll, September 26, 1935, p. 2, HO 45/16428, TNA.

108. 309 Parl. Deb. H.C. (5th ser.) (February 27,1936), col. 627.

109. 98 Parl. Deb. H.L. (5th ser.) (July 23, 1935), col. 754.

110. Scott, "Extract from Minutes," April 15, 1935, p. 10, HO 45/16428, TNA; and Chairman, Air Raid Precautions (Organsation) Sub-Committee, "Policy with Regard to Respirators," July 1935, p. 3, HO 45/16428, TNA.

111. Pritchard, Sumner, Hodgson, Fennelly, and Hodsoll, "Sub-Committee on Policy with Regard to Respirators," March 6, 1934, p. 11, HO 45/16428.

112. R. R. Scott, Air Raid Precautions (Organsation) Sub-Committee, "Policy with Regard to Respirators," Committee of Imperial Defence, A.R.P. (P) 42, October 14, 1935, p. 3, HO 45/16428, TNA.

113. Illeg. To Scott, letter, "Protection of Babies and Infants against Gas," June 11, 1935, p. 1, HO 45/17620, TNA.

114. C. G. Trotman and J. A. Sadd, Defensive Munitions Dept., "The Protection of Babies and Young Children against Gas," May 11, 1936, p. 1, HO 45/17620, TNA.

115. Medical Officer of Health, Metropolitan Borough of Poplar to Commander A. Steele-Perkins, Home Office Air Raid Precautions Department, July 14, 1936, HO 45/17620, TNA.

116. Illeg, "Babies' Device," March 3, 1938, HO 45/17620, TNA.

117. "Anti-Gas Protection for Young Children," 3, HO 45/17620, TNA.

118. "Babies' Device," p. 1, HO 45/17620; and "Anti-Gas Protection for Young Children," p. 4, HO 45/17620.

119. The Ministry of Home Security, "Hitler Will Send No Warning," poster (London: J. Weiner Ltd, c. 1940–1945), Imperial War Museum. Poster can be found at https://commons.wikimedia.org/wiki/File:Hitler_Will_Send_No_Warning_Art .IWMPST13861.jpg.

120. R. S. Woods to Sir George Gater, September 18, 1939, HO 186/2098, TNA. When children played conkers with their respirator containers, they swung them by the straps so that the boxes would hit one another. Usually children played the game with horse chestnuts. Public archeologist Gabriel Moshenska discusses in more details children's perceptions of gas masks as well as some of the drills they experienced and games they tried with their masks and boxes. Gabriel Moshenska, *Material Cultures of Childhood in Second World War Britain* (London: Routledge, 2019), 29–32.

121. Copy of extract from the report of the Regional Police Staff Office, no. 10 region (Manchester), September 19, 1939, p. 1, HO 186/2098, TNA.

122. "Report from Mass-Observation on Gas-Mask Carrying [From Ladbroke Road, London]", May 28, 1940, p. 1, Mass-Observation Online Report, Gas-Mask Carrying, File Report 146, MO; and "Reports and Summaries," p. 22, TC 1938–1945, TC 55: Gas Masks 1939–1943, Box 2: Gas Mask Counts, 1941–43, MO.

123. M.60.B., M.35.D., M.25.B., Mass-Observation, TC 1938–1945, TC 55: Gas Masks 1939–1943, Box 1 Gas Carrying, 55-1-B Gas Mask Questionnaire March 1941, pp. 8 and 12, MO.

124. F.30.B., Gas Mask Questionnaire March 1941, p. 17.

125. 370 Parl. Deb. H.C. (5th ser.) (March 27, 1941), col. 684.

126. Gas Mask Questions, Gas Mask Questionnaire, March 1941, p. 1.

127. "Gas Masks," 1940, p. 5, Data from Sept. 40 Directive (Box 165/212), Mass-Observation Online 191301_1028655-1928661, 55-2-M, MO.

128. "Feelings about Poison Gas," p. 2, Mass-Observation Report Online 662, April 20, 1941, MO.

129. "Gas Masks," 1940, 4.

130. "Gas Masks," 1940, 5.

131. Wiseman, *Gas Warfare*, 19.

132. Armstrong to Gertrude Williams, May 17, 1941, HO 186/2247, TNA.

133. J. Johnson to Mr. Sheepshanks, February 14, 1941, HO 186/2098, TNA. Other reasons included the recognition that cabinet members would often be in violation of the law because they did not always carry their masks, and it would be a burden on foster parents to be responsible for evacuated children. "Difficulties in the Way of an Order about the Compulsory Carrying of Gas Masks," March 19, 1941, HO 186/2098, TNA.

134. Draft report, dictated by Mr. McNulty, "Subject-GAS," March 11, 1941, HO 186/2247, TNA.

135. See, for example, G.P. to Miss Crawten, September 26, 1941, HO 186/2247, TNA; and unsigned memo to Mr. Snelling, April 10, 1941, HO 186/2116, TNA.

136. Special Correspondent, "Where's Your Gas Mask?" *The Evening Chronicle* (Manchester), March 17, 1940, clipping in HO 186/2098, TNA; and Illegible to Sir Wilfred Eady memorandum, March 11, 1940, HO 186/2098, TNA.

137. Unsigned to J. P. McNulty, letter, April 30, 1941, HO 186/2116, TNA.

138. "Hitler Will Send No Warning"; and "Take Your Gas Mask Everywhere," Art. IWM PST 13860, Imperial War Museum, https://www.iwm.org.uk/collections/item/object/8427.

139. Mrs. Gertrude Williams to Dr. E. Armstrong, August 26, 1941, HO 186/2247, TNA.

140. Gertrude Williams to Howard Marshall, June 12, 1941, HO 186/2247, TNA.

141. "Gas Raid Quiz No. 3," draft, HO 186/2247, TNA; and "Gas Raid Quiz No. 4," proof, HO 186/2247, TNA.

142. "Gas Raid Quiz No. 1," proof, HO 186/2247, TNA; and "Gas Raid Quiz No. 6," HO 186/2247, TNA.

143. "Gas Raid Quiz No. 8," proof, HO 186/2247, TNA; and J. Walter Thompson Company Limited, London, "Gas Raid Quiz," draft, unnumbered, May 19, 1941, HO 186/2247, TNA.

144. "Gas Raid Quiz No. 3," proof, HO 186/2247, TNA.

145. "Gas Raid Quiz No. 3," proof.

146. "Gas Raid Quiz, No. 2," proof, HO 186/2247, TNA; and "Gas Raid Quiz, No. 17," proof, HO 186/2247, TNA; and "Gas Raid Quiz, No. 20," proof, HO 186/2247, TNA.

147. "J. Walter Thompson Company Limited, London, "Gas Raid Quiz No. 12," draft, HO 186/2247, TNA.

148. "Gas Raid Quiz, No. 9," proof, HO 186/2247, TNA.

149. For example, inclement weather could inhibit a gas attack. George Wood to Sir George Gater, September 18, 1939, HO 186/2098, TNA.

150. "Gas Raid Quiz, No. 5," proof, HO 186/2247.

151. "Gas Raid Quiz, No. 1" and "Gas Raid Quiz, No. 9," HO 186/2247.

## 3. The Sole Exception to the Rule

1. Winston S. Churchill, "We Shall Fight on the Beaches," June 4, 1940, House of Commons, transcribed at the International Churchill Society, https://winstonchurchill .org/resources/speeches/1940-the-finest-hour/we-shall-fight-on-the-beaches.

2. Field Marshal Sir John Dill, "The Use of Gas in Home Defence," June 15, 1940, pp. 1–2, WO 193/732, TNA.

3. It even went so far as to discuss, with the secretary of state for dominions, the status of global British subjects. Chiefs of Staff Committee, Minutes, C.O.S. (42) 104th Meeting, April 2, 1942, p. 4, CAB 79/20, TNA.

4. General staff, War Office, *Gas Warfare*, June 1922, p. 3, WO 188/144, TNA.

5. Extract from "Summary of Important Decisions in Connection with Policy as Regards Chemical Warfare," WO 188/212, TNA; and "A Summary of Important Notes and Papers in Connection with the Policy of Gas Warfare in Order of Dates from 1899," p. 16–17, WO 188/212, TNA.

6. "Extract from the Minutes of the 341st Meeting Held on December 15, 1938," Committee of Imperial Defence, December 15, 1938, p. 1, CAB 104/146, TNA.

7. Illegible to Wood, September 13, 1939, HO 186/2846, TNA.

8. H. M. Knatchbull-Hugessen to secretary, Committee of Imperial Defence, November 29, 1938, enclosed in Committee of Imperial Defence, "The Use of Poison Gas in War," December 2, 1938, p. 1, CAB 104/146, TNA.

9. "Memorandum Prepared By the War Office and Air Ministry," in Committee of Imperial Defence, "The Manufacture of Toxic Gas for Use in War," August 30, 1938, pp. 2–3, CAB 104/146, TNA.

10. Foreign office to Germany, September 3, 1939, HO 186/2846, TNA.

11. Swiss legation to foreign office, September 8, 1939, HO 186/2846, TNA.

12. From an eye-witness at headquarters, "Full Story of Ypres," *The Times* (London), April 30, 1915, *The Times* Digital Archive.

13. Illegible to Wood, September 13, 1939, HO 186/2846, TNA.

14. Copy of Brazilian Embassy, London to foreign office, June 18/19, 1940, HO 186/2846, TNA.

15. SBL to Mr. Williams, August 7, 1941, HO 186/2247, TNA.

16. C. S. Sugden, "Nature of Enemy Attack," Anglo-French Chemical Warfare Conversations, 1939, Service Discussions, A.F.C.W. (S.) 4, May 5, 1939, CAB 29/162, TNA.

17. M.I. 14, "Possible Use of Gas by Germany," January 17, 1941, p. 1, HO 186/1498, TNA; and Florence E. [Illegible] to minister of home security, March 7, 1943, HO 186/962, TNA.

18. Dan Cruickshank, "The German Threat to Britain in World War Two," BBC, last updated June 21, 2011, http://www.bbc.co.uk/history/worldwars/wwtwo/invasion_ww2_01.shtml.

19. G.M.K. to Lord Privy Seal, "Enemy Use of Mustard Gas," January 21, 1941, CAB 118/26, TNA.

20. Annex to war cabinet, C.O.S. (41) 582, "Chemical Warfare," War Cabinet, September 30, 1941, p. 5, PREM 3/88/1, TNA.

21. W[inston] S. C[hurchill] to General Ismay, June 30, 1940, CAB 120/775, TNA.

22. Dill, "The Use of Gas in Home Defence," p. 1, WO 193/732.

23. Dill, "The Use of Gas in Home Defence," p. 1, WO 193/732.

24. D. F. Anderson, ACIGS(C) to CIGS, June 16, 1940, WO 193/732, TNA.

25. Anderson, June 16, 1940, WO 193/732.

26. Anderson, June 16, 1940, WO 193/732.

27. Compare the summary of viewpoints mentioned in WO 193/732, Sugden, July 8, 1940.

28. Winston Churchill to General Ismay, June 30, 1940, CAB 120/775, TNA.

29. A. C. T. Paget to minister of home defence, July 1, 1940, CAB 120/775, TNA.

30. H. L. Ismay to Sir Thomas Gardiner, July 24, 1940, HO 186/317, TNA. See Peter Fleming, *Operation Sea Lion* (New York: Simon and Schuster, 1957); and G. C. Wynne, *Stopping Hitler: An Official Account of How Britain Planned to Defend Itself in the Second World War* (Yorkshire: Frontline Books, 2017) for detailed accounts of Britain's plans to resist an invasion.

31. M.I. 14, "Possible Use of Gas By Germany," January 17, 1941, HO 186/1498.

32. G.M.K., "Enemy Use of Mustard Gas," CAB 118/26, and gas quizzes in chapter 2.

33. Kenneth N. Crawford to Sugden, minute 15A, August 30, 1940, WO 193/720, TNA.

34. Annex to L. C. Hollis, "Chemical Warfare—Retaliation," C.O.S. (41) 171, March 17, 1941, WO 193/732, TNA; L. Williams to Major W. J. Stirling, November 12, 1941, CAB 21/3192, TNA; D. Brunet, "Large-Scale Gas Attacks on the British Isles during Winter Inversions," June 10, 1941, CAB 21/3192, TNA; and Chiefs of Staff Committee, C.O.S. (41) 156th meeting, minutes, May 2, 1941, p. 4, CAB 79/11, TNA.

35. Chiefs of Staff Committee, C.O.S. (41) 156th meeting, CAB 79/11.

36. "Extract from Minutes of Meeting of the Chiefs of Staff Committee on 20th January 1941," HO 186/1498, TNA.

37. Chief of the Imperial General Staff, "Chemical Warfare: Gas Retaliation in Event of Invasion," Memorandum, C.O.S. (41) 269, April 26, 1941, WO 193/732, TNA.

38. These scholars refer to a decision to retaliate if it is beneficial, not if it is in retaliation for gas, during an invasion. Robert Harris and Jeremy Paxman, *A Higher Form of Killing: The Secret Story of Gas and Germ Warfare* (Chatto & Windus, 1982), 115.

39. Acting assistant C of S G-2 to C of S, memo, December 5, 1940, sub: "British and German Production and Use of Mustard Gas," WPD 165–20, National Archives and Records Administration [hereinafter NARA] cited in Frederic J. Brown, *Chemical Warfare: A Study in Restraints* (Westport, CT: Greenwood Press, Publishers, 1981, reprint of Princeton University Press, 1968), 229, n. 102.

40. Leo P. Brophy and George J. B. Fisher, *The Chemical Warfare Service: Organizing for War* (Washington, DC: Center of Military History, United States Army, 2004), 206 and 227.

41. Brophy and Fisher, *Organizing for War*, 265.

42. Jonathan B. Tucker, *War of Nerves: Chemical Warfare from World War I to Al-Qaeda* (New York: Pantheon Books, 2006), 89.

43. Kim Coleman, *A History of Chemical Warfare* (Houndsmill, Hampshire: Palgrave Macmillan, 2005), 68; and Leo P. Brophy, Wyndham D. Miles, and Rexmond C. Cochrane, *United States Army in World War II: The Technical Services: The Chemical Warfare Service: From Laboratory to Field* (Washington, DC: Office of the Chief of Military History, Department of the Army, 1959), 404–5.

44. Donald H. Avery, *The Science of War: Canadian Scientists and Allied Military Technology during the Second World War* (Toronto: University of Toronto Press, 1998): 124.

45. Michael Bliss, *Banting: A Biography* (Toronto: McClelland and Stewart, 1984), 263.

46. Christopher Robin Paige, *Canada and Chemical Warfare: 1939–1945* (Salt Spring Island, Canada: Spire Publishing, 2011), 41.

47. Paige, *Canada and Chemical Warfare*, 42; and Avery, *Science of War*, 127.

48. E. Ll. Davies to Director of Chemical Warfare, "Defence of England Against C.W. Agents," March 9, 1942, [HQ]S 4352-1-8, vol 1.: Chemical Warfare General Policies, Reel C5002, RG24- C-1, Library and Archives Canada [hereinafter LAC]; and Cabinet War Committee, minutes, March 6, 1942, Minutes and Documents of the Cabinet War Committee, volume VIII, RG 2, 7c, LAC.

49. N. Miller, "Some Considerations Concerning the Employment of Chemical Warfare as Part of a Large-Scale Attack by the Enemy," March 6, 1942, p. 2, S.4354-1-8, vol. 1: Chemical Warfare General Policies, Reel 5002, RG24-C-1, LAC.

50. N. A. White, "C.W. Defence of England in the Event of an Invasion," undated [approximately March 1942], S.4354-1-8, vol. 1: Chemical Warfare General Policies," Reel 5002, RG24-C-1, LAC.

51. Lieutenant-Colonel D. J. C. Wiseman, *The Second World War, 1939–1945, Army: Special Weapons and Types of Warfare*, volume 1: *Gas Warfare* (London [?]: The War Office, 1951), 12.

52. E. Ll. Davies, "Defence of England Against C.W. Agents," March 9, 1942; and Cabinet War Committee, March 6, 1942, Minutes and documents of the Cabinet War Committee.

53. Chiefs of Staff Committee, minutes, C.O.S. (42) 89th Mtg., March 19, 1942, p. 2, CAB 79/19, TNA.

54. Protocols were discussed in 1941, but there were amendments in a 1943 folder, too, suggesting that they remained in force. "Amendment to Departmental Invasion Instructions. Poison Use," circa 1943, p. 1, HO 186/1277, TNA; Illegible to Wing Commander Warburton, "Notification of Use of Poison Gas," April 7, 1941, pp. 13–15, HO186/1495, TNA; and Chiefs of Staff Committee, minutes, C.O.S. (41) 103rd meeting, March 12, 1941, CAB 79/10, TNA.

55. Wiseman, *Special Weapons*, appendices II and III.

56. Wiseman, *Special Weapons*, 13.

57. Wiseman, *Special Weapons*, 6, 7, 5, and 9.

58. Wiseman, *Special Weapons*, 16–17.

59. Wiseman, *Special Weapons*, 6.

60. Bernard Partridge, "Retribution," *Punch*, July 7, 1915, 1.

61. Note that several state parties have since withdrawn reservations, sometimes doing so for CW separately from BW. "Protocol for the Prohibition of the Use in War of Asphyxiating, Poisonous, or Other Gases, and of Bacteriological Methods of Warfare (Geneva Protocol)," June 17, 1925, https://www.state.gov/t/isn/4784.htm, hereinafter "Geneva Gas Protocol."

62. War Cabinet, Joint Planners Staff, "Chemical Warfare: Possible Use of Gas by Italy against Ethiopia," illegible numbers, December 6, 1940, p. 1, CAB 84/24/9, TNA; and C.-in-C., Middle East to The War Office, repeated major-general commanding troops Sudan, December 30, 1940, CAB 120/775, TNA.

63. Joint Planners Staff, "Possible Use of Gas by Italy against Ethiopia," p. 1, CAB 84/24/9.

64. Joint Planners Staff, "Possible Use of Gas by Italy against Ethiopia," p. 1, CAB 84/24/9.

65. Joint Planners Staff, "Possible Use of Gas by Italy against Ethiopia," p. 1, CAB 84/24/9.

66. Joint Planners Staff, "Possible Use of Gas by Italy against Ethiopia," p. 2, CAB 84/24/9.

67. Joint Planners Staff, "Possible Use of Gas by Italy against Ethiopia," p. 2, CAB 84/24/9.

68. [War Office] to commander-in-chief, Middle East, undated [December 1940?], CAB 120/775, TNA.

69. Joint Planners Staff, "Possible Use of Gas by Italy against Ethiopia," p. 2, CAB 84/24/9.

70. Joint Planners Staff, "Possible Use of Gas by Italy against Ethiopia," p. 2, CAB 84/24/9.

71. Joint Planners Staff, "Possible Use of Gas by Italy against Ethiopia," p. 3, CAB 84/24/9.

72. Joint Planners Staff, "Possible Use of Gas by Italy against Ethiopia," p. 3, CAB 84/24/9.

73. Joint Planners Staff, "Possible Use of Gas by Italy against Ethiopia," p. 3, CAB 84/24/9. A factor that was not discussed was the exchange of telegrams with Italy, via Brazil, around June 19, 1940, in which Italy promised Britain it would adhere to the Geneva Gas Protocol. Brazilian Embassy, "No. 36. Received in Foreign Office 19th June 1940," HO 186/2846, TNA. Britain could have publicized this to darken Italy's

name further or to bolster its own actions if it had decided to retaliate in kind. The fact that it did not adds to the argument that Britain did not want to put itself in a position where it felt it had to use gas to respond in kind.

74. D. [?] Williams to J. E. Sainer, August 2, 1940, CAB 21/1258, TNA, illustrates the gentle dismissal of a report brought to the government by a civilian.

75. Winston Churchill to General Ismay for Chiefs of Staff Committee and Others Concerned, December 26, 1940, CAB 120/775, TNA.

76. Churchill to Ismay, December 26, 1940, CAB 120/775.

77. Churchill to Ismay, December 26, 1940, CAB 120/775.

78. Hamilton to Kitchener, July 8, 1915, WO 32/5172, TNA. For World War II awareness of this pretext, see "Threat of Poison Gas Seen in Nazi Lies," October 21, 1939, *Globe and Mail* (Toronto), ProQuest Historical Newspapers.

79. A. Nicholl, "Chemical Warfare—Publicity for Precautionary Measures," in War Cabinet, Chiefs of Staff Committee, C.O.S. (41) 147, March 8, 1941, p. 1, CAB 80/26, TNA.

80. A. Nicholl in C.O.S. (41) 147, March 8, 1941, p. 1, CAB 80/26.

81. Foreign Office to Washington, December 8, 1941, HO 186/2846, TNA. Also see Swedish Legation in London, Note Verbale, December 17, 1941, HO 186/2846, TNA. Note that the United States declared war on Hungary and Rumania in 1942 and severed diplomatic relations with Finland in 1944, but the exchanges about the Geneva Gas Protocol occurred between the attack on Pearl Harbor and war with them.

82. Some members of the public in Canada heard about this but did not exhibit much faith. The Toronto *Globe and Mail* reported that the "assurance . . . may have some value as a curio," but there was nothing in *The Times* (London) during the period and, as events later in the chapter demonstrate, the appeals to Japan seemed to stay secret otherwise. "Notes and Comments," *Globe and Mail* (Toronto), December 10, 1941, ProQuest Historical Newspapers.

83. Buenos Aires to Foreign Office, December 20, 1941, HO 186/2846, TNA.

84. Foreign Office to Argentina, December 23, 1941, HO 186/2846, TNA.

85. Buenos Aires to Foreign Office, no. 113, 23–24 January 23–24, 1942, HO 186/2846, TNA.

86. Illegible to Sheepshanks, Kirwan, Gordon Johnson, Snelling, Armstrong, January 29, 1942, HO 186/2846, TNA.

87. C. Steel to under-secretary of state, War Office, the secretary of the admiralty, the under-secretary of state for air, air ministry, the under-secretary of state, Dominions Office, February 11, 1942, HO 186/2846, TNA; and C. W. Lambert to under-secretary of state, Foreign Office, January 17, 1942, HO 186/2846, TNA.

88. Steel [illegible?], memo, January 29, 1942, FO 371/32486, TNA.

89. Lambert, "Use of Poison Gas," January 17, 1942, HO 186/2846.

90. Scholar John Dower may be the scholar best known for discussing this in John W. Dower, *War without Mercy: Race & Power in the Pacific War* (New York: Pantheon Books, 1986).

91. Sir Alan Campbell, "Obituary: Sir Ashley Clarke," *The Independent*, January 25, 1994, https://www.independent.co.uk/news/people/obituary-sir-ashley-clarke-1409253 .html; and Ashley Clarke, January 30, 1942, FO 371/32486, TNA. For more about Nan-

king see Timothy Brook, "Introduction," in *Documents on the Rape of Nanking*, ed. Timothy Brook (Ann Arbor: The University of Michigan Press, 1999), 2–4.

92. British records did acknowledge that the Chinese ambassador had made claims that the Japanese had used CW and BW repeatedly in China since 1937 in documents shown to Churchill in July of 1942. There is a gap in the early months of 1942, but then the topic becomes an issue of discussion again in June of 1942. See, for example, H. L. Ismay to Winston Churchill, July 9, 1942, CAB 120/775, TNA.

93. "Battle on the Yangtze." *The Times*, October 14, 1941, *The Times* Digital Archive.

94. Steel, "Use of Poison Gas in Warfare," February 11, 1942, HO 186/2846.

95. Steel to under-secretary of state, et al., February 11, 1942, HO 186/2846.

96. Foreign Office to Sir E. Ovey, draft telegram to Japan, "Use of Poison Gas in Warfare: Corres. [*sic*] With Allied and Foreign Govts. [*sic*]," February 1942, HO 186/2846, TNA.

97. Foreign Office to Buenos Aires, March 21, 1942, HO 186/2846, TNA.

98. Foreign Office to Buenos Aires, "Use of Poison Gas in Warfare," March 21, 1942, HO 186/2846, TNA.

99. P. D. [illeg] to Dean and Allen, February 28, 1942, pp. 1–2, FO 371/32486, TNA.

100. C. G. Caines to secretary of state for foreign affairs, Foreign Office, February 21, 1942, p. 1, HO 186/2846, TNA.

101. Steel, "Use of Poison Gas in Warfare," February 11, 1942, HO 186/2846.

102. Caines to secretary of state for foreign affairs, "Use of Poison Gas in Warfare," February 21, 1942, HO 186/2846, TNA; and C. E. Steel to under-secretary of state for air, March 6, 1942, HO 186/2846, TNA.

103. Steel to the under-secretary of state for air, "Use of Poison Gas in Warfare," March 6, 1942, HO 186/2846, TNA.

104. Steel to the under-secretary of state for air, "Use of Poison Gas in Warfare," March 6, 1942, HO 186/2846.

105. D. L. Stewart, February 25, 1942, HO 186/2846, TNA; and Caines to secretary of state for foreign affairs, "Use of Poison Gas in Warfare," p. 21, HO 186/2846, TNA.

106. R. P. Keffel [Keppel?], February 4, 1942, FO 371/32486, TNA.

107. J. G. Ward, February 4, 1942, p. 2, FO 371/32486, TNA.

108. H. W. Malkin, March 19, 1942, folder 14, FO 371/ 32486, TNA.

109. See, for example, Foreign office to Chunking, telegram no. 847, June 18, 1942, PREM 3/65, TNA. Recent scholarship suggests episodic use. Walter Grunden, "No Retaliation in Kind: Japanese Chemical Warfare Policy in World War II," in *One Hundred Years of Chemical Warfare: Research, Deployment, Consequences*, ed. B. Friedrich, D. Hoffman, J. Renn, F. Schmaltz, and M. Wolf (Switzerland: Springer Cham, 2017), 259–60, https://link.springer.com/content/pdf/10.1007%2F978-3-319-51664-6_14.pdf.

110. R. A. Haccius, International Committee of the Red Cross, to W. St. C. Roberts, February 16, 1942, FO 371/32486, Folder 10, TNA.

111. Haccius to Roberts, February 16, 1942, FO 371/32486.

112. File cover memo, undated but circa February 16, 1942, FO 371/32486, folder 10, TNA.

113. Gerald Bailey to Winston Churchill, May 15, 1942, HO 186/2846, TNA.

114. Philip M. Taylor, *Munitions of the Mind: A History of Propaganda*, 3rd ed. (Manchester: Manchester University Press, 2003).

115. Chiefs of Staff Committee, minutes, April 28, 1942, CAB 79/20/33, TNA.

116. "Appreciation of German C.W. Intentions," no. 1, January to March 1942, C.D.R.5/2753, March 24, 1942, p. 4, CAB 120/778, TNA. Also see Conclusions, War Cabinet, 137 (41), December 29, 1941, p. 269, CAB 65/20/29, TNA.

117. War Cabinet, 68 (41), July 10, 1941, p. 134, CAB 65/19/4, TNA.

118. Scholar Richard M. Price, author of an impressive book on poison gas, refers to the statements analyzed in this section as "Reinforcing the Threshold." Price offers valuable insights on the strengths and weaknesses of a concept of a taboo, and he discusses the warnings with that in mind. Richard M. Price, *The Chemical Weapons Taboo* (Ithaca, NY: Cornell University Press, 1997), 116–19.

119. W.M. (42) 36, Minute 3 attachment, "Chemical Warfare and Civilian Anti-Gas Preparations," March 24, 1942, CAB 65/25/36, TNA.

120. Chiefs of Staff Committee, Minutes, April 11, 1942, CAB 79/20/15, TNA; and W.M. (42) 51st Conclusions, Minute 1, Confidential Annex, April 21, 1942, CAB 65/30/5, TNA.

121. W.M. (42) 51st Meeting, 21 April 21, 1942, CAB 65/30/5.

122. Chiefs of Staff Committee, 11 April 11, 1942, CAB 79/20/15.

123. C.R.A., secretary of state for Dominion affairs, memorandum, "Chemical Warfare," in W.P. (42) 171, April 20, 1942, CAB 66/24/1, TNA. This memo also describes the shortage of masks for India.

124. Joint Planning Staff, *Chemical Warfare*, report, April 10, 1942, CAB 79/20/115, TNA acknowledging how "catastrophic" global gas warfare would be.

125. W.M. (42) 51st Meeting, April 21, 1942, CAB 65/30/5.

126. War Cabinet, Joint Planning Staff report, *Chemical Warfare*, J.P. (42) 382, April 10, 1942, CAB 84/44/75, TNA.

127. Noel Mason-MacFarlane to chief of the Imperial General Staff, undated telegram circa April 1942, CAB 84/44/51, TNA. This appears to be after Churchill's warning.

128. Noel Mason-MacFarlane, telegram, circa April 1942, CAB 84/44/51.

129. Chiefs of Staff Committee, minutes, June 19, 1942, CAB 79/21/33, TNA.

130. W.M. (42) 58th Conclusions, minute 2, confidential annex, May 7, 1942, CAB 65/30/9, TNA.

131. Col. William Stirling to Lt. Col. Cuthbert Sugden, May 20, 1942, p. 1, CAB 21/3912, TNA.

132. L. C. Hollis, "Chemical Warfare," Chiefs of Staff Committee, C.O.S. (42) 312, June 18, 1942, CAB 80/37/12, TNA.

133. 30 Military Mission, Moscow to War Office, May 12, 1942 in Chiefs of Staff Committee, C.O.S. (42) 312, June 18, 1942, p. 2, CAB 80/37/12, TNA.

134. Annex III, draft telegram to the British Ambassador in Russia, undated, in Chiefs of Staff Committee, C.O.S. (42) 312, June 18, 1942, p. 3, CAB 80/37, TNA.

135. V. Dykes to Major-General Pope, letter, undated, H.Q.S. 4354-1-8 F.D.-22: Chemical Warfare-General Policy—Defensive, Reel C-5002, RG24-C-1, LAC.

136. Chilean ambassador, Berlin, to minister for foreign affairs, Santiago, May 13, 1942 in "Chilean Ambassador, Berlin, Reports German Examination of Russian Poison Gas," May 17, 1942, HW 1/575, TNA.

137. V. Dykes to Major-General Pope, undated.

138. Appendix A, statement by the president, June 8, 1943 (As quoted in Department of State Bulletin, June 12, 1943) in report by the Joint Staff Planners, *Allied Chemical Warfare Program*, December 10, 1943, p. 4, RG 218, Chemical and Biological Warfare, Box 425, folder "Allied Chemical Warfare Program" CCS 441.5 Sec. 2, NARA. Note that this document contains reports of earlier statements by FDR.

139. Japan largely refrained from chemical warfare after this, although China continued to allege that Japan used CW and Allied intelligence tracked occasional claims of gas and smoke use throughout the war. Still, Japan did not embrace large-scale gas use of the sort that the United States had no choice but to notice. (There is more about this in chapter 6.)

140. E. E. Bridges to General Ismay, July 17, 1942, CAB 120/775, TNA.

141. This was not unique; the Canadian minister of justice argued that Canada would best be served with "[c]oncerted action with the United Kingdom and the American . . . If and when British and American forces adopted chemical warfare, it could be assumed that its prior use by the enemy had been established." Cabinet War Committee, minutes, July 8, 1942, Ministers and Documents of the Cabinet War Committee, volume X, RG 2, 7C, LAC.

142. Cabinet War Committee, minutes, July 8, 1942, Minutes and Documents of the Cabinet War Committee, volume IX, RG 2, 7C, LAC.

143. Cabinet War Committee, July 8, 1942, RG 2, 7C.

144. Kendrick Lee, *Gas Warfare*, vol. II, (Washington, DC: Editorial Research Report, 1943), 129 in RG 218, Chemical and Biological Warfare, Box 425, "Chemical Warfare Program" Folder CCS 441.5 98-27–42, Sec. 1, NARA.

145. W.M. (43) 123rd conclusions, minute 1, confidential annex, September 6, 1943, p. 1, CAB 65/34/20, TNA.

146. The War Cabinet also concluded that the Soviets "should be consulted, since the outbreak of gas warfare would probably be to the disadvantage of the Russian offensive." There was no treaty obligation to warn or even negotiate with the USSR, in other words, but it might be prudent for strategic reasons. W.M. (43) 123rd conclusions, September 6, 1943, p. 2, CAB 65/34/20.

147. W.M. (43) 123rd conclusions, September 6, 1943, p. 2, CAB 65/34/20.

148. George O. Gillingham to General John R. Deane, letter, September 6, 1943, RG 218, Chemical and Biological Warfare, Box 425, "Allied Chemical Warfare Program" CCS 441.5, Sec. 2, NARA.

## 4. The Limits of Friendship

1. As the epigraph suggests, concerns about the battlefield had an impact on discussions off the battlefield. [Re] Memorandum by the Representatives of the British Chiefs of Staff, in Combined Chiefs of Staff, Allied Chemical Warfare Policy, C.C.S. 106/11, January 18, 1944, p. 1, RG 218, Chemical and Biological Warfare, CCS 441.5 (8-27-42) Sec. 2, Box 425, NARA.

2. D. J. C. Wiseman, *Gas Warfare, The Second World War, 1939–1945, Army*, vol. 1, *Special Weapons and Types of Warfare* (London: The War Office, 1951), 118.

3. The USSR and China were not included in the efforts by these three countries to create a joint policy on offensive gas strikes and retaliation, even though Russia at least

had some gas. At a Joint Planning Staff meeting, the discussion on this topic concluded that "because of Russia's independent attitude in these matters she could not be prevailed upon to voluntarily subscribe to this policy and any report which presumed so would not be realistic." "Notes on JPS 43rd Meeting, Allied Chemical Warfare Program," October 28, 1942, RG 165, Records of the War Department General and Special Staffs, Box 576, Folder ABC 475.92, Sec. 1-A (8-28-42), NARA. While they did not discuss China, Chinese authorities repeatedly made unsubstantiated claims that the Japanese used CBW, which is likely to have led the Western Allies to wonder if it would be an unbiased partner in a joint policy. Note to D.U.S. of S., "Toxic Smokes and Lachrymatory Gas used by the Japanese in China," July 11, 1939, HO 186/2775, TNA.

4. Ottawa to Chiefs of Staff, telegram, January 21/22, 1944, file 452-7-3, pt/vol 2, L123, Chemical Warfare-Policy, 1938, 1940–44, vol. 5432, RG24-E-1-B, LAC.

5. The Commonwealth countries joined Britain willingly, but the viceroy of India, the governor of India appointed by London, made the decision for India.

6. The War Office to Britlist, Melbourne, 23 February 1944, p. 2, CAB 119/57, TNA.

7. Susan L. Smith, *Toxic Exposures: Mustard Gas and the Health Consequences of World War II in the United States* (New Brunswick, NJ: Rutgers University Press, 2017), 32.

8. Christopher Robin Paige, *Canada and Chemical Warfare: 1939–1945* (Salt Spring Island, Canada: Spire Publishing, April 2011), 59.

9. British Joint Staff Mission and British Joint Services Mission: Washington Office Records Memorandum by the Canadian Joint Staff Mission, September 9, 1943, CAB 122/1323, TNA, in Paige, *Canada and Chemical Warfare*, 63.

10. Donald H. Avery, *The Science of War: Canadian Scientists and Allied Military Technology during the Second World War* (Toronto: University of Toronto Press, 1998), 124. The United States also conducted work there.

11. Paige, *Canada and Chemical Warfare*, 54, 55.

12. Paige, *Canada and Chemical Warfare*, 55.

13. William Lyon Mackenzie King, Diaries, July 8, 1942, Item 24336, LAC, https://www.bac-lac.gc.ca/eng/discover/politics-government/prime-ministers/william-lyon-mackenzie-king/Pages/item.aspx?IdNumber=24336.

14. Paige, *Canada and Chemical Warfare*, 62.

15. King, Diaries, July 8, 1942.

16. Ross Coen, *Fu-Go: The Curious History of Japan's Balloon Bomb Attack on America* (Lincoln: University of Nebraska Press, 2014), 5; and Leo P. Brophy and George J. B. Fisher, *United States Army in World War II: The Technical Services. The Chemical Warfare Service: Organizing for War* (Washington, DC, Center of Military History, United States Army, 2004, 1959), 199.

17. Paige, *Canada and Chemical Warfare*, 32.

18. "'Originals' of Ontario will Mark Ypres Battle," *Globe and Mail* (Toronto), April 15, 1943, ProQuest Historical Newspapers.

19. Brooks E. Kleber and Dale Birdsell, *United States Army in World War II: The Technical Services, The Chemical Warfare Service, Chemicals in Combat* (Washington, DC, Office of the Chief of Military History, United States Army, 1966), 162.

20. There were some nuances in perspectives toward the Canadian policy, and these changed a bit over time. Paige focuses on early 1942, Paige, *Canada and Chemical Warfare*, 59. Also see King, Diaries, July 8, 1942.

21. Paige, *Canada and Chemical Warfare*, 59.

22. Excellent scholarship exists on the Allied air war in Europe. Biddle is one of the leading historians in this field. See, for example, Tami Davis Biddle, "Air Power and Warfare: A Century of Theory and History," Report, Strategic Studies Institute and U.S. Army War College Press, March 2019, 25–27.

23. Britain was quite concerned about having proper chains for reporting gas attacks. See, for example, Chiefs of Staff Committee, Minutes, C.O.S. (42) 239th Meeting, 17 August 1942, p. 3, CAB 79/22/39, TNA, about not delegating authority to approve a gas response. Chiefs of Staff Committee, C.O.S. (41) 103rd Meeting, March 19, 1941, p. 2, CAB 79/10/3, TNA. There was some recognition that the details about how to retaliate might be left to the military. Chiefs of Staff Committee, Minutes, C.O.S. (41) 156th Meeting, May 2, 1941, p. 4, CAB 79/11/16, TNA.

24. Appendix to Joint Strategic Services Survey, Allied Chemical Warfare Policy, report, enclosure in A. J. McFarland and E. D. Graves, Jr. to Joint Chiefs of Staff, "Allied Chemical Warfare Policy," J.C.S. 176, April 19, 1944, RG 165, Box 576, Folder ABC 475.92 (8-28-42), Sec. 1-B, p. 2, NARA.

25. Cuthbert Sugden to Colonel William G. Stirling, May 19, 1942, p. 1, CAB 21/3912, TNA.

26. Sugden to Stirling, May 19, 1942, pp. 1–2, CAB 21/3912.

27. Also note that there were plans for a "coordinated United Nations chemical warfare procurement and supply program" in progress too. The discussions about each of these were largely kept separate, though. Combined Staff Planners, Report, Allied Chemical Warfare Program, Combined Chiefs of Staff, CCS 106/1, November 7, 1942, RG 218, CCS 441.5 (8-27-42), Box 425, NARA. The Combined Chiefs of Staff ordered the British and the United States to share intelligence to ensure base inventories of CW in theaters where both nations fought, to standardize offensive material, etc. However, there was an awareness that gas could not dominate "a balanced overall munition programme." It took some time to allocate specific responsibilities and to reach agreements about standard characteristics, but by the end of October 1943, practical progress had been made. Britain, for instance, would import mustard gas bombs from the United States. Wiseman, *Gas Warfare*, vol. 1, 122–25.

28. Combined Staff Planners, Report, Allied Chemical Warfare Program, Combined Chiefs of Staff, CCS 106/1, November 7, 1942, RG 218, CCS 441.5 (8-27-42), Boxes 425, pp. 2–3, NARA. Also note that coordinated production was included in the early policy plans, although that was less of an issue that the questions of initiation and retaliation. Chairman of the Inter-Service Committee on Chemical Warfare to Chiefs of Staff Committee, "Allied Chemical Warfare Programme," War Cabinet, Chiefs of Staff Committee, C.O.S. (42) 483, December 14, 1942, p. 1, CAB 80/38, TNA.

29. Robert Bothwell, Ian Drummond, and John English, *Canada, 1900–1945* (Toronto: University of Toronto Press, 1987, pbk. 1990), 337, 352–3; and Paige, *Canada and Chemical Warfare*, 67.

30. King, Diaries, July 8, 1942.

31. Vice-Chiefs of Staff, report, *Chemical Warfare Policy—Association of Commonwealth Governments*, Chiefs of Staff Committee, War Cabinet, COS (44) 184 (O), February 22, 1944, p. 2, CAB 80/80, TNA.

32. Appendix A, "Review of Policy and Developments of Gas Warfare," to the Joint Staff Planners on "Gas Warfare," Report, enclosed in C. H. Donnelly, F. J. Green to the Joint Staff Planners, on "Gas Warfare," January 22, 1944 (J.P. S. 365? (illegible)/1), RG 218, CCS 441.5, Box 425, NARA.

33. H. Redman to Captain Royal, "Allied Chemical Warfare Policy," Letter, September 29, 1943, RG 165, Box 576, Folder ABC 475.92 Sec. 1-A (8-28-42), NARA.

34. Vice-Chiefs of Staff, report, February 22, 1944, CAB 80/80.

35. The language used was that it was "unlikely that the War Cabinet would delegate in advance authority, either to the Chiefs of Staff, or to the Commander-in-Chief, Home Forces, to undertake retaliatory measures in gas without some reference to them," so it was "undesirable to suggest such a course to the Cabinet." War Cabinet, Chiefs of Staff Committee, COS (41) 103, March 19, 1941, p. 2, CAB 79/10/3, TNA.

36. War Cabinet, Chiefs of Staff Committee, COS (42) 352, December 21, 1942, CAB 79/24/52, TNA.

37. Chiefs of Staff Committee, COS (42) 352, December 21, 1942, CAB 79/24/52.

38. Chiefs of Staff Committee, COS (43) 4th Meeting, January 4, 1943, CAB 79/25.

39. Annex from The Joint Chiefs of Staff, Washington, "Memorandum for the Secretary, British Joint Staff Mission," January 11, 1943, in L. C. Hollis, War Cabinet, Chiefs of Staff Committee, "Allied Chemical Warfare Programme," C.O.S. (43) 23, January 19, 1943, CAB 80/39, TNA.

40. "Memorandum for the Secretary, British Joint Staff Mission," January 11, 1943, in Hollis, War Cabinet, Chiefs of Staff Committee, COS (43) 23, January 19, 1943, CAB 80/39.

41. "Allied Chemical Warfare Program," "Notes on JPS 43rd meeting," October 28, 1942, RG 165, Box 576, Folder ABC. 475.92, Sec. 1-A, (8-28-42), NARA.

42. H. R. Moore, A. E. Nye, D. C. S. Evill to Prime Minister Churchill, April 19, 1943, CAB 120/775, TNA; and King, Diaries, July 8, 1942.

43. War Cabinet, Chiefs of Staff Committee, C.O.S. (43) 322 (0), December 30, 1943, CAB 79/68/32, TNA; and Winston Churchill to General Ismay for C.O.S. Committee, February 28, 1944, CAB 120/775, TNA.

44. [Re] Memorandum by the Representatives of the British Chiefs of Staff, Combined Chiefs of Staff, Allied Chemical Warfare Policy, C.C.S. 106/11, January 18, 1944, RG 218, CCS 441.5 (8-27-42), Box 425, NARA.

45. Vice-Chiefs of Staff, Report, February 22, 1944, CAB 80/80.

46. Vice-Chiefs of Staff, Report, February 22, 1944, CAB 80/80.

47. Chiefs of Staff Committee, Minutes, C.O.S. (44) 44th Meeting (0), February 10, 1944, CAB 70/70, TNA.

48. Vice-Chiefs of Staff, Report, February 22, 1944, p. 2, CAB 80/80.

49. Representatives of the British Chiefs of Staff, C.C.S. 106/11, January 18, 1944, RG 218, CCS 441.5 (8-27-42), Box 425, NARA.

50. Representatives of the British Chiefs of Staff, C.C.S. 106/11, January 18, 1944, RG 218, CCS 441.5 (8-27-42), Box 425, NARA.

51. Representatives of the British Chiefs of Staff, C.C.S. 106/11, January 18, 1944, RG 218, Box 425, CCS 441.5 (8-27-42).

52. Annex I, Note to prime minister from L. C. Hollis, February 25, 1944, CAB 80/81, TNA.

53. Alex Danchev, "Sir John Greer Dill," *Oxford Dictionary of National Biography*, January 6, 2011, https://doi-org.unh.idm.oclc.org/10.1093/ref:odnb/32826; and Excerpt, CCS 144th Meeting, April 2, 1944, RG 218, CCS 441.5 (8-27-42), Box 425, NARA.

54. Notes on JPS 143rd Meeting, "Allied Chemical Warfare Policy," April 5, 1944, RG 165, Folder ABC 475.92 8-28-42) Sec. 1-B, Box 576, NARA.

55. United States Chiefs of Staff, Appendix "C" to memorandum in Joint Staff Planners, "Allied Chemical Warfare Policy," Report in Royal and McFarland to the Joint Chiefs of Staff, January 27, 1944, RG 218, CCS 441.5 (8-27-42, Chemical and Biological Warfare), Box 425, NARA.

56. Joint Staff Planners, Report, Enclosure to McFarland and Graves, J.C.S. 176/8, April 8, 1944, RG 165, Box 576, Folder ABC 475.92 (8-28-42) Sec. 1-B, p. 1, NARA.

57. Churchill to General Ismay to Chiefs of Staff Committee, February 28, 1944, PREM 3/89, TNA.

58. War Cabinet, Chiefs of Staff Committee, COS (43) 249 (O), October 14, 1943, CAB 79/66/6, TNA.

59. The War Office to Britlist, Melbourne, February 23, 1944, p. 2, CAB 119/57, TNA.

60. Air Ministry to Britman Washington, March 14, 1944, CAB 119/57, TNA.

61. Chiefs of Staff Committee, Minutes, C.O.S. (44) 94 (O), March 21, 1944, CAB 79/72/4, TNA.

62. J.S.M. Washington to A.M.S.S.O., April 26, 1944, p. 2, CAB 120/775, TNA.

63. J.S.M. Washington to A.M.S.S.O., 26 April 1944, p. 2, CAB 120/775.

64. J.S.M. Washington to A.M.S.S.O., 26 April 1944, p. 2, CAB 120/775.

65. J.S.M. Washington to A.M.S.S.O., 26 April 1944, p. 1, CAB 120/775; and Appendix A of Joint Staff Planners, Report, enclosure to C. H. Donnelly and F. J. Green to Joint Staff Planners, "Implications of Recent Intelligence Regarding Alleged German Secret Weapons," J.P.S. 341/7, March 21, 1944, RG 165, Box 488, Folder ABC 385.2 Germany Sec. 1 20 Dec '43, p. 9, NARA.

66. Owen Wilkes, "Working Paper No. 4: A History of New Zealand Chemical Warfare, 1845–1945," (Auckland: Center for Peace Studies, University of Auckland, August 1993), 45–46.

67. Washington to A.M.S.S.O., April 26, 1944, p. 1, CAB 120/775.

68. Washington to A.M.S.S.O., April 26, 1944, p. 2, CAB 120/775.

69. Excerpts and variations of this plan spread. The Air Chemical Officer, Army Air Forces (I-B Theater) and the IB Air Service Command in conjunction with the Chemical Officers, Tenth US Army Air Force, 14th US Army Air Force "Plan for Air Chemical Warfare against Japanese (China and India-Burma Theaters)," February 1945, pp. 2–3, Air Force Historical Research Agency, Maxwell Air Force Base, Alabama, quotes from an early version of the joint gas warfare policy plan that included Canada.

70. A. J. McFarland and R. D. Coleridge to Combined Chiefs of Staff, "Allied Chemical Warfare Policy," C.C.S. 106/15, April 29, 1944, RG 165, Box 576, Folder ABC 475.92 (8-28-42) Sec. 1-B, NARA.

71. Washington to A.M.S.S.O., April 26, 1944, p. 2, CAB 120/775.

72. Certain accidents occurred, for example, in production and research, but these were either away from the battlefront or in small numbers. There is a growing body of scholarship about casualties deliberately caused in research facilities to test vulnerabilities to gas. These include Ulf Schmidt, *Secret Science: A Century of Poison Warfare and*

*Human Experiments* (Oxford: Oxford University Press, 2015); Bridget Goodwin, *Keen as Mustard: Britain's Horrific Chemical Warfare Experiments in Australia* (St. Lucia: University of Queensland Press, 1998); Susan L. Smith, *Toxic Exposures: Mustard Gas and the Health Consequences of World War II in the United States* (New Brunswick, NJ: Rutgers University Press, 2017); and Rob Evans, *Gassed* (London: House of Stratus, 2000). Harold Johnston, *A Bridge Not Attacked: Chemical Warfare Civilian Research during World War II* (New Jersey: World Scientific, 2003) includes accounts of dangers during research in labs. One worker at the Huntsville arsenal in Alabama recounted the injuries that occurred there. Lois Moore, oral history transcript, by Lisa Craft, May 1999, Lois Moore 99.0350, Institute of World War II and the Human Experience, Florida State University.

73. "Report on the Circumstances in which Gas Casualties Were Incurred at Bari in 2/3 December 1943," n.d., p. 1, WO 204/1105, TNA.

74. "Report on the Circumstances in which Gas Casualties Were Incurred at Bari in 2/3 December 1943," n.d., p. 2, WO 204/1105.

75. For Chief of Staff, Allied Force Headquarters, "Report on Adequacy of Protective Measures at Bari," December 11, 1943, p. 1, WO 204/1105, TNA.

76. Unknown Author to SECTANT, Memo, Undated, CAB 121/101, TNA. Another report listed "approximately 200,000 100-lb. H bombs" among the cargo of the *John Harvey*. Shadle to A-C of S, G-4, "Inspection of the Port of Bari," December 20, 1943, p. 1, WO 204/1102, TNA.

77. Stewart F. Alexander, "Final Report of Bari Mustard Casualties," undated, pp. 3 and 2, WO 188/2050, TNA.

78. C. in C. Mediterranean to Admiralty, December 19, 1943, p. 1, AIR 2/13585, TNA.

79. RR Powell to Commanders-in-Chief, et al., July 5, 1944, pp. 1–2, AIR 2/13585, TNA. The reports vary by a few numbers—Lt. Col. Stewart Alexander's medical report in late December counted 638 mustard gas cases and sixty-nine deaths—but are similar in scope. Stewart Alexander to director, medical service, Allied Force Headquarters Surgeon, NATOUSA, "Toxic Gas Burns Sustained in the Bari Harbor Catastrophe," memo, December 27, 1942, in Glenn B. Infield, *Disaster at Bari* (New York: The Macmillan Company, 1971), 273.

80. Infield, *Disaster at Bari*, 259.

81. A.F.H.Q. Algiers to AGWAR (for Marshall), telegram, January 11, 1944, CAB 121/101, TNA. Note that a report says that the area around the *John Harvey* "was immediately decontaminated by Chemical Warfare Service personnel of the 12th Air Force who were fortunately nearby with the equipment and a large supply of decontamination materials." It is questionable how immediate this was, though, since there were so many casualties and so few knew about the cargo. Charles S. Shadle to A C of S, C-4, "Inspection of the Port of Bari, Italy," December 20, 1943, p. 1, WO 204/1102, TNA.

82. Shadle, "Inspection of the Port of Bari" December 20, 1943, p. 1, WO 204/1102.

83. A.F.H.Q. Algiers to AGWAR, January 11, 1944, CAB 121/101. US hospitals in Bari had not been established yet, and, in fact, the attack in December destroyed most of equipment earmarked for them. Charles M. Wiltse, *United States Army in World War II: The Technical Services, The Medical Department: Medical Service in the Mediterranean and Minor Theaters*, (Washington, DC: Office of Military History: Department of the Army, 1965), 351, https://achh.army.mil/history/book-wwii-medsvcsinmedtrnmnrthrtrs-chapter9.

84. Infield, *Disaster at Bari*, 179 and 190.

85. R.C.I. Chichester-Constable, "Report on the Circumstances in which Gas Casualties were Incurred at Bari on 2/3 December 1943," p. 8, WO 204/1106, TNA.

86. Infield, *Disaster at Bari*, 210.

87. Lowell W. Rooks, January 6, 1944, citing Cable No. W9154/22799, January 2, 1944, WO 204/1105, TNA.

88. In the 1980s when news of the gas at Bari became widely known in Britain, laymen wrote to the government protesting what they saw as a violation of the Geneva Protocol by Britain, even though the United States had shipped the CW and no one had released it deliberately. See, for example, Frank M. Leamon to Mrs. Thatcher, January 21, 1986, PIN 59/448, TNA.

89. A.F.H.Q. Algiers to AGWAR, January 11, 1944, CAB 121/101.

90. Chiefs of Staff Committee, Extract from C.O.S. (44) 33 (O), February 3, 1944, CAB 121/101, TNA.

91. R. Peck to A.U.S. (G), minute, January 24, 1944, AIR 2/13585, TNA.

92. A.F.H.Q. Algiers to AGWAR, January 2, 1944, AIR 2/13585; and C. in C. Mediterranean to Admiralty, December 19, 1943, AIR 2/13585, TNA.

93. L. C. Hollis to General G. M. Molesworth, 26 (unclear date) January 1944, CAB 121/101, TNA.

94. Hollis to Moleworth, 26 (unclear date) January 1944, CAB 121/101. The British Empire's diversity is apparent at Bari. South Africans and a Bechuana (or Basuto) were also on the casualty list. AFHQ Algiers to the War Office, January 1944, AIR 2/13585, TNA.

95. See, for example, the Bertram Stevens case. He was not told about his exposure to gas at Bari. A physician, forty years later, deduced that mustard gas must be behind his ailments. Stevens's appeal to the government to increase his pension became a *cause célèbre*. PIN 59/448, TNA.

96. R.C.T. Chichester-constable to assistant chief of staff, "Board of Officers," January 21, 1944, WO 204/1102, TNA.

97. D. Movements to S.G, minute, May 10, 1944, AIR 2/13585, TNA.

## 5. Rolling the Dice

1. Churchill to General Ismay for the C.O.S. Committee, prime minister's personal minute, D. 217/4, July 6, 1944, CAB 120/775, TNA.

2. Tami Davis Biddle, "On the Crest of Fear: V-Weapons, the Battle of the Bulge, and the Last Stages of World War II in Europe," *The Journal of Military History* 83, no. 1 (January 2019), 173.

3. John Keegan narrates the debate in detail in John Keegan, *Intelligence in War: The Value—and Limitations—of What the Military Can Learn about the Enemy* (New York: Vintage Books: 2004), 258–94.

4. E. J. King-Salter to War Cabinet, Joint Intelligence Sub-Committee, "Operation Bodyline," note in J.I.C. (43) 445 (0), October 29, 1943, p. 1, CAB 121/101, TNA.

5. Vice-Chiefs of Staff to War Cabinet, "Operation Crossbow," Report, War Cabinet, Chiefs of Staff Committee, C.O.S. (43) 754 (O), December 8, 1943, CAB 121/101, TNA.

6. Vice Chief of the Imperial General Staff, "German Long Range Rocket," memorandum in War Cabinet, Chiefs of Staff Committee, C.O.S. (43) 574 (O), September 24, 1943, CAB 80/75, TNA.

7. C.O.S. (43) 754 (O), December 8, 1943, p. 1, CAB 121/101.

8. C.O.S. (43) 754 (O), December 8, 1943, p. 1, CAB 121/101.

9. Vice Chiefs of Staff, C.O.S. (43) 754 (O), December 8, 1943, CAB 121/101.

10. Donald H. Avery, *The Science of War: Canadian Scientists and Allied Military Technology during the Second World War* (Toronto: University of Toronto Press, 1998), 146.

11. Annex, C.O.S. (43) 754 (O), December 8, 1943, p. 3, CAB 121/101; and Annex I, C.O.S. (43) 754 (O), December 8, 1943, pp. 2, 4, CAB 121/101, TNA.

12. Annex I, C.O.S. (43) 754 (O), December 8, 1943, p. 3, CAB 121/101.

13. C.O.S. (43) 754 (O), December 8, 1943, p. 2, CAB 121/101.

14. Eric Golson, "The Economics of Neutrality in World War II," November 11, 2019, VOX CEPR Policy Portal, https://voxeu.org/article/economics-neutrality-world-war-ii.

15. C.O.S. (43) 754 (O), December 8, 1943, p. 2, CAB 121/101.

16. Greig Watson, "Operation Gomorrah: Firestorm created 'Germany's Nagasaki,'" August 2, 2018, BBC, https://www.bbc.com/news/uk-england-43546839. See Keith Lowe, *Inferno: The Devastation of Hamburg, 1943* (New York: Scribner, 2007) about the attack on Hamburg.

17. Annex to C.O.S. (43) 754 (O), December 8, 1943, p. 4, CAB 121/101.

18. Chiefs of Staff Committee, Extract, C.O.S. (44) 229 Meeting (O), October 16, 1944, CAB 121/102, TNA; and Ian Simple, "What Is White Phosphorus?" *The Guardian*, November 19, 2005, https://www.theguardian.com/science/2005/nov/19/thisweekssciencequestions.uknews.

19. Use of WP is a complicated issue in international law today, but scholars are clear that WP is not necessarily a CW, depending on its use. David P. Fidler, "The Use of White Phosphorus Munitions by U.S. Forces in Iraq," *American Society of International Law* 9, no. 37 (December 6, 2005), https://www.asil.org/insights/volume/9/issue/37/use-white-phosphorus-munitions-us-military-forces-iraq. Some go so far as to say that "there does not seem to be any significant disagreement that WP weapons do not fall under the definitions of poison or poisonous gas in the relevant conventions," namely the Geneva Gas Protocol. Stian Nordengen Christensen, "Regulation of White Phosphorous Weapons in International Law," (Brussels: Torkel Opsahl Academic EPublisher, 2016), 1, https://www.toaep.org/ops-pdf/6-christensen. As can be seen in this chapter, the case was not quite that clear in 1944.

20. United States Army, Center of Military History, Anzio Beachhead, 22 January–25 May 1944, CMH Pub 100–10, (Washington, DC, 1990), 32, first printed by Historical Division, War Department, for the American Forces in Action series, 1948, https://history.army.mil/books/wwii/anziobeach/anzio-allied.htm.

21. "White Fire," *Time*, November 29, 1943, vol. 42, p. 68.

22. "Copy of Minute (SHAEF 17211/One) dated 20th May, 1944 from the supreme commander Allied Expeditionary Force to air-commander-in-chief, Allied Expeditionary Air Force," in Annex in Chiefs of Staff Committee, "'Overlord'—The Use of White Phosphorus," C.O.S. (44) 589 (O), July 1, 1944, RG 331, Records of Allied Operational and Occupation Headquarters, Box 128, Folder Chiefs of Staff (44) Minutes, NARA.

23. Leo P. Brophy, Wyndham D. Miles, and Rexmond C. Cochrane, *United States Army in World War II, The Chemical Warfare Service from Laboratory to Field* (Washington, DC: United States. Department of the Army. Office of Military History, 1959), 406.

24. "Copy of letter (SHAEF 17211/One(A)) dated 30 June 1944 from chief of staff to supreme commander Allied Expeditionary Force, to the Secretary, Chiefs of Staff Committee," in War Cabinet, Chiefs of Staff Committee, C.O.S. (44) 589 (O), "'Overlord'—Use of White Phosphorus," July 1, 1944, RG 331, Box 128, Folder COS(44) Minutes, NARA.

25. "Copy of letter . . . dated 30 June 1944," C.O.S. (44) 589 (O), July 1, 1944.

26. "Copy of letter . . . dated 30 June 1944," C.O.S. (44) 589 (O), July 1, 1944.

27. L. C. Hollis to Winston Churchill, June 1, 1944, PREM 3/89, TNA.

28. Hollis to Churchill, June 1, 1944, PREM 3/89.

29. Hollis to Churchill, June 1, 1944, PREM 3/89.

30. Hollis to Churchill, June 1, 1944, PREM 3/89.

31. Hollis to Churchill, June 1, 1944, PREM 3/89.

32. Hollis to Churchill, June 1, 1944, PREM 3/89.

33. Secretary, Chiefs of Staff Committee to chief of staff to the supreme commander, Allied Expeditionary Force, June 1, 1944, PREM 3/89, TNA.

34. Hollis to Churchill, June 1, 1944, PREM 3/89.

35. Hollis to Churchill, June 1, 1944, PREM 3/89.

36. "Annexes I- III in War Cabinet Chiefs of Staff Committee, "'Overlord'—Use of White Phosphorus," C.O.S. (44) 543 (0), June 19, 1944, RG 331, Box 104, Folder COS (44) Minutes, NARA.

37. Anthony Eden (A.E.) to Winston Churchill, P.M./44/422, June 7, 1944, PREM 3/89, TNA.

38. H. L. Ismay to prime minister, June 21, 1944, PREM 3/89, TNA.

39. Chiefs of Staff Committee, "Extract from C.O.S. (44) 339 Meeting (O), October 16, 1944," CAB 121/102, TNA. The assessments about Germany's likely use of gas varied over the last year of the war, but there was almost always concern that Hitler might use it as a "last resort." See, for example, V. Canendish-Bentirck, E. G. N. Rushbrooke, J. A. Sinclair, F. P. Inglis, and M. Y. Watson (Joint Intelligence Subcommittee), "Use of Chemical Warfare by the Germans," J.I.C. (45) 36 (0) Final, January 29, 1945, PREM 3/89, TNA; and V. Cavendish Bentirk, E. G. N. Rushbrooke, J. A. Sinclair, G. W. P. Grant, and C. G. Vickers (the Joint Intelligence Sub-Committee), "Use of Chemical Warfare by the Germans," J.I.C. (45) 52 (O) Final, February 19, 1945, PREM 3/89, TNA.

40. Chiefs of Staff Committee, C.O.S. (44) 239 Meeting (O), October 16, 1944, CAB 121/102.

41. Chiefs of Staff Committee, C.O.S. (44) 239 Meeting (O), October 16, 1944, CAB 121/102.

42. W. R. Sawyer, Lt. Col., "Minutes of a Meeting Held in Office of CCDD 1200 Hrs 26 Apr 44 to discuss Esoid Project," p. 2, vol. 12195, Folder 1/Chemical/1/2 "Policy—Chemical Warfare," Roll T17488, RG 24C-2, LAC.

43. George Merck, a consultant to the secretary of war and a pillar of the pharmaceutical industry, viewed BW as including bacteria "and toxic agents from living organisms (as distinguished from synthetic chemical . . . to produce death or disease." George W. Merck to Secretary of War Robert P. Patterson, letter, October 24, 1945,

p. 1, RG 165, Records of the War Department General and Special Staffs, Box 67, Folder 334, Project 2263, NARA.

44. "Minutes of a Meeting Held . . . 26 Apr 44 to discuss Esoid Project," vol. 12195, Folder 1/Chemical/1/2, Roll T17488, RG 24C-2, LAC.

45. Henry Stimson to chief of staff, "Biological Warfare," Memorandum, January 13, 1944, RG 165, Box 488, Folder ABC 485.2 Germany Sec. 1, December 20, 1943, pp. 1–2, NARA; and Joint Logistics Committee, "British-United States Liaison with Respect to Biological Warfare," p. 2, enclosure to C. H. Donnelly and R. B. Pegram, Joint Logistics Committee, "British-United States Liaison with Respect to Biological Warfare," J.L.C. 122/4, August 4, 1944, RG 218, Records of the U.S. Joint Chiefs of Staff, Box 376, Folder Chemical, Biological & Radiological Warfare JCS 182 (illegible), NARA.

46. One could argue that biological warfare had been used throughout history, from poisoning wells to deliberately infecting (or rather trying to sicken) human targets with smallpox. See Adrienne Mayor, *Greek Fire, Poison Arrows, and Scorpion Bombs: Biological and Chemical Warfare in the Ancient World* (Woodstock, NY: Overlook Duckworth, 2003) for an in-depth discussion. The latter is recognized as one tactic used by Europeans against Native Americans during the colonial period when blankets contaminated with smallpox blisters were transferred to the vulnerable Native Americans who had no immunities to the disease. The result was devastating to some indigenous populations. Elizabeth A. Fenn, *Pox Americana: The Great Smallpox Epidemic of 1775–1782* (New York: Hill & Wang, 2001) discusses the impact on Native Americans and others. However, efforts during the modern era to transmit germs deliberately through modern means had been morally rejected by the general international populations (through the Geneva Gas Protocol, for example, which also banned bacteriological weapons) and practically dismissed by most scientists. George Merck, the head of America's BW committee, reported to Secretary Robert P. Patterson that an earlier version of his group, the WBC Committee, had decided that BW were feasible by February of 1942. George W. Merck to Secretary of War, letter, October 24, 1945, p. 1, RG 165, Box 67, Folder Project 2253, NARA.

47. "Japanese Attempts at Bacteriological Warfare in China," attachment to H. L. Ismay to prime minister [Winston Churchill], July 9, 1942, pp. 3–4, CAB 120/775, TNA; and Frank Snowden, "Latina Province, 1944–1950," *Journal of Contemporary History* 43, no. 3 (July 2008): 509–26, https://www.jstor.org/stable/40542973 analyzes the German effort to encourage malaria in Italy during World War II.

48. Illegible Burns, "MEMORANDUM of Conference on Research in Gas and Bacteriological Warfare," January 3, 1940, vol. 12191, Folder 1-Chemical/1 ("Chemical Warfare"), Roll T17488, RG 24C-2, LAC.

49. John Bryden, *Deadly Allies: Canada's Secret War, 1937–1947* (Toronto: McClelland & Stewart, 1989), 196.

50. "Policy—Chemical Warfare," vol. 12195, Folder 1/Chemical/1/2, Roll T17488, RG 24C-2, LAC; Sawyer, "Minutes of a Meeting Held in Office of CCDD 1200 Hrs 26 Apr 44 to discuss Esoid Project," vol. 12195, RG 24C-2, LAC; and E. G. D. Murray and G. B. Reed to Lt. Gen. K. Stuart, chief of staff, CMHQ, p. 1, vol. 12195, RG 24C-2, LAC.

51. Murray and Reed to Stuart, RG 24C-2, vol. 12195.

52. Sawyer "Minutes of a Meeting Held . . . 26 Apr 44 to discuss Esoid Project," p. 1, vol. 12195, RG 24C-2.

53. Sawyer "Minutes of a Meeting Held . . . 26 Apr 44 to discuss Esoid Project," p. 1, vol. 12195, RG 24C-2.

54. Sawyer, "Minutes of a Meeting Held . . . 26 Apr 44 to discuss Esoid Project," p. 1, vol. 12195, RG 24C-2.

55. K. Stuart to C.O.C.-in. C, First Canadian Army, letter, May 8, 1944, vol. 12195, Folder 1/Chemical/1/2 "Policy—Chemical Warfare," Roll T17488, RG 24C-2, LAC.

56. Joint Intelligence Sub-Committee, "Use of Chemical Warfare by the Germans," War Cabinet, Joint Intelligence Sub-Committee, JIC (44) 89 (O) Final, March 9, 1944, p. 3, CAB 121/101, TNA.

57. Sawyer, "Minutes of a Meeting Held . . . 26 Apr 44 to discuss Esoid Project," p. 2, RG 24C-2, vol. 12195.

58. "Military Considerations Affecting the Initiation of Chemical and Other Special Forms of Warfare," undated (before June 6, 1944), p. 1, PREM 3/89, TNA.

59. There were nervous discussions about potential CW outbreak on D-Day, too, but those are discussed elsewhere and quite separately from BW considerations by those concerned at the time.

60. K. Stuart, "Record of conversation between Lt-Gen. K. Stuart and Lt-Gen. Beedel [sic] Smith, chief of staff to General Eisenhower, 24 Apr. 44," vol. 12195, Folder 1/Chemical/1/2 "Policy—Chemical Warfare," Roll T17488, RG 24C-2, LAC. Bryden, *Deadly Allies*, 124, suggests that the United States was committed, at least for a time, to inoculating.

61. Sawyer, "Minutes of a Meeting Held . . . 26 Apr 44 to discuss Esoid Project," p. 1, vol. 12195, RG 24C-2.

62. Sawyer, "Minutes of a Meeting Held . . . 26 Apr 44 to discuss Esoid Project," p. 2, vol. 12195, RG 24C-2; and K. Stuart, "Record of conversation between Lt-Gen. Sir Archibald Nye, Acting C.I.G.S., and Lt-Gen. K. Stuart, Folder 1/Chemical/1/2 "Policy—Chemical Warfare," at the War Office on 26 Apr. 1944," vol. 12195, Roll T17488, RG 24C-2, LAC.

63. Sawyer, "Minutes of a Meeting Held . . . 26 Apr 44 to discuss Esoid Project," p. 2, vol. 12195, RG 24C-2.

64. This is discussed in more detail later in the chapter. Bryden, *Deadly Allies*, 125–26.

65. Murchie to Stuart, telegram GS 343, May 29, 1944, vol. 12195, Folder 1/Chemical/1/2 "Policy—Chemical Warfare," Roll T17488, RG 24C-2, LAC.

66. Stuart to Murchie, Telegram COS 105, May 31, 1944, p. 1, vol. 12195, Folder 1/Chemical/1/2 "Policy—Chemical Warfare," Roll T17488, RG 24C-2, LAC.

67. Stuart to Murchie, telegram COS 100, May 27, 1944, p. 2, vol. 12195, Folder 1/Chemical/1/2 "Policy—Chemical Warfare," Roll T17488, RG 24C-2, LAC.

68. Everitt George Dunne Murray, "Esoid: Comments on GS 343 and COS 100," no date, p. 2, vol. 12195, Folder 1/Chemical/1/2 "Policy—Chemical Warfare," Roll T17488, RG 24C-2, LAC.

69. EGD Murray, "Esoid: Comments on GS 343 and COS 100," p. 2, RG 24C-2.

70. "Everitt George Dunne Murray," Microbiology Society, https://www.microbiologyresearch.org/sotsog/egd-murray.

71. Colonel John Boyd Coates, Jr., MC, and Ebbe Curtis Hoff, Ph.D., M.D., eds., *Preventive Medicine, Preventive Medicine in World War II*, Volume III: *Personal Health Measures and Immunization* (Washington, DC: Office of the Surgeon General, Department of the

Army, 1955), 312. The vaccine was "both grown and suspended in human serum" through mid-1942 when the military stopped using the inoculation because it was contaminated. Roger E. Thomas, Diane L. Lorenzetti, and Wendy Stragins, "Mortality and Morbidity among Military Personnel and Civilians during the 1930s and World War II from Transmission of Hepatitis during Yellow Fever Vaccination: Systemic Review," *Am. J. Public Health* 103, vol. 3 (March, 2013): e16–e29, doi: 10.2105/AJPH.2012.301158.

72. Stuart to Murchie, telegram, COS 100, May 27, 1944, p. 2, vol. 12195, Roll T17488, Folder 1/Chemical/1/2 "Policy-Chemical Warfare," RG 24C-2, LAC.

73. Table 1, Thomas, Lorenzetti, and Stragins, "Mortality and Morbidity." In the days before D-Day, Maass reported an intermediate number (120) of yellow fever vaccine casualties. Bryden, *Deadly Allies*, 126. Regardless, the Canadians, rightly, rejected the American arguments about the trouble with the yellow fever vaccine as being the reason to dismiss a botulism vaccine.

74. EGD Murray, "Esoid," no date, p.3, vol. 12195, RG 24C-2.

75. Stuart to Murchie, May 27, 1944, p. 2, vol. 12195, RG 24C-2.

76. Murray, "Esoid," no date, p. 3, vol. 12195, RG 24C-2.

77. K. Stuart to G.O.C.-in-C, letter, May 17, 1944, pp. 2–3, vol. 12195, RG 24C-2; and Illeg. to K. Stuart, "Bacteriological Warfare," letter, May 18, 1944, vol. 12195, Folder 1/Chemical/1/2 "Policy—Chemical Warfare," Roll T17488, RG 24C-2, LAC.

78. Illeg. to K. Stuart, May 18, 1944, vol. 12195, RG 24C-2.

79. Bryden, *Deadly Allies*, 126.

80. Bryden suggests that "Canada's defence minister, James Ralston, should have known about Ultra" because he approved some of the costs involved in Canadian efforts to participate on the edges of the radio intercepts involved, but he did not know enough to figure out that US and UK resistance had to do with Ultra messages. Bryden, *Deadly Allies*, 127. Because the other Allies were giving reasons for their reluctance, even if the reasons seemed weak, it does seem likely that it would be difficult for Ralston to penetrate their cover story and find the real reason behind it.

81. Sawyer, "Esoid Project," p.1, vol. 12195, RG 24C-2. This speaks to timeliness and effectiveness.

82. Murchie to Stuart, GS 343 telegram, p. 1, May 25, 1944, vol. 12195, Folder 1/Chemical/1/2 "Policy—Chemical Warfare," Roll T17488, RG 24C-2, LAC.

83. Notes on Esoid Problem," May 18, 1944, pp. 1-3, vol. 12195, RG 24C-2.

84. Cabinet War Committee, 24 May 1944, Minutes and Documents of the Cabinet War Committee, volume XV, RG 2, 7c, LAC.

85. K. Stuart to G. O. C.-in-C First Canadian Army, May 12, 1944, Folder 1/Chemical/1/2 "Policy—Chemical Warfare," vol. 12195, Roll T17488, RG 24C-2, LAC.

86. The exact terms of each of the retaliation promises differs. See chapter 3 for details.

87. Sir Ian Hamilton to Lord Horatio Kitchener, Telegram 6A, July 8, 1915, WO 32/5172, TNA.

88. Bryden, *Deadly Allies*, 124; and Harry Crerar to Ken Stuart, letter, May 18, 1944, p. 1, vol. 12195, Folder 1/Chemical/1/2 "Policy—Chemical Warfare," Roll T17488, RG 24C-2, LAC.

89. Not everyone was convinced that total secrecy would be possible. Crerar to Stuart, May 18, 1944, p. 1, RG 24C-2.

90. Crerar to Stuart, May 18, 1944, p. 1, RG 24C-2.

91. Paul Fussell, *The Boys Crusade: The American Infantry in Northwestern Europe, 1944–1945* (New York: Modern Library Paperback Edition, 2005), 17.

92. Murchie to Stuart, telegram, May 25, 1944, p. 2 Roll T17488, Folder 1/Chemical/1/2 "Policy—Chemical Warfare," vol. 12195, RG 24C-2, LAC.

93. "Esoid Problem," May 18, 1944, p. 1, RG24C-2, LAC; and Stuart to Murchie, Telegram COS 105, May 31, 1944, p. 2, Folder 1/Chemical/1/2 "Policy—Chemical Warfare," vol. 12195, Roll T17488, RG 24C-2, LAC.

94. "Notes on Esoid Problem," May 18, 1944, p. 1, RG 24C-2.

95. "Proposed Cover Plan," Folder 1/Chemical/1/2 "Policy—Chemical Warfare," vol. 12195, Roll T17488, RG 24C-2, LAC.

96. C. P. Fenwick, "Memo for Medical Officers," May 27, 1944, Folder 1/Chemical/1/2 "Policy—Chemical Warfare," vol. 12195, Roll T17488, RG 24C-2, LAC.

97. Coates and Hoff, *Personal Health Measures and Immunization*, 324–25.

98. W. R. Freasby, ed., *Official History of the Canadian Medical Services, 1939–1945*, vol. 2, *Clinical Subjects* (Ottawa: Queen's Printer, 1953), 383, https://www.canada.ca/content/dam/themes/defence/caf/militaryhistory/dhh/official/book-1953-medical-services-2-en.pdf.

99. Stuart to Murchie, COS 100, May 27, 1944, p. 4, RG 24C-2.

100. "Esoid Problem," May 18, 1944, pp. 2–3, RG 24C-2.

101. "Esoid Problem," May 18, 1944, p. 1, RG 24C-2.

102. "Esoid Problem," May 18, 1944, p. 2, RG 24C-2.

103. Crerar to Stuart, May 18, 1944, RG 24C-2.

104. "Notes on the Esoid Problem," May 18, 1944, p. 2, RG 24C-2.

105. "Notes on the Esoid Problem," May 18, 1944, RG 24C-2.

106. Crerar to Stuart, May 18, 1944, RG 24C-2; and Stuart to Murchie, telegram, May 19, 1944, p. 3, Folder 1/Chemical/1/2 "Policy—Chemical Warfare," vol. 12195, Roll T17488, RG 24C-2, LAC; and Stuart to Murchie, Telegram, COS 120, June 8, 1944, p. 1, Folder 1/Chemical/1/2 "Policy—Chemical Warfare," vol. 12195, Roll T17488, RG 24C-2, LAC.

107. Murchie to Stuart, telegram, May 25, 1944, Folder 1/Chemical/1/2 "Policy—Chemical Warfare," vol. 12195, Roll T17488, RG 24C-2, LAC.

108. Murchie to Stuart, May 25, 1944, p. 1, vol. 12195, RG 24C-2, LAC.

109. Bryden, *Deadly Allies*, 127.

110. A. J. McFarland and R. D. Coleridge to Combined Chiefs of Staff, "Allied Chemical Warfare Policy," C.C.S. 106/15, April 29, 1944, RG 165, Box 576, Folder ABC 475.92 (8-28-42) Sec. 1-B, NARA.

111. R (the rest is illegible) at the War Office to Ken Stuart, "Bateriological Warfare," letter, June 19, 1944, p. 1, Folder 1/Chemical/1/2 "Policy—Chemical Warfare," vol. 12195, RG 24C-2, Roll T17488, LAC; and Cabinet War Committee, June 14, 1944, Minute and Documents of the Cabinet War Committee, Volume XV, RG 2, 7c, LAC.

112. R(?) to Ken Stuart, June 19, 1944, vol. 12195, RG 24C-2.

113. Joint Committee on New Weapons and Equipment, "Implications of Recent Intelligence Regarding Alleged German Secret Weapon," Enclosure to F. B. Royal and A. J. McFarland to Joint Chiefs of Staff, "Implication of Recent Intelligence Regarding Alleged German Secret Weapon," J.C.S. 625/1, January 6, 1944, pp. 9–10, RG 218, Box

375, Folder: CS 385.2 (12-17-43) Sec. 1 Chemical, Biological & Radiological Warfare (JCS 1822), NARA.

114. Edyta Janik, Michal Ceremuga, Joanna Saluk-Bijak, and Michal Bijak, "Biological Toxins as the Potential Tools for Bioterrorism," *International Journal of Molecular Science* 20, no. 5 (March 2019): 1181, published online March 8, 2019. NCBI, doi: 10.3390/ijms20051181.

115. Committee on New Weapons and Equipment, "Implications of Recent Intelligence," pp. 9–10, J.C.S. 625/1, January 6, 1944, RG 218, Box 375, NARA.

116. Committee on New Weapons and Equipment, "Implications of Recent Intelligence," J.C.S. 625/1, January 6, 1944, RG 218, Box 375, CCS Folder: Chemical, Biological & Radiological Warfare (JCS 1822), NARA.

117. Alden Waitt to Gas Warfare Subcommittee of the Joint Committee on New Weapons and Equipment and the Combined Chiefs of Staff, "CWS Representative's Report. Enemy Capabilities with Gas," Annex A, pp. 445–46, RG 218, Box 375, Folder: Chemical, Biological, & Radiological Warfare (JCS 1822), NARA; and Joint Committee on New Weapons and Equipment, "Implications of Recent Intelligence Regarding Alleged German Secret Weapon," p. 34, Enclosure in F. B. Royal and A. J. McFarland to Joint Chiefs of Staff, "Implications of Recent Intelligence," JCS 625/4, February 5, 1944, RG 218, Box 375, Folder: Chemical, Biological, & Radiological Warfare (JCS 1822), NARA.

118. "Implications of Recent Intelligence Regarding Alleged German Secret Weapons," Appendix A, pp. 6–7, to Joint Staff Planners, Enclosure, in Joint Staff Planners, "Implications of Recent Intelligence Regarding Alleged German Secret Weapons," J.P.S. 341/5, March 4, 1944, RG 218, Box 376, Folder "Chemical, Biological & Radiological Warfare (JSC 1822)," NARA.

119. "Implications of Recent Intelligence," Appendix A, p. 8, to Joint Staff Planners, Enclosure, in Joint Staff Planners, "Implications of Recent Intelligence," J.P.S. 341/5, March 4, 1944, RG 218, Box 376, NARA.

120. "Joint Staff Planners, "Implications of Recent Intelligence Regarding Alleged German Secret Weapons," p. 3, Enclosure, in Joint Staff Planners, "Implications of Recent Intelligence Regarding Alleged German Secret Weapons," J.P.S. 341/5, March 4, 1944, RG 218, Box 376; and Joint Committee on New Weapons and Equipment, "Implications of Recent Intelligence Regarding Alleged German Secret Weapon," report, enclosed in Joint Chiefs of Staff, "Implications of Recent Intelligence Regarding Alleged German Secret Weapon," J.C.S. 625/4, February 5, 1944, pp. 34–35, RG 218, Box 375, Folder Chemical, Biological & Radiological Warfare (JCS 1822), NARA.

121. Alden Waitt to Gas Warfare Subcommittee of the Joint Committee on New Weapons and Equipment, "Retaliation Gas Warfare Capabilities in European Theater," memorandum, January 27, 1944, pp. 57–63, Annex E in enclosure to Joint Committee on New Weapons and Equipment, "Implications of Recent Intelligence Regarding Alleged German Secret Weapon," in Joint Chiefs of Staff, "Implications of Recent Intelligence Regarding Alleged German Secret Weapon," JCS 625/4, February 5, 1944, RG 218, Box 375, Folder: Chemical, Biological, & Radiological Warfare (JCS 1822), NARA.

122. Joint Staff Planners, "Implication of Recent Intelligence," p. 1, Report, enclosed in Joint Staff Planners, J.P.S. 341/5, March 4, 1944, RG 218, Box 376, NARA.

123. "Extract from a Minute to the Prime Minister from the Home Secretary Dated July4 [*sic*], 1944," PREM 3/89, TNA.

124. "Extract from a Minute to the Prime Minister from the Home Secretary dated July4, 1944 [*sic*]," PREM 3/89.

125. H. L. Ismay to prime minister, July 28, 1944, PREM 3/89, TNA.

126. "Military Considerations," p. 2, PREM 3/89, TNA.

127. Joint Planning Staff, 'Chemical Warfare in Connection with Crossbow," War Cabinet, J.P. (44) 177 [Final], July 5, 1944, p. 2, PREM 3/89, TNA.

128. "Military Considerations," p. 3, PREM 3/89, TNA; and Annex, "The Use of Gas Against Crossbow Installations," to Joint Planning Staff, "Chemical Warfare in Connection with Crossbow," J.P. (44) 177 [Final], July 5, 1944, p. 4, PREM 3/89.

129. "Military Considerations," p. 2, PREM 3/89.

130. Annex, "The Use of Gas against Crossbow Installations and as a Measure of Retaliation against Germany," in J.P. (44) 177 [Final], July 5, 1944, p. 5, PREM 3/89; and L.C. Hollis to Prime Minister, letter, July 5, 1944, p. 1, PREM 3/89, TNA.

131. "Military Considerations," p. 2, PREM 3/89. It is worth noting that India was vulnerable to gas attacks from nearby Japan, but it was facing other challenges already including the Bengal famine and the Indian National Army, serious ones that did not need to be exacerbated.

132. 401 Parl. Deb. H.C. (5th ser.) (July 6, 1944), cols. 1325–27.

133. Winston Churchill to General Ismay for the C.O.S. Committee, Minute, July 6, 1944, p. 2, PREM 3/89: TNA.

134. Churchill to Ismay, July 6, 1944, pp. 1–4, PREM 3/89.

135. Churchill to Ismay, July 6, 1944, p. 2, PREM 3/89.

136. See for example, J. B. S. Haldance, *Callinicus: A Defence of Chemical Warfare* (New York: E.P. Dutton, 1925), 33. Haldane addresses the (in)humane nature of weapons, and thus the concept of psychological trauma. Should one consider mental injury or just focus on physical casualties and death when evaluating the nature and use of gas? Marek Pruszewicz, "How Deadly was the Poison Gas of WW1?" *BBC Magazine*, January 30, 2015, https://www.bbc.com/news/magazine-31042472. It is hard to find exact statistics, though, since it might be hard to tell why someone died or how any of the missing died. Certainly, some of the massive bombs today are more powerful than World War I gases.

137. Churchill to Ismay, July 6, 1944, pp.1, 3, PREM 3/89.

138. Churchill to Ismay, July 6, 1944, p. 1, PREM 3/89.

139. W[inston] S. C[hurchill] to General Ismay for the C.O.S. Committee, July 25, 1944, PREM 3/89, TNA; and "Military Considerations," in Ismay to prime minister, July 28, 1944, p. 3, PREM 3/89.

140. "Military Considerations," p. 3, PREM 3/89.

141. "Military Considerations," p. 3, PREM 3/89.

142. Exact casualty statistics by month are hard to determine. See, for instance Stephen Henden, "Flying Bombs and Rockets," November 2019, http://www.flyingbomb sandrockets.com/Timeline.html. Other sources say November had the most V-2 deaths (168). Harriet Arkell, "Death from above without Warning," *The Daily Mail Online*, September 10, 2014, https://www.dailymail.co.uk/news/article-2750353/Interactive-map -reveals-hundreds-sites-Hitler-s-V2-rockets-killed-thousands-British-civilians-final -months-WW2.html.

143. "Death from above without Warning," and Amanda Mason, "The Blitz around Britain," January 8, 2018, Imperial War Museum, https://www.iwm.org.uk/history/the-blitz-around-britain.

144. Two scholars suggest that in the summer of 1944, with both sides mired in Normandy, Churchill feared that the stalemate would lead to another trench war, complete with the enormous casualties Britain faced in World War I. The fact that a repeat of the previous conflict did not emerge helped restrain Churchill's calls for gas. They suggest that this conclusion emerges from instructions given to the Joint Staff Planners to avoid "stalemate," although that was just one concern along with shortening the war and the likelihood that the V-weapons could stop the war effort. "Instructions to the Joint Planning Staff, 16 July 1944," CAB 84/64, TNA in Robert Harris and Jeremy Paxman, *A Higher Form of Killing: The Secret Story of Gas and Germ Warfare* (London: Chatto & Windus, 1982), 129–30; and Harris and Paxton, *A Higher Form of Killing,* 134. For the impact of V-2 rockets during successful German resistance on Allied movement, see Biddle's description of Arnhem. Biddle, "On the Crest of Fear," 181.


## 6. Critical Timing

1. General Porter thought it was not only an option but a strong one. Major General William N. Porter to Lieutenant General Joseph T. McNerney, letter, December 17, 1943, Enclosure: "Gas Warfare in the Pacific Theatre," p. 1, Record Group 165, Records of the War Department General and Special Staffs, Box 82, File OPD 385 TS Section II, NARA.

2. Porter to McNerney, December 17, 1943, "Gas Warfare in the Pacific Theatre," RG 165, Box 82. This echoes the view that J. B. S. Haldane had expressed after World War I, but the idea that gas could be more humane than other weapons under certain circumstances—such as using tear gas without defensive helmets—did not gain popularity. J. B. S. Haldane, *Callinicus: A Defense of Chemical Warfare* (New York: E.P. Dutton, 1925), 21.

3. Donald Avery, "Canadian Scientists, CBW Weapons and Japan, 1939–1945," in Roy M. MacLeod, ed., *Science and the Pacific War* (Dordrecht, The Netherlands: Kluwer Academic Publishers, 2000), 240.

4. "Protocol for the Prohibition of the Use in War of Asphyxiating, Poisonous, or Other Gases, and of Bacteriological Methods of Warfare (Geneva Protocol)," June 17, 1925, https://www.state.gov/t/isn/4784.htm, hereinafter "Geneva Gas Protocol."

5. This very fear sparked the cover-up of the mustard gas casualties at Bari as discussed in chapter 4.

6. Chinese representatives made repeated allegations that Japan used CBW in their country, but Britain and the United States debated whether these could be confirmed by evidence.

7. Joint Staff Planners, "Implications of Recent Intelligence Regarding Alleged German Secret Weapons (Biological Warfare)," Extract, JPS 137th meeting, March 15, 1944, pp. 1–2, Record Group 218, Records of the US Joint Chiefs of Staff, Box 376, Folder Chemical, Biological & Radiological Warfare (JCS 1822), NARA.

8. Joint Staff Planners, "Implications of Recent Intelligence Regarding Alleged German Secret Weapons (Biological Warfare)," Extract, JPS 137th meeting, March 15, 1944, pp. 1–2, RG 218, Box 376, NARA.

9. John Dower, *War without Mercy: Race and Power in the Pacific* (New York: Pantheon, 1986).

10. William Porter to L. J. Greeley, letter, August 6, 1943, Record Group 175, Records of the Chemical Warfare Service, Box 157, Folder 479.6 (Enemy), NARA.

11. Gallup Organization, Gallup Poll # 1944–0329: World War II/Presidential Election/Country of Birth, Question 5, USGALLUP.111344.R02B, Gallup Organization, (Cornell University, Ithaca, NY: Roper Center for Public Opinion Research, 1944), Dataset; and Gallup Organization, Gallup Poll # 1944–0329: World War II/Presidential Election/Country of Birth, Question 4, USGALLUP.111344.R02A.

12. "Allied Chemical Warfare Policy," in JCS 158th Meeting, Suppl. Min., April 11, 1944, p. 1, RG 218, Box 425, Folder: CCS 441.5 (illeg.-27-42) Sec. 3, NARA.

13. Appendix A to R. B. Pegram, Jr. to Rear Admiral L. D. McCormick, Rear Admiral J. W. Radford, Major General W. A. Wood, Brigadier General P. H. Tansey, Captain R. G. Tobis, and Colonel D. W. Benner, "Capabilities of Implementing Decision to Initiate Retaliatory Chemical Warfare Against the Japanese," Memorandum, August 27, 1944, p. 2, RG 218, Box 426, Folder "Allied Chemical Warfare Program," NARA.

14. Representatives of the British Chiefs of Staff to the Combined Chiefs of Staff, "German War Gases," Memorandum, C.C.S. 883, June 21, 1945, p. 1, RG 165, Box 576, Folder "Allied Chemical Warfare Program," Sec. 3, NARA.

15. Thomas T. Handy to deputy chief of staff, "Letter from the Chief, Chemical Warfare Service, Regarding Prospective Use of Gas," Memorandum, December 27, 1943, p. 1, RG 165, Box 82, NARA.

16. The official history of the CWS claims that the Operations Division of the War Department General Staff (OPD) first considered overtly offensive gas use in June of 1945. Leo P. Brophy and George J. B. Fisher, *The Chemical Service: Organization for War* (Washington, DC: Center of Military History, United States Army, 2004), 87.

17. The War Office (M.I. 10), Notes on Japanese Chemical Warfare, report, June 1942, p. 12, WO 33/2331, TNA. See for, example, Daniel Barenblatt, *A Plague upon Humanity: The Hidden History of Japan's Biological Warfare Program* (New York: HarperCollins Perennial, 2004) for details about Unit 731 or Walter E. Grunden, *Secret Weapons and World War II: Japan in the Shadow of Big Science* (Lawrence: University Press of Kansas, 2005), chapter 5.

18. Foreign Office, United Kingdom to Sir Al Clark Kerr and Sir R. Craigie, May 19, 1938, FO 371/23692, TNA.

19. There are indications that the British investigated claims in 1938 too. Sir Andrew Noble to Viscount Halifax, May 24, 1940, FO 371/24692, TNA. Also see G.S., memorandum, "Japanese Chemical Warfare," January 18, 1942, WO 106/3445, TNA. The history of CBW in China during the 1930s and 1940s is still foggy regarding the exact list of which toxins were used when. Part of the challenge is that it was difficult to confirm, to the Allies' satisfaction, that CBW had been used. The rigor needed seems to resemble the care taken with chains of evidence in criminal cases today. Regardless, as with the chemical warfare in the European theater of World War II, it was the perception of events that proved as influential and enduring as any reality that existed.

20. Noble to Halifax, May 24, 1940, FO 371/24692.

21. O.W. Lambert to The Under-Secretary of State, Foreign Office, February 17, 1942, HO 186/2846, TNA.

22. Anna Feigenbaum, *Tear Gas: From the Battlefields of World War I to the Streets of Today* (London: Verso, 2017), 61.

23. "Enemy Breaches of the Rules of Warfare, &c.: Summary for November 1941 to January 1942," W 1805/117/49, February 3, 1942, p. 2, FO 371/32436, TNA.

24. Chinese Ambassador, London to Foreign Office, Chungking, "Chinese Ambassador, London, Reports Japanese Plans for Use of Poison Gas," December 8, 1941, HW 1/307, TNA.

25. B.A.D. Washington to Admiralty, January 16/17, 1942, WO 106/3445, TNA.

26. General George Marshall to Field Marshall Sir John Dill, *The Papers of George Catlett Marshall,* ed. Larry I. Bland and Sharon Ritenour Stevens (Lexington, VA: The George C. Marshall Foundation, 1981-). Electronic version based on *The Papers of George Catlett Marshall,* vol. 3, *"The Right Man for the Job," December 7, 1941–May 31, 1943* (Baltimore and London: The Johns Hopkins University Press, 1991), p. 67. The George C. Marshall Foundation, marshallfoundation.org, accessed September 27, 2019.

27. Appendix B (hand corrected from "Appendix A") to Enclosure, Joint Staff Planners "Allied Chemical Warfare Program," to Joint Chiefs of Staff, J.C.S. 176/6 (Washington), December 10, 1943, pp. 3–4, RG 218, Box 425, Folder "Allied Chemical Warfare Program," NARA.

28. Major H. A. Delcallier, Chemical Warfare, Proposed General Staff Policy and Plan, December 10, 1941, p. 1, S.4354-1-8, vol. 2, Chemical Warfare-General Policy-Defensive, Reel C5002, RG24-C-1, LAC.

29. Lt-Gen., chief of the General Staff to prime minister, "Production in Canada of MUSTARD GAS, February 1942, p. 2, HQS452-7-3 vol. 1, Vol. 5432, "Chemical Warfare, Policy," RG24-C-1, LAC.

30. Canadian CW Inter-Service Board, Twenty-Ninth Meeting, Minutes, February 22, 1944, p. 3, Chemical Warfare: General Data and Correspondence, vol. 3947, file 1037-33-1, pt. 2, RG 24-D-1-b, LAC.

31. Walter Grunden, "No Retaliation in Kind: Japanese Chemical Warfare Policy in World War II," in *One Hundred Years of Chemical Warfare: Research, Deployment, Consequences,* ed. B. Friedrich, D. Hoffmann, J. Renn, F. Schmaltz, and M. Wolf, (Springer Cham, 2017), https://doi.org/10.1007/978-3-319-51664-6_14. In 2003 about a dozen Chinese individuals won damages from a Japanese court because of injuries from mustard gas the Imperial army abandoned in China; that is not absolute proof, of course, that the Japanese used it. Brendan Koerner, "Who Used Mustard Gas in WWII?" Slate .com, October 1, 2003, https://slate.com/news-and-politics/2003/10/who-used-mustard -gas-in-wwii.html.

32. Delcallier, "Chemical Warfare, Proposed General Staff Policy and Plan, December 10, 1941, p. 1, S.4354-1-8, vol. 2, Reel C5002, RG24-C-1, LAC.

33. F. V. Heakes to C.A.S., February 10, 1942, File HQS 452-7-3, vol. 1, vol. 5432, "Chemical Warfare, Policy," RG24-C-1, LAC.

34. N. R. Anderson to C.A.S., May 26, 1942, vol 5432, file 452-7-3, pt. 1 and vol. 1, "Chemical Warfare Policy," RG24-E-1-b, LAC.

35. Tab "B" "Influences for and against Initiation of the Use of Toxic Gas," Enclosure to "Axis Capabilities and Intentions to Use Gas Warfare, 1943," January 16, 1943, to Joint Intelligence Committee, January 19, 1943, p. 7, RG 218, Box 425, File CCS (Combined Chiefs of Staff), "Chemical Biological Warfare," NARA.

36. This is still a contentious issue, although historians agree it occurred. In 2007, Spain decided not to discuss in parliament whether the nation's army did drop gas in Morocco in the 1920s and whether it should pay compensation. Reuters, "Spain Rejects Move to Discuss Rif Chemical Attack," February 14, 2007, https://www.reuters.com/article/idUSL14606426. There are claims that the British used gas in Iraq during the interwar period, but there seems to be debate among historians about this. See, for example, Geoff Simons, *Iraq: From Sumer to Post-Saddam*, foreword by Tony Benn, 3rd ed. (New York: Palgrave Macmillan, 2004), xvi and 213, in which it is clear that Winston Churchill and others considered using gas, but Britain does not seem to have done so. R. M. Douglas, "Did Britain Use Chemical Weapons in Mandatory Iraq?" *The Journal of Modern History* 81 (December 2009): 859–887 studies the subject carefully and dismisses British use in Iraq.

37. See chapter 2.

38. Research Unit, Military Intelligence Service, WDGS, "Reports of the Incidents of Use of Gas by Japanese," October 6, 1944, in Project 717: "Japanese Use of Gas" October 5, 1944, Record Group 319, Records of the Army Staff, Box 2835, NARA.

39. Research Unit, "Reports of the Incidents of Use of Gas by Japanese," October 6, 1944, in Project 717: "Japanese Use of Gas," October 5, 1944, RG 319, Box 2835; and "Logistical Information," Appendix B, to Joint Logistics Committee, "Capabilities of Implementing a Decision to Initiate Retaliatory Chemical Warfare against the Japanese," Report, in Joint Logistics Committee, "Capabilities of Implementing a Decision to Initiate Retaliatory Chemical Warfare against the Japanese," JLC 144/3, September 21, 1944, p. 21, RG 218, Box 426, Folder 427, NARA.

40. The War Office (M.I. 10), "Notes on Japanese Chemical Warfare," June 1942, p. 57, WO 33/2331, TNA.

41. H. L. Ismay to Churchill, July 9, 1942, CAB 120/775, TNA; and "Japanese Gas Warfare in China," CAB 120/775. After World War II ended, some individuals who took the reports about Japan's use of CBW seriously tried to convince the organizers of the Tokyo War Crimes Trials (more formally known as the International Military Tribunal for the Far East), but a combination of mixed evidence and American political concerns, according to scholar Jeanne Guillemin, quashed this complaint. Guillemin, a scholar of this topic, notes that there were international efforts to find BW evidence in China after the war and before the trials. The American in charge of this search, David Sutton, a civilian attached to the investigative team, was not able to find enough evidence to recommend prosecution for these kinds of crimes. Colonel Thomas Morrow, however, found substantiation of CW activities for acts between 1937 and 1945, although a separate investigation by Lt. Col. John Beebe of the US CWS recorded denials of organized casualty ?? gas use by leading Japanese officials. Among other reasons given explicitly by those who quashed allegations of Japanese CW use in the complaint for the trials, Guillemin suggests that the CWS did not want to have any Japanese gas use publicized because of its own political interests, and she notes that Shiro Ishii, the Japanese BW scientist, was working secretly with the United States after the war. Jeanne Guillemin, "The 1925 Geneva Protocol: China's CBW Charges Against Japan at the Tokyo War Crimes Tribunal," in *One Hundred Years of Chemical Warfare: Research, Deployment, Consequences*, ed. B. Friedrich, D. Hoffmann, J. Renn, F. Schmaltz, and M. Wolf, (Springer Cham, 2017), 273–286, https://doi.org/10.1007/978-3-319-51664-6_15.

42. H. L. Ismay to The Hon. Sir Alexander Cadogan, July 20, 1942, CAB 120/775, TNA.

43. The PWC was actually two interrelated groups, one in London and one in Washington, DC, both nominally supervising, or at least advising, about the Pacific theater (although the Combined Chiefs of Staff took the real lead) and discussing postwar diplomatic relationships. The one in Washington, DC was a body under the auspices of the United States containing Allied nations, dominions, territories, and colonies participating in the Pacific theater, including China. The one in London was more limited in influence. For a more detailed discussion of the PWC, see Thomas P. Maga, "Vison and Victory: Franklin Roosevelt and the PWC, 1942–1944," *Presidential Studies Quarterly* 21, no. 2 (Spring 1991), 351–363, http://www.jstor.com/stable/27550723. Warren F. Kimball, "'Merely a Façade?' Roosevelt and the Southwest Pacific," *The Journal of American-East Asian Relations* 3, no. 2 (Summer, 1994), 103–106, http://www.jstor.com/stable/23613382 offers more details about the relationship of the London body to the American one.

44. Ismay to Cadogan, July 20, 1942, CAB 120/775.

45. H. L. Ismay to prime minister, July 9, 1942, CAB 120/775, TNA.

46. Ismay to prime minister, July 14, 1942, PREM 3/65, TNA.

47. EE.B.[Sir Edward Bridges] to General H. L. Ismay, July 17, 1942, CAB 120/775, TNA.

48. Ismay to Cadogan, July 20, 1942, CAB 120/775.

49. Ismay to Cadogan, July 20, 1942, CAB 120/775.

50. Maurice (Illeg.) at Foreign Office to Ismay, August 19, 1942, CAB 121/100, TNA.

51. Maurice (Illeg.) to Ismay, August 19, 1942, CAB 121/100.

52. Enclosure B to Combined Intelligence Committee to the Combined Chiefs of Staff, "Memorandum for Information No. 56: Axis Capabilities and Intentions, Gas Warfare," Report, April 5, 1943, p. 4, RG 165, Box 576, Folder ABC 475.92 Sec. 1-A 98-28-320, NARA.

53. The War Office (M.I. 10), "Notes on Japanese Chemical Warfare," June 1942, p. 13, WO 33/2331, TNA.

54. The War Office (M.I. 10), "Notes on Japanese Chemical Warfare," p. 56, WO 33/2331.

55. "Japanese Use of Poison Gas," October 5, 1944; and "Condensed Statement of Information available concerning Japanese Use of War Gas," part of the Research Unit: Military Intelligence Service: WDGS, Project No. 717: Japanese Use of Poison Gas, October 5, 1944, pp. 9 and 12, RG 319, Box 2835, NARA.

56. Enclosure "A" "Summary and Conclusions" to Combined Intelligence Committee, "Axis Capabilities and Intentions, Gas Warfare," C.I.C. 15/3, September 30, 1943, p. 4, RG 218, Box 425, CCS 441.5 Sec. 2, NARA.

57. Nor was the United States the only regional belligerent trying to determine whether Japan used gas. According to the New Zealand Deputy Chiefs of Staff, the only evidence of which they were aware was the presence of Japanese CW in the theater, but their judgment came in May, months before the American reports. Owen Wilkes, "A History of New Zealand Chemical Warfare: 1845–1945," (working paper no. 4, Centre For Peace Studies, University of Auckland, 1993), 29.

58. Appendix B, "Logistical Implications" to Joint Logistics Committee, Report: "Capabilities of Implementing a Decision to Initiate Retaliatory Chemical Warfare Against the Japanese," in Joint Logistics Committee, "Capabilities of Implementing a Decision to Initiate Retaliatory Chemical Warfare Against the Japanese," JLC 144/3, September 21, 1944, p. 21, RG 218, Box 426, CCS 441.5 (8-27-42) Sec. 3 "Allied Chemical Warfare Policy," NARA.

59. Thomas Handy to deputy chief of staff, December 27, 1943, p. 1, RG 165, Box 82, OPD 385 TS Sect II, NARA. Also, see Walter Grunden, a scholar of Japanese science during World War II, notes that Japan used gas at Guadalcanal, but, in a footnote, raised the question of whether these were relatively harmless smoke candles or something more. He does not refer to the choking gas that the Military Intelligence Research Unit confirmed, and that was almost certainly potentially lethal, even if fatalities did not result from that particular deployment. Walter Grunden, "No Retaliation in Kind: Japanese Chemical Warfare Policy in World War II," in *One Hundred Years of Chemical Warfare: Research, Deployment, Consequences*, ed. B. Friedrich, D. Hoffmann, J. Renn, F. Schmaltz, and M. Wolf, (Springer Cham, 2017), https://doi.org/10.1007/978-3-319-51664-6_14.

60. Memorandum attached to M.S.J. to General Lincoln, Memorandum, June 4, 1945, p. 5, RG 165, Box 578, Folder ABC 475.92 (February 25, 1944) Sec. 1-C, NARA.

61. Unknown to chief of staff, U.S. Army, "Chemical Warfare Policy," Memorandum, May 21, 1945, RG 165, Box 576, File ABC 475.92 (8-28-42), Sec. 1-B, NARA.

62. For example, see G[eorge] A. L[incoln] to Colonel Johnson, Memorandum, April 3, 1945, RG 165, Box 577, Folder ABC 475.92 (February 25, 1944), NARA; and Joint Staff Planners, "Theater Plans for Chemical Warfare," report enclosed in Joint Staff Planners, "Theater Plans for Chemical Warfare," Memorandum, JPS 484/6, June 4, 1945, RG 165, Box 578, File ABC 475.92 (Feb 25, 1944) Sec. 1-C, NARA.

63. See, for example, concern about India. C.R.A., Secretary of State for Dominion Affairs, "Chemical Warfare," in War Cabinet, W.P. (42) 171, April 20, 1942, CAB 66/24/1, TNA.

64. Illegible, "Comments on C.O.S. (44) 450 (0), May 23, 1944, WO 106/4284A, TNA; Aide for Lt. Gen. Miles Dempsey, "Chemical Warfare," May 21, 1944, WO 205/130, TNA; and Major-General, chief of staff to First United States Army and First Canadian Army, "Personal Anti-Gas Equipment," May 25, 1944, WO 205/130, TNA.

65. Lt. Colonel Kenneth H. Cousland, "'The Great War,' 1914–1918: A Former 'Gunner' of the First World War Looks Back," 56, Liddell Hart Centre for Military Archives, King's College.

66. "Tab B: Influences for and against initiation of the use of toxic gas," in enclosure "Axis Capabilities and Intentions to Use Gas, 1943," January 16, 1943, p. 7, in Joint Intelligence Committee, "Axis Capabilities and Intelligence Gas Warfare," January 19, 1943, RG 218, Box 425, Folder CCS 441.5 (8-27-43) Sec. 1, NARA. Even during World War II, the United States wondered if one reason the Germans had not used gas yet was because the war in Europe was one of movement.

67. William N. Porter to the Joint Committee on New Weapons and Equipment and the Joint Chiefs of Staff, Washington, DC, memo, "Present Status of Development of Toxic Gases," December 6, 1942, p. 6, RG 175, Box 142, NARA.

68. Porter, "Present Status of Development of Toxic Gases," December 6, 1943, p. 6. Also, note that the British had considered using gas in the Empire in the interwar period to lure criminals out of lairs; the idea of clearing Pacific islands by using gas adapted that method to war, although the CWS documents did not make that connection. J. H. T., December 3, 1935, in Cabinet, "Use of Tear Gas in the Colonial Empire," C.P. 226(35), p. 2, CO 323/1341/19, TNA.

69. The Germans launched their first gas attack on the Western Front on April 22, 1915, at Ypres, and the British responded during the battle of Loos, begun September 25, 1915.

70. The War Office to C. in C. India, Rptd. C.C.S., Melbourne, telegram and unidentified quoted telegram, April 24, 1942, WO 106/3445, TNA.

71. Kendrick Lee, "Gas Warfare," August 27, 1943, pp. 128–9, vol. II, no. 8, Washington, DC: Editorial Research Reports, RG 218, Box 425, Folder CCS 441.5 (8-27-42) Sec. 1, NARA. Editorial Research Reports is now part of CQ Researcher. For its history, see CQPress, https://library.cqpress.com/cqresearcher/static.php?page=aboutcqr.

72. The United States kept a list of Chinese and Japanese allegations of gas use published by various press outlets. One interpretation is that these were meant to sway public opinion. "Recent Information Received through Press Channels," RG 319, Box 2835, in Folder Research Unit: Military Intelligence Service, WDGS, "Intelligence Research Project," Project No. 717, October 1944, NARA.

73. Lee, "Gas Warfare," 129.

74. Lee, "Gas Warfare," 128.

75. Enclosure "A" to Combined Intelligence Committee, "Axis Capabilities and Intentions, Gas Warfare, Report," in Combined Intelligence Committee, "Axis Capabilities and Intentions, Gas Warfare," C.I.C. 15/4, October 2, 1943, p. 3, RG 218, Box 425, CCS 441.5, Chemical and Biological Warfare, Box 425, NARA; and Roy B. Snapp to Secretaries, Joint War Plans Committee, Memorandum, "Japanese Chemical Warfare," October 28, 1943, RG 218, Box 425, CCS 441.5 Sec. 2, Chemical and Biological Warfare, NARA.

76. "Condensed Statement of Information Available Concerning Japanese Use of War Gas," p. 3, in "Intelligence Research Project," Project No. 717, RG 319, Box 2835, NARA.

77. Snapp to Joint War Plans Committee, "Japanese Chemical Warfare," October 28, 1943.

78. Excerpt from Hanson Baldwin, "A War without Quarter Forecast in the Pacific," *The New York Times*, January 30, 1944; and Annex B to Enclosure, Joint Staff Planners, "Communication from Apostolic Delegate to Washington Regarding Use of Poison Gas by the Japanese Forces," in Joint Chiefs of Staff, "Communication from Apostolic Delegate to Washington Regarding Use of Poison Gas by the Japanese Forces," J.C.S. 731/1, March 8, 1944, RG 218, Box 425, CCS 441.5 Sec. 2 "Chemical and Biological Warfare," NARA.

79. A. G. Cicognani to Cordell Hull, letter, February 15, 1944, enclosed in E. R. Stettinius, Jr. to Admiral William D. Leahy, letter, February 24, 1944, RG 218, Box 425, CCS 441.5 Sec. 2 "Chemical and Biological Warfare," NARA.

80. E. R. Stettinius, Jr. to Admiral William D. Leahy, letter, February 24, 1944, RG 218, Box 425, CCS 441.5 Sec. 2 "Chemical and Biological Warfare."

81. Joint Staff Planners, "Communication from Apostolic Delegate in Washington regarding Use of Poison Gas by the Japanese Forces," report, enclosure to Joint Chiefs of Staff, March 8, 1944, RG 218, Box 425, CCS 441.5 Sec. 2 "Chemical and Biological Warfare," NARA.

82. Joint Staff Planners, "Communication from Apostolic Delegate in Washington regarding Use of Poison Gas by the Japanese Forces," report; and W.D. Leahy to The Secretary of State, Annex "C" to Joint Chiefs of Staff, "Communication from Apostolic Delegate in Washington regarding Use of Poison Gas by the Japanese Forces," March 8, 1944, RG 218, Box 425, CCS 441.5 Sec. 2 "Chemical and Biological Warfare," NARA.

83. Joint Staff Planners, "Communication from Apostolic Delegate in Washington regarding Use of Poison Gas by the Japanese Forces."

84. William D. Leahy to Cordell Hull, letter, March 10, 1944, RG 218, Box 425, CCS 441.5 Sec. 2 "Chemical and Biological Warfare," NARA.

85. McFarland and Graves, Jr., Note, in Joint Staff Planners, "Retaliatory Measures of Warfare Against Japan," JCS 895, April 18, 1944 and William D. Leahy to The Secretary of State, "Draft Reply to the Department of State," Appendix A, to enclosure A, Joint Staff Planners, "Retaliatory Measures of Warfare Against Japan," Report, in Joint Staff Planners, "Retaliatory Measures of Warfare Against Japan," JCS 825, April 18, 1944, RG 165, Box 577, Folder ABC 475.92 (25 Feb 44) Sec 1-A, NARA.

86. McFarland and Graves, Jr., to Joint Chiefs of Staff, JCS 895, April 18, 1944.

87. Enclosure "B" in Combined Intelligence Committee to Combined Chiefs of Staff, p. 1, "Memorandum for Information No. 56: Axis Capabilities and Intentions, Gas Warfare," April 5, 1943, RG 165, Box 576, Folder ABC 475.92 (8-28-42) Sec. 1-A, NARA.

88. 220 Military Mission [aka Lethbridge Mission, Final Mission Report, vol. 1, 1944, p. 1, Lethbridge 1/2, LHCMA.

89. 220 Military Mission, Lethbridge 1/2, p. 1.

90. Chiefs of Staff Committee, Extract from C.O.S. (44) 120 (?)th meeting (0), April 13, 1944, CAB 121/101, TNA.

91. J.S. Lethbridge, "Chemical Warfare Interim Report (aka Lethbridge Report No. 23)," November 29, 1943, WO 106/4974, TNA.

92. Brunskill, "Comments on Leth [sic] Report No. 23," January 24, 1944, WO 106/4944, TNA.

93. Winston S. Churchill to General Ismay for Chiefs of Staff Committee, July 25, 1944, PREM 3/89, TNA.

94. N. H. Bottomley, "Interim Report: Employment of Chemical Warfare in the War Against Japan," for the Chiefs of Staff Committee, C.O.S. (44) 664 (O), July 27, 1944, p. 1, CAB 80/85/84, TNA.

95. Bottomley, Interim Report: Employment of Chemical Warfare, C.O.S. (44) 664 (O), pp. 1–2, CAB 80/85/84.

96. Bottomley, Interim Report: Employment of Chemical Warfare, C.O.S. (44) 664 (O), p. 2, CAB 80/85/84.

97. Bottomley, Interim Report: Employment of Chemical Warfare, C.O.S. (44) 664 (O), pp. 2–3, CAB 80/85/84.

98. Bottomley, Interim Report: Employment of Chemical Warfare, C.O.S. (44) 664 (O), p. 3, CAB 80/85/84.

99. William N. Porter, Enclosure 1: "Gas Warfare in the Pacific Theatres," in William N. Porter to Lieutenant General Joseph T. McNarney, letter, December 17, 1943, pp. 1, 3, and 4, RG 165, Box 82, File OPD 385 TS Section II, NARA.

100. Porter, "Enclosure 1: Gas Warfare in the Pacific," pp. 1, 4.

101. Porter, "Enclosure 1: Gas Warfare in the Pacific," p. 1.

102. Porter to McNarney, December 17, 1943, "Gas Warfare in the Pacific," p. 1.

103. Porter, "Enclosure 1: Gas Warfare in the Pacific," p. 1.

104. Porter, "Enclosure 1: Gas Warfare in the Pacific," p.1.

105. Porter, "Enclosure 1: Gas Warfare in the Pacific," p. 2.

106. Porter, "Enclosure 1: Gas Warfare in the Pacific," p. 1.

107. Porter, "Enclosure 1: Gas Warfare in the Pacific," p. 1.

108. See, for example, accounts of testing in Florida and Panama from the perspective of an American graduate student assisting with the research. Harold Johnston, *A Bridge Not Attacked: Chemical Warfare Civilian Research during World War II* (New Jersey: World Scientific, 2003), 128–195. Some of the testing by the Allies included human subject research on soldiers, sometimes without their full knowledge, as well as field trials in North America and beyond. There are several works on this topic including Bridget Goodwin, *Keen as Mustard: Britain's Horrific Chemical Warfare Experiments in Australia* (St. Lucia: University of Queensland Press, 1998); Geoff Plunkett, *Chemical Warfare in Australia: Australia's Involvement in Chemical Warfare, 1914-Today* (Sydney: Leech Cup Books, 2013); Ulf Schmidt, *Secret Science: A Century of Poison Warfare and Human Experiments* (Oxford: Oxford University Press, 2015); and Susan L. Smith, *Toxic Exposures: Mustard Gas and the Health Consequences of World War II* (New Brunswick, NJ: Rutgers University Press, 2017).

109. Colonel George Unmacht to General Alden Waitt, letter, December 11, 1942, p. 1, RG 175, Box 135, Folder 322.095, NARA.

110. Porter, "Enclosure 1: Gas Warfare in the Pacific Theatres," p. 2.

111. Porter, "Enclosure 1: Gas Warfare in the Pacific Theatres," p. 2.

112. Alden H. Waitt to chief, Chemical Warfare Services, "Conference with General Styder," Memorandum, January 9, 1944, p. 1, RG 175, Box 143, Folder 377 (General Policy Board), NARA.

113. Combined Staff Planners, "Allied Chemical Warfare Program," enclosure to Combined Staff Planners, "Allied Chemical Warfare Program," C.P.S. 45/4, May 1, 1943, p. 2, RG 218, Box 425, Folder CCS 441.5 Sec. 2: "Allied Chemical Warfare Program," NARA.

114. Thomas T. Handy to the deputy chief of staff, "Letter from the Chief, Chemical Warfare Service, Regarding Prospective Use of Gas," Memorandum, December 27, 1943, pp. 1 and 2, RG 165, Box 82, Folder OPD 385 TS Section II, NARA.

115. Handy to deputy chief of staff, December 27, 1943, p. 1.

116. Handy to deputy chief of staff, December 27, 1943, p. 1.

117. Handy to deputy chief of staff, December 27, 1943, p. 2.

118. Handy to deputy chief of staff, December 27, 1943, p. 2.

119. There had been occasional considerations before this point, which is not surprising because CW always had some adherents in the US military. However, they were neither detailed analyses nor did they always recommend that the United States adopt gas at that time. Notes on CPS 32nd Meeting, "Allied Chemical Warfare Program," September 11, 1942, p. 1, RG 165, Box 576, Folder ABC 475.92, Sec. 1-A (8-28-42), NARA; and

Roy B. Snapp to Joint War Plans Committee, "Japanese Chemical Warfare," Memorandum, October 28, 1943, RG 218, Box 425, Folder CCS 441.5 Sec. 2 "Allied Chemical Warfare Program," NARA.

120. Chief, CWS, Synopsis of Memorandum to the chief of staff, "Use of Gas in the Pacific Theaters (Revised Study)," June 5, 1944, RG 165, Box 576, Folder: "The Use of Gas in the Pacific Theaters, Memorandum to the chief of staff through The Commanding General, Army Service Forces, 20 May 1944," NARA.

121. Brigadier General Alden M. Waitt to Canadian Chemical Warfare Inter-Service Board, Remarks, Ottawa, Canada, January 13, 1944, p. 1, Vol 3947, file 1037-33-1, pt. 2, "Chemical Warfare General Data and Correspondence," RG 24-D-1-b, LAC.

122. George H. Roeder, *The Censored War: American Visual Experience during World War Two* (New Haven, CT: Yale University Press, 1993), 1, 11–12.

123. Porter to McNarney, December 17, 1943, p. 1.

124. David Reynolds, *From Munich to Pearl Harbor: Roosevelt's America and the Origins of the Second World War* (Chicago: Ivan R. Dee, Publisher, 2001), 186.

125. Commander-in-Chief, Army Group, South East Asia to Chief of General Staff, India, Draft memo "CW Policy," February 1944, p. 1, WO 205/130, TNA.

126. 220 Mission, Final Mission Report, vol. 1, p. 259, Lethbridge 1/2, LHCMA.

127. Inter-Services Committee on Chemical Warfare, "Use of Gas in the Assault upon Formosa," War Cabinet Chiefs of Staff Committee, January 24, 1945, C.O.S. (45) 75 (O), pp. 2 and 1, CAB 121/102, TNA.

128. "Use of Gas in the Assault upon Formosa," p. 1.

129. "Use of Gas in the Assault upon Formosa," p. 1.

130. "Use of Gas in the Assault upon Formosa," p. 5.

131. "Use of Gas in the Assault upon Formosa," p. 5.

132. "Use of Gas in the Assault upon Formosa," p. 1.

133. "Use of Gas in the Assault upon Formosa," p. 1.

134. "Use of Gas in the Assault upon Formosa," p. 1.

135. "Use of Gas in the Assault upon Formosa," p. 1.

136. "Use of Gas in the Assault upon Formosa," pp. 2–3.

137. "Use of Gas in the Assault upon Formosa," pp. 1, 3–4.

138. "Use of Gas in the Assault upon Formosa," p. 5.

139. "Use of Gas in the Assault upon Formosa," p. 8.

140. "Use of Gas in the Assault upon Formosa," pp. 8–9.

141. "Use of Gas in the Assault upon Formosa," p. 11.

142. "Use of Gas in the Assault upon Formosa," p. 11.

143. "Use of Gas in the Assault upon Formosa," p. 6.

144. "Use of Gas in the Assault upon Formosa," p. 10.

145. "Use of Gas in the Assault upon Formosa," p. 6.

146. "Use of Gas in the Assault upon Formosa," pp. 11–12.

147. "Use of Gas in the Assault upon Formosa," p. 12.

148. Robert Ross Smith, "Luzon versus Formosa," to be included in *Triumph in the Philippines in United States Army in World War II*, https://history.army.mil/books/70-7_21.htm, 461 and 477.

149. Edmund Russell, *War and Nature: Fighting Humans and Insects with Chemicals from World War I to Silent Spring* (Cambridge: Cambridge University Press, 2001), 20–21.

150. Illegible to Churchill, Memorandum, "Crop Destruction," March 9, 1944, p. 1, PREM 3/89, TNA.

151. Cherwell to Churchill, March 12, 1944; Illegible to Churchill, "Crop Destruction," March 9, 1944, p. 1, PREM 3/89, TNA; and Inter-Services Committee on Chemical Warfare, Report, "Crop Destruction—Security," Chiefs of Staff Committee," COS (45), 417 (O), June 26, 1945, p. 1, CAB 121/102, TNA.

152. Inter-Services Committee on Chemical Warfare to the Chiefs of Staff Committee, report, "Legality of Crop Destruction," July 23, 1945, COS (45) 488 (O), CAB 80/96/12, TNA. Note that it is a CW committee that studies crop destruction in Britain even though it is a BW expert, George Merck, who is responsible for this in the United States. Because of the way 1313 and 1414 worked as well as the organization of committees in the two countries, crop destruction compounds were considered CW (much like botulism was), even though they have BW components. F.W.S. to General Lincoln, "Chemicals for Destruction of Japanese Food Crops," April 25, 1945, p. 1, RG 165, Box 577, Folder ABC 475.92 (February 25, 1944), NARA.

153. Inter-Services Committee on Chemical Warfare "Legality of Crop Destruction," July 23, 1945, COS (45) 488 (O), p. 1, CAB 80/96/12. Whether or not victims or observers would agree that crop destruction chemicals followed the spirit of the law is another question.

154. Cherwell to Churchill, March 12, 1944, PREM 3/89.

155. Illegible to Churchill, "Crop Destruction," March 9, 1944, pp. 1–3, PREM 3/89.

156. Cherwell to Churchill, March 21, 1944, PREM 3/89, TNA; and W.S.C. to Chancellor of the Exchequer, March 17, 1944, PREM 3/89, TNA.

157. Cherwell to Churchill, March 12, 1944, PREM 3/89.

158. W.S.C. to Chancellor of the Exchequer, March 17, 1944, PREM 3/89.

159. George W. Merck to General George C. Marshall, "Destruction of Crops by 'LN' Chemicals," Memorandum, p. 1, March 8, 1945, RG 165, Box 577, Folder ABC 475.92 (February 25, 1944), NARA. LN chemicals, which were known by several names, such as VKA, were also analyzed by civilian experts, namely the National Academy of Sciences, not just the military. "Chemicals for Destruction of Japanese Food Crops," p. 1. Also see Robert Harris and Jeremy Paxman, *A Higher Form of Killing: The Secret Story of Gas and Germ Warfare* (London: Chatto & Windus, 1982), 99, for more details about specific chemicals developed by the United Kingdom and the United States that fall into the collection discussed here.

160. Myron C. Cramer to George Merck and the Secretary of War, "Destruction of Crops by Chemicals," SPJGW 1945/164, March 5, 1945, p. 2, Appendix II to unnamed document, RG 165, Box 577, Folder ABC 475.92 (February 25, 1944), NARA, citing FM 27–10, *Rules of Land Warfare*, par. 24.

161. "Chemicals for Destruction of Japanese Food Crops," p. 1.

162. John Ray Skates, *The Invasion of Japan: Alternative to the Bomb* (Columbia: University of South Carolina Press, 1994), 86, citing Memo, Porter to Commanding General, Army Service Forces, March 30, 1945, Sub: Weekly Progress Report on LN8 Agent, RG 165, ABC 475.92 (February 25, 1944), Sec. 1-B, NARA discusses the efforts Dow Chemicals would have to make to produce the chemicals as scheduled.

163. In fact, the assistant chief of staff, Major General J. E. Hull, believed refusing to categorize crop destruction chemicals as CW might be splitting hairs. He expressed his concern that the Japanese might retaliate with gas by saying that they "might justifiably

consider" the LNs as true CW attacks. J. E. Hull, to chief of staff, "Destruction of Crops by "LN" Chemicals," Summary, March 9, 1945, RG 165, Box 577, Folder 475.92 (25 Feb 44), NARA.

164. "Capability of Japanese to Wage Chemical Warfare," memorandum to DOCS, Ref INT/19/3, May, appendix C in Headquarters Supreme Allied Commander, South East Asia, SAC (45) (106), July 10, 1945, p. 1, WO 204/44, TNA.

165. F.W.S. to General Lincoln, "Proposed Use of Chemical Agents for the Destruction of Japanese Food Crops," Memorandum, May 11, 1945, p. 1, RG 165, Box 577, Folder ABC 475.92 (February 25, 1944), NARA.

166. Joint Staff Planners and the Joint Logistics Committee, "Policy on the Use of Chemical Agents for the Destruction of Japanese Food Crops," report, Enclosure to Joint Staff Planners, "Policy on the Use of Chemical Agents for the Destruction of Japanese Food Crops," J.P.S. 665/2, May 21, 1945, p. 2, RG 165, Box 577, Folder ABC 475.92 (February 25, 1944), NARA.

167. Wolfgang Saxon, "Brig. Gen. George Lincoln Dies; Top Military Planner Was 67," *The New York Times*, May 26, 1975, ProQuest Historical Newspapers; and General Lincoln to Policy Section, "JPS 665/2—Policy on the Use of Chemical Agents for the Destruction of Japanese Food Crops," Memorandum, May 29, 1945, RG 165, Box 577, Folder ABC 475.92 (February 25, 1944), NARA.

168. General George Lincoln to Admiral Duncan; Captain Campbell; Colonel Johnson; and Secretary, Joint Staff Planning, Memorandum, May 26, 1945, RG 165, Box 577, Folder ABC 475.92 (February 25, 1944), NARA.

169. "Proposed Use of Chemical Agents," 1; Cherwell to Churchill, March 12, 1944, PREM 3/89, TNA; and W.S.C. to Chancellor of the Exchequer, March 17, 1944, PREM 3/89.

170. "Capability of Japanese to Wage Chemical Warfare," Ref INT/19/3, May, appendix C in Headquarters Supreme Allied Commander, South East Asia, SAC (45) (106), July 10, 1945, p. 2, WO 204/44.

171. Excerpt from the Joint Logistics Committee Meeting minutes, 8-11-44, RG 218, Box 426, CCS 441.5 (8-27-42), NARA.

172. Chemical Warfare Section, "Revision of S.E.A. Command Chemical Warfare Policy," July 17,1945, p. 3, WO 203/4401, TNA.

173. "Plan Downfall," in Strategic Logistics Branch of the Office of the Director of Plans and Operations, Army Service Forces, War Department, "Operations against the Japanese: Logistic Study" July 5, 1945, Record Group 160, Records of Headquarters Army Service Forces, Box 690, NARA.

174. "Report of the Chief of the Chemical Warfare Service: Employment of Gas" in "Plan Downfall," in Strategic Logistics Branch of the Office of the Director of Plans and Operations, Army Service Forces, War Department, "Operations against the Japanese: Logistic Study" July 5, 1945, RG 160, Box 690, NARA.

175. "Report of the Chief of the Chemical Warfare Service: Employment of Gas" in "Plan Downfall," in Strategic Logistics Branch of the Office of the Director of Plans and Operations, Army Service Forces, War Department, "Operations against the Japanese: Logistic Study" July 5, 1945, RG 160, Box 690, NARA.

176. "Report of the Chief of the Chemical Warfare Service: Employment of Gas" in "Plan Downfall," in Strategic Logistics Branch of the Office of the Director

of Plans and Operations, Army Service Forces, War Department, "Operations against the Japanese: Logistic Study" July 5, 1945, RG 160, Box 690, NARA.

177. Skates, *The Invasion of Japan*, 94.

178. "Report of the Chief of the Chemical Warfare Service: Employment of Gas" in "Plan Downfall," in Strategic Logistics Branch of the Office of the Director of Plans and Operations, Army Service Forces, War Department, "Operations against the Japanese: Logistic Study" July 5, 1945, RG 160, Box 690, NARA.

179. Untitled Report, no date, p. 2, RG 165, Box 578, Folder 475.92 (25 Feb 44) Sec. 1-C, NARA.

180. Report and Tab A attached to M.S.J. to General Lincoln, memorandum, June 20, 1945, pp. 3 and 5–7, RG 165, Box 576, Folder ABC 475.92, Section 1-B (8-28-42), NARA.

181. Report attached to M.S.J. to General Lincoln, June 20, 1945, p. 3.

182. "Report of the Chief of the Chemical Warfare Service: Employment of Gas" in "Plan Downfall," in Strategic Logistics Branch of the Office of the Director of Plans and Operations, Army Service Forces, War Department, "Operations against the Japanese: Logistic Study" July 5, 1945, RG 160, Box 690, NARA.

183. M.S.J. to General Lincoln, Memorandum, June 4, 1945, 165, Box 578, Folder ABC 475.92 (February 25, 1944) Sec 1-C, NARA.

184. Gallup Organization, Gallup Poll # 1945–0343: Aftermath of War/Employment, Question 31, USGALLUP.343T.QT02B1, Gallup Organization, (Cornell University, Ithaca, NY: Roper Center for Public Opinion Research, 1945), Dataset; Gallup Organization, Gallup Poll # 1945–0343: Aftermath of War/Employment, Question 30, USGALLUP.343T.QT02A; Gallup Organization, Gallup Poll # 1945–0347: Starvation in War Effected Countries/Taxes/Peace Terms, Question 20, USGALLUP.347K.QK09; Gallup Organization, Gallup Poll # 1944–0337: World War II/Social Security/Italy and Greece's New Governments/Presidential Election, Question 42, USGALLUP.011745. RK0; and Gallup Organization, Gallup Poll # 349, Question 42, USGALLUP.349T. QT03A.

185. See, for example, Gallup Organization, Gallup Poll # 1944–0329: World War II/Presidential Election/Country of Birth, Question 4, USGALLUP.111344.R02A; and Gallup Organization, Gallup Poll # 349, Question 42, USGALLUP.349T.QT03A.

186. Michael Sherry, *The Rise of American Air Power: The Creation of Armageddon* (New Haven, CT: Yale University Press, 1987), 293, http://www.jstor.com/stable/j.ctt32bx7b.13.

187. Memorandum of Conversation from John J. McCloy, May 29, 1945, Washington DC, #5–147, Record Group 107, Records of the Office of the Secretary of War, Secretary of War Safe, S-1, National Archives and Records Administration, College Park, Maryland, www.marshallfoundation.org and *The Papers of George Catlett Marshall,* ed. Larry I. Bland and Sharon Ritenour Stevens (Lexington, Va.: The George C. Marshall Foundation, 1981). Electronic version based on *The Papers of George Catlett Marshall*, vol. 5, "*The Finest Soldier," January 1, 1945–January 7, 1947* (Baltimore and London: The Johns Hopkins University Press, 2003), 205–207.

188. J. J. Mc[Cloy] to chief of staff, "JCS 825/6 and 825/7," Memorandum, June 15, 1945, RG 165, Box 578, Folder ABC 475.92 (February 25, 1944) Sec 1-C, NARA.

189. "U.S. Chemical Warfare Policy," report, undated, p. 2, enclosure from chief of staff to Admiral King, Memo, undated (circa 1945), RG 165, Box 576, Folder ACB 475.92, Sec. 1-AB (8-28-42), NARA.

190. *The Papers of George Catlett Marshall,* ed. Larry I. Bland and Sharon Ritenour Stevens (Lexington, VA: The George C. Marshall Foundation, 1981-). Electronic version based on *The Papers of George Catlett Marshall,* vol. 5, *"The Finest Soldier,"* January 1, 1945–January 7, 1947 (Baltimore and London: The Johns Hopkins University Press, 2003), 237–238.

191. J. B. Hull, "Gas Warfare," July 5, 1945, RG 165, Box 578, Folder ABC 475.92 (February 25, 1944) Sec 1-C, NARA.

192. Joint Staff Planners, Memorandum, June 1945, RG 165, Box 578, Folder ABC 475.92 (25 Feb 44) Sec 1-C, NARA; and chief of staff, U.S. Army to Joint Chiefs of Staff, "Availability and Production of Chemical Munitions," J.C.S. 825 / 8, July 6, 1945, RG 165, Box 578, Folder ABC 475.92 (February 25, 1944) Sec 1-C, NARA.

193. General Marshall to Admiral Leary, Memorandum, June 21, 1945, RG 165, Box 576, Folder ABC 475.92 Sec. 1-A (8-28-42), NARA.

194. "U.S. Chemical Warfare Policy," report, undated, enclosure from chief of staff to Admiral King, undated (circa 1945), p. 2.

195. "U.S. Chemical Warfare Policy," report, undated, enclosure from chief of staff to Admiral King, undated (circa 1945), p. 3.

196. John D. Chappell, *Before the Bomb: How America Approached the End of the Pacific War* (Lexington: The University Press of Kentucky, 1997), 94.

197. Skates, *The Invasion of Japan,* 96.

198. J. Samuel Walker, *Prompt and Utter Destruction: Truman and the Use of the Atomic Bombs against Japan* (Chapel Hill: The University of North Carolina Press, 2004, rev. ed.), 18 and 22. There was information about the bomb's range, but Truman did not dwell on the report and his advisers assumed the bomb would be used; its consequences did not provide angst to the decision makers the way gas did to people worldwide.

199. Walker, *Prompt and Utter Destruction,* 21–22.

200. Russell, *War and Nature: Fighting Humans and Insects with Chemicals,* 3–4.

## Epilogue

1. It is not only British gas masks, or military ones, that inspire emotional responses. See, for example, Susan Grayzel, "'Macabre and Hilarious': The Emotional Life of the Civilian Gas Mask in France during and after the First World War," in *Total War: An Emotional History,* ed. Claire Langhamer, Lucy Noakes, and Claudia Siebrecht (Oxford: Oxford University Press, 2020), 40–58.

2. Owen Wilkes, "Working Paper No. 4: History of New Zealand Chemical Warfare, 1845–1945," (Auckland: Centre for Peace Studies, University of Auckland, 1993), 41–42.

3. Lois Moore, oral history transcript, by Lisa Craft, May 13, 14, and 17, 1999, pp. 2-4, Lois Moore 99.0350, Institute of World War II and the Human Experience, Florida State University.

4. See, for example, Bridget Goodwin, *Keen as Mustard: Britain's Horrific Chemical Warfare Experiments in Australia* (University of Queensland, 1998); and Susan L. Smith, *Toxic Exposures: Mustard Gas and the Health Consequences of World War II in the United States* (New Brunswick, NJ: Rutgers University Press, 2017). Ulf Schmidt emphasizes Cold War experimentation. Ulf Schmidt, *Secret Science: A Century of Poison Gas and Human Experiments* (London: Oxford University Press, 2015).

5. Frank M. Leamon to Margaret Thatcher, February 21, 1986, PIN 59/448, TNA; W.M. Cheale to Hon. A. MacKay, MP, January 23, 1986, PIN 59/448, TNA; Gerald Bartlett, "Mustard Gas Victims' Pension Review," newspaper clipping, PIN 59/448, TNA; and "Briefing [notes] for the Prime Minister—Thursday 6 March 1986: Mr. Bertram Stevens—War Pensioner Exposed to Mustard Gas," PIN 59/448, TNA. There are numerous letters to Margaret Thatcher and to others in the government about Betram Stevens in PIN 59/448.

6. Barack Obama referred to the use of gas as a "red line" that would prompt US intervention in Syria, although the United States did not respond as promised to its use. See, for example, President Barack Obama, "Remarks by the President to the White House Press Corps," Washington, DC, August 20, 2012, https://obamawhitehouse.archives.gov/the-press-office/2012/08/20/remarks-president-white-house-press-corps.

7. Illegible to prime minister, February 28, 1945, pp. 1–2, PREM 3/89, TNA.

8. Jonathan B. Tucker, *War of Nerves: Chemical Warfare from World War I to Al-Qaeda* (New York: Pantheon Books, 2006), 108.

9. General Sir Nevil Charles Dowell Brownjohn to Prime Minister Sir Winston Churchill, "Policy for Chemical Weapons D(53)17, March 24, 1953, CAB 21/3912, TNA.

10. For example, consider Saddam Hussein's use of CW against the Kurds in Iraq and Egypt's use in Yemen.

11. Jonathan B. Tucker, "A Farewell to Germs: The U.S. Renunciation of Biological and Toxin Warfare, 1969–70." *International Security* 27.1 (Summer 2002): 107–48 for an in-depth account.

12. George Bush and Brett Scowcroft, *A World Transformed* (New York: Knopf, 1998), 441–2.

13. Japan did use gas in China, but Japan had not signed the Geneva Gas Protocol at the time. It ratified the treaty in 1970. "Protocol for the Prohibition of the Use in War of Asphyxiating, Poisonous, or Other Gases, and of Bacteriological Methods of Warfare (Geneva Protocol)," June 17, 1925, https://www.state.gov/t/isn/4784.htm.

14. Michael Bothe, "Convention on the Prohibition of the Development, Production, Stockpiling and Use of Chemical Weapons and on their Destruction," United Nations Audiovisual Library of International Law, accessed January 20, 2022, https://legal.un.org/avl/ha/cpdpsucw/cpdpsucw.html. Note that there is a separate Biological Weapons Convention, unlike the joint ban in the Geneva Gas Protocol.

15. "OPCW by the Numbers," Organisation for the Prohibition of Chemical Weapons, accessed June 5, 2022, https://www.opcw.org/media-centre/opcw-numbers; and "Chemical Weapons Convention," Organisation for the Prohibition of Chemical Weapons, accessed June 5, 2022, https://www.opcw.org/chemical-weapons-convention.

16. Scientific Advisory Board, Organisation for the Prohibition of Chemical Weapons, accessed June 5, 2022, https://www.opcw.org/about-us/subsidiary-bodies/scientific-advisory-board.

17. "OPCW by the Numbers."

18. Dupuy and Hammerman think the Geneva Gas Protocol was enough to influence restraint on nuclear weapons. Trevor N. Dupuy and Gay M. Hammerman,

eds., *A Documentary History of Arms Control and Disarmament* (New York: R. R. Bowker Company, 1973), 124–5.

19. "Timeline of Syrian Chemical Weapons Activity, 2012–2019," Arms Control Association, reviewed March 2019, https://www.armscontrol.org/factsheets/Timeline-of-Syrian-Chemical-Weapons-Activity.

20. Steve Rosenberg, "Alexei Navalny: Report Names 'Russian Agents' in Poisoning Case," December 14, 2020, BBC World, https://www.bbc.com/news/world-europe-55303703; and Gordon Corera, *Russians Among Us: Sleeper Cells, Ghost Stories, and the Hunt for Putin's Agents* (London: William Collins, 2020), 392–4.

21. Inter-Services Committee on Chemical Warfare, "Future of Chemical Warfare Research," Report, C.O.S. (45) 157, July [date illegible], 1945, CAB 121/102, TNA.

22. See, for example, Davide Castelvecchi, "Will Russia Use Chemical Weapons in Ukraine? Researchers Evaluate the Risks," *Nature* 604 (April 5, 2022), 228–229, *doi: https://doi.org/10.1038/d41586-022-00948-0*; and Paul D. Shinkman, "Fears of Flase Flag Operation Grow as Russia Claims Ukraine Poised for Chemical Weapons Attack," May 6, 2022, 5:09 PM, *U.S. News and World Report*, https://www.usnews.com/news/world-report/articles/2022-05-06/russia-claims-ukraine-poised-for-chemical-weapons-attack-as-analysts-fear-false-flag-operation.

# BIBLIOGRAPHY

## Archival Sources

**Air Force Historical Research Agency, Maxwell Air Force Base, Alabama**
US Army Air Force, "Plan for Air Chemical Attack against the Japanese,"
February 1945
**The Avalon Project: Documents in Law, History and Diplomacy, Lillian Goldman Law Library, Yale Law School**
Hague Conventions, Kellogg-Briand Pact, The Versailles Treaty
**Institute on World War II and the Human Experience**
Oral History Program: Lois Moore
**Library and Archives Canada (LAC)**
RG 2 and RG24
William Lyon Makenzie King Diaries
**Liddell Hart Centre for Military Archives, King's College, London**
Kenneth H. Cousland Collection
Major General John Sydney Lethbridge Collection
**The National Archives (TNA) (UK), Kew**
AIR 2
CAB 4, CAB 21, CAB 23, CAB 24, CAB 26, CAB 29, CAB 37, CAB 65, CAB 66, CAB 70m CAB 79, CAB 80, CAB 84, CAB 104, CAB 118, CAB 119, CAB 120, CAB 121, CAB 122
CO 323
FO 371
HO 45, HO 186, HO 197
HW 1
MUN 5
PIN 59
PREM 3
WO 32, WO 33, WO 106, WO 142, WO 188, WO 193, WO 203, WO 204, WO 205
**National Archives and Records Administration (NARA), College Park, Maryland**
RG 160, RG 165, RG 175, RG 218, RG 319, RG 331
**Parliamentary Debates**
House and Senate (Canada), 3$^{rd}$ session
**Parliamentary Debates**
House of Commons and House of Lords (UK), 5$^{th}$ series

**Roper Center for Public Opinion Research, Cornell University**
  Gallup Polls, Gallup Organization,
**Imperial War Museum**
  Art Collection: Art.IWM PST 13861
  Document Collection: Stationery Services (SS) pamphlets on gas
  Photographs: CH 448, D 447, D 3918
**Mass Observation Archives, The Keep, University of Sussex**
  Mass-Observation Online, File Reports 146, 662, 814
  TC 1938–1945, TC 55: Gas Masks 1939–1943
  SxMOA1/2/55/1/A/17
**United States Congress**
  Cong 69S, 146, 151
  Cong 71H, H1824


## Newspapers and Magazines

  *Advocate (Burnie, Tasmania, Australia)*
  *Boston Globe*
  *Daily Mail Online*
  *The Guardian*
  *Illustrated London News*
  *Independent*
  *Maclean's*
  *Nature*
  *New York Times*
  *Punch*
  *Slate*
  *The Times* (London)
  *Time*
  *Globe and Mail* (Toronto)
  *U.S. News and World Report*


## Published Sources

"About *CQ Researcher Online* and Related Resources." CQPress. Accessed January 25, 2022. https://library.cqpress.com/cqresearcher/static.php?page=aboutcqr.

Adams, Valerie. *Chemical Warfare, Chemical Disarmament*. Bloomington: Indiana University Press, 1990.

Avery, Donald H. "Canadian Scientists, CBW Weapons and Japan, 1939–1945." In *Science and the Pacific War*, edited by Roy M. MacLeod, 231–252. Dordrecht, The Netherlands: Kluwer Academic Publishers, 2000.

Avery, Donald H. *The Science of War: Canadian Scientists and Allied Military Technology during the Second World War*. Toronto: University of Toronto Press, 1998.

Barenblatt, Daniel. *A Plague upon Humanity: The Hidden History of Japan's Biological Warfare Program*. New York: HarperCollins Perennial, 2004.

Baudendistel, Ranier. *Between Bombs and Good Intentions: The International Committee of the Red Cross (ICRC) and the Italo-Ethiopian War, 1935–1936*. New York: Berghahn Books, 2006.

Bennett, Huw, Michael Finch, Andrei Mamolea, and David Morgan-Owen. "Studying Mars and Clio: Or How Not to Write about the Ethics of Military Conduct and Military History." *History Workshop Journal* 88 (August 16, 2019): 274–280. https://doi.org/10.1093/hwj/dbz034.

Bernstein, Barton J. "Why We Didn't Use Poison Gas in World War II." *American Heritage* 36, no. 5 (1985): 40–45.

Biddle, Tami Davis. "Air Power and Warfare: A Century of Theory and History." Strategic Studies Institute and U.S. Army War College Press, 2019. http://www.jstor.org/stable/resrep20093.

Biddle, Tami Davis. "On the Crest of Fear: V-Weapons, the Battle of the Bulge, and the Last Stages of World War II in Europe." *The Journal of Military History* 83, no. 1 (January 2019): 157–194.

Bland, Larry I., and Sharon Ritenour Stevens, eds. *The Papers of George Catlett Marshall*. Lexington, VA.: The George C. Marshall Foundation, 1981—. Electronic version based on *"The Finest Soldier," January 1, 1945–January 7, 1947*. Vol. 5 of *The Papers of George Catlett Marshall*. Baltimore: Johns Hopkins University Press, 2003.

Bliss, Michael. *Banting: A Biography*. Toronto: McClelland and Stewart, 1984.

"The Blitz around Britain," Imperial War Museum. Accessed January 8, 2018. https://www.iwm.org.uk/history/the-blitz-around-britain.

Blum, Howard. *Dark Invasion: 1915: Germany's Secret War and the Hunt for the First Terrorist Cell in America*. New York: HarperCollins, 2014.

Bothe, Michael. "Convention on the Prohibition of the Development, Production, Stockpiling and Use of Chemical Weapons and on Their Destruction." In United Nations Audiovisual Library of International Law, September 3, 1992. https://legal.un.org/avl/ha/cpdpsucw/cpdpsucw.html.

Bothwell, Robert, Ian Drummond, and John English. *Canada, 1900–1945*. Toronto: University of Toronto Press, 1990.

Bourke, Joanna. *Fear: A Cultural History*. Emeryville, CA: Shoemaker & Hoard, 2006.

Brook, Timothy, ed. *Documents on the Rape of Nanking*. Ann Arbor: The University of Michigan Press, 1999.

Brophy, Leo P., and George J. B. Fisher. *The Chemical Warfare Service: Organizing for War*. In *United States Army in World War II: The Technical Services*. Washington, DC: Center of Military History, United States Army, 2004.

Brophy, Leo P., Wyndham D. Miles, and Rexmond C. Cochrane. *The Chemical Warfare Service: From Laboratory to Field*. In *United States Army in World War II: The Technical Services*. Washington, DC: Center of Military History, United States Army, 1959.

Brown, Frederic J. *Chemical Warfare: A Study in Restraints*. Westport, CT: Greenwood Press, 1981. First published 1968 by Princeton University Press.

Bush, George, and Brett Scowcroft. *A World Transformed*. New York: Knopf, 1998.

Bryden, John. *Deadly Allies: Canada's Secret War, 1937–1947*. Toronto: McClelland & Stewart, 1989.

Campion, Sarah. *Thirty Million Gas Masks*. Manchester: Peter Davies, 1937.

Cassar, George H. *Trial by Gas: The British Army at the Second Battle of Ypres*. N.p.: Potomac Books, 2014.

Chappell, John D. *Before the Bomb: How America Approached the End of the Pacific War*. Lexington: The University Press of Kentucky, 1997.

"Chemical Weapons Convention." Organisation for the Prohibition of Chemical Weapons. Accessed January 20, 2022. https://www.opcw.org/chemical -weapons-convention.

Christensen, Stian Nordengen. *Regulation of White Phosphorous Weapons in International Law*. Brussels: Torkel Opsahl Academic EPublisher, 2016. https://www.toaep.org/ops-pdf/6-christensen.

Churchill, Winston S. "We Shall Fight on the Beaches," speech to the House of Commons. June 4, 1940. Transcribed at the International Churchill Society. https://winstonchurchill.org/resources/speeches/1940-the-finest-hour/we -shall-fight-on-the-beaches/.

Clarke, I. F. *Voices Prophesying War: Future Wars, 1963–3749*, 2nd ed. Oxford: Clarendon Press, 1992.

Coen, Ross. *Fu-Go: The Curious History of Japan's Balloon Bomb Attack on America*. Lincoln: University of Nebraska Press, 2014.

Coleman, Kim. *A History of Chemical Warfare*. Houndsmill, Hampshire: Palgrave Macmillan, 2005.

Cook, Tim. "'Against God-Inspired Conscience': The Perception of Gas Warfare as a Weapon of Mass Destruction, 1915–1939." *War & Society* 18, no. 1 (May 2000): 45–69.

Cook, Tim. *No Place to Run: The Canadian Corps and Gas Warfare in the First World War*. Vancouver: UBC Press, 1999.

"Convention for the Supervision of Trade in Arms and War Munitions." *The American Journal of International Law* 20, no. 1 (January 1926): 151–154. https://www.jstor.org/stable/2188821.

Coyne, Ana Carden, David Morris, and Tim Wilcox, eds., "The Sensory War: Bodies, Minds, and Environments," in *The Sensory War, 1914–2014*. Manchester: Manchester Art Gallery, 2014.

Corera, Gordon. *Russians among Us: Sleeper Cells, Ghost Stories, and the Hunt for Putin's Agents*. London: William Collins, 2020.

Cruickshank, Dan. "The German Threat to Britain in World War Two." BBC. Updated June 21, 2011. http://www.bbc.co.uk/history/worldwars/wwtwo /invasion_ww2_01.shtml.

Danchev, Alex. "Sir John Greer Dill." In *Oxford Dictionary of National Biography*. Oxford University Press, 2004; online ed., 2011. https://doi-org.unh.idm.oclc .org/10.1093/ref:odnb/32826.

Douglas, R. M. "Did the British Use Chemical Weapons in Mandatory Iraq?" *Journal of Modern History* 81, no. 4 (December 2009): 859–887.

Dower, John W. *War without Mercy: Race & Power in the Pacific War*. New York: Pantheon Books, 1986.

Dupuy, Trevor N., and Gay M. Hammerman, eds. *A Documentary History of Arms Control and Disarmament*. New York: R. R. Bowker Company, 1973.

"Emergency Preparedness and Response: Facts about Sarin." Centers for Disease Control Page, last reviewed April 4, 2018. https://emergency.cdc.gov/agent /sarin/basics/facts.asp.

Emery, Theo. *Hellfire Boys: The Birth of the U.S. Chemical Warfare Service and the Race for the World's Deadliest Weapons*. New York: Little, Brown, 2017.

Evans, Rob. *Gassed*. London: House of Stratus, 2000.

"Evolution of the Status of Participation in the Convention." Organisation for the Prohibition of Chemical Weapons. Updated June 16, 2018. https://www .opcw.org/evolution-status-participation-convention.

Faith, Thomas I. *Behind the Gas Mask: The U.S. Chemical Warfare Service in War and Peace*. Urbana: University of Illinois Press, 2014.

Feigenbaum, Anna. "100 Years of Tear Gas." *The Atlantic*, August 16, 2014. https:// www.theatlantic.com/international/archive/2014/08/100-years-of-tear-gas /378632.

Feigenbaum, Anna. *Tear Gas: From the Battlefields of World War I to the Streets of Today*. London: Verso, 2017.

Fenn, Elizabeth A. *Pox Americana: The Great Smallpox Epidemic of 1775–1782*. New York: Hill & Wang, 2001.

Fidler, David P. "The Use of White Phosphorus Munitions by U.S. Forces in Iraq." *American Society of International Law* 9, no. 37 (December 6, 2005). https:// www.asil.org/insights/volume/9/issue/37/use-white-phosphorus-munitions -us-military-forces-iraq.

Fleming, Peter. *Operation Sea Lion*. New York: Simon and Schuster, 1957.

Foulkes, Charles H. *Gas!: The Story of the Special Brigade*. Edinburgh: William Blackwood, 1934.

Freasby, W. R., ed. *Clinical Subjects*. Vol. 2 of *Official History of the Canadian Medical Services, 1939–1945*. Ottawa: Queen's Printer, 1953. https://www.canada.ca /content/dam/themes/defence/caf/militaryhistory/dhh/official/book-1953 -medical-services-2-en.pdf.

Fujitani, Kevin Takashi. "The United States and Chemical Warfare: The 1925 Geneva Gas Protocol and Its Legacy." MA thesis, University of Hawaii, 1991.

Fussell, Paul. *The Boys Crusade: The American Infantry in Northwestern Europe, 1944–1945*. New York: Modern Library Paperback Edition, 2005.

Girard, Marion. *A Strange and Formidable Weapon: British Responses to World War I Poison Gas*. Lincoln: University of Nebraska Press, 2008.

Golson, Eric. "The Economics of Neutrality in World War II." VOXEU CEPR. November 11, 2019. https://voxeu.org/article/economics-neutrality-world -war-ii.

Goodwin, Bridget. *Keen as Mustard: Britain's Horrific Chemical Warfare Experiments in Australia*. St. Lucia: University of Queensland Press, 1998.

Grayzel, Susan R. *At Home and Under Fire: Air Raids and Culture in Britain from the Great War to the Blitz*. New York: Cambridge University Press, 2013.

Grayzel, Susan R. "'Macabre and Hilarious' The Emotional Life of the Civilian Gas Mask in France during and after the First World War." In *Total War: An Emotional History*, edited by Claire Langhamer, Lucy Noakes, and Claudia Siebrecht, 40–58. Oxford: Oxford University Press, 2020.

Grip, Lina, and John Hart. "The Use of Chemical Weapons in the 1935–1936 Italo-Ethiopian War." In *SIPRI Arms Control and Non-Proliferation Programme, October 2009*. https://www.sipri.org/sites/default/files/Italo-Ethiopian-war.pdf.

Grunden, Walter E. "No Retaliation in Kind: Japanese Chemical Warfare Policy in World War II." In *One Hundred Years of Chemical Warfare: Research, Deployment, Consequences*, edited by B. Friedrich, D. Hoffmann, J. Renn, F. Schmaltz, and M. Wolf. Springer Cham, 2017. https://link.springer.com/content/pdf/10.1007%2F978-3-319-51664-6_14.pdf.

Grunden, Walter E. *Secret Weapons and World War II: Japan in the Shadow of Big Science.* Lawrence: University Press of Kansas, 2005.

Guillemin, Jeanne. "The 1925 Geneva Protocol: China's CBW Charges against Japan at the Tokyo War Crimes Tribunal." In *One Hundred Years of Chemical Warfare: Research, Deployment, Consequences*, edited by B. Friedrich, D. Hoffmann, J. Renn, F. Schmaltz, and M. Wolf. Springer Cham, 2017. https://doi.org/10.1007/978-3-319-51664-6_15.

Haldane, J. B. S. *Callinicus: A Defence of Chemical Warfare.* New York: E. P. Dutton, 1925.

Halsbury, the Earl of. "Gas!" *British Legion Journal*, January 1933, 238–239.

Halsbury, the Earl of. *1944.* London: Thornton Butterworth, 1926.

Harris, Robert, and Jeremy Paxman. *A Higher Form of Killing: The Secret Story of Gas and Germ Warfare.* London: Chatto & Windus, 1982.

Henden, Stephen. "V1 and V2 Timeline." Flying Bombs and Rockets, November 2019. http://www.flyingbombsandrockets.com/Timeline.html.

Hoff, Ebbe Cutris, ed. *Personal Health Measures and Immunization.* Vol. 3 of *Preventive Medicine, Preventive Medicine in World War II*, edited by John Boyd Coates, Jr. Washington, DC: Office of the Surgeon General, Department of the Army, 1955.

Holman, Brett. *The Next War in the Air: Britain's Fear of the Bomber, 1908–1941.* London: Routledge, 2014.

Iarocci, Andrew. "'A Unique Art' Canadian Anti-Gas Respirator Production in the Second World War." *Canadian Military History* 18, no. 4 (2009): 51–64.

Infield, Glen B. *Disaster at Bari.* New York: The Macmillan Company, 1971.

Janik, Edyta, Michal Ceremuga, Joanna Saluk-Bijak, and Michal Bijak. "Biological Toxins as the Potential Tools for Bioterrorism." Special Issue, *International Journal of Molecular Science* 20, no. 5 (March 2019): 1181. https://doi.org/10.3390/ijms20051181.

Johnston, Harold. *A Bridge Not Attacked: Chemical Warfare Civilian Research during World War II.* New Jersey: World Scientific, 2003.

Karagama, Y. G., J. R. Newton, and C. J. R. Newbegin. "Short-Term and Long-Term Physical Effects of Exposure to CS Spray." *Journal of the Royal Society of Medicine* 96, no. 4 (April 2003): 172–174. https://www.ncbi.nlm.nih.gov/pmc/articles/PMC539444.

Keegan, John. *Intelligence in War: The Value—and Limitations—of What the Military Can Learn about the Enemy.* New York: Vintage Books, 2004.

Kimball, Warren F. "'Merely a Façade?' Roosevelt and the Southwest Pacific." *The Journal of American-East Asian Relations* 3, no. 2 (Summer 1994): 103–106. http://www.jstor.com/stable/23613382.

Kleber, Brooks E., and Dale Birdsell. *The Chemical Warfare Service, Chemicals in Combat.* In *United States Army in World War II: The Technical Services.* Washington, DC: Center of Military History, United States Army, 1966.

Langhamer, Claire, Lucy Noakes, and Claudia Siebrecht, eds. *Total War: An Emotional History.* Oxford: Oxford University Press, 2020.

Lister, Tim. "Bellingcat: Russian Scientists Secretly Developing Novichok Nerve Agent, and Working with Military Intelligence." CNN, October 23, 2020. https://www.cnn.com/2020/10/23/europe/bellingcat-russia-novichok -report-intl/index.html.

Lowe, Keith. *Inferno: The Devastation of Hamburg, 1943.* New York: Scribner, 2007.

Lynch, Cecilia. *Beyond Appeasement: Interpreting Interwar Peace Movements in World Politics.* Ithaca, NY: Cornell University Press, 1999.

Lynch, Cecilia. "A Matter of Controversy: The Peace Movement and British Arms Policy in the Interwar Period," in *Arms Limitation and Disarmament: Restraints on War, 1899–1939.* Edited by B. J. C. McKercher. Westport, CT: Praeger, 1992.

Maga, Thomas P. "Vison and Victory: Franklin Roosevelt and the Pacific War Council, 1942–1944." *Presidential Studies Quarterly* 21, no. 2 (Spring 1991): 351–363. http://www.jstor.com/stable/27550723.

Mayor, Adrienne. *Greek Fire, Poison Arrows, and Scorpion Bombs: Biological and Chemical Warfare in the Ancient World.* Woodstock, NY: Overlook Duckworth, 2003.

Moon, John Ellis van Courtland. "Chemical Weapons and Deterrence: The World War II Experience." *International Security* 8, no. 4 (Spring 1984), 3–35.

Morewood, Steven. "'This Silly African Business': The Military Dimension of Britain's Response to the Abyssinian Crisis." In *Collision of Empires: Italy's Invasion of Ethiopia and its International Impact.* Edited by G. Bruce Strang, 73–108. Surrey: Ashgate, 2013.

Moshenska, Gabriel. *Material Cultures of Childhood in Second World War Britain.* London: Routledge, 2019.

The National Archives (UK). Currency Converter: 1270–2017. Accessed January 18, 2022. https://www.nationalarchives.gov.uk/currency-converter/#.

The National Archives (UK). "UK Population Change." Archived January 5, 2016. https://webarchive.nationalarchives.gov.uk/ukgwa/20160105160709 /http://www.ons.gov.uk/ons/resources/figure2s_tcm77-292368.png.

Oanda, "Currency Converter." Accessed January 18, 2022. https://www.oanda.com /currency/converter/.

Obama, Barack. "Remarks by the President to the White House Press Corps." Washington, DC, August 20, 2012. https://obamawhitehouse.archives.gov /the-press-office/2012/08/20/remarks-president-white-house-press-corps.

O'Brien, Terence. *Civil Defence.* London: Her Majesty's Stationery Office and Longmans, Green, 1955.

"OPCW Fact-Finding Mission Confirms Use of Chemical Weapons in Khan Shaykhun on 4 April 2017." Organisation for the Prohibition of Chemical Weapons, June 30, 2017. https://www.opcw.org/news/article/opcw-fact-finding-mission -confirms-use-of-chemical-weapons-in-khan-shaykhun-on-4-april-2017/.

"OPCW by the Numbers." Organisation for the Prohibition of Chemical Weapons, Updated January 3, 2022. https://www.opcw.org/media-centre/opcw-numbers.

Owen, Wilfred. "Dulce et Decorum Est." *Poems*. Poetry Foundation. Accessed January 4, 2022. First published 1921 by Viking Press. https://www.poetryfoundation.org/poems/46560/dulce-et-decorum-est.

Paige, Christopher Robin. *Canada and Chemical Warfare, 1939–1945*. Salt Spring Island, Canada: Spire Publishing, 2011.

Plunkett, Geoff. *Chemical Warfare in Australia: Australia's Involvement in Chemical Warfare, 1914-Today*. Sydney: Leech Cup Books, 2013.

Prentiss, Austin M. *Chemicals in War: A Treatise on Chemical Warfare*. New York: McGraw-Hill, 1937.

Price, Richard M. *The Chemical Weapons Taboo*. Ithaca, NY: Cornell University Press, 1997.

"Professor Everitt George Dunne Murray (1890–1964)." Microbiology Society. Accessed January 22, 2022. https://www.microbiologyresearch.org/sotsog/egd-murray.

Pruszewicz, Marek. "How Deadly Was the Poison Gas of WW1?" *BBC Magazine*, January 30, 2015. https://www.bbc.com/news/magazine-31042472.

Root, Elihu. "International Law at the Arms Conference." *Proceedings of the American Society of International Law at its Sixteenth Annual Meeting, Washington D.C., April 27–29, 1922*. Washington, DC: The Society, 1922.

Richelson, Jeffrey T. *A Century of Spies: Intelligence in the Twentieth Century*. New York: Oxford University Press, 1995, 1997.

Roberts, Adam. "Land Warfare: From Hague to Nuremberg." In *The Laws of War: Constraints on Warfare in the Western World*, edited by Michael Howard, George J. Andreopoulos, and Mark R. Shulman, 116–139. New Haven, CT: Yale, 1994.

Robinson, Julian Perry. *The Rise of CB Weapons*. Vol. 1 of *The Problem of Chemical and Biological Warfare*. Stockholm: Almqvist and Wiksell, 1971.

Rosenberg, Steve. "Alexei Navalny: Report Names 'Russian Agents' in Poisoning Case." BBC World, December 14, 2020. https://www.bbc.com/news/world-europe-55303703.

Russell, Edmund. *War and Nature: Fighting Humans and Insects with Chemicals from World War I to Silent Spring*. Cambridge: Cambridge University Press, 2001.

Saint-Amour, Paul K. *Tense Future: Modernism, Total War, Encyclopedic Form*. Oxford: Oxford University Press, 2015.

"The Sarin Gas Attack in Japan and the Related Forensic Investigation." Organisation for the Prohibition of Chemical Weapons. Accessed January 15, 2022. First published June 1, 2001 in *Synthesis*. https://www.opcw.org/media-centre/news/2001/06/sarin-gas-attack-japan-and-related-forensic-investigation.

"Scientific Advisory Board: Keeping Pace with Scientific and Technological Change." Organisation for the Prohibition of Chemical Weapons. Accessed February 13, 2022. https://www.opcw.org/about-us/subsidiary-bodies/scientific-advisory-board.

Scott, James Brown, ed. *The Proceedings of The Hague Peace Conferences, Translation of Official Texts, Conference of 1899*. New York: Oxford University Press, 1920.

"The Shape of Things to Come." IMDB. Accessed January 2022. https://www.imdb.com/title/tt0079894/.

Sherry, Michael. *The Rise of American Air Power: The Creation of Armageddon.* New Haven, CT: Yale University Press, 1987. http://www.jstor.com/stable/j .ctt32bx7b.13.

Skates, John Ray. *The Invasion of Japan: Alternative to the Bomb.* Columbia: University of South Carolina Press, 1994.

Simons, Geoff. *Iraq: From Sumer to Post-Saddam,* 3rd ed. Houndsmill, Basingstoke, Hampshire: Palgrave Macmillan, 2004.

Schmidt, Ulf. *Secret Science: A Century of Poison Warfare and Human Experiments.* Oxford: Oxford University Press, 2015.

Smith, Robert Ross. "Luzon versus Formosa," to be included in *Triumph in the Philippines in United States Army in World War II,* by Robert Ross Smith. In *United States Army in World War II: The War in the Pacific.* Washington, DC: Center of Military History, United States Army, 1993. https://history.army .mil/books/70-7_21.htm.

Smith, Susan L. *Toxic Exposures: Mustard Gas and the Health Consequences of World War II in the United States.* New Brunswick, NJ: Rutgers University Press, 2017.

Snowden, Frank. "Latina Province, 1944–1950," *Journal of Contemporary History* 43, no. 3 (2008): 509–526. https://www.jstor.org/stable/40542973.

Sobek, Allison. "How Did the Women's International League for Peace and Freedom Campaign against Chemical Warfare, 1915–1930?" Revised and updated by Melissa Doak. Binghamton: State University of New York at Binghamton, 2001. https://documents.alexanderstreet.com/d/1000682890.

Spiers, Edward M. *Chemical Warfare.* Urbana: University of Illinois Press, 1986.

Stansky, Peter. *The First Day of the Blitz: September 7, 1940.* New Haven, CT: Yale University Press, 2007.

Taylor, Philip M. *Munitions of the Mind: A History of Propaganda,* 3rd ed. Manchester: Manchester University Press, 2003.

"Things to Come." IMDB. Accessed January 2022. https://www.imdb.com/title /tt0028358/.

Thomas, Roger E., Diane L. Lorenzetti, and Wendy Stragins. "Mortality and Morbidity Among Military Personnel and Civilians during the 1930s and World War II from Transmission of Hepatitis during Yellow Fever Vaccination: Systemic Review." *Am. J. Public Health* 103, no. 3 (March 2013): e16–e29. https://doi.org/10.2105/AJPI I.2012.301158.

Thuillier, Sir Henry F. *Gas in the Next War.* London: Geoffrey Bles, 1939.

"Timeline of Syrian Chemical Weapons Activity, 2012–2018." Arms Control Association. Updated May 2021 by Masterson, Julia, and Leanne Quinn. https://www.armscontrol.org/factsheets/Timeline-of-Syrian-Chemical -Weapons-Activity.

Trumpeter, Ulrich. "The Road to Ypres: The Beginnings of Gas Warfare in World War I." *The Journal of Modern History* 47 (September 1975): 460–480.

Tucker, Jonathan B. "A Farewell to Germs: The U.S. Renunciation of Biological and Toxin Warfare, 1969–70." *International Security* 27, no. 1 (Summer 2002): 107–148,

Tucker, Jonathan B. *War of Nerves: Chemical Warfare from World War I to al-Qaeda.* New York: Pantheon Books, 2006.

Union of Democratic Control. *Poison Gas.* London: Farleigh Press, 1935.

United States Army. *Anzio Beachhead, 22 January—25 May 1944*. Washington, DC: Center of Military History, 1990. First Published 1948 by Historical Division, War Department, for the American Forces in Action series. https://history .army.mil/books/wwii/anziobeach/anzio-allied.htm and https://history .army.mil/html/books/100/100-10/CMH_Pub_100-10.pdf.

U.S. Department of State. *Foreign Relations of the United States, 1921*. Vol. 1. Washington, DC: Government Printing Office, 1936. https://history.state.gov /historicaldocuments/frus1921v01/d87.

Wagner, Kim A. "Expanding Bullets and Savage Warfare." *History Workshop Journal* 88 (August 14, 2019): 281–287. https://doi.org/10.1093/hwj/dbz044.

Wagner, Kim A. "Savage Warfare: Violence and the Rule of Colonial Difference in Early British Counterinsurgency." *History Workshop Journal* 85 (January 3, 2018): 217–237. https://doi.org/10.1093/hwj/dbx053.

Walker, J. Samuel. *Prompt and Utter Destruction: Truman and the Use of the Atomic Bombs against Japan*, rev. ed. Chapel Hill: The University of North Carolina Press, 2004.

Wells, H. G. *The Shape of Things to Come*. New York: Macmillan, 1933.

Wilkes, Owen. *Working Paper No. 4: A History of New Zealand Chemical Warfare, 1845–1945*. Auckland: Center for Peace Studies, University of Auckland, August 1993.

Wiltse, Charles M. *Medical Service in the Mediterranean and Minor Theaters*. In *United States Army in World War II: The Technical Services, The Medical Department*. Washington, DC: Office of Military History: Department of the Army, 1965. https://achh.army.mil/history/book-wwii-medsvcsinmedtrnmnrthrtrs -chapter9.

Wiseman, D. J. C. *Gas Warfare*. Vol. 1. of *The Second World War, 1939–1945, Army: Special Weapons and Types of Warfare*. N.p.: The War Office, 1951.

Women's International League for Peace and Freedom. *Can We Outlaw Poison Gas?* Washington, DC: Women's International League for Peace and Freedom, 1927. In The Records of the Women's International League for Peace and Freedom, U.S. Section, 1919–1959. Swarthmore College Peace Collection. Mircrofilm, Reel 33, Frames 281–84. In Sobek, Allison. *How Did the Women's International League for Peace and Freedom Campaign against Chemical Warfare, 1915–1930?* Binghamton: State University of New York at Binghamton, 2001. https://documents.alexanderstreet.com/d/1000679974.

Wroughton, Lesley. "U.S. Imposes Sanctions on Russia for Nerve Agent Attack in UK." Reuters. Updated August 8, 2018. https://www.reuters.com/article/us -britain-poison-skripal-usa/u-s-imposes-sanctions-on-russia-for-nerve-agent -attack-in-uk-idUSKBN1KT2FC.

Wynne, G. C. *Stopping Hitler: An Official Account of How Britain Planned to Defend Itself in the Second World War*. Yorkshire: Frontline Books, 2017.

Yetman, Daniel. "How Does Tear Gas Affect the Human Body?" *Healthline*, May 28, 2020. https://www.healthline.com/health/tear-gas-effects.

# Index

Figures are indicated by f.

Abyssinia
    CW used on, 2–3, 41–46, 45f, 74, 90, 174, 179, 207
    Geneva Gas Protocol and, 43–44, 222nn9–10
    League of Nations and, 44, 46, 90
    in World War II, 90–93
ACS. See American Chemical Society
aerial bombing
    CW and, 25, 46
    of Dresden, 10, 204
    expectation of, 10–11, 25
    of Japan, 166, 204
Afghanistan, 27
Agent Orange, 9
agreements, interwar. See interwar period, CW agreements of
American Chemical Society (ACS), 21, 35–36
American Legion, 21, 36
Anderson, Desmond F., 84–85
Anderson, John, 62
Anglo-French Chemical Warfare Conversations, 82
anti-botulism vaccine, 138
    Britain and, 148–53, 155–57
    Canada and, 5, 134, 145–57
    CWS and, 145–46
    D-Day and, 146, 148, 153–54
    fear and, 154–55
    Germany and, 153, 155–56
    joint CW policy and, 156
    safety of, 149–50
    secrecy of, 153–55
    US and, 145–46, 148–53, 155–57
anti-gas, 24–25, 41, 46. See also masks
    Britain compared with other countries, 54–57
    British and US, 110

British and World War I, 62
British commercial efforts, 47, 59–61
British compulsion of, 71–72
in British Empire, 77
British food protection, 63–64
British government preparation, 57–59
British group protection, 61–64
British press on, 50–52, 57
British production of, 53–54
British propaganda encouraging, 68, 69f, 72–74
British public apathy about, 68–70, 75
British World War II civilian preparation, 42, 62, 85, 152–54
Canadian, 51, 55, 57, 74, 87
Canadian press on, 51
capes, 12, 54, 54f, 179, 190
eye shields, 54, 54f, 56
French, 51–52, 54–55
German, 52–53
Japanese, 189
mustard gas and, 12, 61
Russian, 51–52, 54, 68
shelters, 12, 55, 59–63
for soldiers, 54f, 57–59, 70, 179, 190
uneven distribution of, 204–5
US, 50–51, 55–57, 74–75, 87, 110
US press on, 50–51
World War I, 4, 12, 62, 179, 203, 204f
anti-gas lobby, US, 21–22, 35–37, 39
antipersonnel weapon, WP as, 138–44
Article 171. See Treaty of Versailles
asphyxiating projectiles, banning, 13, 17
Asquith, Herbert, 13
atomic bomb. See nuclear weapons
Attlee, Clement, 201
Attu, 181
Aum Shinrikyo, 10
Austrian Ministry of Defense, 52

Avery, David, 151
Axis, 208. *See also* Germany; Italy; Japan
    Britain and CW use against, 76–79
    Britain and retaliation against, 108
    FDR and retaliation against, 87, 90, 107–8,
        115, 136, 152, 157, 167, 197, 211n7
    pretext of CW and, 167, 193

babies, masks for, 66f, 67–68
bacteriological warfare, 9
    Geneva Gas Protocol on, 7, 29, 33, 146,
        246n46
    Joint Committee on New Weapons and
        Equipment on, 158–59
Bailey, Gerald, 100
Baldwin, Stanley, 46
Banting, Frederick, 87, 110–11
Bari, Italy, mustard gas incident, 128f, 153,
    178
    Britain and, 111, 126–27, 130–31, 205,
        243n95
    casualties, injuries from, 127–30, 205, 209,
        243n95
    cover-up of, 130–31
    CWS and, 129, 242n81
    Geneva Gas Protocol and, 243n88
    joint CW policy and, 126–27, 131–32
    Stevens injured in, 205, 209, 243n95
Bennett, Richard, 33
biological toxins, 158
biological weapons (BW), 98, 137, 153,
    246n46. *See also* bacteriological warfare
    Britain and, 146, 150–51, 156, 158
    Canada on, 87
    China and, 146, 255n41
    crop destroyers and, 191–93
    Geneva Gas Protocol prohibiting, 15, 29,
        33, 146
    Germany and, 146, 148–51, 155–60,
        215n44
    Japan and, 146, 170, 255n41
    Joint Committee on New Weapons and
        Equipment on, 158–59
    marginal role of, 146
    US eradicating arsenal of, 207
    US on, 145–46, 158–60, 168
    in World War I, 215n44
Biological Weapons Convention, 266n14
Blitz, 10, 42, 135
    casualties from, 164
    shelters in, 62
Boothby, Robert, 41, 46
Borah, William E., 35, 37

botulism, as CW, 9, 134, 155
Bridges, Edward, 176
Britain, 37, 212n11. *See also* anti-gas;
        Churchill, Winston; retaliation, British
    Abyssinia and, 2–3, 41, 43–46, 45f, 74,
        90–93
    Anglo-French Chemical Warfare
        Conversations, 82
    anti-botulism vaccine and, 148–53, 155–57
    Bari mustard gas incident and, 111,
        126–27, 130–31, 205, 243n95
    Blitz, 10, 42, 62, 135, 164
    BW and, 146, 150–51, 156, 158
    cabinet, 31–32, 79, 91, 176, 229n133
    Canada and, 6, 20, 33–34, 78, 86–88, 110,
        112–13, 119
    Chiefs of Staff Committee, 88, 94, 110,
        118, 120–22, 144, 160–64, 169, 188, 191
    commercial anti-gas in, 47, 59–61
    Committee of Imperial Defence, 31–32, 79
    Coventry bombing, 204
    crop destroyers of, 191–94
    CW attacks anticipated by, 41–43, 82–85
    CW considered by interwar, 258n68
    CW stock and production of, 89, 184, 189
    Empire of, 31, 34, 77, 112, 258n68
    on first use, 76–77, 82–89, 93
    food and anti-gas in, 63–64
    on French CW plans, 79
    gas quiz campaign, 72–73
    Geneva Gas Protocol and, 15, 18, 23,
        29–34, 38–40, 80–82, 89, 93–94, 96, 98,
        100–102, 137, 142–43, 165, 185, 192,
        243n88
    guarantees requested by, 79–82
    on high explosives, 162
    Imperial War Museum advertisements,
        203, 204f
    Inter-Services Committee on Chemical
        Warfare, 184, 188–91, 208–9
    Inter-Service Sub-Committee on
        Biological Warfare, 156
    interwar CW agreements and, 15, 18–20,
        23, 27–34, 38–40, 44–46
    Iraq and, 27, 255n36
    joint CW policy and, 16, 42, 112, 115–27
    Joint Intelligence Committee, 136, 193
    Joint Intelligence Sub-Committee, 101,
        148
    JPS, 19, 90, 103, 237n3
    on lethal gas, 27, 38, 82
    masks in, 53–54, 58–75, 66f, 69f
    no-first-use policy and, 16, 112, 115

on nonlethal gas, 15, 23–24, 27, 171
Noxious Gases treaty and, 97–98
phosgene gas and, 87, 160
press in, 50–52, 57
production of anti-gas, 53–54
pro-gas in, 19, 24–26, 88, 168
propaganda on anti-gas, 68, 69f, 72–74
psychological CW of, 77–80, 99–102
public apathy and anti-gas in, 68–70, 75
public opinion in interwar, 24–26, 41,
    46–47
Russia and, 6, 94, 101–6, 108–9, 123, 138,
    162
shelters in, 59–63
on tear gas, 15, 27, 171
US compared with, 7, 19
V-weapons response of, 16, 133, 135–38,
    157, 159–64
V-weapons used against, 5, 133–35, 157,
    160, 164
War Cabinet, 85–86, 88, 94, 102, 105, 117,
    121, 176
World War I and, 3, 13–14, 17, 27, 62, 89,
    133, 180
on WP, 139–45
Britain, Germany and
    CW against Germany considered, 76–77,
        85–86, 133–35, 138, 206
    CW threat from Germany, 140, 142–43,
        145, 204
    invasion threat from Germany, 16, 82–83,
        87–89, 206
    mustard gas against Germany considered,
        85–86
    retaliation and V-weapons, 157, 160–63
    retaliation policy and, 28, 77, 79–82, 85,
        88–89, 92–94, 102–3, 105–6, 123, 135–36,
        164
    World War I and, 13–14
Britain, Japan and
    CW of Japan, 170–72, 175–78
    CW use against Japan, 167–70, 183–84,
        188–91, 197, 201–2
    retaliation policy and, 96–98, 107, 168, 176
    telegraph exchanges between, 94–100
British Commonwealth. *See* Commonwealth
Brooke, Alan, 86, 135
Brunskill, Gerald, 184
Bryden, John, 248n80
Bush, George H. W., 207
Bush, Vannevar, 158
Bushido, spirit of, 95–98
BW. *See* biological weapons

cabinet, British, 176, 229n133
    Committee of Imperial Defence and,
        31–32, 79
    retaliation policy and, 79, 91
Cabinet War Committee (Canada), 108, 125
Campion, Sarah (Mary Rose Coulton), 48–50
Canada, 18, 164, 234n82
    anti-botulism vaccine and, 5, 134, 145–57
    anti-gas in, 51, 55, 57, 74, 87
    on BW, 87
    Cabinet War Committee, 108, 125
    Chemical Warfare Inter-Service Board, 187
    Commonwealth and, 6, 112–13, 120
    CW readiness of, 87–88
    CW use against Japan and, 167, 187, 202
    FDR and, 119–20
    first use and, 86–87
    Geneva Gas Protocol and, 15, 20–21, 25,
        33–35, 38–40, 113
    interwar public opinion in, 26
    on Japanese CW use, 173–74
    joint CW policy and, 16, 19, 112–13, 115,
        119–22, 125–26
    masks in, 55
    Noxious Gases treaty and, 20, 33
    press and anti-gas in, 51
    retaliation policy and, 107–8, 115
    sovereignty of, 15, 20, 34–35, 115, 119–22,
        154–55, 157
    Suffield Experimental Station, 113, 114f,
        119
    in Western Allies, 6–7, 157
    in World War I, 13–14, 114
capes, 12, 54, 54f, 179, 190
CBW. *See* chemical and biological weapons
CC (lethal gas), 186
Cecil (lord), 44
chemical and biological weapons (CBW),
    152–53
    crop destroyers and, 191–93
    fear and, 154
    Geneva Gas Protocol and, 146, 192
    Germany and, 137, 148, 155–59, 164
    Japan and, 146, 170–71, 175–76, 187, 200,
        255n41
    US on, 158–59
*Chemicals in War* (Prentiss), 52
Chemical Warfare Inter-Service Board
    (Canada), 187
Chemical Warfare Service (CWS) (US), 87,
    160, 255n41
    anti-botulism vaccine and, 145–46
    Bari mustard gas incident and, 129, 242n81

Chemical Warfare Service (CWS) (*continued*)
CW use against Japan and, 167, 169, 179, 186–87, 189, 194, 196–97
interwar, 21, 27–28, 55–56
chemical weapons (CW). *See specific topics*
Chemical Weapons Convention (CWC), 15, 29, 207–9
Cherwell (lord), 192
Chiang Kai Shek (Jiang Jieshi), 178, 199
Chiefs of Staff Committee (Britain), 110
Churchill and, 144, 160, 162–64
on CW plans, 88, 160–63, 169
on Japan, 188, 191
on joint CW policy, 118, 120–22
on retaliation, 94, 120–22, 160–63
children, masks for, 66f, 67–68
China
BW and, 146, 255n41
Japanese CW allegations against, 181
Japanese CW and, 3, 94–96, 98, 105, 167, 169–75, 182, 185, 201, 237n3, 237n139, 266n13
joint CW policy and, 237n3
US and, 178, 199
Western Allies and, 3, 6, 175–77, 237n3
chlorine gas, 9, 13, 17, 61
choking gas, 177, 257n59
Churchill, Winston, 119–20, 175–76
Chiefs of Staff Committee and, 144, 160, 162–64
on crop destroyers, 192
CW accepted by, 24, 27, 76, 82, 133, 160, 162–63
CW use against Japan and, 184, 201–2
FDR and, 7, 87, 106–10, 115, 152, 157, 162, 167, 173
on first use, 82–85, 93
on Iraq, 255n36
on joint CW policy, 124
retaliation policy and, 87, 90, 93–94, 103, 105–6, 123, 125, 136, 152, 157, 160, 162–63, 167–68
Russia and, 102, 105–6
on V-weapons, 157, 160, 162–64
on WP, 144
Cicognani, Amleto Giovanni, 182–83
Clarke, Ashley, 96
Cold War, 206–7
Combined Chiefs of Staff
Bari mustard gas incident and, 130
joint CW policy and, 118–20, 123, 125, 156
Combined Intelligence Committee, 176–77, 183

commercial anti-gas efforts, 47, 59–61
Committee of Imperial Defence (Britain), 31–32, 79
Commonwealth, 31, 77, 106. *See also* Canada; New Zealand
Canada and, 6, 112–13, 120
Japan and, 96, 107, 170
joint CW policy and, 112–13, 118–20, 125–26
Convention for the Supervision of Trade in Arms and War Munitions, 219n50
Cooper, Duff, 101–2
Coronet. *See* Operation Coronet
Coulton, Mary Rose. *See* Campion, Sarah
Coventry, bombing of, 204
Cramer, Myron C., 192
Cranborne (viscount), 41, 45, 223n14
Crerar, Harry, 153
crop destroyers, 191–94
CW (chemical weapons). *See specific topics*
CWC. *See* Chemical Weapons Convention
CWS. *See* Chemical Warfare Service

Dandurand, Raoul, 33, 35
D-Day, 16, 111, 136
anti-botulism vaccine and, 146, 148, 153–54
CW and, 133–34, 247n59
WP and, 139, 141–44
Delcellier, H. A., 173
Dill, John, 76, 83–84, 123, 172
dogs, masks for, 60–61, 60f
Domenet, Paul, 204f
Dower, John, 168
Dresden, bombing of, 10, 204
"Dulce et Decorum Est" (Owen), 1
Dunkirk evacuations, 76, 82–83
Dupuy, Trevor N., 266n18

Eden, Anthony, 96–98, 143, 175–76
Eisenhower, Dwight David, 139–42, 165
emergency period (US), 56
Empire, British, 31, 34, 77, 112, 258n68
Esoid. *See* anti-botulism vaccine
Ethiopia. *See* Abyssinia
Expeditionary Air Force, Allied, 139, 141
eye shields, 54, 54f, 56

Faith, Thomas, 55
FDR. *See* Roosevelt, Franklin Delano
fear, 3, 42
anti-botulism vaccine and, 154–55
CW as weapon of, 4

masks and, 203, 204f, 209
press and managing, 52–53
in World War I, 13–14, 203, 204f
fiction, CW in, 47–50, 216n20
Finland, 94, 100
firebombing, 10, 137
First Gulf War, 207
first use. *See also* no-first-use policy
Britain on, 76–77, 82–89, 93
Canada and, 86–87
Churchill and, 82–85, 93
joint CW policy and, 116–17
US and, 86–88
First World War. *See* World War I
First World War Galleries, Imperial War
Museum, 203, 204f
Fitzgerald, Roy, 37
Florida, 186
flu vaccine, 154
food, anti-gas and, 63–64
Formosa, 188–91, 201
France, 153, 161
Anglo-French Chemical Warfare
Conversations, 82
anti-gas in, 51–52, 54–55
Geneva Gas Protocol and, 30–31, 33, 89
interwar CW agreements and, 27–31, 33,
79, 89
masks produced by, 51
occupation of, 77
retaliation policy of, 30–31, 79
tear gas used by, 13
Fries, Amos, 21, 22f, 55
Fuller, J. F. C., 25–26
Fussell, Paul, 153

Gallacher, William, 65
gas, lethal, 26, 257n59. *See also* mustard gas
Anglo-French Chemical Warfare
Conversations on, 82
Britain on, 27, 38, 82
CC, 186
chlorine, 9, 13, 17, 61
Japan and, 171–73
lewisite, 14, 22, 171, 224n45
nerve gas, 10, 137, 169, 204, 207–8, 212n9
phosgene, 9, 12, 61, 87, 147, 159–60, 167,
186, 196, 203
Zyklon B, 3
gas, nonlethal, 21, 44
Britain on, 15, 23–24, 27, 171
Japan using, 171
tear gas, 9–10, 13, 15, 22, 27, 171

gas, types of, 9–12
Gascoyne-Cecil, Robert. *See* Cranborne
gas defenses. *See* anti-gas
gas quiz campaign, British, 72–73, 85
Gauss, Clarence, 182
Geneva Gas Protocol, 3, 52, 202, 207, 266n18
Abyssinia and, 43–44, 222nn9–10
on bacteriological warfare, 7, 29, 33, 146,
246n46
Bari mustard gas incident and, 243n88
Britain and, 15, 18, 23, 29–34, 38–40,
80–82, 89, 93–94, 96, 98, 100–102, 137,
142–43, 165, 185, 192, 243n88
BW prohibited in, 15, 29, 33, 146
Canada and, 15, 20–21, 25, 33–35, 38–40,
113
CBW and, 146, 192
flaws of, 7–8, 15, 18, 20, 30, 205
France and, 30–31, 33, 89
Germany and, 81, 89, 93
Italy and, 43, 82, 222nn9–10
Japan and, 7, 29–30, 94–98, 170–71, 185,
200, 266n13
League of Nations and, 29
retaliation and, 89–90, 125–26, 167, 185
tear gas and, 171, 201
US and, 6–7, 15, 18, 22–23, 26, 29, 34–39,
86, 115, 142, 157, 181, 183, 185,
200–201, 206
WP and, 140, 142–43, 244n19
Germany, 37, 208, 257n66
anti-botulism vaccine and, 153, 155–56
anti-gas in, 52–53
British invasion threat from, 16, 82–83,
87–89, 206
British retaliation and V-weapons, 157,
160–64
British retaliation policy on, 28, 77, 79–82,
85, 88–89, 92–94, 102–3, 105–6, 123,
135–36
BW and, 146, 148–51, 155–60, 215n44
CBW and, 137, 148, 155–59, 164
CW attacks anticipated from, 41–42, 80,
82–85, 134
CW considered against, 76–77, 85–86,
133–35, 138, 206
CW threat from, 140, 142–43, 145, 204
Dresden bombing, 10, 204
FDR warnings and, 136
Geneva Gas Protocol and, 81, 89, 93
Hague Conventions violated by, 8, 13, 17,
28, 80, 115
Hitler, 4, 74, 145

Germany (*continued*)
  interwar CW agreements and, 18, 27, 38, 81, 89, 93, 97
  masks produced by, 52
  mustard gas considered against, 85–86
  mustard gas research of, 80
  Nazi-Soviet Non-Aggression Pact, 101–3
  nerve gas of, 10, 137, 169, 204, 207, 212n9
  Operation Sea Lion, 16, 82, 89, 206
  pretext of CW and, 93, 130, 141, 145, 153, 176
  Russia and, 13, 101–6
  Treaty of Versailles and, 18, 27, 81, 97
  V-weapons, 5, 16, 133–38, 157, 159–64, 204
  Weimar literature, 223n23
  World War I CW use of, 13–14, 46, 80, 114–16, 180, 207
  WP used by, 140–41
  Zyklon B used by, 3
Giffard, George, 188
Grayzel, Susan, 63
Great Britain. *See* Britain
Great War. *See* World War I
Grew, Joseph, 2
Grey, Edward, 17
Griesbach, William, 34
Grunden, Walter, 257n59
Guadalcanal, 177–78, 186
guarantees, Britain requesting, 79–82
Guillemin, Jeanne, 255n41
Gulf War, First, 207

Hague Conventions (1899), 11, 29, 34, 36, 98
  asphyxiating projectiles banned by, 13, 17
  Germany and, 8, 13, 17, 28, 80, 115
  Land Warfare Regulations, 143
Hague Conventions (1907), 17, 27, 98, 115
Haldane, J. B. S., 251n36
Halifax (lord), 39, 79
Halsbury (lord), 3, 24, 48, 50
Hamburg, firebombing of, 137
Hamilton, Cicely, 47–48
Hammerman, Gay M., 266n18
Handy, Thomas, 186–87
Hart, Basil Liddell, 221n3
Hawaii, 186
high explosives, 64–65, 160, 178, 200
  Britain on, 162
  CW combined with, 61, 196, 204
  CW compared with, 52, 83, 190, 218n38
  shelters for, 57, 61–62, 70
  against Tarawa, 185

Hiroshima, nuclear bombing of, 10, 166, 197, 200, 207
Hitler, Adolf, 4, 74, 145
Hollis, Leslie, 141–42
Holocaust, 3
Hoover, Herbert, 18, 21
Hull, J. E., 262n163
Hungary, 94, 100
Huntsville Arsenal, Alabama, CW injuries in, 205, 209, 241n72
Hussein, Saddam, 10, 266n10

ICI. *See* Imperial Chemical Industries
ICRC. *See* International Committee of the Red Cross
*Idiot's Delight* (Sherwood), 49–50
*Illustrated London News* (*ILN*) (magazine), 50–52
Imperial Chemical Industries (ICI), 191–92
Imperial War Museum (Britain), 203, 204f
India, 77, 112, 119, 123, 130, 204
influenza vaccine, 154
International Committee of the Red Cross (ICRC), 30, 100, 183, 222n9
International Military Tribunal for the Far East (Tokyo War Crimes Trials), 255n41
Inter-Services Committee on Chemical Warfare (Britain), 184, 188–91, 208–9
Inter-Service Sub-Committee on Biological Warfare (Britain), 156
interwar period, 203
  Abyssinia CW attacks in, 2–3, 41–46, 45f, 74, 90, 174, 179, 207
  Britain and mustard gas in, 27, 45f
  British considering CW in, 258n68
  CW attacks expected in, 2–3, 10, 25
  CWS in, 21, 27–28, 55–56
  press in, 50–52, 57
  public opinion in, 19, 24–26, 35–37, 41, 46–47
  Washington Naval Conference, 15, 18, 20, 22, 27–30, 33, 97–98
  Western Allies in, 15–16, 74–75
interwar period, CW agreements of. *See also* Geneva Gas Protocol
  Britain and, 15, 18–20, 23, 27–35, 38–40, 44–46
  Canada and, 15, 18, 20–21, 25, 33–35, 38–40
  France and, 27–31, 33, 79, 89
  Germany and, 18, 27, 38, 81, 89, 93, 97
  Japan and, 38
  League of Nations and, 28–29, 38

no-first-use policy and, 7, 33, 116
Noxious Gases treaty, 15, 18, 20, 22, 28–30, 33, 97–98
Treaty of Versailles, 15, 18, 20, 22, 27, 29–30, 81, 97–98, 202
US and, 15, 18, 21–23, 26–27, 29, 34–39
Iraq
Britain and, 27, 255n36
First Gulf War, 207
Kurds in, 10, 266n10
Irwin, Will, 21–22
Ismay, Hastings, 175–76
Israel, 208
Italy
Abyssinia CW use by, 2–3, 41–46, 45f, 74, 90, 174, 179, 207
Abyssinia in World War II and, 90–93
Bari mustard gas incident, 8, 111, 126–31, 126–32, 128f, 153, 178, 205, 209, 242n81, 243n88, 243n95
Britain and CW use of, 41, 43–46, 45f, 74, 90–93
British retaliation policy and, 90–93, 108
Geneva Gas Protocol and, 43, 82, 222nn9–10
mustard gas used by, 42–43, 45f, 174, 179, 207
World War II and CW use by, 90–93
WP use in, 140

Japan, 38, 102
aerial bombing of, 166, 204
anti-gas of, 189
British retaliation policy and, 96–98, 107, 168, 176
British telegraph exchanges with, 94–100
Bushido, spirit of, 95–98
BW and, 146, 170, 255n41
CBW and, 146, 170–71, 175–76, 187, 200, 255n41
China and CW of, 3, 94–96, 98, 105, 167, 169–75, 182, 185, 201, 237n3, 237n139, 266n13
on Chinese CW use, 181
Commonwealth and, 96, 107, 170
crop destroyers considered against, 192–94
FDR warning, 99, 106–8, 167–69, 175–78, 185, 194
Geneva Gas Protocol and, 7, 29–30, 94–98, 170–71, 185, 200, 266n13
Hiroshima bombing, 10, 166, 197, 200, 207
lethal gas and, 171–73
New Zealand and CW of, 256n57

no-first-use policy and, 168
nonlethal gas used by, 171
Noxious Gases treaty and, 97–98
nuclear weapon use against, 2, 5, 10, 166, 170, 197, 199–200, 202, 207
Operation Coronet against, 195f, 196
Operation Downfall against, 8, 193–94, 195f, 196–97, 199
Operation Olympic against, 195f, 196–97, 199
pretext of CW and, 176, 180–81
as pro-gas, 94
race and, 168, 173–74, 201
retaliation policy on, 96–99, 106–8, 167–69, 174–79, 185, 194
Russia and, 5, 174
Tokyo subway nerve gas attack, 10, 209
Tokyo War Crimes Trials, 255n41
US retaliation policy on, 99, 106–8, 167–69, 175–78, 183, 185, 194
on US with CW, 181
Western Allies and CW of, 170–78, 194
Japan, CW use against, 2, 164–66, 180–81
Britain on, 167–70, 183–84, 188–91, 197, 201–2
British Chiefs of Staff Committee on, 188, 191
Canada and, 167, 187, 202
Churchill and, 184, 201
CW conflict with avoided, 170–79
CWS on, 167, 169, 179, 186–87, 189, 194, 196–97
Formosa and, 188–91, 201
joint CW policy and, 199
mustard gas considered, 167, 184–86, 198
Operation Downfall and, 8, 194, 195f, 196–97
phosgene gas considered, 167, 186, 196
Porter on, 167, 169, 185–87, 189, 191, 197
Truman and, 170, 199–200
US and planning for, 5–6, 167, 187, 189, 194, 195f, 196–99
US considering, 168–70, 182–83, 185–86, 200–202
US Joint Chiefs of Staff on, 198–99
US public opinion on, 169, 185, 188, 197–98, 200
Jiang Jieshi (Chiang Kai Shek), 178, 199
*John Harvey* (US ship), 128–29
Joint Chiefs of Staff (US), 124, 182–83, 191
on CBW question, 158
on CW against Japan, 198–99
in CW decision-making, 121

Joint Chiefs of Staff (US) (*continued*)
    on Japanese CW, 172
    on joint CW policy, 118
Joint Committee on New Weapons and
    Equipment (US), 158–59
joint CW policy, of Western Allies, 6, 78, 86,
    110–11, 199
    agreement on, 125–26
    anti-botulism vaccine and, 156
    Bari mustard gas incident and, 126–27,
        131–32
    Britain and, 16, 42, 112, 115–27
    British Chiefs of Staff Committee on, 118,
        120–22
    British retaliation and, 117, 121–23
    Canada and, 16, 19, 112–13, 115, 119–22,
        125–26
    China and, 237n3
    Combined Chiefs of Staff and, 118–20,
        123, 125, 156
    Commonwealth and, 112–13, 118–20,
        125–26
    decision-making power in, 120–21
    no-first-use policy and, 19, 23, 116–17
    Russia and, 237n3
    sovereignty and, 117–26, 131
    US and, 39, 114–16, 118–27, 131
    V-weapons and, 16, 137–38, 159
Joint Intelligence Committee (Britain), 136, 193
Joint Intelligence Sub-Committee (Britain),
    101, 148
Joint Logistics Committee (US), 174, 177,
    193–94
Joint Planning Staff (JPS) (Britain), 19, 90,
    103, 237n3
Joint Staff Planners (US), 124, 159–60, 183,
    252n144
JPS. *See* Joint Planning Staff

Kellogg, Frank, 35–36
Kellogg-Briand Pact, 219n57
King, Ernest, 198–99
King, William Lyon Mackenzie, 33, 35, 119
Kitchener, Horatio, 13–14
Koo, Wellington, 175–76
Kurds, 10, 266n10

Lambie, T. A., 43
Lampel, Peter Martin, 223n23
Lang, Cosmo Gordon, 44
League of Nations, 170
    Abyssinia CW attacks and, 44, 46, 90
    interwar CW agreements and, 28–29, 38

Lee, Kendrick, 181
Leigh-Mallory, Trafford, 139, 141, 143
Lethbridge, John Sydney, 183–84
Lethbridge Mission, 170, 183–84, 201
lewisite, 14, 22, 171, 224n45
*Life* (magazine), 52–53
Lincoln, George, 193–94, 197
literature, CW in, 47–49, 47–50, 216n20,
    223n23

MacArthur, Douglas, 121, 181
*Maclean's* (magazine), 51
Magruder, John, 171
Mahan, Alfred, 13
Makua, Hawaii, 186
Malaya, 171–72, 175
Malkin, William, 98–99
Manhattan Project, 166
Manion, Robert, 34
Marley (lord), 65–66
Marshall, George, 2, 124, 169, 172, 185,
    198–99
masks, 11, 24, 54f, 226n72
    for babies and young children, 66f, 67–68
    in Britain, 53–54, 58–75, 66f
    British propaganda encouraging, 68, 69f,
        72–74
    Canada preparing, 55
    compulsion of, 71–72
    cost and providing, 64–67
    in "Dulce et Decorum Est," 1
    fear and, 203, 204f, 209
    France producing, 51
    Germany producing, 52
    in Imperial War Museum advertisement,
        203, 204f
    as individual protection, 12, 64–72, 66f, 69f
    in military, 70, 179, 190
    for pets, 60–61, 60f
    press on, 51–52
    public apathy about, 68–70, 75
    in Russia, 68
    shelters and, 61–62
    soldiers wearing, 70, 179, 190
    testing, 12
    in *Thirty Million Gas Masks*, 48–49
    US preparing, 56
    in World War I, 4, 12, 203, 204f
Mason-Macfarlane, Noel, 104
McCloy, John J., 2, 198
Merck, George W., 192, 245n43, 246n46
Military Intelligence Service Research Unit
    (US), 177, 257n59

Moore, Lois, 205, 209, 241n72
Morocco, 2, 174, 201, 222n8, 255n36
Morrison, Herbert, 62, 69–70, 160–61
munitions workers, CW injuries of, 205, 209, 241n72
Murray, E. G. D., 149–50
mustard gas, 159–60. *See also* Bari, Italy, mustard gas incident
   in Abyssinia, 42–43, 45f, 174, 179, 207
   anti-gas against, 12, 61
   Bari explosion of, 8, 111, 126–32, 128f, 153, 178, 205, 209, 242n81, 243n88, 243n95
   Britain considering use of, 85–86
   contemporary use of, 10
   German research on, 80
   harm caused by, 9–12, 43, 129, 186, 205
   interwar Britain on, 27, 45f
   against Japan, considering, 167, 184–86, 198
   Japan reportedly having, 171, 173
   treatment for, 129, 153
   in World War I, 12, 186

National Peace Council, 100
Native Americans, 246n46
Navalny, Alexei, 208
Nazi-Soviet Non-Aggression Pact, 101–3
nerve gas, 208
   Germans developing, 10, 137, 169, 204, 207, 212n9
   organophosphate, 10
   sarin, 10, 207
   tabun, 10, 207
New Zealand, 125, 204–5, 212n11, 256n57
*1944* (Halsbury), 3, 48, 50
Nixon, Richard, 207
no-first-use policy
   Britain and, 16, 112, 115
   interwar CW agreements and, 7, 33, 116
   Japan and, 168
   joint CW policy and, 19, 23, 116–17
   US, 86, 115, 200
Normandy, invasion of. *See* D-Day
Noxious Gases treaty. *See* Treaty Regarding the Use of Submarines and Noxious Gases in Warfare
nuclear weapons, 2, 5, 16, 170, 202
   CW prevention and, 208
   in First Gulf War retaliation policy, 207
   Hiroshima bombing, 10, 166, 197, 200, 207
   secrecy around, 166
   Truman and, 166, 199–200

Obama, Barack, 266n6
Olympic. *See* Operation Olympic
OPCW. *See* Organisation for the Prohibition of Chemical Weapons
OPD. *See* Operations Division
Operation Barbarossa, 42, 77, 82
Operation Bodyline, 135, 164
Operation Coronet, 195f, 196
Operation Crossbow, 135, 164
Operation Downfall, 8, 193–94, 195f, 196–97, 199
Operation Olympic, 195f, 196–97, 199
Operation Overlord, 148
Operations Division (OPD) (US), 186–87
Operation Sea Lion, 16, 82, 89, 206
Organisation for the Prohibition of Chemical Weapons (OPCW), 208
organophosphate, 10
Ottoman Empire, 93–94
Owen, Wilfred, 1, 209

Pacific War Council (PWC), 175–76
Paige, Christopher Robin, 113, 116
Panama, 186
Parsons, Charles, 35–36
Pershing, John, 21, 35–36
pesticides, 191
Peter, Marc, 183
pets, masks for, 60–61, 60f
phosgene gas, 9, 61, 147
   Britain and, 87, 160
   against Japan, considering, 167, 186, 196
   US and, 87, 159–60, 167, 186, 196
   in World War I, 12, 203
poison gas. *See specific topics*
*Poison Gas* (Lampel), 223n23
Portal, Charles, 104, 144
Porter, William, 178, 181
   CW advocated by, 166, 169
   on CW use against Japan, 167, 169, 185–87, 189, 191, 197
   on retaliation policy, 169
post–World War II era, 206–8
Prentiss, Augustin M., 52
press
   on anti-gas, 50–53
   British, 50–52, 57
   Canadian, 51
   management of fear and, 52–53
   on masks, 51–52
   US, 50–51
pretext, of CW
   Axis and, 167, 193

pretext (*continued*)
   Germany and, 93, 130, 141, 145, 153, 176
   Japan and, 176, 180–81
   retaliation and, 92–94, 102, 130, 145, 180–81
Price, Richard M., 236n118
pro-gas
   in Britain, 19, 24–26, 88, 168
   Japan as, 94
   in US, 19, 21, 22f, 23, 28, 35–37, 39, 199
propaganda, anti-gas, 68, 69f, 72–74
protocol. *See* Geneva Gas Protocol
prussic acid, 171–72
psychological chemical warfare (psychological CW)
   British, 77–80, 99–102
   US, 78
public opinion
   apathy on anti-gas, 68–70, 75
   British, 24–26, 41, 46–47
   Canadian, 26
   interwar, 19, 24–26, 35–37, 41, 46–47
   US interwar, 19, 26, 35–36
   US on Japan and CW, 169, 185, 188, 197–98, 200
PWC. *See* Pacific War Council

Rabinowitch, Israel, 87, 110–11
race, Japan and, 168, 173–74, 201
Ralston, James, 33, 107–8, 248n80
Redman, Harold, 120
Research Unit, Military Intelligence Service, 177, 257n59
respirators. *See* masks
retaliation, 164
   Canada and, 107–8, 115
   FDR on, 87, 90, 99, 107–8, 115, 136, 152, 157, 167, 197, 211n7
   French policy, 30–31, 79
   Geneva Gas Protocol and, 89–90, 125–26, 167, 185
   against Japan, 96–99, 106–8, 167–69, 174–79, 185, 194
   pretext for, 92–94, 102, 130, 145, 180–81
   sovereignty and, 115
   US First Gulf War policy, 207
   US policy, 87, 90, 115, 125, 136, 152, 157, 211n7
   US policy and Japan, 99, 106–8, 167–69, 175–78, 183, 185, 194
   of Western Allies, 77–78, 87–90, 106–9, 116–27
retaliation, British, 30–31, 78
   cabinet and policy of, 79, 91

Churchill and, 87, 90, 93–94, 103, 105–6, 123, 125, 136, 152, 157, 160, 162–63, 167–68
Committee of Imperial Defence on, 31–32, 79
German V-weapons and, 157, 160–64
Germany and, 28, 77, 79–82, 85, 88–89, 92–94, 102–3, 105–6, 123, 135–36
Italy and, 90–93, 108
Japan and, 96–98, 107, 168, 176
joint CW policy and, 117, 121–23
Russia and, 102–3, 105–6
Reynolds, David, 188
ricin, 158
Rif. *See* Morocco
Romania, 94, 100
Roosevelt, Franklin Delano (FDR), 124–25, 127, 170, 197, 199, 225n66
   Canada and, 119–20
   Churchill and, 7, 87, 106–10, 115, 152, 157, 162, 167, 173
   CW opposed by, 4, 7, 15, 18, 86–87, 115, 126, 167–68, 183, 187–88, 200
   Germany and, 136
   Japan and, 99, 106–8, 167–69, 175–78, 183, 185, 194
   no-first-use policy of, 200
   on retaliation, 87, 90, 107–8, 115, 136, 152, 157, 167, 211n7
Rumania. *See* Romania
Russell, Edmund, 201
Russia, 212n9, 237n146
   anti-gas in, 51–52, 54, 68
   Britain and, 6, 94, 101–6, 108–9, 123, 138, 162
   Churchill and, 102, 105–6
   in Cold War, 207
   CW considered by, 32
   distrust of, 6, 102–6, 138
   Germany and, 13, 101–6
   Japan and, 5, 174
   joint CW policy and, 237n3
   masks in, 68
   Nazi-Soviet Non-Aggression Pact, 101–3
   in *1944*, 48
   political enemies poisoned by, 10, 208
   possibility of gas war and, 136–38, 161–62
   Stalin, 102, 105, 162, 199
   in Ukraine, 209
   US and, 6, 138, 199

sarin, 10, 207
Second World War. *See specific topics*

SHAEF. *See* Supreme Headquarters Allied Expeditionary Force
*The Shape of Things to Come* (Wells), 24, 48
shelters
  anti-gas, 12, 55, 59–63
  in Britain, 59–62
  commercial anti-gas, 59–60
  for high explosives, 57, 61–62, 70
  masks and, 61–62
Sherry, Michael, 198
Sherwood, Robert, 49–50
shortages, 4
Skirpal, Sergei, 10, 208
smallpox, 246n46
Smith, Walter Bedell, 140, 148
soldiers, anti-gas for, 54f, 57–59, 70, 179, 190
sovereignty, 8, 111–12
  Canadian, 15, 20, 34–35, 115, 119–22, 154–55, 157
  joint CW policy and, 117–26, 131
  retaliation policy and, 115
Soviet Union. *See* Russia
Spain, 3, 137, 222n8, 255n36. *See also* Morocco
Stalin, Joseph, 102, 105, 162, 199
Stevens, Bertram, 205, 209
Stimson, Henry, 2, 145, 188, 192–93, 198
Stuart, Ken, 148–50, 152, 154–56
Suffield Experimental Station, Canada, 113, 114f, 119
Sugden, C. S., 118
Supreme Headquarters Allied Expeditionary Force (SHAEF), 148, 150–51, 160
Syria, 8, 10, 208–9, 266n6

tabun, 10, 207
Tarawa, 185, 191
Taylor, John Thomas, 36
Taylor, Philip, 100
tear gas, 9–10
  Britain on, 15, 27, 171
  France using, 13
  Geneva Gas Protocol and, 171, 201
  US domestic use of, 22–23, 171, 201
Thatcher, Margaret, 205
*Theodore Savage* (Hamilton), 47–48
*Thirty Million Gas Masks* (Campion), 48–50
Thuillier, Henry, 24
Tokyo subway nerve gas attack, 10, 209
Tokyo War Crimes Trials (International Military Tribunal for the Far East), 255n41
transnational history, 7

treaties. *See* Chemical Weapons Convention; Geneva Gas Protocol; Hague Conventions; Treaty of Versailles; Treaty Regarding the Use of Submarines and Noxious Gases in Warfare
treatment, for mustard gas, 129, 153
Treaty of Versailles, 20
  Article 171, 27, 97
  CW under, 15, 18, 27, 29–30, 97–98, 202
  Germany and, 18, 27, 81, 97
  US and, 22
Treaty Regarding the Use of Submarines and Noxious Gases in Warfare (Noxious Gases treaty), 15, 18, 22, 28–30
  Britain and Japan on, 97–98
  Canada and, 20, 33
Trenchard, Hugh, 32–33
Truman, Harry, 166, 170, 199–200
Tyson, Lawrence, 37

UDC. *See* Union for Democratic Control
UK. *See* Britain
Ukraine, 209
Ultra, 151
UN. *See* United Nations
Union for Democratic Control (UDC), 24
United Kingdom. *See* Britain
United Nations (UN), 118, 239n27
United States (US), 84, 94, 164, 257n66. *See also* Roosevelt, Franklin Delano
  anti-botulism vaccine and, 145–46, 148–53, 155–57
  anti-gas lobby in, 21–22, 26, 35–37, 39
  anti-gas of, 50–51, 55–57, 74–75, 87, 110
  Axis and warnings of, 87, 90, 107–8, 115, 136, 152, 157, 167, 197, 211n7
  Bari mustard gas incident, 8, 111, 126–32, 128f, 153, 178, 205, 209, 242n81, 243n88, 243n95
  Britain compared with, 7, 19
  on BW, 145–46, 158–60, 168, 207
  Canada and, 6, 20, 34, 39, 112–13, 115, 119–20
  on CBW, 158–59
  China and, 178, 199
  Cold War, 206–7
  on crop destroyers, 192–94
  CWS, 21, 27–28, 55–56, 87, 129, 145–46, 160, 167, 169, 179, 186–87, 189, 194, 196–97, 242n81, 255n41
  CW stock of, 184, 189
  emergency period in, 56
  First Gulf War retaliation policy, 207

United States (US) (*continued*)
  first use and, 86–87, 86–88
  Geneva Gas Protocol and, 6–7, 15, 18,
    22–23, 26, 29, 34–39, 86, 115, 142, 157,
    181, 183, 185, 200–201, 206
  Hague Conventions and, 17, 115
  high explosives used by, 185
  interwar CW agreements and, 15, 18,
    21–23, 26–27, 29, 34–39
  interwar public opinion in, 19, 26, 35–36
  Joint Chiefs of Staff, 118, 121, 124, 158,
    172, 182–83, 191, 198–99
  joint CW policy and, 39, 114–16, 118–27,
    131
  Joint Logistics Committee, 174, 177,
    193–94
  Joint Staff Planners, 124, 159–60, 183,
    252n144
  lewisite developed by, 14, 224n45
  masks for, 56
  Military Intelligence Service Research
    Unit, 177, 257n59
  munitions worker injuries in, 205, 209,
    241n72
  no-first-use policy of, 85, 115, 200
  OPD, 186–87
  phosgene gas and, 87, 159–60, 167, 186,
    196
  press of, 50–51
  pro-gas in, 19, 21, 22f, 23, 28, 35–37, 39,
    199
  psychological CW of, 78
  retaliation policy, 87, 90, 115, 125, 136,
    152, 157, 211n7
  Russia and, 6, 138, 199
  on Syria, 266n6
  on tear gas, 22–23, 171, 201
  V-weapons studied by, 135
  Washington Naval Conference and, 27
  in World War I, 14
  on WP, 134, 139–42, 144
United States, Japan and. *See also* Japan, CW
    use against
  CW allegations against US, 181
  CW conflict avoided, 170–79
  CW considered against Japan, 168–70,
    182–83, 185–86, 200–202
  CW plans against Japan, 5–6, 167, 187,
    189, 194, 195f, 196–99
  Operation Coronet, 195f, 196
  Operation Downfall, 8, 193–94, 195f,
    196–97, 199
  Operation Olympic, 195f, 196–97, 199

  public opinion on CW and, 169, 185, 188,
    197–98, 200
  retaliation policy and, 99, 106–8, 167–69,
    175–78, 183, 185, 194
Unmacht, George, 186
US. *See* United States
USSR. *See* Russia

vaccines
  anti-botulism, 5, 134, 138, 145–57
  flu, 154
  yellow fever, 150
Vatican, 182–83
V-E Day. *See* Victory in Europe Day
Vengeance weapons (V-weapons), 204
  Britain attacked with, 5, 133–35, 157, 160,
    164
  British response to, 16, 133, 135–38
  British retaliation policy and, 157,
    159–64
  casualties from, 164
  Churchill on, 157, 160, 162–64
  CW delivery with, 159, 161
  joint CW policy and, 16, 137–38, 159
  US on, 135
  V-1 flying bombs, 5, 16, 133–34, 160–61
  V-2 rockets, 5, 16, 133–34, 160–61
Victory in Europe Day (V-E Day), 5, 169, 200,
    206
Vietnam, 9
V-weapons. *See* Vengeance weapons

Wadsworth, James W., Jr., 35, 37
Waitt, Alden, 160, 187
War Cabinet (Britain), 94
  CW use and approval of, 85–86, 88, 117,
    121
  on Japan, 176
  on Russia, 102, 105
Washington Naval Conference
  Noxious Gases treaty, 15, 18, 20, 22, 28–30,
    33, 97–98
  US and, 27
WDC. *See* World Disarmament Conference
weapons of mass destruction (WMD), 10,
    135, 148, 152, 155, 208
Wedemeyer, Albert, 178, 199
Weimar Germany, literature of, 223n23
Wells, H. G., 24, 48
Western Allies, 2, 4, 114f, 205. *See also* joint
    CW policy, of Western Allies; *specific
    countries*
  anti-gas of, 74–75, 87, 204

Bari mustard gas incident and, 8, 126–27, 130–32, 153
Canadian role in, 6–7, 157
China and, 3, 6, 175–77, 237n3
in Cold War, 206–7
cooperation of, 106–9
CW policy of, 6, 9, 112–16
on CW use against Japan, 164–69, 180–83, 185, 187–91, 194, 201–2
CW use considered by, 5, 133–34, 179–80, 206, 208
first use and, 86–87
Geneva Gas Protocol and, 7, 38, 140
in interwar period, 15–16, 74–75
on Japanese CW, 170–78, 194
Japanese CW conflict avoided by, 170–79
no-first-use policy and, 7, 19, 23, 116–17, 168
psychological CW of, 77–79
retaliation policy of, 77–78, 87–90, 106–9, 116–27
Russia and, 136
transnational analysis of, 7
V-weapons and, 16, 135, 137–38
on WP, 134, 138–45
white phosphorus (WP), 205
as antipersonnel weapon, 138–44
Britain on, 139–45
as CW, 138–39, 145
D-Day and, 139, 141–44
Geneva Gas Protocol and, 140, 142–43, 244n19
Germany using, 140–41
US on, 134, 139–42, 144
Wilbur, Curtis, 21–22
WILPF. See Women's International League for Peace and Freedom

Wilson, G. S., 149
Winter, Jay, 7, 212n14
WMD. See weapons of mass destruction
Women's International League for Peace and Freedom (WILPF), 21, 26
World Disarmament Conference (WDC), 18, 33, 38, 42, 96
World War I, 26, 37, 153
anti-gas in, 4, 12, 62, 179, 203, 204f
Britain and, 3, 13–14, 17, 27, 62, 89, 133, 180
BW in, 215n44
CW ban attempted after, 15–16
fear in, 13–14, 203, 204f
Hague Conventions and, 8, 13, 17, 28, 34, 80, 115
masks in, 4, 12, 203, 204f
pesticides in, 191
World War I, CW in, 1–2, 4, 19, 168, 179, 202
Britain and, 27, 89, 133
Canada and, 13–14, 114
fiction and, 47–48
German, 13–14, 46, 80, 114–16, 180, 207
mustard gas, 12, 186
Ottoman Empire and, 93–94
phosgene gas, 12, 203
prussic acid, 171
US developing, 14
varieties of, 9, 11–12
World War II. See specific topics
WP. See white phosphorus

X. See anti-botulism vaccine

yellow fever vaccine, 150

Zyklon B, 3

CPSIA information can be obtained
at www.ICGtesting.com
Printed in the USA
LVHW031501230323
742394LV00013B/739/J

9 781501 768361